# Global Energy Justice

We need new ways of thinking about, and approaching, the world's energy problems. Global energy security and access is one of the central justice issues of our time, with profound implications for happiness, welfare, freedom, equity, and due process. This book combines up-to-date data on global energy security and climate change with fresh perspectives on the meaning of justice in social decision-making. Benjamin K. Sovacool and Michael H. Dworkin address how justice theory can help people to make more meaningful decisions about the production, delivery, use, and effects of energy. Exploring energy dilemmas in real-life situations, they link recent events to eight global energy injustices and employ philosophy and ethics to make sense of justice as a tool in the decision-making process. They go on to provide remedies and policies that planners and individuals can utilize to create a more equitable and just energy future.

BENJAMIN K. SOVACOOL is Professor of Business and Social Sciences and Director of the Center for Energy Technologies, AU-Herning, Aarhus University, Denmark. He is also Associate Professor at Vermont Law School, where he manages the Energy Security and Justice Program at the Institute for Energy and the Environment (IEE).

MICHAEL H. DWORKIN is a Professor of Law and Director of the IEE at Vermont Law School.

# Global Energy Justice

## Problems, Principles, and Practices

BENJAMIN K. SOVACOOL
*Aarhus University*
and
MICHAEL H. DWORKIN
*Vermont Law School*

CAMBRIDGE
UNIVERSITY PRESS

# CAMBRIDGE
## UNIVERSITY PRESS

University Printing House, Cambridge CB2 8BS, United Kingdom

Cambridge University Press is part of the University of Cambridge.

It furthers the University's mission by disseminating knowledge in the pursuit of education, learning and research at the highest international levels of excellence.

www.cambridge.org
Information on this title: www.cambridge.org/9781107665088

© Benjamin K. Sovacool and Michael H. Dworkin 2014

First published 2014

A catalogue record for this publication is available from the British Library

Library of Congress Cataloguing in Publication data
Sovacool, Benjamin K.
Global energy justice: problems, principles, and practices / Benjamin K. Sovacool, Aarhus University, and Michael H. Dworkin, Vermont Law School.
  pages  cm
ISBN 978-1-107-66508-8 (paperback)
1. Energy policy.  2. Social justice.  I. Dworkin, Michael H.  II. Title.
HD9502.A2S6763  2014
333.79–dc23

2014010871

ISBN 978-1-107-04195-0 Hardback
ISBN 978-1-107-66508-8 Paperback

*The science of political economy, and the distribution of resources, bears a nearer resemblance to the science of morals and politics than to mathematics.*

*Thomas Malthus, 1820*

*To Ethan and Zachary Sovacool, and Samuel and Alice Dworkin, so that you might live in a better, more energy-just world.*

# Contents

| | | |
|---|---|---|
| *List of figures* | *page* xiii | |
| *List of tables* | xvi | |
| *Acknowledgements* | xviii | |
| *List of abbreviations* | xx | |
| 1 | Introduction | 1 |
| 2 | The global energy system | 31 |
| 3 | Virtue and energy efficiency | 88 |
| 4 | Utility and energy externalities | 125 |
| 5 | Energy and human rights | 157 |
| 6 | Energy and due process | 191 |
| 7 | Energy poverty, access, and welfare | 223 |
| 8 | Energy subsidies and freedom | 256 |
| 9 | Energy resources and future generations | 288 |
| 10 | Fairness, responsibility, and climate change | 319 |
| 11 | The imperative of making just energy decisions | 353 |
| *Index* | 378 | |

# Analytical table of contents

| | |
|---|---:|
| *List of figures* | *page* xiii |
| *List of tables* | xvi |
| *Acknowledgements* | xviii |
| *List of abbreviations* | xx |
| **1  Introduction** | **1** |
| "Energy justice" as a concept and a tool | 5 |
| Energy as a concept | 6 |
| Justice as a concept | 9 |
| Energy justice as a concept | 13 |
| Chapters to come | 18 |
| What is reality? | 19 |
| What is justice? | 20 |
| What is to be done? | 20 |
| Parallel frameworks | 21 |
| Novelty and contribution | 22 |
| Focus on justice | 22 |
| Interdisciplinary methodology | 25 |
| Broad definition of decision-makers | 25 |
| Global comparisons | 26 |
| Towards energy justice | 29 |
| **2  The global energy system** | **31** |
| Introduction | 31 |
| Fundamental concepts | 32 |
| Fuels, prime movers, delivery mechanisms, and end-uses | 36 |
| Resources and fuels | 36 |
| Prime movers and end-uses | 38 |
| Internal combustion engines | 38 |
| Jet turbines | 40 |
| Households and other devices | 41 |
| Delivery mechanisms | 44 |
| Pipelines | 44 |

| | | |
|---|---|---|
| Tankers | | 45 |
| Electric transmission and distribution | | 46 |
| Towards global energy systems | | 47 |
| Extractive industries | | 49 |
| Oil and gas | | 49 |
| Coal | | 53 |
| Uranium | | 55 |
| Critical materials | | 57 |
| Electricity | | 60 |
| Transport | | 61 |
| Agriculture | | 65 |
| Environmental and social impacts | | 68 |
| Climate change | | 68 |
| Air pollution | | 74 |
| Water use and contamination | | 79 |
| Land use and deforestation | | 82 |
| Other pollution | | 83 |
| Conclusion | | 86 |
| 3 | Virtue and energy efficiency | 88 |
| | What is reality? | 90 |
| | Energy conversion and use | 90 |
| | Aging capital stock and blackouts | 95 |
| | Declining energy payback ratios | 100 |
| | Social barriers to energy-efficient behavior | 101 |
| | Opportunity costs | 106 |
| | What is justice? | 108 |
| | An ideal state | 109 |
| | Happiness | 110 |
| | Balance | 111 |
| | What is to be done? | 113 |
| | Electricity demand-side management | 113 |
| | Transportation demand-side management | 116 |
| | Reductions in energy intensity | 117 |
| | Energy-efficiency labeling and fuel economy standards | 118 |
| | Smarter grids and electricity pricing | 119 |
| | Information and awareness campaigns | 123 |
| 4 | Utility and energy externalities | 125 |
| | What is reality? | 126 |
| | Climate change | 127 |

Electricity generation                                       129
Automobiles and transport                                    130
Oil and gas production                                       132
Mountaintop removal coalmining                               133
Uranium mining                                               135
Nuclear waste storage and decommissioning                    136
Indoor air pollution                                         139
What is justice?                                             139
Jeremy Bentham                                               141
John Stuart Mill                                             143
Henry Sidgwick                                               144
What is to be done?                                          145
Placing a price on carbon                                    145
Accurate price signals and tax shifting                      147
Environmental bonds                                          153

5   Energy and human rights                                  157
What is reality?                                             158
Occupational hazards and accidents                           159
Human rights abuses                                          165
Corruption                                                   169
Social and military conflict                                 172
What is justice?                                             174
Immanuel Kant                                                175
What is to be done?                                          179
Energy truth commissions and inspection panels               180
Improved impact assessments                                  181
Extractive industry transparency initiatives                 184
Protect, respect, and remedy                                 187

6   Energy and due process                                   191
What is reality?                                             193
Unfair negotiations                                          193
Involuntary resettlement                                     195
Improper licensing and deception                             199
Community marginalization                                    202
What is justice?                                             206
Due process                                                  206
Procedural justice                                           208
What is to be done?                                          213
Better information disclosure
    and auditing                                             213

Broader public involvement and participatory energy
decision-making 214
Community-based energy research 215
Participatory technology assessment and consensus
conferences 215
Debates, referendums, review boards,
and consultation 218
Free prior informed consent 220

7 Energy poverty, access, and welfare 223
What is reality? 224
Accessibility, energy poverty, and drudgery 225
Fuel poverty, health, and excess winter deaths 231
Intellectual property 233
What is justice? 237
John Rawls 238
Amartya Kumar Sen 242
Martha C. Nussbaum 243
What is to be done? 246
Investing in small-scale renewable energy 246
Harnessing the "pro-poor public private
partnership" approach 249
Social pricing and assistance programs 253

8 Energy subsidies and freedom 256
What is reality? 258
Defining subsidies 258
Government deficits 262
Increased consumption and reduced efficiency 265
Anticompetitive behavior and poor investment 267
Energy shortages and exacerbation of poverty 269
Externalities and emissions 271
Subsidy "lock-in" and "addiction" 272
What is justice? 273
Robert Nozick 274
Milton Friedman 275
Libertarian theory in a nutshell 276
What is to be done? 279
Eliminating inappropriate subsidies 280
Subsidy impact studies 282
Sunset clauses 285
Adjustment packages 286

9    Energy resources and future generations              288
     What is reality?                                     291
        Long-lived nuclear waste                          291
        Resource depletion                                294
     What is justice?                                     300
        Ronald Dworkin                                    301
        Brian Barry                                       303
        Edith Brown Weiss                                 305
     What is to be done?                                  310
        Efficiency and innovation                         311
        Natural resource funds                            314
        Renewable energy                                  315

10   Fairness, responsibility, and climate change         319
     What is reality?                                     320
        Towards global calamity                           321
     What is justice?                                     326
        Respect for future generations                    327
        Honoring subsistence rights                       329
        Responsibility and corrective justice             330
     What is to be done?                                  332
        Greenhouse development rights                      333
        Community-based adaptation                         336
        Mitigation stabilization wedges                    339

11   The imperative of making just energy decisions        353
     The perversity of energy injustice                    356
     The necessity of comprehensive intervention           358
     The import of values behind technologies              362
     Presenting an energy justice framework                366
        Availability                                       367
        Affordability                                      368
        Due process                                        368
        Information                                        369
        Sustainability                                     369
        Intragenerational equity                           370
        Intergenerational equity                           370
        Responsibility                                     371
        Synthesis                                          371
     The criticality of choice                             375

Index                                                     378

# Figures

1.1 Descriptive, normative, and prescriptive components
of energy justice                                                    *page* 19
1.2 Balance of carbon dioxide emissions embodied in
imports and exports of the largest trading countries                       28
2.1 A comparison of densities for common fuels                             39
2.2 Trends in luminous efficiency for various lighting devices,
1850–2010                                                                  42
2.3 World population growth (right axis), per capita gross
domestic product (left axis), and primary energy use (left
axis), 1800–2010                                                           48
2.4 Share of global greenhouse gas emissions by sector, gas,
and country, 2010                                                          70
2.5 Projected greenhouse gas emissions, 1900–2100                          72
2.6 Atmospheric concentration of carbon dioxide (ppm),
1900–2000                                                                  72
2.7 Temperature change from preindustrial times (°C),
1900–2100                                                                  73
2.8 Cities with high concentrations of particulate matter
pollution, 2008–2009 ($PM_{10}$ concentration
micrograms/m$^3$)                                                          78
2.9 Global freshwater evaporated from dam reservoirs
(km$^3$/year), 1900–2010                                                   80
3.1 Inefficiencies involved in modern forms of energy
conversion and use                                                         93
3.2 Wasted energy in the global energy system, 2012                        94
3.3 Age of US coal generators by capacity, in 2012                         96
3.4 Average load factor for the US electric grid, 1955–2010                96
3.5 Energy payback ratios for various energy fuels and
technologies                                                              101
3.6 McKinsey cost curve for carbon dioxide abatement
options                                                                   115

3.7 Energy-efficiency savings in eleven Organisation for
    Economic Co-operation and Development Countries,
    1973–2006                                                                118
3.8 Malaysian electricity bill showing ascending block-rate
    tariffs                                                                  122
4.1 Oil and gas production near Baku, Azerbaijan                            133
4.2 Mountaintop removal coalmining near Kayford
    Mountain, West Virginia                                                  134
4.3 The dangers of household cooking and indoor air
    pollution                                                                140
5.1 Comparison of occupational and accident risks
    associated with various energy systems                                  165
6.1 The Three Gorges Dam in China                                           197
7.1 Bedouin villages in Southern Israel without access to the
    electricity grid that surrounds them                                    227
7.2 Annual deaths worldwide by cause, 2012 and 2030                         228
7.3 Key characteristics of the "pro-poor public private
    partnership" approach                                                   250
8.1 Subsidies for gasoline and diesel in selected countries                264
8.2 Global energy research expenditures, 1974–2010
    (millions of US$)                                                       270
8.3 Top thirty "most effective" policies for promoting clean
    energy (n = 181)                                                        281
9.1 Major global energy reserves for leading energy nations,
    2012                                                                    295
9.2 Global production of fossil fuels, 1800–2200                            297
9.3 Estimated direct economic costs of oil dependence to the
    United States, 1970–2010 (billions of US$)                             298
9.4 Average energy use of a new refrigerator in the United
    States (kilowatt-hours), 1950–2014                                      313
10.1 Average emissions rates for cumulative carbon dioxide
    emissions by country, 1880–2004                                        325
10.2 Example of a per capita emissions "contraction and
    convergence" strategy, 1980–2040                                       332
10.3 Stabilization "wedges" and "triangles" for mitigating
    emissions                                                              341
10.4 Base energy technology scenario for the Western United
    States, 2020–2050                                                      347

10.5  Growth rates of selected renewable energy technologies
     (%), 2010–2012                                                    348
10.6  Global investment rates in selected renewable energy
     technologies (billions of US$), 2007–2012                          348

# Tables

1.1 Energy justice concepts and contexts                              *page* 14
1.2 Parallel terminology for our analytical framework                      21
2.1 Fundamental differences between energy resources
and fuels                                                                  36
2.2 Major producers of crude oil and natural gas liquids
(thousand barrels per day) and reserves (million barrels),
1995–2010                                                                  50
2.3 Major producers of natural gas (billion cubic meters)
and reserves (billion cubic meters), 1995–2010                             51
2.4 Top ten largest oil and gas companies by reserves
and production                                                             52
2.5 Number of coalmines worldwide                                          54
2.6 Top coal producers worldwide (million tons)                            54
2.7 Global production of uranium, 2005–2012 (metric tons)                  56
2.8 Top uranium mining companies, 2012                                     57
2.9 Materials for nuclear and renewable power plant
construction (tons/installed GW equivalent)                               58
2.10 World production of petroleum liquids by region,
2009–2040 (million barrels per day)                                        63
2.11 Global environmental degradation associated with
energy use                                                                 68
2.12 Global leaders in carbon dioxide equivalent emissions
from deforestation                                                         83
2.13 Major sources of global energy pollutants                            84
3.1 Lifecycle equivalent carbon dioxide emissions (grams
of $CO_2$/kWh) for selected "clean" sources of modern
energy                                                                    107
3.2 Carbon-to-cost ratio for "clean" sources of modern
energy                                                                    108
3.3 Comparison between conventional electricity grids
and "smart grids"                                                         120

4.1 Approximate causes of death in the United States, 2011    131

4.2 Negative externalities associated with various energy systems (cents/kWh in 1998 dollars)    149

4.3 Examples of environmental and energy tax shifting    152

5.1 Major coalmining accidents in the United States, 1940–2010    160

5.2 Major cases of energy-related corruption, 1960–2010    170

5.3 Impact-benefit agreements in Canada, 2012    185

6.1 Participatory technology assessments undertaken from 2005 to 2009    217

7.1 Number and share of population without access to modern energy services, 2009    226

7.2 Average excess winter mortality in twelve countries, 2008    232

7.3 Community improvement from the Cinta Mekar Microhydro Project, 2004–2008    252

8.1 Types of global energy subsidies    259

8.2 VAT energy subsidies removed in Europe, 1983–2005    282

8.3 Successful examples of national subsidy reform, 1952–2012    283

9.1 Life expectancy of proven fossil-fuel and uranium resources, 2012    296

9.2 Prices of end-use energy in Britain, 1300–2000 (1900 = 100)    312

9.3 Renewable energy technologies and associated fuel cycles    316

10.1 Criteria and indicators for Shue's "standard of decent living"    330

10.2 Characteristics of a greenhouse development rights framework based on responsibility and capacity    335

10.3 Examples of infrastructural, organizational, and social adaptation projects in the Asia-Pacific    340

10.4 Sixteen climate stabilization wedges    343

10.5 Top five countries for renewable energy growth and cumulative investment, 2010    349

11.1 Energy justice conceptual framework    367

# Acknowledgements

The Energy Security and Justice Program at Vermont Law School's Institute for Energy and the Environment investigates how to provide ethical access to energy services and minimize the injustice of current patterns of energy production and use. It explores how to equitably provide available, affordable, reliable, efficient, environmentally benign, proactively governed, and socially acceptable energy services to households and consumers. One track of the program focuses on lack of access to electricity and reliance on traditional biomass fuels for cooking in the developing world. Another track analyzes the moral implications of existing energy policies and proposals, with an emphasis on the production and distribution of negative energy externalities and the impacts of energy use on the environment and social welfare.

This book is one of three produced by the Program. The first, *Energy Security, Equality, and Justice*, maps a series of prominent global inequalities and injustices associated with modern energy use. The second, *Energy and Ethics: Justice and the Global Energy Challenge*, presents a preliminary energy justice conceptual framework and examines eight case studies where countries and communities have overcome energy injustices. The third, *Global Energy Justice: Problems, Principles, and Practices*, matches eight philosophical justice ideas with eight energy problems, and examines how these ideals can be applied in contemporary decision-making.

Also, the global energy justice team would like to thank many people along the way who made the completion of this book – which took half a decade to compile and write – possible. At the top of this list are Lilei Chow and Loring Starr, for their endless, much-needed love and support. In the academic world, we are thankful to Maria D'Amico at McGill University, Mark Jaccard from Simon Fraser University, and Thomas Homer-Dixon from the Balsillie School of International Affairs for thoughtful discussions with the authors on some of the topics of this book. Also, we thank Markus Gehring from the University of

Cambridge, John Haffner from Ontario Power Generation, Richard Janda from McGill University, Robb Miller from Ecofuels Canada, and Lavania Rajamani from Queens' College in Cambridge for participating in energy justice related workshops at the Vermont Law School. David Contrada from the Institute for Energy and Environment at Vermont Law School, and Tracy Bach and Burns Weston from the Climate Legacy Initiative at Vermont Law School, deserve a special mention for writing excellent articles that certainly clarified our understanding of energy justice. Michael gives a heartfelt thanks to Professor Murray Dry of Middlebury College, who, long ago, showed him how the words of the ancient Greeks could help us define a justice worth aspiring to in today's world. In addition, we express deep gratitude to Barry Barton for both specific comments on Chapter 1 and the chance (for one of us) to spend a semester teaching and learning at the Center for Energy Resources and Environmental Law at Waikato University's Te Piringa Faculty of Law in New Zealand. We are also grateful to Professor Aleh Cherp and the Central European University in Budapest, Hungary, for an Erasmus Mundus Visiting Fellowship (for the other of us) with the Erasmus Mundus Masters Program in Environmental Sciences, Policy, and Management (MESPOM), which has supported elements of the work reported here. None of the people indicated here necessarily endorses or agrees with our argument in part or overall; and all errors are the fault of the authors alone.

# Abbreviations

| | |
|---|---|
| AC | alternating current |
| ASE | Alliance to Save Energy |
| BTC | Baku–Tbilisi–Ceyhan |
| BTU | British Thermal Unit |
| CAFE | Corporate Average Fuel Economy |
| CCS | carbon capture and sequestration |
| CFL | compact fluorescent lamp |
| CI | Conservation International |
| COP | Conference of Parties |
| COP15 | Fifteenth Session of the Conference of Parties |
| $CO_2$ | carbon dioxide |
| CRS | Compagnies Républicaines de Sécurité |
| DOE | Department of the Environment |
| dwt | deadweight |
| EIA | Environmental Impact Assessment |
| EITI | extractive industry transparency initiative |
| EJ | exajoule |
| EPA | Environmental Protection Agency |
| EPR | energy payback ratio |
| ESCO | energy service company |
| EU | European Union |
| FCPA | Foreign Corrupt Practices Act |
| FIT | feed-in tariff |
| 5P | pro-poor public private partnership |
| FPIC | free prior informed consent |
| GAO | Government Accountability Office |
| GDP | gross domestic product |
| GDR | greenhouse development rights |
| GHG | greenhouse gas |
| GW | gigawatt |
| GWh | gigawatt-hour |

| | |
|---|---|
| HVDC | high-voltage direct current |
| IAEA | International Atomic Energy Agency |
| IAP | indoor air pollution |
| IBA | Impact-Benefit Agreement |
| IEA | International Energy Agency |
| IEEE | Institute of Electrical and Electronics Engineers |
| IISD | International Institute for Sustainable Development |
| IMF | International Monetary Fund |
| IPCC | Intergovernmental Panel on Climate Change |
| ITT | Ishpingo Tambococha Tiputini |
| IUCN | International Union for Conservation of Nature |
| JDZ | Joint Development Zone |
| kV | kilovolt |
| kW | kilowatt |
| kWh | kilowatt-hour |
| LED | light-emitting diode |
| LIHEAP | Low Income Home Energy Assistance Program |
| LNG | liquefied natural gas |
| LPG | liquid petroleum gas |
| MJ | megajoule |
| MMSD | Mining Minerals and Sustainable Development |
| mpg | miles per gallon |
| MTVF | mountaintop mining with valley fill |
| MW | megawatt |
| MWh | megawatt-hour |
| NAPAs | National Adaptation Programs of Action |
| NASA | National Aeronautics and Space Administration |
| NEITI | Nigerian Extractive Industries Transparency Initiative |
| $NO_x$ | nitrogen oxide |
| NRC | National Research Council |
| NREL | National Renewable Energy Laboratory |
| OECD | Organisation for Economic Co-operation and Development |
| ORML | Oil Revenue Management Law |
| ORNL | Oak Ridge National Laboratory |
| PM | particulate matter |
| ppm | parts per million |
| PSI | Paul Scherrer Institute |

| | |
|---|---|
| PTA | participatory technology assessment |
| PUC | Public Utilities Commission |
| PV | photovoltaic |
| RCI | Responsibility and Capacity Indicator |
| REDD | Reducing Emissions from Deforestation and Degradation |
| REEEP | Renewable Energy and Energy-Efficiency Partnership |
| REN21 | Renewable Energy Policy Network for the 21st Century |
| RGGI | Regional Greenhouse Gas Initiative |
| SCORE | Sarawak Corridor of Renewable Energy |
| SDG&E | San Diego Gas and Electric |
| $SO_2$ | sulfur dioxide |
| SRRP | Saskatchewan Rate Review Panel |
| T&D | transmission and distribution |
| TRI | Toxics Release Inventory |
| TW | terawatt |
| TWh | terawatt-hour |
| ULCC | ultra-large crude carrier |
| UN | United Nations |
| UNEP | United Nations Environment Program |
| UNESCAP | United Nations Economic and Social Commission for Asia and the Pacific |
| UNFCCC | United Nations Framework Convention on Climate Change |
| UNPFII | United Nations Permanent Forum on Indigenous Issues |
| US EIA | United States Energy Information Administration |
| VLCC | very large crude carriers |
| V2G | vehicle-to-grid |
| W | Watt |
| WEC | World Energy Council |
| WHO | World Health Organization |
| $ | United States dollar unless otherwise noted |

# 1 | Introduction

Some may think that decisions about energy can be made on a purely technical or technological basis, without the need to be "distracted" by abstract questions of justice. We disagree, not only because typical controlling statutes for electric utilities require pursuit of outcomes that are "just and reasonable," but also since in *substance* energy problems raise moral issues decisively and differentially affected by the outcomes of policy decisions.[1] People are starting to recognize that the world of energy involves fundamental ethical questions. Thirty years ago, electrons, barrels of oil, and justice would have seemed like a jumble of topics, but now their combination makes sense.

Consider the following example.[2] It is a quiet summer afternoon in Ohio, in the middle of a moderate, but hardly unique, warm spell. Imagine that you are sitting in the control room of the Ohio electric grid, in your third year on the job, feeling competent enough to be comfortable covering the shift while those around you go to get a sandwich or to work on maintenance routines. You look up at the "big-board" showing how much power is being carried by each major transmission line, how that compares to its design-limits, and how Ohio's grid ties into the systems feeding the rest of northeastern North America. You know that you are responsible for a small, but vital, part of "the Eastern Interconnect" which serves 200 million people spread over a million square miles of the US and Canada.

---

[1] By "decisively," we mean that some decisions will foreclose options that cannot readily be revisited or reopened; by "differentially," we mean that some decisions will lead to outcomes that are morally and materially different from other decisions that could have been made.

[2] Our discussion here is simplified for illustrative principles. However, it is inspired by an important actual event. For a readable, fascinating, and authoritative analysis of that real world example, see the US–Canada Power System Outage Task Force, *Final Report on the August 14, 2003 Blackout in the United States and Canada: Causes and Recommendations* (Washington, DC: US Department of Energy, April 2004).

Things seem calm, until you notice that one important line, serving 2 million people in and around Cleveland, is rapidly overheating. You take a few minutes to try to lower the load upon that line by opening up alternative lines, but few are available and they do not adequately compensate. Now you face a major choice: should you deliberately disconnect the Cleveland region from the larger power grid? If you do, 2 million people will certainly lose all electric power immediately and without notice, and it may well take two to four days to reconnect them. But, if you do not disconnect the region around Cleveland, there is a small but real chance – your best guess is 5 percent – that the entire Eastern Interconnect will be affected and that 50 million people, or more, will lose power and need at least four days (since a larger area will take more time to fix) to be fully reconnected.

You would love to gather more information, to ask your boss to make a decision, or to convene a meeting of experts and the representatives of the millions of people who could be affected either way. But, alas, the reality is that, at the rate the key line is overheating, you have only a few minutes to decide "what's the right thing to do?"[3] Will you, *should you*, expose hundreds of millions of people to a real chance of losing all electric power for days, or will you disconnect the line to Cleveland, knowing that there is a certainty that 2 million real, identifiable people will lose electricity for at least two days in order to reduce the risk that the same thing might happen to 50 million others, or perhaps more?

What will you decide? And *how* will you decide?

As it happens, several philosophers of justice have thought about similar questions in the past. One of them, an Englishman named Jeremy Bentham, proposed a theory that is labeled as utilitarianism and which is sometimes summed up as seeking "the greatest good of the greatest number." Using some basic arithmetic, a Benthamite could describe a choice of disconnecting 2 million people for at least two days as "four million person-days without power." In contrast, a 5 percent chance of disconnecting 50 million people for four days could be

---

[3] This phrase, "What's the Right Thing to Do?," is the title of Michael Sandel's book, which, as the subtitle makes clear, focuses on justice theory as a guide to decisions and actions, not merely as a form of contemplation. See Michael J. Sandel, *Justice: What's the Right Thing to Do?* (New York: Farrar, Straus, and Giroux, 2009).

described as expecting "10 million person-days without power." Thus, under Bentham's approach, disconnecting Cleveland is the ethical choice. Why? Because it avoids the risk of an expected 10 million person-days without power as a result of inaction, compared to a mere 4 million person-days without power if Cleveland is disconnected.[4] However, German philosopher Immanuel Kant would disagree. He would state the importance of individual freedom in contrast to cumulative social benefit. Kant's ideas could lead one to conclude that if individuals should not be sacrificed for greater social goods, then a specific city full of specific people should not be harmed to protect the expected well-being of a greater number of others.

Bentham and Kant hardly exhaust the range of justice theory on this example. Aristotle's concept of justice focuses on the idea of "virtue," defined as being "fit" for the true purposes of a person, an object, or a society (such as a polis, or a municipality). Suppose you knew that the city at risk, Cleveland in this case, was unusually productive, or unusually unproductive, as measured by its contribution to America's gross domestic product (GDP) – or its Human Development Index. Or what if it was about to host some important international event, such as the Olympics or the World Series (of American baseball)? Would that make it a more – or less – "virtuous" city? Would you think it right to take higher risks to keep Cleveland on the electric grid if you knew that it was "punching above its weight" in contributions to our economic prosperity? What if it housed a vital center for contributions to our military security? Is that the kind of "virtue" that you think should best be taken into account in deciding if it is "just and reasonable" to impose greater risks on others in order to keep Cleveland from a disconnection?

You are most likely *not* sitting in an electricity control room as you read this book. But real people must make similar decisions every minute. And despite the moral implications of those decisions, our species is drifting into a future threatened with climate change and

---

[4] In a simple version of utilitarian theory, you, sitting in the control room of the Ohio grid, might do some very simple arithmetic and say that a 100 percent chance of an outage for at least two days for 2 million people around Cleveland equals an expectation of at least 4 million person-days without power. However, a 5 percent chance of an outage for at least 50 million people for at least four days equals an expectation of at least 10 million person-days without power – which means the decision to disconnect Cleveland is the proper one.

rising sea levels, burgeoning amounts of energy-related pollution, aggra-vated scarcity and insecurity of energy fuels, the proliferation of nuclear weapons, and a host of other hazards. This creates pressing ethical conundrums with no easy resolution. It is becoming increasingly clear that routine energy analyses do not offer suitable answers to these sorts of issues. The enduring questions they provoke involve aspects of equity and morality that are seldom explicit in contemporary energy planning and analysis.

Essentially, this is because our current global energy system is prehistoric – both in terms of the fuels it utilizes, and also in the intellectual assumptions underpinning it. We rely on dwindling reserves of fossilized fuels that have existed for millions of years to provide a majority of our energy needs and services. These have paradoxically returned us to dependence on a sort of hunter-gatherer lifestyle, with global fossil-fuel hunting expeditions using more expen-sive and sophisticated technology to discover and develop untapped reserves.[5] The belief in limitless opportunities for energy use to grow within a limited globe is also prehistoric in a sense, for it contravenes even rudimentary lessons from physics, thermodynamics, ecology, and biology.

However, our moral systems are also ill-equipped to handle the complexity and expansiveness of modern-day energy and climate prob-lems. As one sign of this, a recent study from psychologists and environ-mental scientists at the University of Oregon concluded that human moral systems are not well attuned to address the crisis of climate change given its complexity, the difficulty of assigning blame, and our own complicity in causing it.[6] They noted that cognitively, climate change is abstract, complex, and nonlinear, making it hard to predict the trajectory of future emissions pathways, and harder still to connect them with actual consequences on the ground. It becomes even more difficult when most of the impacts from climate change will occur in the future, making them temporally distant, and when those impacts are asymmetric, such as increased rainfall in some areas, and decreased rain in others. Climate change, moreover, is largely unintentional, making it

---

[5] Kurt Yeager, *Electricity and the Human Prospect: Meeting the Challenges of the 21st Century* (Palo Alto: Electric Power Research Institute, 2004).
[6] Ezra M. Markowitz and Azim F. Shariff, "Climate Change and Moral Judgment," *Nature Climate Change* 2 (March 2012), pp. 243–247.

relatively "blameless" and lacking features of intentional moral transgressions such as murder or cheating. In the case of climate change, there was never any real intention to do harm – and in some cases, there was the opposite, such as building coal-fired power stations to provide jobs, improve economic security, or expand access to modern energy services. Lastly, climate change must overcome our guilty bias; that is, humans do not like to feel guilty, and will derogate evidence of their own role in causing a problem. The implication is that individuals will work to avoid feelings of responsibility for climate change; some will even have optimistic biases, downgrading any negative information they receive and counterbalancing it with almost irrational exuberance.

Clearly, we need new ways of thinking about, and approaching, the world's energy problems – and the issues at hand make global energy security and access among the central justice issues of our time, with profound implications for happiness, welfare, freedom, equity, and due process. Any decent and stable society must grapple with the injustices surrounding energy and the environment.

## "Energy justice" as a concept and a tool

The concept of "energy justice" gives us a way to better assess and resolve these dilemmas. We define an energy-just world as one that equitably shares both the benefits and burdens involved in the production and consumption of energy services, as well as one that is fair in how it treats people and communities in energy decision-making. In other words, we see importance to both substantive outcomes and decisional procedures. Energy justice, thus, involves the right of all to access energy services, regardless of whether they are citizens of more or less greatly developed economies. It encompasses how negative environmental and social impacts related to energy are distributed across space and time, including human rights abuses and the access that disenfranchised communities do or should have to remedies. Energy justice ensures that energy permitting and siting do not infringe on basic civil liberties and that communities are meaningfully informed and represented in energy decisions.

To better illuminate the moral aspects of our energy systems, this introductory chapter begins by defining the concepts of "energy," of "justice," and of "energy justice." It then previews the chapters to come and highlights four factors distinguishing this book from other types of energy analysis and scholarship.

## Energy as a concept

The global energy system consists of infrastructures for the extractive industries, electricity, transport, and agriculture. However, it is far more than that alone. The poet and painter William Blake (1757–1827) once wrote that "energy is eternal delight." It seems that the very word "energy" first appeared in English in the sixteenth century, and then it had no scientific meaning. It simply referred to forceful or vigorous language, and it was not until the 1800s that the concept of "energy" encompassed anything resembling its modern form, when natural philosophers began to use it to describe phenomena such as the motion of the planets, transfer of heat, and operation of machinery. The concept continued to evolve into today's common scientific definition that energy is the capacity to do work, or the ability to move an object against a resisting force.

Even now, the notion of "energy" is a broad idea and envelops a number of disciplines. In a scientific sense, Newtonian physics functions within the fundamental empirical truth of the first law of thermodynamics, which states that energy is neither created nor destroyed, but rather changes form.[7] For scientists and engineers, the term "primary energy" means the energy "embodied" in natural resources, such as coal, crude oil, natural gas, uranium, and even sunlight, wind, geothermal heat, or falling water, which may be mined, stored, harnessed, or collected but not yet converted into other forms of energy. Sometimes analysts use the term "end-use energy" to refer to the energy content of primary energy supplied to the consumer at the point of end-use, such as kerosene, gasoline, or electricity, delivered to homes and factories. The phrases "useful energy," "useful energy demands," and "energy services" refer to what "end-use energy" is transformed into: heat for a stove, mobility in an automobile, or mechanical energy for air circulation. "Energy services" are often measured in units of heat, or work, or temperature, but these are in essence surrogates for measures of satisfaction experienced when human beings

---

[7] National Aeronautics and Space Administration (NASA), *Conservation of Energy*, found at: www.grc.nasa.gov/WWW/K-12/airplane/thermo1f.html, accessed July 5, 2010.

consume or experience them. Energy services can thus be regarded as the benefits that energy carriers produce for human well-being.[8]

Biology and life sciences recognize life as a continuous input of energy, (almost) all of which originates from the sun: light energy transforms into chemical energy to produce water and minerals, while any "lost" energy is merely converted into heat as the energy is passed along different trophic levels.[9] Minerals, then, can be understood as units of energy – like food calories – and can be measured by the energy required to raise 1 kilogram of water 1 degree Celsius.[10]

Of course, in our daily lives, we use the word "energy" and its derivatives in many other ways. We use "energetic" as an adjective to describe people on a spectrum from "energetic at a high-octane level" to "not having enough energy to get out of bed." When we speak as energy consumers, we refer to energy sources to fuel our cars, light our homes, and heat or cool our buildings. Politicians speak about "energy security" to describe the merits of purchasing – or conquering – petroleum from foreign countries. Engineers focus on the efficiency and reliability of energy systems looking for "line losses" or "redundancy" or "fuel efficiency." Anthropologists note that we need energy for needs and aspirations, that we do not need "electrons" or "kilowatt-hours" but instead well-lit studying areas, warm rooms, and cold beers – we seek comfort, cleanliness, and convenience.[11]

Drawing from both these scientific and social conceptions, by "energy" we therefore refer to the sociotechnical system in place to convert energy fuels and carriers into services – thus not just technology or hardware such as power plants and pipelines, but also other elements of the "fuel cycle" such as coalmines and oil wells in addition to the institutions and agencies, such as electric utilities or transnational

---

[8]  B.K. Sovacool, "Conceptualizing Urban Household Energy Use: Climbing the 'Energy Services Ladder,'" *Energy Policy* 39(3) (March 2011), pp. 1659–1668.

[9]  Marietta College, *Environmental Biology – Ecosystems*, found at:www.marietta. edu/~biol/102/ecosystem.html#Energyflowthroughtheecosystem3, accessed July 5, 2010, and What Is Life: A Life Science Education Forum, *What is Life? Principles of Biology*, found at: www.whatislife.com/principles/principles05-energy.htm, accessed July 5, 2010.

[10]  Jim Painter, "How Do Food Manufacturers Calculate the Calorie Count of Packaged Foods?," in *Scientific American*, July 31, 2006, found at www. scientificamerican.com/article/how-do-food-manufacturers/.

[11]  Elizabeth Shove, *Comfort, Cleanliness, and Convenience: The Social Organization of Normality* (Oxford: Berg Press, 2003).

corporations, that manage the system, as well as the households and enterprises that consume or put that energy to work.

As we shall see, decision-makers grapple with both (1) the benefits of energy technologies that are constantly completing much work for the human race, and (2) the costs required to maintain these benefits. Energy systems and technologies can be socially advantageous, providing underlying and basic work in order for human beings to pursue other aspects of life. Immense human achievements have been made possible through concentrated energy, including longer life expectancy through improved healthcare as well as the energy requirements for humanity to land on the moon and send probes to Mars. The past CEO of the Electric Power Research Institute has even gone so far as to declare that "energy is the elemental force upon which all civilizations are built, and technology provides the means to harness energy."[12] Energy is, according to the late economist E.F. Schumacher, "not just another commodity, but the precondition of all commodities, a basic factor equal with air, water, and earth."[13]

Nonetheless, little in life comes free of cost, and energy systems indeed require inputs (e.g. natural resources) and produce both desired and undesired outputs (e.g. pollution) that must be accounted for. It is the responsibility of those managing the system to weigh the benefits of energy services – like heat in our homes, light at night, hot showers, quick transportation – against the economic, social, and environmental costs it takes to produce and maintain these benefits. Developing, implementing and maintaining the energy systems that support these services require significant human involvement, essentially reminding us that "energy works for humanity but it must also be worked for."[14] Consequent costs on a macro scale create a tension between societal damages and the benefits that energy systems provide. A fair weighing of these benefits and costs is essential for determining the outcomes among which decision-makers must choose. Indeed, major statutes, such as the Federal Power Act in the United States, explicitly set the goal of "just and reasonable" outcomes for processes such as setting

---

[12] Yeager, *Electricity*, p. 3.

[13] Geoffrey Kirk, *Schumacher on Energy: Speeches and Writings of E.F. Schumacher* (London: Jonathan Cape, 1977).

[14] John G. Clark, *The Political Economy of World Energy: A Twentieth Century Perspective* (Chapel Hill: University of North Carolina Press, 1990), p. 1.

prices for energy. But to define a "just" result, we need to consider an age-old question: what exactly is justice?

## Justice as a concept

Justice as a fundamental concept has been debated for well over 2,000 years. As one recent philosophical textbook put it:

> If the concept of human rights is of relatively recent origin, just the opposite could be said about the concept of justice: It is a moral concept with a rich and long history, stretching back before the time of Plato and Aristotle and running as a constant thread from ancient thought to the twenty-first century.[15]

Admittedly, justice is a difficult notion to tie down. As philosopher Scott Gordon puts it, "justice is the central concern of law and jurisprudence and a large part of the social sciences, and it is also a major one of philosophy, theology, and the arts."[16] For the Greeks, justice involved living a virtuous life, but did not ban slavery; for modern libertarians, it is about minimizing government intervention and control over individual choices; for social philosophers, it can be about equality and welfare. For Christians, justice refers to divine law commanding human behavior, with stipulations in the Bible such as the "Golden Rule" and the "Ten Commandments."[17] For European philosophers during the eighteenth and nineteenth centuries such as Thomas Hobbes and John Locke, justice was derived from "natural law" and, like physics or gravity, an absolute concept consisting of moral rules and principles.[18] The criminal justice system in most countries sets laws specifying rules to be obeyed and penalties imposed when one breaks them. Some believe therefore that justice is inherently tied to the law, and to

---

[15] Lawrence M. Hinman, *Ethics: A Pluralistic Approach to Moral Theory*, 4th edn. (Belmont, CA: Thomson and Wadsworth, 2008), p. 233.

[16] Scott Gordon, *Welfare, Justice, and Freedom* (New York: Columbia University Press, 1980).

[17] Jose Ambrozic, "Beyond Public Reason on Energy Justice: Solidarity and Catholic Social Teaching," *Colorado Journal of International Environmental Law and Policy* 21(2) (Spring 2010), pp. 381–398.

[18] See Thomas Hobbes, *Leviathan*, 11.1–2; Robert P. Kraynak, "The Behemoth: Doctrinal Politics and the English Civil War," ch. 3 in *History and Modernity in the Thought of Thomas Hobbes* (Ithaca: Cornell University Press, 1990), pp. 32–68; Leo Strauss, *Natural Right and History* (University of Chicago Press, 1953), p. 181; and John Locke, *Second Treatise of Government*.

retributive or preventive orders made by a judge or an official authority like Congress. Others believe justice concerns individual liberty, and the ability of each citizen to freely pursue – and hopefully realize – their own individual desires. Many modern notions of justice focus on the concept of "fairness" and attempt to create the conditions for fair social structures, which in turn produce a fair distribution of goods and services.

One recurring theme is that the concept of justice may be less important for what it *is* than for what it *does*. In this sense, the concept of justice is a tool with multiple functions:

- It links individual wishes to the values of a larger body and, thus, to the implicit or explicit coercive pressures of society as a whole;
- It serves to resolve disputes in ways that extend beyond mere individual preferences and, thus, reduces the demeaning impact otherwise felt by those whose wishes are rejected;
- It enables us to make better choices, even in the absence of disputes, by distinguishing between more and less "just" outcomes expected from our decisions;
- It promotes mental health and psychological well-being since being dealt with "justly" enables us to feel healthy, virtuous, sane, and "right."

In this "functional" sense, we can discuss what justice is, not by reviewing multiple a priori definitions of the term, but by observing its effect on actual decisions.[19]

One image of justice that has persisted throughout Western culture since at least the time of Plato and Aristotle is the statue of Lady Justice. Today, she can be seen sitting pensive-like and blindfolded holding in one hand a sword, and in the other hand a scale.[20] Upon first reflection, one may observe that Lady Justice is female, and in fact, most icons of justice, across cultures, have been female. The blindfold seems to imply that justice should be impartial, and that decisions based upon either political or personal associations, or upon factors outside of the strict issue at stake, are unjust. The sword gives Lady Justice a certain authority in her decision, while the scale implies a combination of balancing a number of interests with an empirical objectivity to her conclusions.

---

[19] This is analogous to estimating the mass of the moon, not by direct measurement, but by calculating its effects upon the oceanic tides and then calculating the mass necessary for a moon at a known distance to create that tidal change.

[20] Dennis E. Curtis and Judith Resnik, "Images of Justice," *Yale Law Journal*, 96 (1986–1987), pp. 1727–1772, at p. 1729.

All of these aspects of justice do seem to reflect an intuitive sense of what it is about. But what is a more concrete definition? Maybe no one has said it better than celebrated philosopher John Rawls, who noted that

> Justice is the first virtue of social institutions, as truth is of systems of thought. A theory however elegant and economical must be rejected or revised if it is untrue; likewise laws and institutions no matter how efficient and well-arranged must be reformed or abolished if they are unjust. Each person possesses an inviolability founded on justice that even the welfare of society as a whole cannot override. For this reason justice denies that the loss of freedom for some is made right by a greater good shared by others. It does not allow that the sacrifices imposed on a few are outweighed by the larger sum of advantages enjoyed by many. Therefore in a just society the liberties of equal citizenship are taken as settled; the rights secured by justice are not subject to political bargaining or to the calculus of social interests.[21]

Justice primarily involves the distribution of what Rawls calls the "primary goods" of rights and liberties, powers and opportunities, and income and wealth. These, according to Rawls, should be distributed in a manner a hypothetical person would choose if, at that time, they were ignorant of their own status in society.[22] Or, as justice theorist Michael J. Sandel has eloquently written, "to ask whether a society is just is to ask how it distributes the things we prize ... A just society distributes these goods in the right way; it gives each person his or her due."[23] Decision-makers, public and private, should strive to act as impartial persons implementing equitable actions in the world. In order to achieve their goal of justice, decision-makers must be blind to partiality and political bargaining, and must weigh benefits and costs empirically and objectively – making justice in this sense a matter of maintaining or restoring balance and proportion.

At the same time, equity and distributive justice deal with the distribution of material outcomes, or public goods such as resources or wealth and public bads such as pollution or poverty. Procedural justice is concerned with how decisions are made in the pursuit of social goals, or who is involved and has influence in decision-making. It thus has four

---

[21] John Rawls, *A Theory of Justice* (Cambridge, MA: Belknap Press, 1971), pp. 3–4.
[22] *Ibid.*   [23] Sandel, *Justice: What's the Right Thing to Do?*, p. 19.

important elements: (1) access to information; (2) access to and meaningful participation in decision-making; (3) lack of bias on the part of
decision-makers; and (4) access to legal processes for achieving
redress.[24] Modern justice consequently has societal as well as individual
dimensions: it refers to the healthy functioning of society in addition to
the fair treatment of the individual in day-to-day interactions. It boils
down to who gets what, and the processes and procedures that govern
how we decide the principles of that distribution.

These modern conceptualizations of justice mirror scholarship emerging from the recent field of environmental justice. Environmental justice is
commonly defined as the distribution of environmental hazards and
access to all natural resources; it includes equal protection from burdens,
meaningful involvement in decisions, and fair treatment in access to the
benefits.[25] Justice theorist Gordon Walker defines environmental justice's
two central issues as (1) how some consume key environmental resources
at the expense of others and (2) how the power to affect change and
influence decision-making is unequally influenced.[26] Ecological justice or

---

[24] Gordon Walker, *Environmental Justice: Concepts, Evidence, and Politics*
(London: Routledge, 2012).

[25] For a sample of this thinking, see R. Hofrichter (ed.), *Toxic Struggles: The Theory
and Practice of Environmental Justice* (Philadelphia: New Society, 1993);
R. Wilkinson, *Unhealthy Societies: The Afflictions of Inequality* (London:
Routledge, 1996); E.M. Hockman and C.M. Morris, "Progress towards
Environmental Justice: A Five-Year Perspective of Toxicity, Race, and Poverty in
Michigan, 1990–1995," *Journal of Environmental Planning and Management*
41(2) (1998), pp. 157–176; N. Low and B. Gleeson, *Justice, Society, and Nature:
An Exploration of Political Ecology* (London: Routledge, 1998); D. Schlosberg,
*Environmental Justice and the New Pluralism: The Challenge of Difference for
Environmentalism* (Oxford University Press, 1999); L.W. Cole and S.R. Foster,
*From the Ground Up: Environmental Racism and the Rise of the Environmental
Justice Movement* (New York University Press, 2000); P. Novotny, *Where We
Live, Work, and Play: The Environmental Justice Movement and the Struggle for
a New Environmentalism* (Westport: Praeger, 2000); R.D. Bullard and G.
S. Johnson, "Environmental Justice: Grassroots Activism and the Impact on
Public Policy Decision-Making," *Journal of Social Issues* 56(3) (2000),
pp. 555–578; E.M. McGurty, "Warren County, NC, and the Emergence of the
Environmental Justice Movement," *Society and Natural Resources* 13 (2000),
pp. 373–387; W.M. Bowen and M.V. Wells, "The Politics and Reality of
Environmental Justice," *Public Administration Review* 62(6) (2002),
pp. 688–698; John Byrne (ed.), *Environmental Justice: Discourses in the
International Political Economy* (Brunswick, NJ,: Transaction Publishers, 2002).

[26] Walker, *Environmental Justice*.

"inter-species equity"[27] concerns itself with equitable relations between humanity and the natural world, or how human beings interact with nonhuman beings.[28]

## Energy justice as a concept

Drawing from these divergent strands of thought, we define "energy justice" as a global energy system that fairly disseminates both the benefits and costs of energy services, and one that has representative and impartial energy decision-making. It involves the following key elements:

- Costs, or how the hazards and externalities of the energy system are imposed on communities unequally, often the poor and marginalized;
- Benefits, or how access to modern energy systems and services are highly uneven;
- Procedures, or how many energy projects proceed with exclusionary forms of decision-making that lack due process and representation.

Following from these three elements, an energy-just world would be one that promotes happiness, welfare, freedom, equity, and due process for both producers and consumers. It would distribute the environmental and social hazards associated with energy production and use without discrimination. It would ensure that access to energy systems and services is equitable. It would guarantee that energy procedures are fair and that stakeholders have access to information and participation in energy decision-making.[29]

Essentially, our concept of energy justice connects energy policy and technology with the topics, philosophical concepts, influences, applications, injustices, and solutions summarized in Table 1.1 – using

---

[27] Stephen H. Schneider and Janica Lane, "Dangers and Thresholds in Climate Change and the Implications for Justice," in W. Neil Adger, Jouni Paavola, Saleemul Huq, and M.J. Mace (eds.), *Fairness in Adaptation to Climate Change* (Cambridge, MA: MIT Press, 2006), pp. 23–51.

[28] See Clare Palmer, "Does Nature Matter? The Place of the Nonhuman in the Ethics of Climate Change," in Denis G. Arnold (ed.), *The Ethics of Global Climate Change* (Cambridge University Press, 2011), pp. 272–291; B.H. Baxter, "Ecological Justice and Justice as Impartiality," *Environmental Politics* 3 (Autumn 2002), pp. 43–64; Andrew Dobson, *Green Political Thought* (London: Routledge, 2000); and Low and Gleeson, *Justice, Society, and Nature*.

[29] Tamara Steger, *Making the Case for Environmental Justice in Central and Eastern Europe* (Budapest: CEU Center for Environmental Law and Policy, March 2007).

Table 1.1 *Energy justice concepts and contexts*

| Topic | Concept(s) | Major philosophical influence(s) | Applications to energy | Injustices | Solutions |
|---|---|---|---|---|---|
| Energy efficiency | Virtue | Plato and Aristotle | Energy efficiency: high penetration of efficient service | Inefficiencies involved in energy supply, conversion, distribution, and end-use | Fuel economy standards, energy-efficiency labeling, industrial retrofits, utility-scale demand-side management, ascending block rate pricing, advanced metering and smart grids, training and capacity building, consumer education and awareness |
| Energy externalities | Utility | Jeremy Bentham, John Stuart Mill, Henry Sidgwick | Well-being: less suffering, pain, externalities, and disasters associated with energy production and use | The imposition of negative social and environmental costs on society such as traffic congestion, the extractive industries affiliated with energy production, the | Passage of a carbon tax, accurate price signals and tax shifting, and environmental bonds |

| | | | | resource curse, nuclear waste, air pollution, GHG missions, and water consumption | |
| --- | --- | --- | --- | --- | --- |
| Human rights and social conflict | Human rights | Immanuel Kant | Universal human rights: an obligation to protect human rights in the production and use of energy | The violation of civil liberties – in some extreme cases death and civil war – undertaken in pursuit of energy fuels and technology, as well as the contribution of energy production to military conflict | Extractive industries transparency initiatives, energy truth commissions and inspection panels, improved social/EIAs for energy projects, availability of legal aid to vulnerable groups |
| Energy and due process | Procedural justice | Edward Coke, Thomas Jefferson, Jürgen Habermas | Due process: free prior informed consent (FPIC) for the siting of energy projects; fair representation in energy decision-making | Approaches to energy siting that ignore or contravene free, fair, and informed consent, and/or do not conduct adequate social and EIAs | Better information disclosure, broader community involvement and participation |
| Energy poverty | Welfare and happiness | John Rawls, Amartya Sen, Martha Nussbaum | Accessibility and subsistence: an energy system that gives people an equal shot | Lack of access to electricity and technology, dependence on | Social pricing and assistance programs as well as pro-poor public private |

**Table 1.1** (*cont.*)

| Topic | Concept(s) | Major philosophical influence(s) | Applications to energy | Injustices | Solutions |
|---|---|---|---|---|---|
| | | | of getting the energy they need, energy systems that generate income and enrich lives | traditional solid fuels for cooking, and time-intensive fuelwood and water collection and processing of food in emerging economies, borne mostly by women and children | partnerships for microhydro units, solar home systems, improved cookstoves, biogas digesters, and small-scale wind turbines, mechanical energy for pumping, irrigation, and agricultural processing |
| Energy subsidies | Freedom | Robert Nozick, Milton Friedman | Libertarianism: energy decisions not unduly restricted by government intervention | Gross subsidies that involve an involuntary wealth transfer to recipients, essentially raiding the pocket books of the unwilling | Elimination of inappropriate subsidies, subsidy impact assessments, sunset clauses, and adjustment packages for those dependent on subsidies |
| Energy resources | Posterity | Ronald Dworkin, Brian Barry, Edith Brown Weiss | Resource egalitarianism: an obligation to | Exhaustion of depletable energy reserves and fuels | Improved energy efficiency, establishment of |

| | | | minimize resource consumption and ensure adequate reserves for future generations | | national resource funds, commercial-scale deployment of renewable electricity and biofuels |
| Climate change | Fairness, responsibility, and capacity | Peter Singer, Henry Shue, Paul Baer, Stephen M. Gardiner, Dale Jamieson, Simon Caney | Intergenerational equity: an obligation to protect future generations from energy-related harms | A daunting suite of negative impacts from climate change including ocean acidification, food insecurity, climate refugees, and the increased frequency and severity of natural and humanitarian disasters | Greenhouse development rights (GDR), community-based adaptation, mitigation through stabilization wedges |

eight distinct energy problems to illustrate eight justice themes. The first four of these justice concepts – virtue, utility, human rights, and procedural justice – come primarily from classical theorists, the next four – welfare, freedom, posterity, and responsibility – come from modern thinkers.

In laying out this roadmap, we do not mean to imply that these philosophers always agree on justice concepts or say the same thing. We sample theoretical and applied concepts from a variety of thinkers in our sections on justice principles within each chapter even when these thinkers present contradicting ideas. Not all of the principles are equal or consistent. Aristotle's notions of justice are primarily based on virtue, things a good society should affirm, with an objective sense for what "good" is. Under this interpretation, justice is giving people what they deserve, and one cannot figure out "justice" without reflecting on the most desirable way of life, taken as an absolute. Modern philosophers such as Immanuel Kant and John Rawls, by contrast, do not rest their principles on personal virtue. Instead, their concepts represent each person's ability to choose their own conception of a good life (although Kant's concept of rational choice seems to incorporate a definition of rationality that implies what many might call "virtue.") As Michael Sandel sums it up, "ancient theories of justice start with virtue, while modern theories start with freedom."[30] These different justice ideas and principles can conflict, or in some cases devolve into "a volley of dogmatic assertions, an ideological food fight."[31] We recognize the potential for indigestion; however, given the world's hunger for some sense of justice, we continue the analogy by trying to arrange the tastiest morsels into a well-balanced meal.

## Chapters to come

The chapters to come explore the following eight justice principles by matching each to particular energy problems:

- Virtue with energy efficiency;
- Utility with energy externalities;
- Energy with human rights;
- Energy decisions with due process;

---

[30] Sandel, *Justice: What's the Right Thing to Do?*, p. 9.    [31] *Ibid.*, p. 23.

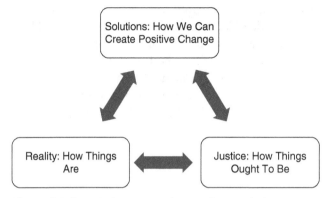

**Figure 1.1** Descriptive, normative, and prescriptive components of energy justice

- Energy poverty with welfare;
- Energy subsidies with freedom;
- Energy resources with future generations; and
- Fairness and responsibility with climate change.

Each of these eight core chapters offers a different way of thinking about three eternal questions:

1. What is reality?
2. What is justice? and
3. What is to be done?

As Figure 1.1 illustrates, part of each chapter is normative, showing how things ought to be; part is descriptive, providing the evidence for how things are; and part is prescriptive, showing how we can influence positive change.

## What is reality?

The first part of each chapter critically presents the injustices of current energy patterns: growing insecurities in everyday life, national policy, and global geopolitics, widening economic disparities in terms of access, subsidies, and distribution, and accelerating environmental degradation across air, water, and land, including the specter of irreversible climate change. Weaving together various global energy injustices, a series of dilemmas become apparent: how do we achieve energy security and access for all in a world of limited and constrained resources? How do we assign blame and responsibility for climate change – based on past culprits (i.e. large emitters such as the United States or Western Europe) or future ones (i.e. Brazil, China, Russia, India, and other growing economies)? How do we maintain a degree of equity and affordability for energy services if they become more expensive as we start to price externalities?

## What is justice?

The next part of each chapter begins by identifying some key traditions and sources by which such dilemmas can be assessed. Any meaningful global justice inquiry, including in the context of energy issues, ought to take account of this diverse normative background. This part of each chapter provides an appropriate orientation for considering, balancing, and prioritizing various justice claims that arise in energy patterns and decisions. This component of each chapter also focuses intently on what ethicist Brian Barry has called the "retail" and "wholesale" attributes of justice: wholesale attributes deal with whether institutions are fair and impartial, retail attributes deal with whether individual outcomes are equitable.[32]

## What is to be done?

This contrast between idealized aspirations to justice and modern energy realities invites reconciliation in the third and final section of each chapter. That final section invokes policy and behavioral solutions, doing so because our energy challenges call on both our public and individual resources. This is because justice is not only descriptive and normative, but also prescriptive.[33] As justice scholar Gordon Walker puts it, "most fundamentally, [justice] is about the way that people

---

[32] Brian Barry, *Theories of Justice* (Los Angeles: University of California Press, 1989), pp. 354–355.

[33] See Serge-Christophe Kolm, *Modern Theories of Justice* (Cambridge, MA: MIT Press, 1996). Kolm writes that justice enables us to answer the question "what should be done?" in society, finding the conditions that promote what is right or good for humans as individuals and groups.

Table 1.2 *Parallel terminology for our analytical framework*

| Philosophy/ethics | Law | Military | Management consulting |
|---|---|---|---|
| What is reality? | What are the relevant facts? | Situation assessment | Problem set |
| What is justice? | What is the applicable law? | Mission definition | Decision criteria |
| What is to be done? | What remedy is right? | Execution strategy | Work product |

should be treated, the way the world should be."[34] We must make informed and difficult decisions as to whether various energy sources should be expanded, managed more responsibly, or eliminated in light of justice principles and local needs. Human beings, much like energy itself, are capable of overcoming seemingly insurmountable barriers once they build into a critical mass – but that energetic potential must be guided by sound moral principles.

## Parallel frameworks

Organizing each chapter around these fundamental parts creates a framework that allows us to examine the philosophical underpinnings of our ideal energy policy while crafting a realistic and comprehensive response to the energy issues that challenge us all. Each chapter effectively begins by (1) gathering the facts; (2) consulting the principles, and (3) devising a solution. Professionals in many fields work though a similar pattern. Table 1.2 gives examples from four such fields.

In our chapters, first we lay out the facts, then we decide how to weigh the merits of outcomes that may occur, then we decide upon next steps that seem likely to lead to more desirable outcomes. For example, a lawyer faced with a complex legal problem will first often create a detailed outline of the *facts* of her case. Similarly, a consultant tasked with developing solutions for a client would begin by creating a *problem set*. A military commander, when briefing troops for deployment,

---

[34] Walker, *Environmental Justice*, p. 1.

would begin with the *situation* component of an Operations Order, describing the current situation in the field.

Second, we ask "What is justice?" This requires us to consider our moral and ethical obligations in developing a just global energy policy. There are parallels to this question in a number of fields. Lawyers decide how to interpret a fact pattern by examining the relevant *decision rules*, i.e. the applicable *rules of law*. A consultant will consider the *decision criteria* that govern his *problem set*. And a Marine Corps commander would develop the *mission* component of an Operations Order, giving the objective of the mission to which he has been assigned. The common element among these differing phrases is that each describes a set of criteria that will label some expected outcomes as desirable and others as unwanted, thus guiding us to more optimal outcomes.

Third, we consider the practical options for implementing the justice goals that we have suggested above. We discuss a broad range of options for meeting this challenge, cutting across the domains of electricity supply, transportation and mobility, infrastructure and buildings, and disaster management and resilience. Again, this analysis parallels that of a lawyer attempting to meet the requirements of the *rule of law* by designing a legal *remedy*, or of a consultant using his *problem set* and decision criteria to finalize a *work product*. Similarly, a military commander would move to the *execution* phase of an Operations Order, in which she would discuss how to coordinate an attack and what tools and materials would be necessary to do so.

## Novelty and contribution

In embarking upon this path, our book differs from other scholarship on energy security and climate change in four meaningful ways.

### *Focus on justice*

First and foremost, our book's focus on the interplay of justice and practical decision-making related to energy is distinctive, as justice is an often neglected aspect of energy and climate planning. Generally, pragmatic decisions about the fundamental infrastructure of society are given little or no consideration in the literature of justice theory. Indeed, the list of work on "energy justice" is remarkably short; our own review of the scientific and energy policy literature (in early 2013) found only five articles published with "energy" and "justice" in their titles in the past four decades.[35] When broadened to include all disciplines and items such as working papers and books, the number of publications with "energy" and "justice" in their titles grows only by nineteen more – and even then, none present a deep, philosophical exploration of justice principles and how they apply to contemporary energy decisions.[36]

[35] These are, in chronological order, M. Perez-Guerrero, "Role of Energy in the Life of Mankind: Lifestyles and Distributive Justice," *Studies in Environmental Science* 16 (1982), pp. 551–564; Alvin M. Weiberg, "Immortal Energy Systems and Intergenerational Justice," *Energy Policy* (February 1985), pp. 51–59; Catherine Gross, "Community Perspectives of Wind Energy in Australia: The Application of a Justice and Community Fairness Framework to Increase Social Acceptance," *Energy Policy* 35 (2007), pp. 2727–2736; Richard Cowell, Gill Bristow, and Max Munday, "Acceptance, Acceptability and Environmental Justice: The Role of Community Benefits in Wind Energy Development," *Journal of Environmental Planning and Management* 54(4) (May 2011), pp. 439–557; and Gordon Walker and Rosie Day, "Fuel Poverty as Injustice: Integrating Distribution, Recognition, and Procedure in the Struggle for Affordable Warmth," *Energy Policy* 49 (October 2012), pp. 69–75.

[36] These are, in chronological order, Ian G. Barbour, *Technology, Environment, and Human Values* (Westport: Praeger, 1980); David A.J. Richards, *Contractarian Theory, Intergenerational Justice, and Energy Policy* (Center for Philosophy and Public Policy Working Paper, University of Maryland, 1981); Derek Parfit, *Energy Policy and the Further Future* (Center for Philosophy and Public Policy Working Paper, University of Maryland, 1981); Brian Barry, *Intergenerational Justice in Energy Policy* (Center for Philosophy and Public Policy Working Paper, University of Maryland, 1981); Dan M. Berkovitz, "Pariahs and Prophets: Nuclear Energy, Global Warming, and Intergenerational Justice," *Columbia Journal of Environmental Law* 17(2) (1992), pp. 245–326; Kevin V. Clarke, "Environmental Justice and Native Americans at the Department of Energy Hanford Site," *Fordham Environmental Law Journal* 10(3) (1999), pp. 319–330; Steven M. Hoffman, "Negotiating Eternity: Energy Policy, Environmental Justice, and the Politics of Nuclear Waste," *Bulletin of Science, Technology & Society* 21(6) (December 2001), pp. 456–472; Alan Ramo, "California's Energy Crisis – The Perils of Crisis Management and a Challenge to Environmental Justice," *Albany Law Environmental Outlook Journal* 7(1) (2002), pp. 1–26; Jason Pinney, "Federal Energy Regulatory Commission and Environmental Justice: Do the National Environmental Policy Act and the Clean Air Act Offer a Better Way," *Boston College Environmental Affairs Law Review* 30(2) (2003), pp. 353–398; George E. Touché, "Ecological Sustainability, Environmental Justice, and Energy Use: An Annotated Bibliography," *Journal of Planning Literature* 19(2) (November 2004), pp. 206–223; Ida Martinac, "Considering Environmental Justice in the Decision to Unbundle Renewable Energy Certificates," *Golden Gate University Law Review* 35(3) (Spring 2005), pp. 491–530; Marcos A. Orellana, "Indigenous Peoples, Energy and Environmental Justice – The Pangue/Ralco Hydroelectric

Furthermore, a series of recent content analyses of the top energy technology and policy journals confirms the perceived unimportance of justice as both a methodological and topical issue. These analyses demonstrated that out of 5,318 authors publishing in these journals over a period of ten years, only six had training in philosophy and/or ethics and only one used the word "justice" in their title and/or abstract.[37]

Yet as one Brookings Institution study recently noted:

Decisions or indecisions today can impose heavy costs on our descendants or, at a minimum, limit the choices they will have. That is why there is an unprecedented need to merge the reality of an international community with the established principle of intergenerational responsibility.[38]

Our book does merge the realities of energy injustice with principles from justice theory, but grounds the justice discussion in real world case studies, connecting lofty ideals with empirical examples. It aims to give students, consumers, planners, and policymakers both purpose and direction concerning their choices about energy production and use.

Project in Chile's Alto BioBio," *Journal of Energy & Natural Resources Law* 23(4) (November 2005), pp. 511–528; David V. Carruthers, "Environmental Justice and the Politics of Energy on the US–Mexico Border," *Environmental Politics* 16(3) (June 2007), pp. 394–413; Virginia Sharpe, "Clean Nuclear Energy? Global Warming, Public Health, and Justice," *Hastings Center Report* 38(4) (July/August 2008), pp. 16–18; Steven Chermak, "Conducted Energy Devices and Criminal Justice Policy," *Criminology and Public Policy* 8(4) (November 2009), pp. 861–864; Lakshman Guruswamy, "Energy Justice and Sustainable Development," *Colorado Journal of International Environmental Law and Policy* 21(2) (Spring 2010), pp. 231–276; Elise Aiken, "Energy Justice: Achieving Stability in Oil-Producing African Nations," *Colorado Journal of International Environmental Law and Policy* 21(2) (Spring 2010), pp. 293–322; Beth Osnes, "Engaging Women's Voices for Energy Justice," *Colorado Journal of International Environmental Law and Policy* 21(2) (Spring 2010), pp. 341–354; and Ambrozic, "Beyond Public Reason on Energy Justice."

[37] B.K. Sovacool, S. Saleem, A.L. D'Agostino, C.R. Ramos, K. Trott, and Y. Ong, "What About Social Science and Interdisciplinarity? A 10-Year Content Analysis of *Energy Policy*," in D. Spreng, T. Flueler, D.L. Goldblatt, and J. Minsch (eds.), *Tackling Long-Term Global Energy Problems: The Contribution of Social Science* (New York: Springer, 2012), pp. 47–72; and A.L. D'Agostino, B. K. Sovacool, K. Trott, C.R. Ramos, S. Saleem, and Y. Ong, "What's the State of Energy Studies Research? A Content Analysis of Three Leading Journals from 1999–2008," *Energy* 36(1) (January 2011), pp. 508–519.

[38] William Antholis and Strobe Talbott, *Fast Forward: Ethics and Politics in the Age of Global Warming* (Washington, DC: Brookings Institution Press, 2010), p. 112.

## Interdisciplinary methodology

A second aspect of this book is our belief that, because of its focus on justice, an understanding of philosophy, law, and ethics, along with politics, economics, sociology, psychology, and history, is elemental in ensuring that decision-makers comprehend the depth and range of their energy actions. Our book therefore involves moving well beyond the "dominant" approach of determining how we address climate change, or respond to energy problems, which remains focused almost exclusively on economic cost-benefit analysis.[39] Our book furthermore refuses to follow the usual dichotomies in energy scholarship and analysis (such as supply vs. demand, technology vs. behavior, science vs. social science), and, through our focus on justice, integrates elements of each.

## Broad definition of decision-makers

An important third element of our book is that we look at various types of energy decisions and thus decision-makers, including policymakers and regulators as well as ordinary students, jurists, homeowners, businesspersons, investors, and consumers. Some decisions are readily identified as critical or regulatory, because they are presented either in an adversarial format or as a "yes" or "no" request for approvals. Examples include requests for permits to build or buy power plants, or to drill within recognized boundaries. Policymakers, administrative officials, and bureaucrats routinely make these sorts of decisions, often with written narratives explaining the bases for a decision and sometimes subject to external reviews. A relatively small number of them therefore act as critical "gatekeepers," given that in the next twenty years (from 2010 to 2030) fewer than 700 state regulators in the United States will serve in office and each one will approve about $6.5 billion in utility capital investment during their term.[40]

Many decisions, however, do not follow that pattern and are not so readily labeled. Often, this is because no specific decision-maker has clearly identified authority over the practice. Furthermore, many

[39] Derek Bell, "Justice and the Politics of Climate Change," in Constance Lever-Tracy (ed.), *Routledge Handbook of Climate Change and Society* (London: Routledge, 2010), pp. 423–441.

[40] Ron Binz, Richard Sedano, Denise Furey, and Dan Mullen, *Practicing Risk-Aware Electricity Regulation* (Boston, MA: CERES and RAP, 2012).

internal company decisions are never exposed to such transparency or "sunshine." Many times, those who are unaware of the significance of their own acts make the most important decisions. For instance, each of a hundred million individuals may "decide" to turn a light switch on, yet none of them may be aware that the cumulative effect of such decisions will require the production of more energy, raise economic costs for all (by requiring new capital investments), raise reliability risks for all (by straining existing transmission systems), and raise environmental cots for all (through a "demand" to flood a valley for a dam, to drill deeper and further for gas or petroleum, or to burn enough coal to kill thousands through accelerated lung diseases caused by breathing particulate emissions).

Therefore, because vital outcomes can be driven by labeled and unlabeled, public and internal, and conscious and unconscious decisions, we do not limit our discussions in this book solely to formal decision-making and dispute resolution. Instead, we sketch out a range of decision-making that can be labeled "polycentric," "multiscalar," or "multidisciplinary" but which, regardless of a label, invites you, our readers, to consider the wide range of human actions that "cause" both just and unjust outcomes in our world.[41] The book therefore discusses "top-down" justice solutions such as national legislation and policy mechanisms alongside "bottom-up" elements such as changes to individual lifestyle and community-based climate change adaptation.

## Global comparisons

Lastly, we offer a comparative, global focus with examples from every populated continent. Most books assessing energy technology or policy take a parochial view that emphasizes one or two countries, whereas our book investigates the dynamics of energy around the globe. This is because energy issues are now global in scope. For example, global

[41] For more on this point, see Elinor Ostrom, "Polycentric Systems for Coping with Collective Action and Global Environmental Change," *Global Environmental Change* 20 (2010), pp. 550–557; B.K. Sovacool, "An International Comparison of Four Polycentric Approaches to Climate and Energy Governance," *Energy Policy* 39(6) (June 2011), pp. 3832–3844; and M.H. Dworkin, R. Sidortsov, and B.K. Sovacool, "Rethinking the Scale, Structure & Scope of US Energy Institutions," *Daedalus: Journal of the American Academy of Arts and Sciences* 142(1) (Winter 2013), pp. 129–145.

trade in oil and gas amounts to roughly $1.2 trillion per year and two-thirds of all oil and gas is traded internationally[42] in addition to another $1 trillion in annual revenues from the extractive industries sector, of which coal is the largest contributor. No less than 200 billion barrels of crude oil, worth some $20 trillion, are priced off the Brent benchmark, the world's largest, each year.[43]

No nation is energy independent, nor is any nation immune from energy disruptions across the globe. Saudi Arabia is the largest exporter of crude oil but must import refined gasoline. Russia exports natural gas but must import uranium. The United States is a net exporter of coal but imports oil and liquefied natural gas (LNG). Australia exports coal and uranium but must import refined diesel fuel. The nuclear accident in Fukushima, Japan in March 2011 promptly affected not only the global price of uranium (since supply exceeded demand due to the unexpected shutdown of dozens of Japanese reactors), but also alternatives to uranium such as oil, coal, and natural gas, which saw their prices rise dramatically. Higher global prices for LNG occurred as more cargoes were diverted from Europe to Japan to make up for its shortfall in electricity.[44] Global uranium prices dropped 25 percent, and gas and coal prices increased 13.4 percent and 10.8 percent, respectively, underscoring the global ramifications of a single energy-related event.[45]

Indeed, one recent study analyzed trade figures from 113 countries across 57 industry sectors and concluded that almost one quarter of global emissions of carbon dioxide ($CO_2$) were from internationally traded commodities and products each year.[46] In some countries such as France and the United Kingdom, the number was greater than 30 percent – that is, almost one third of emissions were affiliated with imported products; others, such as China, India, Russia, and countries from the Middle East, were net carbon exporters, as shown in Figure 1.2. Follow-up research has confirmed that 37 percent of global

[42] Based on UN Trade Commission data for 2011.
[43] "Trading in Oil: Libor in a Barrel," *Economist*, May 18, 2013.
[44] Guy Chazan, "Japan to Use More LNG," *Wall Street Journal*, March 16, 2011, p. 25.
[45] Philip Stafford, Javier Blas, and Jack Farchy, "Nuclear Problems Put Energy Markets in a Spin," *Financial Times*, March 17, 2011, p. 15.
[46] Steven J. Davis and Ken Caldeira, "Consumption-Based Accounting of $CO_2$ Emissions," *Proceedings of the National Academy of Sciences* (March 8, 2010), pp. 1–6.

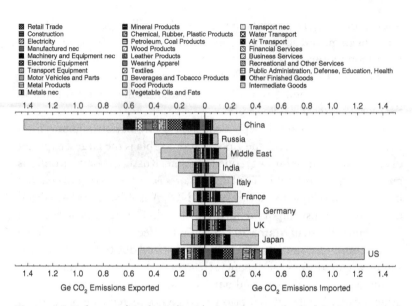

**Figure 1.2** Balance of carbon dioxide emissions embodied in imports and exports of the largest trading countries
*Note:* 'nec': 'not elsewhere classified'; 'Ge': 'gigaton equivalent'.
*Source:* Adapted from Steven J. Davis and Ken Caldeira, "Consumption-Based Accounting of $CO_2$ Emissions," *Proceedings of the National Academy of Sciences* (March 8, 2010), pp. 1–6; and Steven J. Davis, Glen P. Peters, and Ken Caldeira, "The Supply Chain of $CO_2$ Emissions," *Proceedings of the National Academy of Sciences* 108(45) (November 8, 2011), pp. 18554–18559.

emissions were from fossil fuels traded internationally – that is, they were not consumed in their countries of origin – and that an additional 23 percent of global emissions were embodied in traded goods and spread across a supply chain involving two or more countries.[47] As the energy analyst and editor Fereidoon P. Sioshansi recently put it, "We in the rich countries are as much responsible for the pollution in [China and India] because we buy their cheap finished products – and paradoxically, they are happy to lend us money so we can buy even more."[48]

[47] Steven J. Davis, Glen P. Peters, and Ken Caldeira, "The Supply Chain of $CO_2$ Emissions," *Proceedings of the National Academy of Sciences* 108(45) (November 8, 2011), pp. 18554–18559.
[48] Fereidoon P. Sioshansi, "Can We Have Our Cake and Eat It Too? Energy and Environmental Sustainability," *Electricity Journal* 24(2) (March 2011), pp. 76–85.

Just as the world as a whole has become increasingly interdependent, so has the world of energy – the energy industry, its resources and shortages, its people, its prices, and its pollution. This interdependence demands that a systematic assessment of energy justice take a concomitant global focus.

## Towards energy justice

In sum, we hold that without any proper sense of justice, energy security and policy can become a contradiction in terms.[49] They can involve the extraction of depletable natural resources, consolidated in the hands of a few countries, some of which commit human rights abuses; and they can unevenly disperse the harms of energy production and use – consuming water, producing millions of tons of solid waste, GHGs, mercury, particulate matter (PM), and other noxious pollutants into the atmosphere, causing widespread social inequity. The existing energy system can concentrate environmental hazards among the poor and geographically disadvantaged, forcing Appalachia and Navajo Counties, or the Roma in Europe or Kurds in the Middle East, to pay the environmental costs of distributing "clean electrons" to Los Angeles, New York, London, and Cairo,[50] and requiring least developed countries to bear the brunt of the impacts of climate change, even though they contributed least to the problem. The system can make the cleaner places more habitable and the displaced more resentful. The social and environmental costs of energy – known long before the publication of this book – provoked *The Economist* to make the startling claim that "using energy in today's ways leads to more environmental damage than any other peaceful human activity."[51]

The chapters to follow offer readers and energy decision-makers a hopeful way out of this quagmire. Though parts of the following

---

[49] Matthew F. Smith and Naing Htoo, "Energy Security: Security for Whom?," *Yale Human Rights and Development Law Journal* 11 (2008), pp. 217–258.

[50] See Hoffman, "Negotiating Eternity." As he has written regarding nuclear energy, "There is an enormous gap between the distribution of nuclear costs and benefits: Whereas the overwhelming majority of nuclear-generated electricity flows to customers east of the Mississippi, the front-end activities, with all their adverse impacts, are largely experienced by residents of Indian country."

[51] "A Power for Good, a Power for Ill," *Economist*, August 31, 1991.

chapters painstakingly detail the injustices associated with energy production and use, other sections apply useful justice principles so that
decision-makers of all shapes and sizes can create a more just energy
system. In closing, we are reminded of the words from Irish statesman
Edmund Burke, who wrote more than two centuries ago that

> The state is more than a partnership agreement in the trade of pepper and
> coffee, calico, or tobacco . . . It is a partnership in all science; a partnership in
> all art; a partnership in every virtue and in all perfection. As the end of such a
> partnership cannot be obtained in many generations, it becomes a partnership
> not only between those who are living, but between those who are living,
> those who are dead, and those who are [yet] to be born.[52]

Burke's conception of the nation-state expands to encompass all people's shared responsibility for stewardship of the global future. It is this
noble and just energy future that our book strives to contribute to.

---

[52] Edmund Burke (1729–1797), *Reflections on the French Revolution*, The Harvard
Classics (1909–1914), paragraph 165, as quoted in Yeager, *Electricity*.

# 2 | *The global energy system*

## Introduction

Joan Brown, a college student in Atlanta, Georgia, wakes up in the morning to an electronic alarm clock before she microwaves breakfast, takes a hot shower, grabs a latte at Starbucks, and drives her Sport Utility Vehicle to campus – where she texts her boyfriend during class and checks email on her iPad.[1] Gertrude Smith, a widowed grandmother living in London, the United Kingdom, drinks watered down milk for breakfast (to make the carton last longer), walks everywhere, uses discarded newspapers as makeshift lampshades, and reuses her bathwater to clean dishes and clothes. She pays her energy bills with jars of coins.[2] Tiemoko Sangare, a farmer in Tanzania, spends half of his day searching for wood and water and the other half cultivating crops by hand. He has never had a hot shower or bath, and rises and rests according to the sun, with no indoor lighting at night. Sometimes, if his yields are good, he can afford to purchase charcoal at the local market near Dar es Salaam.[3]

These examples show that we are in the midst of a transformational shift in the use of energy – with some, like Ms. Brown, adopting very energy-intensive living. Modern forms of energy have also become key to industrialized lifestyles across the globe, with the late German parliamentarian Hermann Scheer once remarking that energy and raw materials are the *"nervus rerum,"* the "nerve of all things," for our

---

[1] Inspired by M.A. Brown and B.K. Sovacool, *Climate Change and Global Energy Security: Technology and Policy Options* (Cambridge, MA: MIT Press, 2011).
[2] Inspired by "Poverty in Austerity: Still with Us," *Economist*, July 3, 2010, pp. 51–52.
[3] Inspired by James T. Murphy, "Making the Energy Transition in Rural East Africa: Is Leapfrogging an Alternative?," *Technological Forecasting & Social Change* 68 (2001), pp. 173–193.

economies.[4] However, these examples also reveal that the global energy system – the backbone of modern lifestyles and economic development – reflects and perpetuates vast inequities and inequalities. For some of us, lack of access to energy services is a mere inconvenience; for others, such as Mr. Sangare, it is a matter of life or death. Some of us consume staggering amounts of liquid fuels and electricity – and have significantly large carbon footprints – while others go completely without modern energy services and contribute almost nothing to climate change.[5]

As we have seen, across societies and across millennia, analysts have often begun by asking "What is reality?" or "What are the relevant facts?"[6] We, too, begin with that question, and, in this chapter, we offer an introduction to the terminology commonly used to discuss energy systems, and a review of the key elements of the energy systems created and relied upon by humanity across the globe. The chapter depicts the present configuration of the global energy system as categorized into four distinct subsectors: the extractive industries, electricity, transport, and agriculture. The chapter finishes by investigating the waste products of the global energy system, including its link to global climate change. Essentially, the chapter succinctly provides everything readers need to know to comprehend fully the chapters to come.

## Fundamental concepts

In its broadest sense, the word "energy" is a concept developed by human beings to make sense of a large number of distinct phenomena. Those phenomena include things as different as muscle power in humans and animals, wind blowing through sails, burning whale oil to produce light, or combusting oil to warm one's home. Energy is also embodied in materials as diverse as steel and silk, as well as in wooden

---

[4] Hermann Scheer, *The Solar Economy: Renewable Energy for a Sustainable Global Future* (London: Earthscan, 2002), p. 3.

[5] Gordon Walker, *Environmental Justice: Concepts, Evidence, and Politics* (London: Routledge, 2012).

[6] There are, of course, an almost infinite variety of facts that could be cited as relevant. Selecting and ordering those facts requires value judgments about which ones are most likely to be most relevant, or, in the legal phrase, "probative." Thus, there is an inevitable iterative process involving selection of facts, as we do in this chapter, and consideration of values, as we do in the other chapters to come.

homes and in leather furniture. The word "energy" derives from the ancient Greek word *energia*, which literally meant "activity in work." So today, when we use the word energy we are often describing the ability to become something else, or the process of becoming something else: coal combusted with oxygen becomes heat, carbon dioxide, and air pollution, for example, which in turn can be captured by water and transformed into steam, which can then pass through turbine blades to generate electricity.[7] The term energy describes not only the thermal, chemical, and mechanical processes above, but biological processes as well. In human beings and animals, carbohydrates and fats are our major energy sources; cellulose is the major energy source for plants.

Regardless of its different forms, energy is governed by the four laws of thermodynamics, two of which are most relevant.[8] The First Law of Thermodynamics, also known as the "Law of Conservation," states that the total amount of energy and matter in the universe remains constant, merely changing from one form to another. This means that all of the energy has to end up somewhere, either in its original form or in a different form. Thus, energy is always conserved, it cannot be created or destroyed. One vital corollary of this fundamental truth is that energy, when wasted, cannot be used for its intended purpose. Thus, energy lost as waste heat in an old-fashioned incandescent light bulb cannot be used by real people ("end-use customers") for desired goals such as light, motive power, or cooling.

The Second Law of Thermodynamics, also known as the "Law of Entropy," states that in all energy exchanges, if no energy enters or leaves the system, the potential energy of the system will always be less than that of the initial state. Thus, the efficiency of any energy conversion process will always be less than 100 percent and entropy, or the measure of disorder in the universe, always increases. As the disorder increases, energy is transformed into less usable forms. A car that has run out of gas will not run again until you walk 10 miles to a gas station and return with petrol to refuel the car.

---

[7] Duane Chapman, *Energy Resources and Energy Corporations* (Ithaca: Cornell University Press, 1983).

[8] As a brief aside, the other two laws of thermodynamics are important, but less relevant for this book: the Third Law concerns Absolute Zero, and the "Zeroth" Law concerns temperature.

These two laws are incredibly important both for science and for comprehending how our global energy system works. As Frederick Soddy wrote in his classic 1912 *Matter and Energy*,

The laws expressing the relations between energy and matter are not solely of importance in pure science. They necessarily come first ... in the whole record of human experience, and they control, in the last resort, the rise or fall of political systems, the freedom or bondage of nations, the movements of commerce and industry, the origin of wealth and poverty and the general physical welfare of the [species].[9]

The most basic ways of measuring energy concern the British Thermal Unit (BTU) and the calorie. The BTU is the amount of heat necessary to raise the temperature of 1 pound of water 1 degree Fahrenheit. The calorie is also defined as the energy necessary to raise the temperature of 1 gram of water 1 degree Centigrade. The two are related, with 1,000 calories equivalent to almost 4 (3.97) BTUs.

The electricity industry uses its own vocabulary for units of energy and, given its importance in the overall energy picture, that vernacular deserves a brief discussion. Fundamentally, it measures two very different dimensions of electricity generation, supply and use. The first measures installed energy capacity and the second measures electricity consumption over various periods of time.

Electricity capacity is measured in Watts (W) and in multiples of Watts, such as kilowatts (a thousand Watts), megawatts (a million Watts), gigawatts (a billion Watts), and terawatts (a trillion Watts), expressed, respectively, as kW, MW, GW, and TW. These distinctions of scale have an importance that is far greater than their simple differences of appearance when printed out on a page. For example, a measurement in Watts would be typical for quantifying the energy use of a household appliance, such as a 100 W incandescent light bulb. A measurement in kW might most often be used to describe the instantaneous peak demand of an entire household. A measure of some level of MWs would be typical for the total instantaneous demand of a neighborhood or a small town of a few thousand households (or for describing the output of a "small" power plant sized and built to serve that

---

[9] Frederick Soddy, *Matter and Energy* (London: Oxford University Press, 1912), pp. 10–11.

scale). Discussions of GW (each GW being a thousand MW) would be usual if describing the instantaneous cumulative power needs of large cites or provinces or states made up of millions of households. And, at a level a thousandfold larger, a discussion of TW would be appropriate for describing the "single-moment" needs of a highly developed continent such as North America or Europe. Overall, at whatever scale, a discussion of Watts or multiples of Watts can tell us something vital about how to "size" the infrastructure needed to meet peak demands for electric power. Thus, it is an essential part of knowing how big to make key elements such as power plants or transmission lines or in-house wiring or coils within an appliance.

However, and vitally, a discussion of instantaneous demand alone does not tell us anything about duration of demand over time. And duration of demand over time is vital because it informs us how much fuel will be needed to run a system, it is a key input for estimating ongoing labor hours and operating costs, it describes what kind of reliability will be needed, and, perhaps most saliently, it helps us estimate the scale of GHG emissions that are likely to result over time. For these purposes, a simple measure of instantaneous Watts or MW will not provide everything we need to know. Instead, we use a different measurement, a Watt-hour and its multiples: kilowatt-hours (kWh), megawatt-hours (MWh), gigawatt-hours (GWh), and terawatt-hours (TWh), each one being a thousandfold larger than the one before. With this measurement, we can describe the differences between two power plants that might have the same size instantaneous capacity (for example, 500 MW) but where one plant could actually produce twice as much energy throughout the year as the other. Similarly, we can use differences in demand over time (for example, 8,000 kWh compared to 15,000 kWh) to note that a typical British household uses only about one half as much electricity as an average Canadian one over a year.

The sections of the chapter to come categorize energy, or better said the process of converting energy into useful modern services, according to five things:

- Basic resources and fuels such as a lump of coal, a cubic meter of natural gas, or a barrel of crude oil;
- Prime movers such as engines, turbines, and household appliances, the so-called "end-uses" of energy within our homes, vehicles, and factories;

Table 2.1 *Fundamental differences between energy resources and fuels*

|           | Renewable                                                         | Nonrenewable                                                             |
| --------- | ----------------------------------------------------------------- | ----------------------------------------------------------------------- |
| Primary   | Solar radiation, plant mass, wind, moving water                   | Coals, crude oils, natural gases, uranium, other minerals               |
| Secondary | Biodiesel, ethanol, refuse-derived fuel, processed wood pellets, electricity | Charcoal, coke, coal gas, refined crude oils, nuclear fuel rods, electricity |

- Intermediary delivery mechanisms such as pipelines, tankers, and electric transmission and distribution (T&D) networks;
- Vertically and horizontally layered global energy systems and end-users (such as the extractive industries, electricity sector, transport sector, and agriculture);
- Critical outputs, such as waste and carbon dioxide.

## Fuels, prime movers, delivery mechanisms, and end-uses

The human utilization of energy has a long history, with somatic energy, the basic conversion of food into muscle power, existing whenever the first *Homo sapiens* digested food. Deliberate "extrasomatic" energy conversion began about 800,000 years ago, with the control of fire.[10] Now, modern energy use involves resources and fuels, prime movers, and delivery mechanisms. Resources and fuels can be renewable and nonrenewable, as well as primary or secondary. Prime movers refer to the technologies or devices that use energy and convert it into useful things. Delivery mechanisms refer to the elaborate infrastructures that have arisen to move resources and fuels to their final points of consumption where they can be utilized by prime movers.

### Resources and fuels

Energy resources and fuels can be divided into renewable and non-renewable, primary and secondary according to the matrix presented in Table 2.1.[11] Renewable resources include solar radiation and all of its

[10] Vaclav Smil, *Energy Transitions: History, Requirements, Prospects* (Santa Barbara: Praeger, 2010).
[11] This section draws from the masterful overview provided in *ibid*.

biospheric transformations, such as plant mass, wind, and moving water, temperature differences between the surface and depths of water, and geothermal heat. They share one common characteristic: natural processes regenerate each faster than they are likely to be depleted by any probable system of usage. Nonrenewable resources include fossil fuels, coals, and hydrocarbons, deposits that are the product of transformations of ancient biomass, buried in the earth, processed by high pressures and temperatures for millions to hundreds of millions of years. They all share the dominant presence of carbon, whose content can be close to 100 percent for the best anthracite coals or as low as 75 percent for natural gas and methane.

The value of each of these resources is closely linked to a concept called "energy density," or the amount of useful power that can be extracted from any specified mass of the resource. This notion of density is critical because it tells us how hard it may be to move an energy fuel from where we find it to where we want it. For example, if we want to bring some energy to an existing factory and we own a truck that can carry 1,000 kilograms (roughly 1 ton), would we prefer to send it out to bring back wood, or oil, or coal? The answer will depend on price and preexisting systems, but it will always be closely related to the energy density of fuels, which can vary greatly among the nonrenewable options. The density of coals can range from 8 megajoules per kilogram (MJ/kg) for low-quality lignite to 30 MJ/kg for the best anthracite, with most coals falling between 20 and 25 MJ/kg. Crude oils are more constant at 40 to 42 MJ/kg, making them much denser (and more useful), and natural gases rest in the middle with between 35 and 40 MJ/kg.

In Table 2.1, primary types of resources refer literally to the stores of chemical energy inherent in harvested wood or crop residues, or extracted from the earth, such as fossil fuels. Their combustion provides heat (thermal energy) or light (electromagnetic and radiant energy). Secondary fuels have to be processed, which changes their physical state, such as making solid briquettes by compressing coal dust, or harnessing charcoal from trees (which, by the way, can have an energy density as good as the best coals, at 30 MJ/kg). Electricity is unusual, in that it can be both primary and secondary: primary when converted from renewable flows, secondary when released from the combustion of fossil fuels or second-order renewable fuels such as refined biofuels, compacted wood pellets, or refuse-derived fuel (which comes from treated, sorted, and processed municipal solid waste).

*Prime movers and end-uses*

Prime movers are "energy converters able to produce kinetic mechanical energy in forms suitable for human uses."[12] That's a fancy way of saying that they are the technology that converts primary and secondary fuels into useful and usable energy services. Understanding prime movers matters, if for no less reason than that Aristotle begins his treatise on *Metaphysics* by writing that "the things best to know are first principles and causes. For through them and from them all other things may be known."[13] Without prime movers, all of the dazzling technological advances human civilization has made over the past millennia would remain nothing more than unrealized concepts.

Human muscles are the classic prime movers; those muscles enabled us to hunt, gather, and farm, or in the Biblical phrase, to be "hewers of wood and haulers of water" until and as we learned to domesticate animals. The first mechanical prime movers were simple sails, water wheels, and windmills; the industrial revolution had its steam engines and forges; the modern era has internal combustion engines, jet turbines, compact fluorescent light bulbs, and household electric appliances. We will discuss a few of these modern prime movers in turn.

### Internal combustion engines

The idea of using hot gas rather than steam as a working medium in an engine existed for almost 100 years before the first commercial internal combustion engines were designed and operated in the 1860s, yet they were quick to gain favor after the 1890s, due to their rapid starting and relatively quick acceleration and power. High-compression nonsparking internal combustion engines were invented and developed to commercial application by Nikolaus A. Otto in the 1870s and Rudolf Diesel in the 1890s. Compared to steam engines, these internal combustion engines had an overall thermal efficiency of 17 percent (compared to 3–4 percent) and were 94 percent smaller by weight, and they had a mass-to-power ratio nearly 70 percent better. The next step was the invention and design of sparking, four-stroke internal combustion engines, more efficient and powerful than earlier models, fueled by

[12] *Ibid.*, p. 6.
[13] Thanks to Professor Smil for this find, which he presents in Vaclav Smil, *Prime Movers of Globalization: The History and Impact of Diesel Engines and Gas Turbines* (Cambridge, MA: MIT Press, 2010).

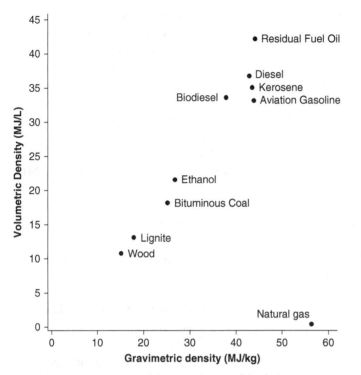

**Figure 2.1** A comparison of densities for common fuels
*Source:* Adapted from Vaclav Smil, *Prime Movers of Globalization: The History and Impact of Diesel Engines and Gas Turbines* (Cambridge, MA: MIT Press, 2010).

gasoline, which had the much enhanced volumetric and gravimetric densities shown in Figure 2.1.

Besides the superior technical attributes of such engines and the refined liquid fuels feeding them, it was perhaps nontechnical factors that played the greatest role in their widespread dissemination. Military needs during the two World Wars prioritized energy dense, liquid fuels to support mechanized combat in rural areas; during this time, research on engine designs continued. After the end of World War II, the worldwide guarantee of safe shipping routes (provided by the United States navy), coupled with international trade agreements and accords, simultaneously emboldened further demand for mobility and raised incomes so people could afford to pay for it.

Today, modern diesel engines power marine ships, railways, and heavy trucks (among other things). The world's most powerful diesel engines are the two-stroke machines operating at low speeds developed for ultra-large crude carriers, bulk carriers, and container ships – they operate at slower speeds so they can use heavier fuel oil and so that they have less wear. The capacity of diesel engines for ships has grown remarkably from 1900 to 2010. Most recently, from 1996 to 2008, global maritime traffic has increased by 60 percent and containerized shipping has expanded 3.5-fold. Today, nearly 100,000 ocean-going commercial ships are used to transport goods, and 97 percent of these are powered by diesel engines, some having rated capacities in excess of 50 MW or even 80 MW. Annual fuel consumption in ocean shipping reaches about 370 million tons, equivalent to 10 percent of the world's oil consumption, and it emits 1.2 billion tons of carbon dioxide, or about 4 percent of global emissions. Compared to national totals, this makes the maritime shipping industry as large a source of carbon dioxide as Japan or India.[14]

Diesel engines are not limited to shipping; because of their fuel efficiency and relatively infrequent need for maintenance, they dominate the railway industry – almost all containers on flat car trains rely on diesel locomotives. Moreover, about 85 percent of high-usage trucks (those driven more than 120,000 kilometers per year) have diesel engines (though only 6 percent of all trucks used for local transport are diesel-powered). The number and size of diesel and sparking internal combustion engines in passenger transport is truly staggering. To quote just one estimate, the 191 million automobiles in the United States already have an equivalent electrical capacity of 2,865 GW (i.e. 2.865 TW) – an amount more than *twice* the country's fleet of operating power plants.[15]

### Jet turbines
The gas turbine prototypes designed by Frank Whittle and Hans-Joachim Pabst von Ohain in the 1930s, and commercialized by Rolls-Royce and General Electric in the 1940s, became the basis for turbofan

[14] Smil, *Energy Transitions*.
[15] Willet Kempton, "Vehicle to Grid Power," *NREL Analysis Seminar* (Washington, DC: National Renewable Energy Laboratory (NREL), September 28, 2005).

engines and jet turbines which now power aircraft, and some natural gas-fired power plants. Larger turbofans could provide greater efficiency, thrust, and ease of maintenance than the propellered aviation engines they replaced. During takeoff, turbine rotor blades can reach more than 1,500°C, a temperature higher than the melting point of rotating metal. Consequently, such engines need elaborate internal air cooling, with every blade acting as a heat exchanger. These engines, though, consume about half as much fuel per unit of thrust as the engines of the 1950s. This probably explains why jet aircraft account for upwards of 95 percent of all commercial airliners worldwide, and why these jet-aircraft designs were adopted for the electricity industry, which often uses combined-cycle natural gas turbines to generate power.

### Households and other devices

A totally different type of prime mover rarely actually moves. Homes throughout the globe have a variety of different electric appliances that convert electricity into light, entertainment, refrigeration, and heat, from televisions and mobile phones to refrigerators and toasters.[16]

Perhaps the most elemental of household needs is illumination. Indeed, at the beginning of the era of electricity, many suppliers were actually called "Power and Light" companies because light was the primary commodity they offered. Over the past few centuries, human beings have moved away from fires and candles to electric lights. The economist William D. Nordhaus has compellingly traced improvements in lighting efficiency from the oil lamps of the Paleolithic era up to today's modern technology, and documented that the rate of improvement per year (in terms of lumens delivered) was about 0.0004 percent during ancient times but 0.04 percent during the nineteenth century and 3.6 percent from 1800 to 1992. As he writes:

Each new lighting technology represented a major improvement over its predecessor. What is striking, as well, is that in each technology there have been dramatic improvements. The Welsbach gas mantle improved the efficiency of

---

[16] This section draws from original arguments presented in B.K. Sovacool, "Conceptualizing Urban Household Energy Use: Climbing the 'Energy Services Ladder,'" *Energy Policy* 39(3) (March 2011), pp. 1659–1668; B.K. Sovacool, "Security of Energy Services and Uses within Urban Households," *Current Opinion in Environmental Sustainability* 3(4) (September 2011), pp. 218–224.

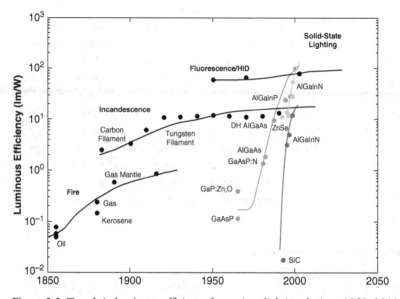

**Figure 2.2** Trends in luminous efficiency for various lighting devices, 1850–2010
*Source:* Adapted from Chart 25.1 from Cutler J. Cleveland and Christopher
G. Morris, *Handbook of Energy Volume I: Diagrams, Charts, and Tables*
(London: Elsevier Science, 2013).

gas lamps by a factor of seven, and another 100 percent improvement was seen
between the kerosene lantern of the 1880s and today's Coleman lantern. There
were marked improvements in the ordinary light bulb in the four decades after
Edison's first carbon-filament lamp, with most of the gain achieved by 1920.

Overall, Nordhaus calculates that the efficiency of lighting has
increased by a factor of 1,200 from the times of Babylon to now.[17]
Figure 2.2 tracks some of the most recent efficiency improvements from
1850 to the present.

Human beings seem to recognize the brilliance (or luminance) of
these improvements, and purchase a mammoth number of modern
bulbs. According to one light bulb manufacturing company, every
year consumers in the United States spend about $1 billion to purchase

[17] William D. Nordhaus, "Do Real-Output and Real-Wage Measures Capture
   Reality?," in Timothy F. Bresnahan and Robert J. Gordon (eds.), *The Economics
   of New Goods* (Chicago University Press, 1996), pp. 27–70.

2 billion light bulbs, working out to 5.5 million bulbs bought *per day*.[18] Though their estimate would not include other types of bulbs such as light-emitting diodes (LEDs) and compact fluorescent lamps (CFLs), which have longer product lifetimes, the *Wall Street Journal* reports that there are a total of 4 billion electric incandescent bulbs in the United States and roughly 12 billion such bulbs around the world.[19]

Of course, we desire far more than light within our modern homes. Using the most recently available data, about 1.4 billion televisions exist throughout the world, with 400 million alone in China and 219 million in the United States.[20] Presuming that each one uses 200 Watts of electricity, powering all of those televisions for one hour needs 280 billion kWh of electricity. That's more electricity than Australia uses for an entire year. Similarly, however, the transformation from vacuum tube to plasma and then from plasma to LED radically improved television picture quality, battery life, and energy efficiency, thereby reducing electricity demand by an amount that is also strategically important in a global sense.

Refrigerators operate continuously and therefore consume about 17 percent of the average household's electricity – more than any other appliance. About 10 million new refrigerators are sold every year in the United States, adding to the existing stock of 140 million refrigerators nationwide (though some of these older refrigerators are certainly discarded). Still, the United States is home to more refrigerators than households, the explanation being that one quarter of all homes have at least two refrigerators.[21] Moreover, this only scratches the surface of appliance use, since many homes possess everything from microwaves, ovens, dishwashers, water heaters, and laundry machines to furnaces, stereos, electric can openers, electric blankets, and clocks.[22] The American Council for an Energy-Efficient Economy, a think tank,

---

[18] Sylvania, "Lighting: About Us," Press Release, August 4, 2011.

[19] "Congress Working on Light Bulb Phase Out," *Wall Street Journal*, September 13, 2007.

[20] Nation Master Statistics, "Televisions (Most Recent) By Country," November 2011, available at www.nationmaster.com/graph/med_tel-media-televisions.

[21] "Keeping a Second Fridge at Home? You're Not Alone," *USA Today*, March 21, 2010.

[22] Readers interested in the history of these other types of appliances should sample Ruth Schwartz Cohen, *More Work for Mother: The Ironies of Household Technology from Open Hearth to the Microwave* (New York: Basic Books, 1983); and Elizabeth Shove, *Comfort, Cleanliness, and Convenience: The Social Organization of Normality* (Oxford: Berg Press, 2003).

estimated in 2013 that the United States was home to more than 2 billion "power-hungry" devices, such as televisions and computers, as well as commercial equipment such as elevators and icemakers, which together used more energy than scores of individual countries, and cost $70 billion in energy expenses annually.[23]

## Delivery mechanisms

Energy resources and prime movers need delivery infrastructure to connect them, and while such transportation and distribution systems are breathtakingly variegated, the three most prominent are pipelines, tankers, and electric T&D lines. Taken together, this infrastructure occupies a substantial chunk of land, with one assessment estimating that roughly 30,000 square kilometers – the size of Belgium – are currently dedicated exclusively to supporting the oil, gas, coal, and electricity industries.[24]

### Pipelines

Technically, a pipeline refers to any facility "through which liquids (crude oil and petroleum products), gases (natural gas, carbon dioxide, steam) or solids (slurries) are transported."[25] Pipelines have been around for a long time, with China using clay pipes to move natural gas as early as 500 years before the birth of Jesus Christ. Despite the availability of other forms of transport such as road and rail, pipelines are the most used mechanism to transport oil and natural gas from producing fields and refineries to gas stations and consumers, and by a wide margin. Pipelines account for 66 percent of all hydrocarbons transported globally (by volume) compared to only 27 percent for ship tankers, 4 percent for railways, and 3 percent for trucks and automobiles.[26] The single longest pipeline in the world, the Enbridge Pipeline System, transports crude oil from Canada to eastern Canada and the United States. It spans more

[23] American Council for an Energy-Efficient Economy (ACEEE), *Miscellaneous Energy Loads in Buildings* (Washington, DC, 2013); see also ACEEE Press Release, "Power-Hungry Devices Use $70 Billion of Energy Annually," June 26, 2013.
[24] Smil, *Energy Transitions*, p. 117.
[25] International Pipeline & Offshore Contractors Association, *Onshore Pipelines: The Road to Success* (International Pipeline & Offshore Contractors Association, September 2011).
[26] *Ibid.*

than 5,000 kilometers (3,100 miles) and it delivers 1.4 million barrels of oil per day – about 1.5 percent of global supply – to refineries spread across Ontario and the American Midwest.

The American Society of Mechanical Engineers estimates that the total length of pipelines around the world exceeds 3.5 million kilometers, and that 64 percent carry natural gas, 19 percent carry petroleum products, and 17 percent carry crude oil.[27] Every year, about 32,000 kilometers of onshore pipelines are added to this stock at an annual cost of $28 billion in addition to $5 billion worth of 8,000 kilometers of offshore pipelines. Individual pipeline systems can be truly huge. As one example, if you laid the Canadian pipeline system end to end, it would circle the world seventeen times.[28]

### Tankers

Three types of merchant ships – very large crude carriers (VLCCs), ultra-large crude carriers (ULCCs), and LNG tankers – carry prodigious volumes of hydrocarbons across the world's seas and oceans each year. A VLCC refers to an oil tanker with between 200,000 and 400,000 metric tons of deadweight (dwt); ULCCs are up to 550,000 dwt; and most LNG tankers with insulated membranes carry between 150,000 and 266,000 cubic meters of natural gas. The world's fleet of 474,800 oil tankers[29] (big and small) moves about 2.6 billion metric tons of oil and refined petroleum products every year, amounting to one third (34 percent) of all seaborne trade by volume, and clocking an astounding 11.7 billion nautical miles collectively traveled.[30] The world's fleet of about 380 LNG tankers hauls 331 billion cubic meters of natural gas every year[31] – enough to meet the combined needs of Iran, Germany, and Japan.

[27] Phil Hopkins, *Oil and Gas Pipelines: Yesterday and Today* (Pipeline Systems Division International Petroleum Technology Institute, American Society of Mechanical Engineers, 2007).

[28] Liz Kilmas, "Obama during Debate: There's Enough Pipeline to Wrap Around the Earth Once," *The Blaze*, October 16, 2012.

[29] Table 24.28 from Cutler J. Cleveland and Christopher G. Morris, *Handbook of Energy Volume I: Diagrams, Charts, and Tables* (London: Elsevier Science, 2013).

[30] Erik Ranham, "Just How Many VLCCs Do We Need?," Intertanko, March 2012.

[31] Tim Colton, LNG Carriers in Service or under Construction (Ship Building History Website, October 2012, available at www.shipbuildinghistory.com/today/highvalueships/lngactivefleet.htm).

All three categories of vessels have grown considerably in size. The average oil tanker during World War II, for instance, was only 530 feet long and had a capacity of 16,500 dwt. The ULCCs of the 1970s, by contrast, were more than 1,300 feet long and had an average capacity of 500,000 dwt. The world's biggest supertanker, built in 1979 and recently decommissioned, was appropriately named the *Happy Giant*; it was so large that when its 46 tanks and 340,000 square feet of storage were filled with oil, it could not fit into the English Channel.[32]

For various legal and logistical reasons, most oil tankers and LNG carriers are not owned by oil companies or sovereign countries themselves, but by independent shipping firms. As one example, a VLCC might be built in South Korea at the Hyundai Shipyard, owned by Texaco in the United States, fly the Liberian flag, and transport oil purchased by the highest bidder until it is broken apart forty years later in Bangladesh. During their month-long journeys around the world, such tankers are at the ever-present mercy of storms, poor navigation, pirates, and cracking hulls, all of which can contribute to major spills such as those that befell the Exxon *Valdez* in Alaska or the Liberian-owned *Presige* off the coast of Spain. However, chronic spills and "routine" releases of oil do more collective damage each year than major disasters. Columbia Law School Professor Michael J. Graetz estimates that every year, perfectly functioning ships discharge large quantities of oil-polluted ballast water and fuel oil that add up to five *Valdez* spills.[33]

### Electric transmission and distribution

In order to move electrons from power plants into your home, electric power systems need elaborate T&D networks consisting of transformers, conductors, insulators, wires, and substations. To understand the basics about how these networks function, readers need to remember at least two characteristics: instantaneousness and variability. The first and most important principle of electric T&D is that it must meet customer demand, often called "load," instantaneously. The second

[32] William B. Hayler and John M. Keever, *American Merchant Seaman's Manual* (Centreville, MD: Cornell Maritime Press, 2003); see also Mark Huber, *Tanker Operations: A Handbook for the Person-in-Charge (PIC)* (Centreville, MD: Cornell Maritime Press, 2001).

[33] Michael J. Graetz, *The End of Energy: The Unmaking of America's Environment, Security, and Independence* (Cambridge, MA: MIT Press, 2011).

important principle of power systems is that customer demands change continuously and exhibit daily, weekly, and seasonal load cycles.

At each moment, the supply of power must meet the demand of customers and utilities must maintain power frequency and voltages within appropriate limits across the entire transmission system. The two critical terms here are "frequency" and "voltage." The design of consumer equipment such as motors, clocks, and electronics often assumes a relatively constant power frequency of 60 Hz for proper operation in the US. Many types of customer equipment require voltage to fall within a narrow range in order to function properly. If delivered voltage is too low, electric lights dim and electric motors function poorly and can overheat. Overly high voltages shorten lives of lamps substantially and increase motor power, which can damage attached equipment.[34]

Most transmission lines rely on high-voltage three-phase alternating current (AC), though single-phase AC is sometimes used for railways and high-voltage direct current (HVDC) can be used for exceptionally long distances. Electricity is transmitted at high voltages, 110 kilovolts (kV) or above in most cases, to reduce the energy lost moving electrons through the line. The United States has at least 500,000 miles of high-voltage transmission lines (160,000 miles of these lines are 500 kW or above) and millions of miles of distribution lines. Globally, about 4 million miles of transmission lines have been built and about 150,000 miles of new transmission lines are added each year worth $184 billion, with the fastest growth in China.[35] As a crude sign of their capital investment, at a replacement cost of $1 to $4 million per mile[36] the world has invested $16 trillion in its network of high-voltage transmission lines. The highest transmission towers crisscrossing the Yangtze River in China reach 1,132 feet – almost as high as the Empire State Building in New York, which rises 1,224 feet.

## Towards global energy systems

Humanity does not utilize electricity and fossil fuels in a vacuum; instead, our society depends on it and other modern energy services to

---

[34] See US Office of Technology Assessment, *Energy Efficiency: Challenges and Opportunities for Electric Utilities* (Washington, DC: US Government Printing Office, September 1993).
[35] ABS Energy Research, *Global Transmission & Distribution Report*, 2010.
[36] American Electric Power, "Transmission Facts," October 2012.

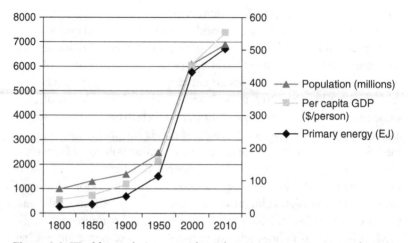

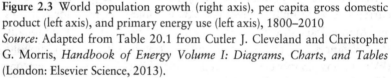

**Figure 2.3** World population growth (right axis), per capita gross domestic product (left axis), and primary energy use (left axis), 1800–2010
*Source:* Adapted from Table 20.1 from Cutler J. Cleveland and Christopher G. Morris, *Handbook of Energy Volume I: Diagrams, Charts, and Tables* (London: Elsevier Science, 2013).

enable lighting, communication, transport, commerce, manufacturing, and industry. Perhaps for these reasons, Figure 2.3 illustrates how as the human population has grown, so has its use of primary energy, and so has its economic development. Complex global energy systems have therefore arisen to connect energy resources and fuels, prime movers, and delivery infrastructure. Humanity as a whole used about 500 exajoules (EJ) of energy in 2005, but demand for energy will grow 45 percent between now and 2030, and this amount will almost triple by the end of the century. Between 2011 to 2035, the International Energy Agency (IEA) expects an additional $38 trillion to be invested in the global energy sector. In 2011, the world also received a sobering 81 percent of its energy from fossil fuels.[37]

The four most important global energy systems involve (1) the extractive industries, (2) electricity, (3) transport, and (4) agriculture. Though they are certainly interconnected, it is helpful as a first step to look at them distinctly.

---

[37] International Energy Agency, *World Energy Outlook 2011* (Paris: OECD, 2011), p. 2. See also International Energy Agency, *Key World Energy Statistics 2011* (Paris: OECD, 2011).

## Extractive industries

The extractive industries most related to energy production encompass the mining of coal and the production of crude oil and natural gas. The extractive industries and mining sector overlaps with parts of the electricity and transport sector, providing raw fuels such as crude oil, unprocessed natural gas, unwashed coal, and nonenriched uranium through a series of hundreds of thousands of mines, onshore wells, and offshore drilling platforms. Yet it also consumes fossil fuels directly for industrial processes; in 2010, for instance, the extractive industries sector accounted for roughly 19 percent of global electricity usage but a whopping 78 percent of fossil-fuel usage.[38] The extractive industries also provide the material inputs – copper, rare earth elements, alumina, and others – needed to manufacture power plants, cars, transmission lines, and other electronic devices, something we call "critical materials." In essence, the demand for all of these resources reminds us that "energy" must be mined, leached, processed, and turned into usable products that can be bought and sold.

### Oil and gas

Crude oil, by definition, is a "naturally occurring, unrefined petroleum product composed of hydrocarbon deposits," whereas natural gas is "a mixture of hydrocarbon gases that occurs with petroleum deposits, principally methane together with varying quantities of ethane, propane, butane, and other gases."[39] At ambient temperatures, crude oil is a liquid and natural gas is gaseous. Oil and gas are both energy fuels as well as the raw materials used to manufacture items such as fertilizer, rubber, and plastic. In both its liquid and gaseous form, petroleum has been used by humans for at least 5,000 years, with oil used before the modern era to keep fires ablaze and in warfare, and natural gas utilized for light.[40] Modern human civilization, however, produces radically different quantities of the stuff. In 2010, the world produced 83.2 million barrels of oil *per day* (see Table 2.2), an increase from the mere 68.8 million barrels per day produced in 1995. Only 30 percent of

[38] Table 20.11 from Cleveland and Morris, *Handbook of Energy*.
[39] World Petroleum Council, *Guide to Oil and Gas* (London: World Petroleum Council, 2009), p. 2.
[40] Fred Halliday, *The Middle East in International Relations: Power and Ideology* (New York: Cambridge University Press, 2005), p. 270.

Table 2.2 *Major producers of crude oil and natural gas liquids (thousand barrels per day) and reserves (million barrels), 1995–2010*

|  |  | 1995 | 2000 | 2005 | 2010 |
|---|---|---|---|---|---|
| Producers | Russia | 6,168 | 6,527 | 9,636 | 10,450 |
|  | Saudi Arabia | 8,922 | 9,068 | 10,604 | 9,761 |
|  | United States | 8,526 | 8,020 | 7,067 | 7,805 |
|  | Iran | 3,702 | 3,760 | 4,239 | 4,259 |
|  | China | 2,986 | 3,253 | 3,628 | 4,103 |
|  | Canada | 2,399 | 2,723 | 3,052 | 3,367 |
|  | Mexico | 3,067 | 3,450 | 3,760 | 2,953 |
|  | United Arab Emirates | 2,493 | 2,622 | 2,995 | 2,848 |
|  | Venezuela | 3,018 | 3,220 | 3,011 | 2,438 |
|  | Nigeria | 2,039 | 2,160 | 2,518 | 2,436 |
|  | First ten countries | 43,318 | 44,802 | 50,511 | 50,420 |
|  | Rest of the world | 25,516 | 30,436 | 31,554 | 32,821 |
|  | World | 68,834 | 75,238 | 82,065 | 83,241 |
| Reserves |  |  |  |  |  |
|  | Europe | 19,267 | 21,249 | 18,044 | 14,000 |
|  | Russia and Central Asia | 55,833 | 56,395 | 77,227 | 98,281 |
|  | Middle East | 623,043 | 675,638 | 729,341 | 753,358 |
|  | Africa | 63,332 | 76,078 | 101,973 | 119,114 |
|  | Asia – Pacific | 44,674 | 43,986 | 36,293 | 40,136 |
|  | Americas | 340,239 | 328,970 | 323,296 | 338,654 |
|  | World | 1,146,388 | 1,202,316 | 1,286,174 | 1,363,543 |

*Source:* Adapted from *Eni's World Oil and Gas Review* (2011).

this oil was produced in the Middle East, with the rest coming from no less than 150 countries around the world.[41] The world has similarly increased its natural gas production from 2,167 billion cubic meters in 1995 to 3,231 billion cubic meters in 2010. Table 2.3 shows how the top ten countries account for about two-thirds of the global total, and it also presents major known reserves by region.

The corporations selling most of these hydrocarbons used to be predominantly privately owned conglomerates such as ExxonMobil,

[41] Eni, *The World Oil and Gas Review* (2011 edn.).

**Table 2.3** *Major producers of natural gas (billion cubic meters) and reserves (billion cubic meters), 1995–2010*

|  |  | 1995 | 2000 | 2005 | 2010 |
|---|---|---|---|---|---|
| Producers | Russia | 573.13 | 561.43 | 615.22 | 624.61 |
|  | United States | 518.31 | 533.06 | 502.78 | 600.15 |
|  | Canada | 155.35 | 176.94 | 183.76 | 157.66 |
|  | Iran | 42.51 | 59.46 | 99.54 | 146.41 |
|  | Qatar | 8.76 | 25.98 | 47.70 | 127.97 |
|  | Norway | 33.70 | 55.20 | 89.50 | 108.73 |
|  | China | 17.91 | 27.15 | 49.23 | 96.60 |
|  | Indonesia | 69.97 | 72.44 | 78.17 | 91.47 |
|  | Algeria | 55.65 | 83.33 | 90.19 | 86.57 |
|  | Saudi Arabia | 33.17 | 40.85 | 66.32 | 79.77 |
|  | First ten countries | 1,508.47 | 1,635.84 | 1,822.41 | 2,119.93 |
|  | Rest of the world | 659.24 | 828.20 | 1,011.76 | 1,111.44 |
|  | World | 2,167.71 | 2,464.03 | 2,834.18 | 3,231.37 |
| Reserves |  |  |  |  |  |
|  | Europe | 8,104 | 9,199 | 7,544 | 6,788 |
|  | Russia and Central Asia | 51,405 | 51,670 | 52,675 | 59,516 |
|  | Middle East | 45,994 | 54,742 | 72,513 | 75,437 |
|  | Africa | 9,858 | 11,434 | 14,078 | 14,720 |
|  | Asia – Pacific | 12,481 | 12,182 | 13,886 | 15,727 |
|  | Americas | 14,292 | 14,137 | 14,425 | 17,375 |
|  | World | 142,134 | 153,364 | 175,121 | 189,563 |

*Source:* Adapted from *Eni's World Oil and Gas Review* (2011).

British Petroleum, Shell, and Chevron; however, they have been overtaken in recent years by the National Oil Companies shown in Table 2.4. Their operations involve exploring for oil and gas, drilling exploratory wells, producing and transporting that oil, and in some cases processing it at the world's 760 commercial refineries. The technology behind these activities can be breathtakingly complex. For instance, the offshore oil platform *Deepwater Horizon* owned by British Petroleum, the one that famously caused the largest oil spill in

Table 2.4 *Top ten largest oil and gas companies by reserves and production*

| Rank | Company | Worldwide liquids reserves (billion barrels) | Worldwide natural gas reserves (trillion cubic feet) | Total reserves in oil equivalent barrels (billion barrels) | Company | Production (million barrels per day) |
|---|---|---|---|---|---|---|
| 1 | Saudi Aramco | 260 | 254 | 303 | Saudi Aramco | 11.0 |
| 2 | National Iranian Oil Company | 138 | 948 | 300 | National Iranian Oil Company | 4.0 |
| 3 | Qatar Petroleum | 15 | 905 | 170 | Kuwait Petroleum Corporation | 3.7 |
| 4 | Iraq National Oil Company | 116 | 120 | 134 | Iraq National Oil Company | 2.7 |
| 5 | Petróleos de Venezuela | 99 | 171 | 129 | Petróleos de Venezuela | 2.6 |
| 6 | Abu Dhabi National Oil Company | 92 | 199 | 126 | Abu Dhabi National Oil Company | 2.6 |
| 7 | Kuwait Petroleum Corporation | 102 | 56 | 111 | Petróleos Mexicanos | 2.5 |
| 8 | Nigerian National Petroleum Corporation | 36 | 184 | 68 | Nigerian National Petroleum Corporation | 2.3 |
| 9 | Libya NOC | 41 | 50 | 50 | Libya NOC | 2.1 |
| 10 | Sonatrach | 12 | 159 | 39 | Lukoil | 1.9 |

*Source:* Adapted from British Petroleum's *Statistical Review of World Energy 2012.*

US history in the Gulf of Mexico in 2010, drilled to a measured depth of 35,000 feet – a depth equal to the height that many commercial airlines *fly* at. The shale gas wells being exploited by ExxonMobil are as long as more than *ten* Empire State Buildings.

## Coal

Another fossil fuel extracted out of the earth is coal, removed through a variety of techniques including surface and opencast mining, underground and deep mining, and mountaintop valley fill operations (known informally as "mountaintop removal"). Opencast mining occurs when seams lie near the surface, and it is done with goliath-size draglines, power shovels, bulldozers, bucket wheel excavators, conveyors, and dump trucks. This type of mining is cheaper, but rarer due to the depth of seams; about 80 percent of coalmining in Australia uses this surface-mining method, along with 67 percent of mining in the United States, but globally it is used for only 10 percent of mining operations.[42] Underground mining involves cutting a network of "rooms" into a coal seam, or using hydraulically powered support beams to create artificial roofs and longwalls. Mountaintop removal, as the name implies, involves dynamiting the crowns off mountains and hills to capture the coal within them. According to the most recent data available, the world was home to about 24,000 coalmines (see Table 2.5). Unlike the oil and gas market, which is controlled by a few firms, Table 2.6 shows how the top ten coalmining companies produce about a quarter of the global total. Another notable difference is that only 15 percent of coal production is destined for the global coal market; the remainder is used domestically.[43]

Coalmines, like oil and gas infrastructure, can become quite deep and large. The world's largest coalmine by volume of production is the Black Thunder Mine in Wyoming, a facility that produces some 120 million tons of coal per year from its six draglines, 22 power shovels, and 148 haul trucks – enough to fill 25 *miles* of railroad cars per day. The deepest coalmine in the world is the Jindřich II Mine in the Rosice-Oslavany coal basin in the Czech Republic, with shafts reaching 1,500 meters into the

---

[42] World Coal Association, "Coal Mining," 2012, available at www.worldcoal.org/coal/coal-mining/.
[43] World Coal Mining, Industry Overview, 2013, available at www.mbendi.com/indy/ming/coal/p0005.htm.

Table 2.5 *Number of coalmines worldwide*

| | Total number of coalmines | % Underground | % Opencast | Production (million tons) | % Production |
|---|---|---|---|---|---|
| China | 18,557 | 95 | 5 | 3,471 | 49.5 |
| USA | 1,458 | 40 | 60 | 1,004 | 14.1 |
| India | 562 | 64 | 36 | 585 | 5.6 |
| European Union | 846 | 28 | 72 | 56.1 | 4.2 |
| Rest of the world | 2,577 | – | – | 2,849.4 | 26.6 |
| World | 24,000 | 90 | 10 | 7,695.4 | 100 |

*Source:* Adapted from the World Coal Association's website in November 2013.

Table 2.6 *Top coal producers worldwide (million tons)*

| | Company | 2010 Production |
|---|---|---|
| 1. | Coal India | 431 |
| 2. | Shenhua Group | 352 |
| 3. | Peabody Energy | 198 |
| 4. | Datong Coal | 150 |
| 5. | Arch Coal | 146 |
| 6. | China Coal | 138 |
| 7. | BHP Billiton | 104 |
| 8. | Shanxi Coal | 101 |
| 9. | RWE Power | 99 |
| 10. | Anglo American | 97 |

*Source:* Adapted from the International Energy Agency's *World Energy Outlook 2012.*

ground, almost twice as deep in length as the world's tallest building, the Burj Khalifa in Dubai (which stands at 830 meters).

Although the United States, Russia, China, Australia, and India hold the largest coal reserves, it is China alone that dominates the market, being home to almost *half* of global production in 2013 and responsible for 75 percent of all new coalmines added that same year. The production of coal that year in China was more than three times that of global trade in coal. Despite this internal production, China also overtook Japan to become the largest importer of coal, and Indonesia overtook Australia to be the world's largest exporter on a tonnage basis.[44]

## Uranium

Another energy commodity extracted from the earth is uranium. Uranium mining is water and volume intensive, since quantities of uranium are mostly prevalent at very low concentrations.[45] Uranium is mined in three different ways: underground mining, open-pit mining, and in-situ leaching. Underground mining extracts uranium much like other minerals, such as copper, gold, and silver, and involves digging narrow shafts deep into the earth.[46] Open-pit mining, the most prevalent type, is similar to strip mining for coal, where upper layers of rock are removed so that machines can extract uranium. Open-pit mining ceased in the United States in 1992 due to concerns about environmental contamination and the quality of uranium, as most ore there is located in lower-grade sandstone deposits.[47] Uranium miners perform in-situ leaching by pumping liquids into the areas surrounding uranium deposits.[48] These liquids include acid or alkaline solutions to weaken the calcium or sandstone surrounding uranium ore.[49] Operators then pump the uranium up into recovery wells at the surface, where it is collected.[50] In-situ leaching is more cost effective than underground mining because it avoids the significant expense of excavating underground sites and often takes less time to implement.[51] Nonetheless, it uses significantly more water – as much as 7 to 8 gallons (26 to 30 liters) for every kWh of nuclear power generated.[52] Table 2.7 shows the top

[44] International Energy Agency, *Medium-Term Coal Market Report 2012: Market Trends and Projections to 2017* (Paris: OECD, 2012).
[45] For an overview of uranium mining and the front end of the nuclear fuel cycle, see B.K. Sovacool, "Valuing the Greenhouse Gas Emissions from Nuclear Power: A Critical Survey," *Energy Policy* 36(8) (August 2008), pp. 2940–2953.
[46] *Ibid.*
[47] See EPA, *Uranium Mining and Extraction Processes in the United States* (Washington, DC: EPA, 2006)
[48] Sovacool, "Valuing the Greenhouse Gas Emissions."   [49] *Ibid.*   [50] *Ibid.*
[51] EPA, *Technologically Enhanced Naturally Occurring Radioactive Materials from Uranium Mining* (Washington, DC: EPA, 2008, Appendices 1 and 2).
[52] US Department of Energy, *Energy Demands on Water Resources* (Sandia National Laboratory 2006), p. 51.

**Table 2.7** *Global production of uranium, 2005–2012 (metric tons)*

| Country | 2005 | 2006 | 2007 | 2008 | 2009 | 2010 | 2011 | 2012 |
|---|---|---|---|---|---|---|---|---|
| Kazakhstan | 4,357 | 5,279 | 6,637 | 8,521 | 14,020 | 17,803 | 19,451 | 21,317 |
| Canada | 11,628 | 9,862 | 9,476 | 9,000 | 10,173 | 9,783 | 9,145 | 8,999 |
| Australia | 9,516 | 7,593 | 8,611 | 8,430 | 7,982 | 5,900 | 5,983 | 6,991 |
| Niger | 3,093 | 3,434 | 3,153 | 3,032 | 3,243 | 4,198 | 4,351 | 4,667 |
| Namibia | 3,147 | 3,067 | 2,879 | 4,366 | 4,626 | 4,496 | 3,258 | 4,495 |
| Russia | 3,431 | 3,262 | 3,413 | 3,521 | 3,564 | 3,562 | 2,993 | 2,872 |
| Uzbekistan | 2,300 | 2,260 | 2,320 | 2,338 | 2,429 | 2,400 | 2,500 | 2,400 |
| USA | 1,039 | 1,672 | 1,654 | 1,430 | 1,453 | 1,660 | 1,537 | 1,596 |
| China | 750 | 750 | 712 | 769 | 750 | 827 | 885 | 1,500 |
| Malawi | | | | | 104 | 670 | 846 | 1,101 |
| Ukraine | 800 | 800 | 846 | 800 | 840 | 850 | 890 | 960 |
| South Africa | 674 | 534 | 539 | 655 | 563 | 583 | 582 | 465 |
| India | 230 | 177 | 270 | 271 | 290 | 400 | 400 | 385 |
| Brazil | 110 | 190 | 299 | 330 | 345 | 148 | 265 | 231 |
| Czech Republic | 408 | 359 | 306 | 263 | 258 | 254 | 229 | 228 |
| Romania | 90 | 90 | 77 | 77 | 75 | 77 | 77 | 90 |
| Germany | 94 | 65 | 41 | 0 | 0 | 8 | 51 | 50 |
| Pakistan | 45 | 45 | 45 | 45 | 50 | 45 | 45 | 45 |
| France | 7 | 5 | 4 | 5 | 8 | 7 | 6 | 3 |
| Total world | 41,719 | 39,444 | 41,282 | 43,853 | 50,772 | 53,671 | 53,493 | 58,394 |
| Tons U$^3$O$^8$ | 49,199 | 46,516 | 48,683 | 51,611 | 59,875 | 63,295 | 63,084 | 68,864 |
| % World demand | 65 | 63 | 64 | 68 | 78 | 78 | 85 | 86 |

*Source:* Adapted from the World Nuclear Association's website in December 2013.

Table 2.8 *Top uranium mining companies, 2012*

| Company | Tons U | % |
|---------|--------|---|
| KazAtomProm | 8,863 | 15 |
| Areva | 8,641 | 15 |
| Cameco | 8,437 | 14 |
| ARMZ – Uranium One | 7,629 | 13 |
| Rio Tinto | 5,435 | 9 |
| BHP Billiton | 3,386 | 6 |
| Paladin | 3,056 | 5 |
| Navoi | 2,400 | 4 |
| Other | 10,548 | 18 |
| Total | 58,394 | 100% |

*Source:* Adapted from the World Nuclear Association's website in December 2013.

global uranium producers from 2005 to 2012, Table 2.8 the top uranium mining companies in 2012 which marketed 82 percent of the world's production. Geographically, Canada, Kazakhstan, and Australia account for more than half of global production.

### Critical materials
Lastly, the energy system needs not only fuels to function, but also ordinary materials – concrete, aluminum, copper, steel, fiberglass – as well as so-called "rare earth" minerals. Energy infrastructure, everything ranging from power plant boilers and control rooms to natural gas pumping stations and wind turbines, requires large amounts of materials in order to be built and operated safely. As Table 2.9 illustrates, these material needs can become quite large. A single 1,000 MW nuclear reactor, the standard size, will need upwards of 179,000 tons of concrete, 36,000 tons of steel, and 729 tons of copper, among other items.[53] Many renewable sources of energy are even more material intensive in various ways, such as hydroelectric dams that, on a per GW basis, need three times as much concrete as a nuclear reactor, or

[53] B.K. Sovacool, "Exploring the Hypothetical Limits to a Nuclear and Renewable Electricity Future," *International Journal of Energy Research* 34 (November 2010), pp. 1183–1194.

Table 2.9  *Materials for nuclear and renewable power plant construction (tons/installed GW equivalent)*

| | Biomass | Nuclear | Wind | Geothermal | Hydroelectric | Solar |
|---|---|---|---|---|---|---|
| Aluminum | 255 | 18 | 0 | 255 | 240 | 22,500 |
| Cadmium | 0 | 0 | 0 | 0 | 0 | 40 |
| Chromium | 122 | 0 | 0 | 122 | 100 | 0 |
| Concrete | 74,257 | 179,681 | 305,891 | 74,257 | 578,704 | 60,000 |
| Copper | 454 | 729 | 211 | 454 | 550 | 2,000 |
| Fiberglass | 0 | 0 | 19,863 | 0 | 0 | 0 |
| Gallium | 0 | 0 | 0 | 0 | 0 | 3.5 |
| Germanium | 0 | 0 | 0 | 0 | 0 | 2 |
| Glass* | 0 | 0 | 0 | 0 | 0 | 13 |
| Indium | 0 | 0 | 0 | 0 | 0 | 20 |
| Lead | 0 | 46 | 0 | 0 | 0 | 0 |
| Manganese | 112 | 434 | 0 | 112 | 80 | 0 |
| Molybdenum | 42 | 0 | 0 | 42 | 0 | 0 |
| Nickel | 10 | 125 | 0 | 10 | 5 | 0 |
| Plastic | 0 | 0 | 0 | 0 | 0 | 3,250 |
| Silicon | 0 | 0 | 0 | 0 | 0 | 6,500 |
| Silver | 0 | 0.5 | 0 | 0 | 0 | 0.3 |
| Steel | 40,293 | 36,068 | 84,565 | 51,044 | 32,604 | 75,000 |
| Tellurium | 0 | 0 | 0 | 0 | 0 | 46.7 |
| Vanadium | 4 | 0 | 0 | 4 | 0 | 0 |
| Total | 115,550 | 217,101 | 410,530 | 126,300 | 612,283 | 169,363 |

* Glass materials are reported in square kilometers rather than metric tons.

*Source:* Adapted from B.K. Sovacool, "Exploring the Hypothetical Limits to a Nuclear and Renewable Electricity Future," *International Journal of Energy Research* 34 (November 2010), pp. 1183–1194.

wind turbines which require 20,000 tons of fiberglass per installed GW. Other critical materials, somewhat harder to find, include lithium, cobalt, and indium, key both to batteries for electric vehicles and for the manufacturing of solar photovoltaic (PV) panels.

Another class of inputs, equally important but far more difficult to extract, fall into the "rare earth minerals" category. The term "rare earth minerals" – also called "rare earth elements" and "rare earth metals" – refers to seventeen chemical elements in the periodic table: fifteen lanthanides in addition to scandium and yttrium, found in the same ore deposits.[54] These minerals are called "rare" not because they are about to run out, but because they are not concentrated near the earth's surface and require more energy-intensive effort (and greater cost) to extract. Despite the difficulty of acquiring them, they are needed to make metal alloys, enable circuits in electronics, form catalysts, provide phosphors for lighting, build magnets for generators, and manufacture catalytic converters for automobiles.

For instance, a typical hybrid electric vehicle such as the Toyota Prius needs 2.2 pounds (1 kilogram) of neodymium, and expected growth in demand for electric vehicles will see the need for rare earth minerals such as dysprosium, neodymium, and praseodymium grow 790 percent from 2010 to 2015.[55] Similarly, large capacity wind turbines need magnets composed of neodymium, iron, and boron; energy-efficient fluorescent lights need yttrium, terbium, europium, lanthanum, and cerium; LEDs need cerium and europium phosphors. Nuclear fuel bundles rely on gadolinium, a rare earth mineral, as well as cobalt, indium, and several heavy rare earth minerals. Rare earth minerals are even needed in the fluid of cracking catalysts that convert heavy oil into gasoline and lighter distillates.[56]

Access to these rare earth minerals, however, is limited, and concentrated in a few countries, making most energy-consuming nations highly dependent on dwindling, imported supplies. Demand for such

---

[54] Adrian P. Jones, Francis Wall, and C. Terry Williams (eds.), *Rare Earth Minerals: Chemistry, Origin and Ore Deposits* (London: Chapman and Hall Mineralogy Series, 1996).

[55] Nayantara D. Hensel, "An Economic and National Security Perspective on Critical Resources in the Energy Sector," in Sai Felicia Krishna-Hensel (ed.), *New Security Frontiers: Critical Energy and the Resource Challenge* (London: Ashgate, 2012), pp. 113–138.

[56] *Ibid.*

minerals has also grown rapidly in the past few years. The US Department of Energy, for example, conducted a "criticality assessment" of rare earth minerals in 2011 to determine if adequate supply would exist for various energy technologies from 2012 to 2015.[57] It concluded that five rare earth elements – dysprosium, terbium, europium, neodymium, and yttrium – were found to be critical to the manufacturing of wind turbines, electric vehicles, and efficient lights, but were unlikely to be of sufficient supply at current costs. It also found a "near-critical" projected shortfall of the other elements cerium, indium, lanthanum, and tellurium. It warned that the growing demand for other products that also need rare earth elements, such as mobile phones, computers, and flat panel televisions, could lead to further shortfalls.

## Electricity

Reliance on electricity from power plants, where large amounts of the energy embodied in coal, oil, gas, and uranium end up, has grown significantly due to instant and effortless access, its easily adjustable flow, facilitation of high precision speed and process controls, cleanliness and silence at the point of use. Electricity now energizes not only lights, refrigerators, televisions, and radios but also vehicles, electric fireplaces, electric arc furnaces, and movable sidewalks. In 1900, less than 2 percent of the world's electricity came from fossil fuels, but by 1950 the number had jumped to 30 percent and it passed 80 percent in 2000.[58] Humans have also become more dependent on information and media technology such as the internet and televisions, which have corresponded with a dramatic increase in the manufacturing of information storage, telecommunications, and electronics as well as the energy needed to operate such devices.[59]

Thus, as of early 2012, roughly 170,000 generators provided electricity worldwide at more than 75,000 power plants – about half of

[57] US Department of Energy, *Critical Materials Strategy* (Washington, DC, December 2011).

[58] Vaclav Smil, "Energy in the Twentieth Century: Resources, Conversions, Costs, Uses, and Consequences," *Annual Review of Energy and Environment* 25 (2000), pp. 21–51.

[59] *Ibid.*

them coal-fired, 440 of them nuclear-powered. In the United States, the electricity sector is so big that it consists of almost 20,000 power plants, 410 underground natural gas storage fields, and 125 nuclear waste storage facilities, in addition to T&D lines, transformers, substations, distribution points, electric motors, and electric appliances. It is the most capital-intensive sector of economic activity for the country and represents about 10 percent of sunk investment. Expenditures on electricity reached $374 billion in 2012 (2.5 percent of the nation's GDP in that year),[60] and the country had more electric utilities and power providers than Burger King restaurants.[61] Particular forms of electricity supply, such as nuclear power, differ further still by necessitating their own collection of facilities unique to the fuel cycle, such as uranium mines, uranium mills, enrichment facilities, fuel cladding facilities, temporary waste sites, permanent waste repositories, research laboratories, and research reactors.

## Transport

The introduction of mobile engines and inexpensive liquid fuels has enhanced personal mobility and facilitated new modes of transport. The number of mass-produced motorized vehicles jumped from a few thousand in 1900 to more than 700 million in 2000 along with a notable increase in vacation travel and nonessential trips. In 1900, for instance, there were only 8,000 cars in the United States and just 15 kilometers of paved roads.[62] The mobility of people has been matched by the increasing movement of goods and services as trade and commerce have accelerated. In 2000, trade alone accounted for 15 percent of global economic activity, most of it through diesel-powered rail, freight, trucks, and tankers.

---

[60] US EIA, *An Updated Annual Energy Outlook 2009 Reference Case Reflecting Provisions of the American Recovery and Reinvestment Act and Recent Changes in the Economic Outlook*, SR/OIAF/2009–03 (Washington, DC: DOE, 2009), Tables A1 and A8, available at www.eia.doe.gov/oiaf/servicerpt/stimulus/excel/aeostimtab_18.xls.

[61] Benjamin K. Sovacool, *The Dirty Energy Dilemma: What's Blocking Clean Power in the United States* (Westport: Praeger, 2008), p. 17.

[62] Norman Myers and Jennifer Kent, *Perverse Subsidies: How Tax Dollars Can Undercut the Environment and the Economy* (Washington, DC: Island Press, 2001).

The transport system that resulted now needs to deliver more than 20 million barrels of oil per day to the United States alone, or 86.7 million barrels of oil per day worldwide. As Table 2.10 indicates, oil production is expected to rise even further to 115 million barrels per day by 2040. This massive system of oil extraction, production, and refining is backed by almost 800 refineries and almost 1 million gasoline stations, to the world's roughly 1 *billion* automobiles which drive on 11.1 million miles of paved roads – enough to drive to the moon and back forty-six times.[63] These roads require $200 million of maintenance per day, and constitute a paved area equal to all arable land in Ohio, Indiana, and Pennsylvania. The transport system also creates 7 billion pounds of un-recycled scrap and waste each year. The United States has a voracious appetite for oil, with consumption having climbed 25 percent since the mid-1980s, though it also imports oil from more than sixty different countries (the largest amount coming from Canada, followed by Saudi Arabia).

The rise of the coveted automobile is often characterized as one of the great achievements of the twentieth century. During the first half of the century, the gasoline-powered vehicle evolved from a fragile, cantankerous, and faulty contraption to a streamlined, reliable, fast, luxurious, and widely affordable product.[64] These automotive engineering feats were enhanced by the creation of interstate highway systems and urban infrastructure that have offered many people unprecedented mobility.

Yet consumers worldwide have precious little choice surrounding their fuels for transport: the United States relies on crude oil to meet 94 percent of its transportation demand, for the world the number rises to 96 percent (electricity, natural gas, and biofuels meet the rest).[65] In the developed world, the car maintains its enduring stranglehold over public transportation options. Statistics agencies in many North American states and provinces report that over 80 percent of their

---

[63] A. Goldthau and B.K. Sovacool, "The Uniqueness of the Energy Security, Justice, and Governance Problem," *Energy Policy* 41 (February 2012), pp. 232–240.

[64] W.M. Shields, "The Automobile as an Open to Closed Technological System: Theory and Practice in the Study of Technological Systems" (Ph.D. dissertation, Virginia Polytechnic Institute and State University, 2007).

[65] International Energy Agency, *Key World Energy Statistics 2011*.

**Table 2.10** *World production of petroleum liquids by region, 2009–2040 (million barrels per day)*

| | History | | | | Projections | | | | Ave. annual % change, |
|---|---|---|---|---|---|---|---|---|---|
| | 2009 | 2010 | 2015 | 2020 | 2025 | 2030 | 2035 | 2040 | 2010–2040 |
| OECD Americas | 23.1 | 23.5 | 23.9 | 24.3 | 24.1 | 23.9 | 24.0 | 24.5 | 0.1 |
| United States | 18.6 | 18.9 | 19.1 | 19.5 | 19.2 | 18.7 | 18.6 | 18.6 | 0.0 |
| Canada | 2.2 | 2.2 | 2.3 | 2.2 | 2.2 | 2.2 | 2.2 | 2.3 | 0.1 |
| Mexico/Chile | 2.4 | 2.4 | 2.5 | 2.6 | 2.8 | 3.1 | 3.3 | 3.6 | 1.3 |
| OECD Europe | 15.0 | 14.8 | 13.5 | 13.7 | 13.7 | 13.8 | 14.0 | 14.1 | -0.2 |
| OECD Asia | 7.7 | 7.7 | 8.2 | 8.1 | 8.1 | 8.1 | 8.0 | 7.9 | 0.1 |
| Japan | 4.4 | 4.4 | 4.6 | 4.4 | 4.3 | 4.2 | 4.1 | 3.9 | -0.4 |
| South Korea | 2.2 | 2.3 | 2.4 | 2.5 | 2.6 | 2.6 | 2.7 | 2.7 | 0.6 |
| Australia/New Zealand | 1.1 | 1.1 | 1.2 | 1.2 | 1.2 | 1.2 | 1.2 | 1.3 | 0.5 |
| Total OECD | 45.8 | 46.0 | 45.6 | 46.2 | 46.0 | 45.8 | 46.0 | 46.4 | 0.0 |
| Non-OECD | | | | | | | | | |
| Non-OECD Europe and Eurasia | 4.8 | 4.8 | 5.8 | 5.9 | 6.0 | 6.4 | 6.7 | 6.9 | 1.2 |
| Russia | 2.9 | 3.0 | 3.4 | 3.5 | 3.6 | 3.8 | 3.9 | 3.9 | 0.9 |
| Other | 1.8 | 1.8 | 2.4 | 2.4 | 2.4 | 2.6 | 2.8 | 3.0 | 1.7 |
| Non-OECD Asia | 18.4 | 19.8 | 22.5 | 25.9 | 29.1 | 32.0 | 35.4 | 39.0 | 2.3 |
| China | 8.5 | 9.3 | 11.6 | 13.6 | 15.4 | 16.6 | 18.2 | 19.8 | 2.5 |
| India | 3.1 | 3.3 | 3.7 | 4.4 | 5.1 | 6.1 | 7.1 | 8.2 | 3.1 |
| Other | 6.7 | 7.2 | 7.2 | 7.9 | 8.6 | 9.3 | 10.1 | 11.0 | 1.4 |

**Table 2.10** (*cont.*)

| | History | | | Projections | | | | | Ave. annual % change, |
|---|---|---|---|---|---|---|---|---|---|
| | 2009 | 2010 | 2015 | 2020 | 2025 | 2030 | 2035 | 2040 | 2010–2040 |
| Middle East | 6.5 | 6.7 | 8.1 | 8.4 | 8.6 | 8.9 | 9.4 | 9.9 | 1.3 |
| Africa | 3.3 | 3.4 | 3.5 | 3.6 | 3.8 | 4.0 | 4.2 | 4.5 | 1.0 |
| Central and South America | 5.7 | 6.0 | 6.5 | 6.6 | 6.8 | 7.3 | 7.7 | 8.2 | 1.0 |
| Brazil | 2.5 | 2.6 | 2.8 | 3.0 | 3.1 | 3.3 | 3.5 | 3.8 | 1.2 |
| Other | 3.3 | 3.4 | 3.6 | 3.7 | 3.8 | 4.0 | 4.2 | 4.4 | 0.9 |
| Total non-OECD | 38.7 | 40.7 | 46.4 | 50.5 | 54.3 | 58.6 | 63.4 | 68.6 | 1.8 |
| Total world | 84.5 | 86.7 | 92.0 | 96.6 | 100.3 | 104.5 | 109.4 | 115.0 | 0.9 |

*Source:* Adapted from US EIA, *International Energy Statistics Database* (as of November 2012).

workforce commutes by car. In other words, gasoline vehicles have become a transportation monoculture – cars and petroleum dominate. Automobile domination is evidenced by the fact that public transport accounts for only about 3 percent of passenger travel in the US,[66] and rail transport accounts for less than 1 percent.[67] Gasoline domination is evidenced by the fact that today nonpetroleum fuels (including electricity, biofuels, and natural gas) account for only 6 percent of US transportation fuel consumption (up from 2 percent in 2007).[68] The motorization of America has resulted in more than one auto for every licensed US driver.

In the developing world, dirt-cheap cars are gaining momentum in a marketplace of billions. Throughout India, China, and Indonesia middle-class families are laden three or four to a single scooter, choking through diesel-exhaust on overcrowded roads. Although 85 percent of the world's population does not have access to a car, they aspire to car ownership, especially residents of the rapidly growing South and East Asia nations. In China, the conventional vehicle fleet is expected to grow tenfold from 37 million in 2005 to 370 million by 2030.[69] In total, within a couple of decades, the world is projected to have 2 billion gasoline-powered automobiles – twice the number that currently exists.[70] If China continues its car-centric development model, it could by itself add another billion cars by the end of the century.

## Agriculture

In the agricultural sector, humanity has changed its land use and dietary patterns and attuned our crops to be dependent on fossil-fuel-based fertilizers, borrowing their energy to produce food. The industrial food system depends on the same sources of fossil fuels as the electricity and transport sector, meaning farmers around the world have become more energy-intensive. The land use implications are

[66] Federal Highway Administration, www.fhwa.dot.gov/ohim/tvtw/tvtpage.cfm.
[67] Brown and Sovacool, *Climate Change*.
[68] US EIA, *Annual Energy Outlook 2009*, Tables A2 and A17.
[69] Daniel Sperling and Deborah Gordon, *Two Billion Cars: Driving Toward Sustainability* (New York: Oxford University Press, 2009).
[70] *Ibid.*

massive: about half of global usable land is now in pastoral or intensive agriculture.[71]

Indeed, food now travels more than it did in 1980, with the average bite of food that most people eat traveling 1,500 to 2,500 miles (2,414 to 4,023 kilometers) to reach their mouths. Even locally grown food is often shipped from a nearby farm to be washed and packaged somewhere else, then transported back home. One study looking at cans of strawberry yogurt produced in Germany found that the average carton traversed 8,000 kilometers (4,970 miles) of roads for production and distribution.[72]

Classic agricultural practices attempted to match the growing patterns of food staples to the land; we now conform the land to produce crops that are in demand and highly profitable. Historically, for example, sound farming practices honed through centuries of local knowledge avoided growing only crops without also raising livestock. Farmers raised mixed crops and not monocultures, took care to preserve the soil and prevent erosion, and minimized waste by mixing vegetable and animal wastes into humus and fertilizer. The process of growth and decay balanced each other, care was taken to store rainwater, and both plants and animals were well equipped to protect themselves from pests and disease.[73]

Modern industrial farming inverts or ignores these practices. Farming is no longer based on natural energy flows and instead transforms ecosystems through the use of fertilizer, pesticides, and herbicides. The use of fossil fuels and chemicals deeply alters the land functionally, and it also makes the entire infrastructure of commercial agriculture dependent on high energy flows to ensure speed of transportation and communication and large-scale production and storage.[74]

People in industrialized countries also consume so much food that land in other parts of the world must be altered to support their habits.

[71] Brown and Sovacool, *Climate Change*.

[72] Herbert Girardet and Miguel Mendonca, *A Renewable World: Energy, Ecology, Equality* (London: Green Books, 2009), p. 187.

[73] Albert Howard, *An Agricultural Testament* (London: Oxford University Press, 1943).

[74] Roy A. Rappaport, "The Flow of Energy in an Agricultural Society," *Scientific American* 25 (1971), pp. 116–132.

The average ecological footprint for someone in the US is about 24 acres (9.7 hectares).[75] Yet the country only has about 13 acres (5.3 hectares) per person (and not all of it is productive), creating a deficit of at least 11 acres (4.5 hectares) per person. Quite simply, the physical territory of the US (as well as Japan, Germany, and many other industrialized countries) is insufficient to meet the demands of their high-consumption lifestyles.[76]

Although cropping and agriculture have always taken different forms in different regions, global food production has become more energy-intensive and transformed by the availability of fossil fuels and electricity. These high-energy inputs are used directly by farm equipment and irrigation systems, indirectly to produce machinery and agricultural chemicals, and as essential feedstocks in the synthesis of nitrogen fertilizers. In 1900, the world's farm machinery had a global capacity of about 10 MW, and nitrogen applied to inorganic fertilizers (mostly in Chile) amounted to only 360,000 tons. Yet in 2000, the total capacity of tractors and harvesters was about 500,000 MW, the Haber-Bosch synthesis fixed about 80 million tons of fertilized nitrogen, pumped irrigation served more than 100 million hectares (247 million acres) of farmland, and cropping was highly dependent on energy-intensive fertilizers and pesticides.

Put in other terms, the century saw a 150-fold increase in fossil fuels and electricity used in global cropping, yet only a sixfold increase in yields and a fourfold increase in productivity.[77] Larger farms are now worked with larger machines, need more fertilizers and pesticides, rely on centralized and energy-intensive delivery patterns, and depend more on packaging and processing.[78] Even if fossil-fuel use did not pose grave dangers to the environment and climate, the process would be unsustainable. As Berkeley Professor Michael Pollan has noted,

---

[75] A person's ecological footprint is the land needed to supply his or her needs relating to food, housing, energy, transport, and consumer goods and services. L. Walker and W. Rees, "Urban Density and Ecological Footprints: An Analysis of Canadian Households," in Mark Roseland (ed.), *Eco-City Dimensions: Healthy Communities, Healthy Planet* (Gabriola Island, BC, Canada: New Society Publishers, 1997).

[76] Miranda A. Schreurs, "Divergent Paths: Environmental Policy in Germany, the United States, and Japan," *Environment* 45(8) (2003), pp. 9–17.

[77] Smil, "Energy in the Twentieth Century."

[78] Girardet and Mendonca, *A Renewable World*, p. 188.

Table 2.11 *Global environmental degradation associated with energy use*

| Dimension | Energy contribution to the problem |
| --- | --- |
| Climate change | 66.5% of global carbon dioxide emissions come from energy supply and transport, a further 13.5% come from agriculture |
| Air pollution | About 80% of global $SO_2$ emissions, 80% of PM emissions, and 70% percent of $NO_x$ emissions come from the energy and transport sectors |
| Water availability and quality | 25% of global water supply is lost due to evaporation from reservoirs and another 10–15% of global freshwater is used in thermoelectric power plants; agriculture accounts for 70% of global water consumption |
| Land use change | At least 15% of land use change is caused by the direct clearing of forests for fuelwood and the expansion of plantations for energy crops; about 30% of global land area is occupied by farms and agricultural systems |

"from the standpoint of industrial efficiency, it's too bad we can't simply drink the petroleum directly."[79]

## Environmental and social impacts

This final part of this chapter discusses key energy "impacts" or "outputs" such as waste, pollution, and environmental degradation. The global energy system's wastefulness and inefficiency – for more on this, see Chapter 3 – leads to environmental damage across at least four dimensions summarized in Table 2.11: climate change, air pollution, water quality and availability, and land use change.

### Climate change

The most urgent and dire output from the global energy system is the emission of carbon and carbon dioxide into the atmosphere, which is

[79] Michael Pollan, *The Omnivore's Dilemma: A Natural History of Four Meals* (New York: Penguin, 2006), p. 46.

rapidly losing its ability to safely store and sink it. Basically, scientists and policymakers have treated the atmosphere as an "unlimited sink" with the capacity to safely store as much carbon as we could hurl at it, with the idea that "the solution to pollution is dilution."[80] However, since the 1960s scientists have realized that very real limits exist for the atmosphere's ability to process carbon.

Figure 2.4 shows that most of global GHG emissions come from energy supply and use, agriculture, and transport, and it depicts the individual countries most responsible for those emissions. Note three things about this figure. First, that emissions of carbon dioxide are *not* the only problem; so are emissions of methane, nitrous oxide, and human-made high global warming potential gases such as HFC-23 and sulfur hexafluoride. Second, longstanding industrialized countries no longer make up the bulk of emissions; note the presence of China, India, Brazil, and Indonesia. Third, each country's emissions profile is different, with some (such as the United States and China) coming primarily from energy and transport and others (such as Brazil and Indonesia) coming from deforestation and changes in land use.

Now, whenever discussing the atmospheric capacity to store carbon dioxide, it is important to think about a carbon budget of 1 trillion tons of carbon – that is the ultimate ceiling on what scientists say we can safely emit in total.[81] Right now, humanity is emitting about 50 billion tons of carbon dioxide equivalent per year, or 14.1 billion tons of carbon (which is 3.67 times the weight of carbon dioxide). Between 1751 and 2012, we have emitted a total of about 435 billion tons of carbon. That means we have roughly 565 tons left that we can emit, or forty years of emissions at today's rate.

Here's the rub: *five times* that amount of carbon – 2,795 billion tons – is currently contained in all the proven coal, oil, and gas reserves of fossil-fuel companies and countries. Essentially, this is the fossil fuel we are planning on burning, but it will completely blow our budget. As science writer Bill McKibben explains:

---

[80] Naomi Oreskes and Erik M. Conway, "The Collapse of Western Civilization: A View from the Future," *Daedalus* 142(1) (Winter 2013), pp. 40–58.

[81] Hal Harvey, Franklin M. Orr, Jr., and Clara Vondrich, "A Trillion Tons," *Daedalus* 142(1) (Winter 2013), pp. 8–25.

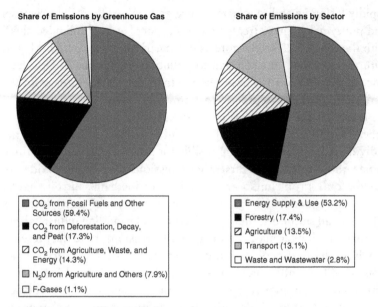

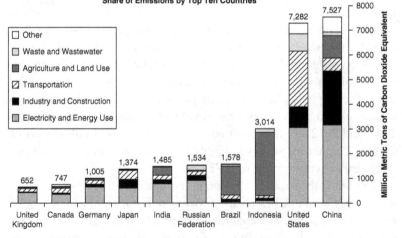

**Figure 2.4** Share of global greenhouse gas emissions by sector, gas, and country, 2010

*Source:* Adapted from M.A. Brown and B.K. Sovacool, *Climate Change and Global Energy Security: Technology and Policy Options* (Cambridge, MA: MIT Press, 2011).

2,795 gigatons is such a big deal. Think of two degrees Celsius as the legal drinking limit – equivalent to the 0.08 blood-alcohol level below which you might get away with driving home. The 565 gigatons is how many drinks you could have and still stay below that limit – the six beers, say, you might consume in an evening. And the 2,795 gigatons? That's the three 12-packs the fossil-fuel industry has on the table, already opened and ready to pour. We have five times as much oil and coal and gas on the books as climate scientists think is safe to burn. We'd have to keep 80 percent of those reserves locked away underground to avoid that fate.[82]

Worse still, those 2,795 billion tons of carbon are worth about $27 trillion in today's (undiscounted) money, which means writing off 80 percent of that is asking fossil-fuel companies to abandon $20 trillion in assets. Yet, as climate scientist James Hansen and his colleagues have noted, "burning all fossil fuels would produce a different, practically uninhabitable, planet."[83]

This dilemma – the inability for companies and consumers to agree to forgo these fuels – may be why under a business as usual scenario, the IPCC forecasts that annual emissions of all GHGs will rise from 52.5 billion tons of carbon dioxide (14.1 billion tons of carbon) today to 140 billion tons of carbon dioxide (38.1 billion tons of carbon) by 2100 – almost a threefold increase, as Figure 2.5 depicts.

As a result of these emissions, carbon dioxide concentrations, usually measured in parts per million (ppm), have been steadily rising. Figure 2.6 shows carbon dioxide concentrations for the past 1,100 years, measured from the air trapped in ice samples and directly in Hawaii.[84] The atmospheric concentration of carbon dioxide reached 340 ppm in 2000. These concentrations have risen to 400 ppm this year (408 ppm when all GHGs are accounted for), and will rise further to 1,410 ppm for all gases by 2100 under business as usual. Put another way, global temperatures rise by about 1.5°C for every trillion tons of carbon put into the atmosphere. The world has pumped out half a trillion tons of carbon since 1750, and temperatures have risen by 0.8°C. At current

---

[82] Bill McKibben, "Global Warming's Terrifying New Math," *Rolling Stone* (July 19, 2012), pp. 32–44.

[83] James Hansen, Makiko Sato, Gary Russell, and Pushker Kharecha, "Climate Sensitivity, Sea Level, and Atmospheric $CO_2$," NASA Goddard Institute for Space Studies and Columbia University Earth Institute, New York, 2013.

[84] David J.C. MacKay, *Sustainable Energy – Without the Hot Air* (Cambridge: UIT, 2008).

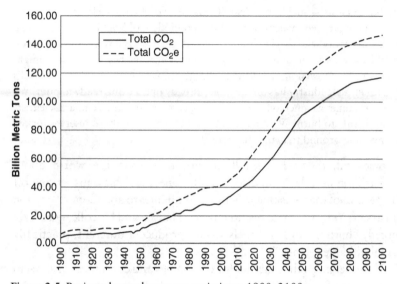

**Figure 2.5** Projected greenhouse gas emissions, 1900–2100
*Source:* Projections assume IPCC's A1FI scenario with growth allocations to
countries based on the 2011 *International Energy Outlook*.

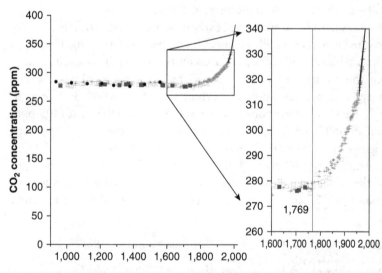

**Figure 2.6** Atmospheric concentration of carbon dioxide (ppm), 1900–2000
*Source:* Adapted from David J.C. MacKay, *Sustainable Energy – Without the
Hot Air* (Cambridge: UIT, 2008).

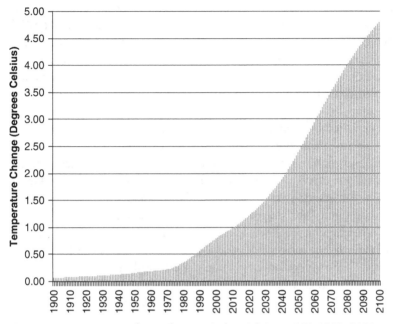

**Figure 2.7** Temperature change from preindustrial times (°C), 1900–2100
*Source:* Projections assume IPCC's A1FI with growth allocations to countries based on the 2011 *International Energy Outlook*.

rates, the next half-trillion tons will be emitted by 2045; the next after that before 2080.[85]

This will not be good for ordered civil society, to put it mildly. So far, since the industrial revolution our emissions have raised the temperature of the planet just under 1 degree Celsius. Already, those emissions have induced much greater damage than anticipated, in the form of melting sea ice, ocean acidity, and feedback loops. Thomas Lovejoy, once the World Bank's chief biodiversity advisor, explained it this way: "if we're seeing what we're seeing today at 0.8°C, two degrees is simply too much."[86] However, Figure 2.7 illustrates that expected emissions and concentrations will result in a temperature change of 4.81°C by 2100. The World Bank, hardly known for a liberal stance on climate

[85] "Climate Science: A Sensitive Matter," *Economist*, March 30, 2013, pp. 77–79.
[86] Quoted in McKibben, "Global Warming's Terrifying New Math."

policy, has warned that warming of 4°C could occur as early as the 2060s if economies grow faster than expected.[87] It concluded that a 4°C change would be "devastating" with "the inundation of coastal cities; increasing risks for food production potentially leading to higher malnutrition rates; many dry regions becoming dryer, wet regions wetter; unprecedented heat waves in many regions, especially in the tropics; substantially exacerbated water scarcity in many regions; increased frequency of high-intensity tropical cyclones; and irreversible loss of biodiversity, including coral reef systems." Critically, a 4°C world is "so different from the current one" as to almost be unimaginable; certainly it is not one that our existing civilizations are adapted to survive. Or, as Kevin Anderson, past Director of the Tyndall Centre for Climate Change, put it, "A 4 degrees C future is incompatible with an organized global community, is likely to be beyond 'adaptation,' is devastating to the majority of ecosystems, and has a high probability of not being stable."[88] For more on how these impacts will play out, readers can jump ahead to Chapter 10.

## Air pollution

The degradation of airsheds is a serious energy-related concern in at least two respects: outdoor air pollution contributes to degraded human health and increased hospital admissions, and indoor air pollution (IAP) causes premature deaths, mostly of women and children. Such pollution is significantly caused by energy production and use, with about 80 percent of sulfur dioxide ($SO_2$) emissions, 80 percent of PM emissions, and 70 percent of nitrogen oxide ($NO_x$) emissions coming from the energy and transport sectors.[89]

$SO_2$ is a pollutant responsible for lake- and forest-damaging acid precipitation and is a precursor to the development of small particles that damage human health. Most $SO_2$ (around 70 percent) comes from electricity generation in most countries, with a further 10 percent

---

[87] Potsdam Institute for Climate Impact Research and Climate Analytics, *Turn Down the Heat: Why a 4°C Warmer World Must Be Avoided* (Washington, DC: World Bank, December 2012).

[88] Quoted in Paddy Manning, "Too Hot To Handle: Can We Afford a 4 Degree Rise?," *Sydney Morning Herald*, July 9, 2011.

[89] World Resources Institute, *Earth Trends Database*, accessed January 2012.

coming from the transportation sector.[90] $NO_x$ emissions react with volatile organic compounds in the atmosphere (gasoline vapors or solvents, for example) and produce compounds that can result in severe lung damage, asthma, and emphysema. $NO_x$ is also a major source of ground-level ozone (smog). It contributes to acid rain and pollutes surface water. The largest sources of nitrogen oxides are automobiles, refineries, and power plants, which account for about 80 percent of emissions in most countries.[91]

Emissions of $SO_2$ and $NO_x$ create problems when they react together in the atmosphere to form compounds that are transported long distances and induce acidification of lakes, streams, rivers, and soils, a process known as acid deposition.[92] Acid rain from $SO_2$ and $NO_x$ compounds can render many bodies of water unfit for certain fish and wildlife species. Acidic deposition can also mobilize toxic amounts of aluminum, increasing its availability for uptake by plants and fish, which are then ingested by humans. The past six decades have seen a tenfold increase in the acidity of rain and snow over millions of square kilometers.[93]

PM is not a specific pollutant itself, but instead is a mixture of fine particles of harmful pollutants such as soot, acid droplets, and metals. PM is the generic term for the mixture of these microscopic solid particles and liquid droplets in the air. Because its make-up is often complex, PM is by far the most difficult pollutant to detect and monitor. The most widely studied are those particles with an aerodynamic diameter of 10 microns or less ($PM_{10}$) and those with a diameter of 2.5 ($PM_{2.5}$) microns or less. Inhalation of PM is strongly associated with heart disease and chronic lung disease.[94] Since microscopic solids or

[90] US EPA, *Air Pollution Facts* (Washington, DC: Air and Radiation Division, 2003).
[91] David R. Wooley, *A Guide to the Clean Air Act for the Renewable Energy Community* (Washington, DC: Renewable Energy Policy Project, 2000), pp. 7–14.
[92] Rodney Sobin, "Energy Myth Seven: Renewable Energy Systems Could Never Meet Growing Electricity Demand in America," in B.K. Sovacool and M. A. Brown (eds.), *Energy and American Society – Thirteen Myths* (New York: Springer, 2007), pp. 171–199.
[93] John P. Holdren and Kirk R. Smith, "Energy, the Environment, and Health," in Tord Kjellstrom, David Streets, and Xiadong Wang (eds.), *World Energy Assessment: Energy and the Challenge of Sustainability* (New York: UN Development Program, 2000), pp. 61–110.
[94] Wooley, *A Guide to the Clean Air Act*.

liquid droplets are so small, they can get deep into the body and cause serious health problems. Numerous scientific studies have linked PM exposure to:

- Irritation of the airways, coughing, or difficulty breathing;
- Decreased lung function;
- Aggravated asthma;
- Development of chronic bronchitis;
- Irregular heartbeat;
- Nonfatal heart attacks;
- Premature death in people with heart or lung disease.[95]

Roughly 50 percent of PM pollution comes from power plants, with the transportation sector accounting for 30 percent (wildfires and dust storms are the other primary sources).[96]

Cumulatively, the impacts of this pollution are quite severe. In a national survey of air quality, the American Lung Association warned that 81 million people live in areas of the United States with unhealthy short-term levels of air pollution. The Association noted that 66 million of these Americans reside in places with unhealthy year-round levels of particle pollution, 136 million in areas with unhealthy levels of ozone, and 46 million in counties with all three forms of pollution.[97] Lung diseases now affect more than 10 percent of the population and are the third leading cause of death for Americans.[98] Nationwide, the Environmental Protection Agency (EPA) has designated 474 counties "nonattainment areas" for unsafe levels of ozone and 224 counties as unsafe areas for fine PM.[99] That is, these counties are so degraded that no additional pollution is authorized under federal law. These areas include all the eastern states from Maine south to

---

[95] US EPA, *Particulate Matter: Health and Environment* (Washington, DC: Air and Radiation Division, 2006).

[96] Angela Ledford, *The Dirty Secret behind Dirty Air* (Boston, MA: Clean Air Taskforce, June 2004).

[97] American Lung Association, *Summary of the American Lung Association's Annual Clean Air Test* (Washington, DC: American Lung Association, 2005).

[98] J.J. Romm and C.A. Ervin, *How Energy Policies Affect Public Health* (Washington, DC: Solstice, 2005).

[99] D.A. Jacobson, "Increasing the Value and Expanding the Market for Renewable Energy and Energy Efficiency with Clean Air Policies," *Environmental Law Review* 37 (2007), pp. 10135–10137.

Georgia as well as Alabama, Arizona, California, Colorado, Illinois, Indiana, Kentucky, Louisiana, Michigan, Missouri, Nevada, Ohio, Tennessee, Texas, West Virginia, and Wisconsin. It may come as no surprise, then, that at the high end of the range, the health costs related to power plant pollution could approach $700 billion each year.[100]

This trend is not limited to the United States. The regional network on air-quality management Clean Air Asia aggregated data from more than 300 Asian cities in sixteen countries in 2012 and found that levels of PM were below "safe" targets in only sixteen cities, most of them in Japan. This means that more than 94 percent of cities sampled have air unsafe to breathe. Moreover, outdoor air pollution is projected to cause more than 3.6 million deaths per year by 2030 throughout the region, mostly in China and India.[101] In China, PM pollution causes at least $63 to $272 billion in damages or as much as 3.3 percent to 7.0 percent of national GDP.[102] In early 2013, air pollution became so bad in China that it soared "beyond index" and resulted in the cancellation of commercial airline flights; the World Health Organization (WHO) reported concentrations of $PM_{2.5}$ as high as 1,000 micrograms in many major urban areas, when safe limits are set at no more than 25 micrograms.[103] Figure 2.8 shows seventeen cities around the world with the rates of PM well above safety standards, with each one showing levels above 10 micrograms of PM per cubic meter.

A completely separate type of air pollution is indoors, rather than outdoors, where billions of homes rely on the burning of firewood, dung, charcoal, kerosene, and coal for warmth and heat. As the WHO

---

[100] See M.A. Delucchi, J.J. Murphy, and D.R. McGubbin, "The Health and Visibility Cost of Air Pollution: A Comparison of Estimation Methods," *Journal of Environmental Management* 64 (2002), pp. 139–152; I. Romieu, J.M. Samet, K.R. Smith, and N. Bruce, "Outdoor Air Pollution and Acute Respiratory Infections among Children in Developing Countries," *Journal of Occupational and Environmental Medicine* 44 (2002), pp. 640–649; K. Katsouyanni and G. Pershagen, "Ambient Air Pollution Exposure to Cancer," *Cancer Causes and Control* 8 (1997), pp. 284–291.

[101] Bettina Wassener, "Asian Cities' Air Quality Getting Worse, Experts Warn," *New York Times*, December 5, 2012.

[102] See X. Deng, "Economic Costs of Motor Vehicle Emissions in China: A Case Study," *Transportation Research* 11(3) (2006), pp. 216–26; and Anthony J. McMichael, "Seeing Clearly: Tackling Air Pollution in China," *Lancet* 370, September 15, 2007, pp. 927–928.

[103] "Wrapped in Smog: Something in the Air?," *Economist*, January 19, 2013, p. 47.

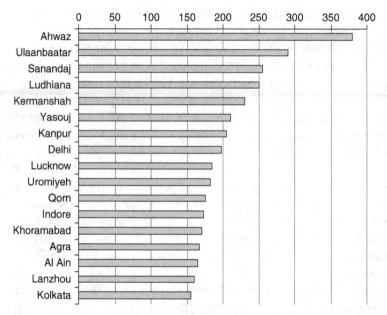

**Figure 2.8** Cities with high concentrations of particulate matter pollution, 2008–2009 (PM$_{10}$ concentration micrograms/m$^3$)
*Source:* Adapted from Asian Development Bank, "Asia's Energy Challenge: Critical Energy Needs for the Asian Century," *Asian Development Outlook 2013* (Manila: Asian Development Bank, 2013), pp. 53–118.

explains: "The inefficient burning of solid fuels on an open fire or traditional stove indoors creates a dangerous cocktail of not only hundreds of pollutants, primarily carbon monoxide and small particles, but also nitrogen oxides, benzene, butadiene, formaldehyde, polyaromatic hydrocarbons and many other health-damaging chemicals."[104] There is both a dangerous spatial and temporal dimension to such pollution. Spatially, it is concentrated in small rooms and kitchens rather than outdoors, meaning that many homes have exposure levels to harmful pollutants sixty times the rate acceptable outdoors in city centers in North America and Europe.[105] Temporally, this pollution from stoves is released at precisely the same times when people are present cooking, eating, or sleeping, with women typically

---

[104] WHO, *Fuel for Life* (Geneva: WHO, 2006), p. 8.    [105] *Ibid.*

spending three to seven hours a day in the kitchen.[106] For more on the health impacts of this IAP, readers are invited to skip ahead to Chapter 4 (which discusses it as an "externality") and Chapter 7 (which discusses the case for expanding access to modern energy services).

## Water use and contamination

The degradation of water quality and availability is a third serious effect of our energy systems. For instance, thermoelectric power plants running on coal, natural gas, oil, and uranium require immense amounts of water to cool the combustion process, and more than fifty countries rely primarily on hydroelectric dams to generate power in their electricity sectors. These collective power plants withdraw trillions of gallons of water from rivers and streams, consume billions of gallons of water from local aquifers and lakes, and contaminate water supplies at various parts of their fuel cycle. A conventional 500 MW coal plant, for instance, consumes about 7,000 gallons (26,498 liters) of water per minute, or the equivalent of seventeen Olympic-sized swimming pools every day.[107] Oil and gas production facilities, refineries, ethanol distilleries, and manufacturing firms also rely on prodigious amounts of water to transform raw commodities into usable energy fuels, services, and products.

Globally, agriculture is the overall largest user of freshwater, and the energy sector comes second, with hydropower, nuclear power, and thermal power generation accounting for about 15 percent of global water use – that is, they use roughly 583 billion cubic meters of water, an amount equal to the annual discharge of the entire Ganges River Basin in India.[108] Furthermore, the United Nations (UN) estimates that the volume of water evaporated from reservoirs is estimated to exceed

---

[106] Jamil Masud, Diwesh Sharan, and Bindu N. Lohani, *Energy for All: Addressing the Energy, Environment, and Poverty Nexus in Asia* (Manila: Asian Development Bank, April 2007).

[107] Benjamin K. Sovacool and Kelly E. Sovacool, "Identifying Future Electricity Water Tradeoffs in the United States," *Energy Policy* 37(7) (2009), pp. 2763–2773.

[108] UNEP, *An Overview of the State of the World's Fresh and Marine Waters* (New York: UNEP, 2008); see also International Energy Agency, *World Energy Outlook 2012* (Paris: OECD, 2012).

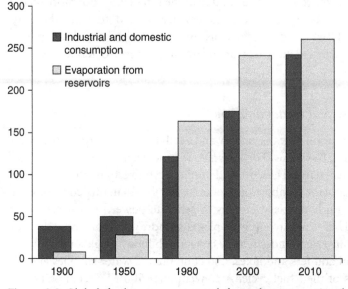

**Figure 2.9** Global freshwater evaporated from dam reservoirs (km³/year), 1900–2010
*Source:* Adapted from UNEP, *An Overview of the State of the World's Fresh and Marine Waters* (New York: UNEP, 2008).

the combined freshwater needs of industry and domestic consumption, which represent about 25 percent of global water use, as Figure 2.9 shows. As the UN concluded, hydroelectric dams therefore "greatly contribute to water losses around the world, especially in hot tropical regions."[109]

Oil and gas production is also exceptionally water intensive. Drilling for oil and gas involves bringing large quantities of rock fragments, called "cuttings," to the surface, and these cuttings are coated with drilling fluids, called "drilling muds," which operators use to lubricate drill bits and stabilize pressure within oil and gas wells. The quantity of toxic cuttings and mud released for each facility is gargantuan, ranging from 60,000 to 300,000 gallons (606,000 to 1.14 million liters) per day. In addition to cuttings and drilling muds, vast quantities of water contaminated with suspended and dissolved solids are also brought to the surface, creating what geologists refer to as "produced

[109] UNEP, *An Overview.*

water."[110] The average offshore oil and gas platform in the United States releases about 400,000 gallons of produced water every day.[111]

The extraction of coal is similarly water intensive and damaging to watersheds. Coalmining, for instance, can remove mountaintops in a process that clears forests and topsoil before it uses explosives to break up rocks, pushing mine spoils into adjacent streams and valleys. This can cause acid drainage into river systems.[112] Mountaintop mining with valley fill (MTVF) operations in the Appalachian region of the United States have so far converted 1.1 million hectares of forest into surface mines and buried more than 2,000 kilometers of freshwater streams and rivers.[113]

Nuclear power plants, too, can create wastewater contaminated with radioactive tritium and other toxic substances that can leak into nearby groundwater sources. In December 2005, for example, Exelon Corporation reported to authorities that its Braidwood reactor in Illinois had since 1996 released millions of gallons of tritium-contaminated wastewater into the local watershed; this prompted the company to distribute bottled water to surrounding communities while local drinking water wells were tested for the pollutant.[114] In New York, a faulty drain system at Entergy's Indian Point Nuclear Plant on the Hudson River caused thousands of gallons of radioactive waste to be leaked into underground lakes.[115] Such examples are not isolated and have not been chosen selectively: as of February 2010, 27 of the 104 reactors operating in the United States have been documented leaking radioactive tritium into watersheds.[116]

---

[110] David Waskow and Carol Welch, "The Environmental, Social, and Human Rights Impacts of Oil Development," in Svetlana Tsalik and Anya Schiffrin (eds.), *Covering Oil: A Reporter's Guide to Energy and Development* (New York: Open Society Institute, 2005), pp. 101–123.

[111] *Ibid.*    [112] Sobin, "Energy Myth Seven."

[113] Emily S. Bernhardt and Margaret A. Palmer, "The Environmental Costs of Mountaintop Mining Valley Fill Operations for Aquatic Ecosystems of the Central Appalachians," *Annals of the New York Academy of Sciences* 1223 (2001), pp. 39–57.

[114] Illinois Sues Exelon for Radioactive Tritium Releases since 1996, Environmental New Service, Mar. 21, 2006, available at www.ens-newswire.com/ens/mar2006/2006–03–21–02.asp.

[115] Abby Luby, "Leaks at Indian Point Created Underwater Lakes," *North Country News*, Feb. 28, 2008, available at www.abbylu.com/pdfs/ENVIRONMENT/indianpointleaks.pdf.

[116] "Leaks Spotlight Aging Nuclear Plants," Associated Press, February 1, 2010.

## Land use and deforestation

The production of energy can negatively affect land in many ways, from converting forests into plantations for energy crops to access roads to dams and oil and gas facilities opening up areas to deforestation. One conservative estimate suggests that 15 percent of land use changes are caused by the clearing of forests for fuelwood and for energy crop plantations.[117]

Much of the world's farming, livestock production, and changes in land use have taken place in former forests and tropical forests (sometimes called "land use and land-use change and forestry," or LULUCF). This transformation of forestland into other uses is problematic because it directly releases carbon into the atmosphere. Forests cover about 30 percent of global land area, storing 683 billion tons of carbon, more than the total amount of carbon contained in the atmosphere. Through the carbon cycle, forests remove an additional 3 billion tons of carbon dioxide each year through growth, and they also absorb about 30 percent of carbon dioxide emissions from fossil-fuel combustion.[118] Put another way, forests store about 45 percent of terrestrial carbon and can sequester additional carbon dioxide emissions directly out of the air. As forests grow, they sink carbon dioxide from the atmosphere in their roots, branches, and leaves (their "biomass"), in essence making $CO_2$ a part of the natural landscape.[119] Yet when forests are cleared, harvested, or catch fire, their stored carbon is emitted back into the atmosphere. About 36 percent of the carbon added to the atmosphere from 1850 to 2000 came from the elimination and conversion of forests.[120]

Yet the rate of deforestation worldwide averaged 13 million hectares a year between 1990 and 2005.[121] Indonesia and Brazil account for

---

[117] Virginia H. Dale, Rebecca A. Efroymson, and Keith L. Kline, "The Land Use–Climate Change–Energy Nexus," *Landscape Ecology* 26 (2011), pp. 755–773.

[118] Girardet and Mendonca, *A Renewable World*, p. 188.

[119] Charlotte Streck, "Forests, Carbon Markets, and Avoided Deforestation: Legal Implications," *Carbon & Climate Law Review* 2(3) (2008), pp. 239–247.

[120] Charlotte Streck, Lucio Pedroni, Manuel Porrua, and Michael Dutschke, "Creating Incentives for Avoiding Further Deforestation: The Nested Approach," in Charlotte Streck, Robert O'Sullivan, Toby Janson-Smith, and Richard G. Tarasofsky (eds.), *Climate Change and Forests: Emerging Policy and Market Opportunities* (Washington, DC: Brookings Institution Press, 2008), pp. 237–249.

[121] UN Food and Agricultural Organization, *Global Forest Resource Assessment* (Rome: Food and Agricultural Organization, 2006).

Table 2.12 *Global leaders in carbon dioxide equivalent emissions from deforestation*

| Country | % Share of emissions from deforestation |
|---|---|
| Indonesia | 33.7 |
| Brazil | 18.0 |
| Malaysia | 9.2 |
| Myanmar | 5.6 |
| Democratic Republic of the Congo | 4.2 |
| Zambia | 3.1 |
| Nigeria | 2.6 |
| Peru | 2.5 |
| Papua New Guinea | 1.9 |
| Total | 80.8 |

*Source*: Adapted from Doug Boucher, *Out of the Woods: A Realistic Role for Tropical Forests in Curbing Global Warming* (Washington, DC: Union of Concerned Scientists, 2008).

about half the emissions from deforestation, which also explains why they are (respectively) the third and fourth largest emitters of GHGs overall, behind China and the US. Indeed, Table 2.12 shows that just nine countries account for more than 80 percent of all GHG emissions from deforestation.[122]

## Other pollution

Tragically, these four major outputs – carbon, air pollution, water pollution, and the degradation of land – are not the global energy system's only four, just the most significant. There are various other pollutants shown in Table 2.13 related to energy production and use, including biologically and climatologically active elements and compounds such as lead, cadmium, methane, and mercury, each deserving of more detail that we are unable to provide due to limitations on space.[123]

---

[122] Doug Boucher, *Out of the Woods: A Realistic Role for Tropical Forests in Curbing Global Warming* (Washington, DC: Union of Concerned Scientists, 2008).

[123] Holdren and Smith, "Energy, the Environment, and Health."

Table 2.13 *Major sources of global energy pollutants*

| Insult/source | Tons emitted/year | Human disruption index | Share of human disruption caused by | | | |
|---|---|---|---|---|---|---|
| | | | % Commercial energy supply | % traditional energy supply | % agriculture | % manufacturing & other |
| Lead emissions to atmosphere | 12,000 | 18 | 41 (fossil-fuel burning, including additives) | Negligible | Negligible | 59 (metal processing, manufacturing, refuse burning) |
| Oil added to oceans | 200,000 | 10 | 44 (petroleum harvesting, processing, and transport) | Negligible | Negligible | 56 (disposal of oil wastes, including motor oil changes) |
| Cadmium emissions to atmosphere | 1,400 | 5.4 | 13 (fossil-fuel burning) | 5 (traditional fuel burning) | 12 (agricultural burning) | 70 (metals processing, manufacturing, refuse burning) |
| Sulfur emissions to atmosphere | 31 million (sulfur) | 2.7 | 85 (fossil-fuel burning) | 0.5 (traditional fuel burning) | 1 (agricultural burning) | 13 (smelting, refuse burning) |
| Methane flow to atmosphere | 160 million | 2.3 | 18 (fossil-fuel harvesting and processing) | 5 (traditional fuel burning) | 65 (rice paddies, domestic animals, land clearing) | 12 (landfills) |
| Nitrogen fixation (as $NO_x$ and ammonium) | 140 million (nitrogen) | 1.5 | 30 (fossil-fuel burning) | 2 (traditional fuel burning) | 67 (fertilizer, agricultural burning) | 1 (refuse burning) |

| Mercury emissions to atmosphere | 2,500 | 1.4 | 20 (fossil-fuel burning) | 1 (traditional fuel burning) | 2 (agricultural burning) | 77 (metals processing, manufacturing, refuse burning) |
|---|---|---|---|---|---|---|
| Nitrous oxide flows to atmosphere | 33 million | 0.5 | 12 (fossil-fuel burning) | 8 (traditional fuel burning) | 80 (fertilizer, land clearing, aquifer disruption) | Negligible |
| Particulate emissions to atmosphere | 3.1 billion | 0.12 | 35 (fossil-fuel burning) | 10 (traditional fuel burning) | 40 (agricultural burning) | 15 (smelting, nonagricultural land clearing, refuse) |
| Nonmethane hydrocarbon emissions to atmosphere | 1,000 million | 0.12 | 35 (fossil-fuel processing and burning) | 5 (traditional fuel burning) | 40 (agricultural burning) | 20 (nonagricultural land clearing, refuse burning) |
| Carbon dioxide flows to atmosphere | 50 billion (carbon) | 0.05 | 75 (fossil-fuel burning) | 3 (net deforestation for fuelwood) | 15 (net deforestation for land clearing) | 7 (net deforestation for lumber, cement manufacturing) |

Source: Adapted from John P. Holdren and Kirk R. Smith, "Energy, the Environment, and Health," in Tord Kjellstrom, David Streets, and Xiadong Wang (eds.), World Energy Assessment: Energy and the Challenge of Sustainability (New York: UN Development Program, 2000), pp. 61–110.

## Conclusion

In sum, the history of the global energy system can be interpreted as one progressing from simple to complex systems. During the days of old, the simplest gathering of wood did not need special delivery mechanisms. The early infrastructures of the industrial revolution were also relatively modest, like a gravel road leading to a coal seam. Nineteenth-century mines became slightly more complicated, as they were connected to markets by railroads and employed shipping by barges. The next generation of mines needed intricate systems of technology such as steam-powered pumping and ventilation systems and power shovels to reach deeper seams. Hydrocarbons introduced a whole new level of complexity, as they needed pipelines to carry oil and gas, fuels that also need to be pretreated, refined and stored. Electricity was even more demanding, as it necessitated expansive T&D lines and large numbers of converters ready to soak up all supply, from lights and appliances to electric motors and furnaces, all combined with an expectation that supply would be matched to demand on virtually an instantaneous basis.

Yet, the influence and impact of the global energy system and its subsystems involving mining, oil and gas development, electricity, transport, and agriculture on the earth's climate has become so pronounced that the planet has actually entered a new geological epoch, transitioning from the 12,000 year old *Holocene* to the fittingly titled *Anthropocene*, which means "human" and "new."[124] If the entire 4.5 billion year history of the Earth is condensed into a single day, human beings do not even appear until 1 minute and 17 seconds to midnight, and the entire industrial age lasts less than a second. Think about this simple fact: the global energy system has managed to exceed the buffering capacity of the atmosphere and disrupt the global climatic system in less than 1 second of the Earth's twenty-four-hour history. "Human activity is the most powerful geological force altering the face of the planet," writes population ecologist William Rees, "and the erosive pace is accelerating."[125] If we could speed up time, the global

---

[124] Paul J. Crutzen and E.F. Stoermer, "The Anthropocene," *IGBP Newsletter* 41, May 2000.

[125] William Rees, "Contemplating the Abyss: The Role of Environmental Degradation in the Collapse of Human Societies," in Laura Nader (ed.), *The Energy Reader* (London: Wiley–Blackwell, 2010), pp. 61–64.

economy and its energy infrastructure would appear to be literally crashing into the earth like an asteroid.[126]

The chapters to come suggest a better way forward – a roadmap for slowing, and even reversing, the metaphorical asteroid strike by pursuing energy options that are more fair, equitable, and just. Having reviewed the key terminology and facts about current energy systems, we now turn to consideration of the values or "concepts of justice" that do play a decisional role in energy policy and personal choices. The chapters ahead weave together both pragmatic examples and theoretical analyses, beginning, in Chapter 3, with an Aristotelian question: What is the purpose of our energy institutions and technologies?

---

[126] James Gustave Speth, *The Bridge at the End of the World: Capitalism, the Environment, and Crossing from Crisis to Sustainability* (New Haven: Yale University Press, 2008).

# 3 | Virtue and energy efficiency

Pretend that the management committee of a large electric utility is reaching a point where standard projections indicate that demand from customers will soon exceed their ability to provide power. Two options have been presented to senior management. One is to spend $3 billion to build a new generating station which is expected to produce enough energy to meet demand growth for ten years at a cost of approximately 5 cents per kWh at the busbar, which would mean a cost delivered to consumers of about 8 cents per kWh. Another option is to invest $2 billion in insulating the homes and businesses of customers, which is expected to avoid the otherwise anticipated increase in demand for at least ten years, at a cost of approximately 3 to 4 cents per kWh, which with overhead will equal 4 to 5 cents per kWh on customer bills.

Which of these alternatives would you choose? Should you be affected by the fact that traditional rulemaking will grant your shareholders a high probability of earning an 8 to 10 percent return on the $3 billion investment in the power plant, while the direct expenses of insulation are recovered, but generate no return on investment?

Now, suppose that the regulatory authority is relatively progressive, and will allow a return of 8 percent on the $2 billion insulation investment. Knowing that an 8 percent on a $2 billion investment earns shareholders less than 8 percent on a $3 billion investment, why would you recommend the less profitable efficiency measures?

What guidance do traditional ethics thinkers offer here? As one answer, this chapter presents one of the oldest concepts of justice: that of virtue. We explore some of the questions posed by Plato and Aristotle about the purposes of things, institutions, and social goals. Long ago, these thinkers suggested that the concept of "virtue" could guide our judgment about what to do and how to distinguish between expected end results. But this concept of "virtue" had a special meaning. It was tied to an internal essential purpose of an object, an institution, or a goal.[1] In one famous example, we are asked, "Who should own a beautifully made flute?" Should it be the maker who devoted time and skill to its creation? Should it be the listener who most greatly needs the beauty of music added to an otherwise drab existence? Should it be the person who can pay the most to possess the lovely object?[2] Aristotle's answer is that it should be none of these; but rather, it should be the flute player who will most skillfully use it to produce music. If the purpose of a flute is to create blissful sounds, then its ownership should be assigned to whoever will most effectively make music. Similarly, other objects each have their own internal essential purpose, and each should properly be assigned to a role that will help its purpose be most efficiently achieved.

In order to understand Aristotelian concepts of virtue, it thus becomes necessary to ask the essential purpose for which an object exists. If we apply this concept to an electric utility or an energy company, we can readily say that the company is most "virtuous" if it most efficiently fulfills its essential purpose, i.e. to provide electricity or energy services. However, perhaps this question is not as easy as it seems to some. For example, if the purpose of a flute was to provide income to flute makers, would it not be most "virtuous" to assign ownership of all flutes to the craftsmen who created them? Similarly, if we believe that the purpose of an electric company is to return a profit to investors, would it not follow that the most "virtuous" company would be the one with the highest profit margins, regardless of its effectiveness at delivering energy services? How are we to resolve this apparently circular issue?

If we need to know the true purpose of an entity in order to define its most "virtuous" behavior, how do we determine that purpose? Here Aristotle's concepts guide us to a question that can be answered. For example, the essential purpose of an electric utility or an energy company can be determined by looking at its Certificate of Public Good or its Articles of Incorporation. If those legal instruments define the purpose of the company as serving the general good of society, then we can judge the virtue or merit of its actions by how closely they serve that general good. If they contain no explicit statement of purpose, we then

---

[1] This concept is sometimes referred to as teleological.
[2] This point follows in part Michael J. Sandel's *Justice: What's the Right Thing to Do?* (New York: Farrar, Straus, and Giroux, 2009) but also draws more directly on Aristotle's *Politics*, ch. 12.

have to ask the more difficult question of whether there is an implied purpose of general good inherent in the laws and regulations that allow it to exist and prosper. In either case, Aristotle's guidance leads us not to an immediate answer, but to a manageable set of answerable questions that can allow decision-makers to choose among varying policies and results.

Drawing from the ancient writings of Plato and Aristotle, we argue in this chapter that a virtuous energy system would be one that does not waste energy. Contemporary energy policy and technology analysis reveals, however, that the global energy system promotes a number of inefficiencies related to energy supply, conversion, and end-use. Thankfully, the final part of the chapter presents a series of mechanisms and practices ranging from fuel economy standards and energy-efficiency programs to smarter pricing and smarter grids that can overcome the troubling vices of the current global energy system.

## What is reality?

Contrary to the ideals of Aristotle and Plato, numerous inefficiencies plague the global energy system: those involved in energy conversion, aging equipment and capital stock, declining energy payback ratios (EPRs), social barriers to efficient behavior, and opportunity costs.

### Energy conversion and use

The modern energy system involves a number of troubling inefficiencies in the way it converts raw energy and fuels into useful energy services, drifting far from an ideal state of perfection. To remind readers of just a little basic science, the first law of thermodynamics stipulates that energy is a constant that can neither be created nor destroyed. It can and does change form, but as it does the amount of useful energy decreases. Consider what it takes for you to transform a dull-looking slice of white bread into a delicious piece of crunchy toast. Now, even before you flip a switch, press a button, or turn a knob, six sets of energy losses typically will occur.

First, all the way back at the power plant, the chemical energy from combusted fuel is converted into thermal energy to produce steam, with a majority of the energy discharged into the surrounding environment as low-temperature waste heat and exhaust. Second, similar losses occur as the thermal energy is converted to mechanical energy to spin turbines. And third, mechanical energy is converted, with losses, to electrical energy to produce an electric current. Cumulatively, these three sets of energy losses are staggeringly large: most power plants convert the potential chemical energy of coal and other fuels into usable energy at a rate of about 33 percent, with the remaining two-thirds simply wasted. Two Oak Ridge National Laboratory (ORNL) researchers have suggested that the poor thermal efficiency of US power plants translates into enough potential power lost every year to meet the needs of five to ten cities the size of Manhattan.[3]

A fourth loss occurs when some of this remaining energy is used by the plant itself in order to operate, run its pollution controls, conduct emissions monitoring, and power other equipment. Conventional coal plants with air pollution controls use 10 percent of their own electricity within the facility; nuclear plants use around 9 percent of their energy to run fuel and cooling cycles.

A fifth loss occurs as electricity enters the T&D grid. T&D lines do not conduct electricity with perfect efficiency. The average transmission line is about 90 percent efficient, with performance worsening in hotter weather, over longer distances, and as loads increase. Thus, any increase in load for one specific customer will increase line losses for the system as a whole, resulting in higher costs for all other customers.

Finally, at your home, a sixth loss occurs as the toaster converts the electrical energy coming out of your socket back into heat to toast your slice of bread. Accounting for all six sets of losses, what you are left with as you set the toaster is only 27.6 units of usable energy out of every 100 units you started with. In terms of making toast, it would have been nearly four times more efficient just to burn a lump of coal and place your bread over the flame (if that lump of coal was magically transported to your kitchen with no extractive or transportation inefficiencies).[4]

Each time energy is converted from fuel to steam to mechanical energy to electricity to end-use, a substantial amount of energy is lost. For lighting, it is even worse: one study found that converting coal at a power

[3] Jan Berry and Steve Fischer, "More than 200 Hospitals Nationwide Are Recycling Energy for Peak Performance," *Distributed Energy* (January/February 2004), p. 32.

[4] Patricia Nelson Limerick, Claudia Puska, Andrew Hildner, and Eric Skovsted, *What Every Westerner Should Know About Energy* (Boulder: Center of the American West, 2003).

plant into luminance from an incandescent bulb inside a home wastes nearly 97 percent of the original energy potential![5] Converting to a compact fluorescent bulb would improve this end-use efficiency about fourfold, but would do little to account for the remaining "upstream" inefficiencies.

It gets worse. The six sets of losses described above do not include inefficiencies that occur between the extraction of fuels and their arrival at the power plant. The goliath-size draglines, bulldozers, dump trucks, barges, and trains that extract and transport coal are not calculated in this exercise, but they represent significant energy costs nonetheless. The net energy loss of decommissioning the energy-intensive materials and processes used to construct and then take apart a conventional power plant after its useful operating life also is not included. The energy use associated with cleaning up air pollutants that have already been emitted and treating polluted water (both energy-intensive activities) also is excluded. So our toast example actually significantly underestimates the amount of total energy lost within the current system.

Similar inefficiencies exist in the next largest energy sector: transportation. A typical internal combustion engine in an automobile only utilizes about 10 percent of the energy content of the gasoline to move the car, with the rest of the energy, again, being lost as heat.[6] These efficiencies are governed by the fundamental way that the chemical energy of fuels is converted in heat engines, illustrated with Figure 3.1. And, in the industrial sector, typical pumping systems convert only 9.5 percent of original energy inputs into useful outputs, losing the rest along the way.[7]

These types of inefficiencies within the electricity, transport, and industrial sectors mean that the United States wastes more energy each year than Japan harnesses for its entire economy.[8] The US EPA projected in 2011 that as much as one third of all energy used in the commercial

[5] Amory B. Lovins, "Energy Myth Nine – Energy Efficiency Improvements Have already Reached their Potential," in B.K. Sovacool and M.A. Brown (eds.), *Energy and American Society – Thirteen Myths* (New York: Springer, 2007), p. 239.

[6] Robert Bent, Lloyd Orr, and Randall Baker (eds.), *Energy: Science, Policy, and the Pursuit of Sustainability* (Washington, DC: Island Press, 2002).

[7] Amory Lovins and the Rocky Mountain Institute, *Reinventing Fire: Bold Business Solutions for the New Energy Era* (White River Junction: Chelsea Green Publishing Company, 2011), p. 142.

[8] John A. "Skip" Laitner, testimony before the House Committee on Science and Technology (September 25, 2007), 4.

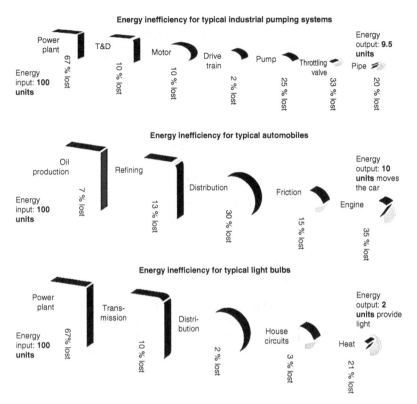

Figure 3.1 Inefficiencies involved in modern forms of energy conversion and use

sector is "wasted or inefficiently used" and another study concluded that only 13 percent of primary energy currently used in the United States ends up as "useful energy services."[9] Additionally, about twenty huge power plants operate to energize US appliances and equipment that are turned off, just to keep them in standby mode.[10] Similarly, in 2012 the Lawrence Livermore National Laboratory estimated energy use in the United States at about 95.1 quadrillion BTUs, or "quads," yet it noted that only 37 quads were converted into "energy services," the rest – a confounding 58.1 quads – was wasted as "rejected" or "nonproductive"

[9] Fereidoon P. Sioshansi, "Can We Have Our Cake and Eat It Too? Energy and Environmental Sustainability," *Electricity Journal* 24(2) (March 2011), pp. 76–85.
[10] Lovins, "Energy Myth Nine."

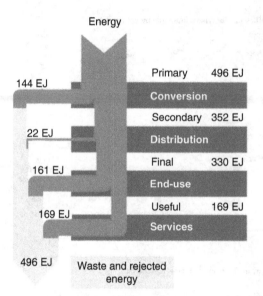

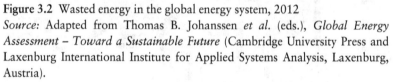

**Figure 3.2** Wasted energy in the global energy system, 2012
*Source:* Adapted from Thomas B. Johanssen *et al.* (eds.), *Global Energy Assessment – Toward a Sustainable Future* (Cambridge University Press and Laxenburg International Institute for Applied Systems Analysis, Laxenburg, Austria).

energy. Figure 3.2 indicates that 36.8 percent of total energy is "wasted" or "rejected" as it travels through the global energy system.

Energy inefficiencies also afflict the US military, impacting national security. American armed forces now risk most of their causalities in combat from convoys and their guards, primarily distributing inefficiently used fuel,[11] and by one estimate 50 percent of the energy used by the Air Force is spent hauling energy fuels.[12] The economist Herman E. Daly once calculated that a single B-1 Bomber was so large, and fuel thirsty, that it needed as much as 1 billion gallons of fuel per year, more than the fuel needed to run all of the buses in all of the cities and

---

[11] Amory Lovins, "Preface to the Chinese Edition of *Winning the Oil Endgame*," February 29, 2008.
[12] Interview with Michal Quah, Energy Studies Institute, Singapore, June 14, 2009.

towns of the United States for a year.[13] The amount the US military spends annually on air conditioning for troops in Iraq and Afghanistan may exceed $20 billion – more than the entire budget for the National Aeronautics and Space Administration (NASA), more than British Petroleum paid in damages from the *Deepwater Horizon* spill, equal to what the G-8 pledged to foster new democracies in Egypt and Tunisia.[14]

### Aging capital stock and blackouts

A second type of inefficiency involves aging energy equipment and infrastructure. Most nuclear plants worldwide were installed in 1984 and 1985, meaning that the average age of a nuclear facility is now approaching thirty years.[15] The mean age of a coal-fired power plant in the United States is above thirty years, and some plants are more than seventy years old – generating electricity before the Dodgers left Brooklyn in 1957 and Neil Armstrong walked on the moon in 1969. Figure 3.3 illustrates how, as of 2012, only 7 percent of coal-fired power plants in the United States were less than twenty years old; and Figure 3.4 reveals how, perhaps oddly, the average load factor for the country's fleet of power plants has gone *down* from a high of almost 70 percent to below 50 percent in 2010 – due in part to aging equipment, and to increased air-conditioning loads in the summer.

Similarly, by 2017, roughly *half* of all large-scale hydroelectric dams in the United States will need to undergo a federal relicensing process because they are getting too old.[16] As Vikram Budhraja, former senior Vice President at Southern California Edison, argued:

The biggest problem facing the electric industry is to modernize the current infrastructure. We have power plants that are operating with an average age of thirty to forty years. We really need to replace them, modernize, and upgrade them, as well as build additional capacity to meet population increase

---

[13] Herman E. Daly, *Steady-State Economics* (Washington, DC: Island Press, 1991), p. 169.

[14] National Public Radio, "Among the Costs of War: Billions a Year in A.C.?," June 25, 2011.

[15] Trevor Findlay, *The Future of Nuclear Energy to 2030 and its Implications for Safety, Security, and Nonproliferation* (Waterloo, Ontario: Center for International Governance Innovation, 2010).

[16] Scott Sklar and Todd R. Burns, *Hydroelectric Energy: An Overview* (Washington, DC: The Stella Group, 2003), p. 5.

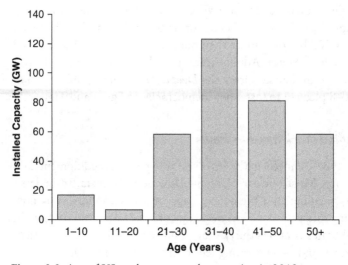

**Figure 3.3** Age of US coal generators by capacity, in 2012
*Source:* Adapted from Union of Concerned Scientists, *Ripe for Retirement* (Washington, DC: November 2012).

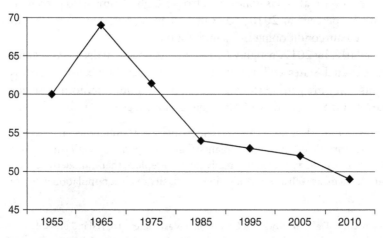

**Figure 3.4** Average load factor for the US electric grid, 1955–2010
*Source:* Adapted from Jon Wellinghoff, "A Day in the Life of the Grid," presentation to the Vermont Law School, July 26, 2013.

and economic growth throughout the country. The industry needs to diversify the resource mix with renewables and replace aging power plants. The industry needs to invest in new grid technologies for reliability, market efficiency, and security.[17]

Generally, while energy end-use measures such as refrigerators, motors, and cars are replaced every few years, roads, highways, urban infrastructure, and power plants are only replaced on average every forty to fifty years, with an upper range of 140 years.[18]

Thus, the late physicist Alvin M. Weinberg once joked that some energy systems last so long, it would be fair to call them "immortal" since they distribute benefits and costs long after they have been amortized.[19] Some dams, for example, have been operating for *hundreds* of years. The Lake of Homs Dam on the Orontes River in North Africa has been operating in various configurations for more than 1,700 years; in Spain, the Dam of Almendralejo was built in 1747 containing a small hydropower device; Niagara Falls between Canada and the United States has dams operating for more than 120 years. Weinberg also notes that the byproducts of nuclear reactors will last for tens of thousands of years into the future. And, of course, the heavy metals such as lead and mercury released by power plants could last even longer.

Yet, as power plants get older, they become less efficient. One Institute of Electrical and Electronics Engineers (IEEE) study looked at inputs and outputs for natural gas power plants over the course of their lifetime, including inputs such as trained staff and date of commencement and outputs such as electrical energy delivered and operating hours. The study found that as the age of a plant increases, the total number of hours that a plant is in operation during each year declined. Moreover, as power plants get older, constant expenses go up as well as variable expenses and reduced efficiency. Efficiency generally drops as much as

---

[17] Quoted in Benjamin K. Sovacool, *The Dirty Energy Dilemma: What's Blocking Clean Power in the United States* (Westport: Praeger, 2008).

[18] Marilyn A. Brown and Sharon (Jess) Chandler, "Governing Confusion: How Statutes, Fiscal Policy, and Regulations Impede Clean Energy Technologies," *Stanford Law and Policy Review* 19(3) (2008), pp. 472–509; G. Unruh, "Escaping Carbon Lock-In," *Energy Policy* 30 (2002), pp. 317–325.

[19] Alvin M. Weinberg, "Immortal Energy Systems and Intergenerational Justice," *Energy Policy* 13(1) (February 1985), pp. 51–59.

15 percent after ten years of operation, especially for units with more than 6,000 hours of annual operation.[20]

The power grid is also aging. The US T&D network has become so prone to failure that the American Society of Civil Engineers gave it a "D+" grade and warned that it was in "urgent need of modernization."[21] In New York, for instance, the underground electricity grid is so degraded that it costs local utilities over $1 billion a year just to replace corroded cable needed to make the system function at current demand levels. James Gallagher, the Director of the Office of Electricity and Environment for the New York State Public Service Commission, comments that the billion dollars "doesn't even allow us to get proactive to get ahead of the problem. The scale of the challenge is enormous."[22]

The ultimate consequence of aging and inefficient infrastructure is an increased incidence of severe blackouts and power outages. Between 1964 and 2005, for instance, the IEEE estimates that no less than seventeen major blackouts have affected more than 195 million residential, commercial, and industrial customers in the United States, with seven of these major blackouts occurring in the past ten years. Sixty-six smaller blackouts (affecting between 50,000 and 600,000 customers) occurred from 1991 to 1995 and seventy-six occurred from 1996 to 2000, and that is for the United States alone. The costs of these blackouts are monumental: the Department of the Environment (DOE) estimates that power outages and power quality disturbances cost customers as much as $206 billion annually, or more than the entire nation's electricity bill for 1990. In the developing world, countries tend to lose 1 to 2 percent of GDP growth potential due to blackouts, overinvestment in backup electricity generators, and inefficient use of resources.[23] Nigerians for instance live with such persistent power outages that one government official characterized the power supply

---

[20] S. Sofianopoulou, V. Dedoussis, K. Konstas, and A. Kassimis, "Efficiency Evaluation of Natural Gas Power Plants Using Data Envelopment Analysis," *Industrial Engineering and Engineering Management* 8 (2009), pp. 315–319.

[21] Elisabeth Rosenthal, "Ahead of the Pack on Cleaner Power," *International Herald Tribune*, September 30, 2010, p. VI.

[22] Quoted in Sovacool, *The Dirty Energy Dilemma*.

[23] UN Development Program, *Energy for a Sustainable Future: The Secretary-General's Advisory Group on Energy and Climate Change Summary Report and Recommendations* (New York: UN Development Program, 2010).

as "epileptic."[24] The Nepal Electricity Authority supplies electricity to Nepal's capital Kathmandu for less than eight hours per day, with load shedding accounting for the remaining sixteen hours.[25] In the bazaars at night, more shops rely on candles to light their wares than on electric bulbs. In February 2010, the Philippines suffered a nationwide electricity breakdown that spanned three weeks of plant failures and rolling blackouts – caused by El Niño-induced droughts, curbing the country's hydroelectric capacity, and exacerbated by human error, historical underinvestment in the energy sector, improper facility maintenance and delayed emergency response measures.[26] In July of 2012, India suffered an "unprecedented grid failure" that affected 670 million people – more than half the country's population, or roughly 10 percent of the world's population, in a single blackout.[27]

Finally, most developing countries must rely on older end-use devices such as electric appliances and heating systems. Examples include lighting equipment in China that is generally 50 percent less efficient than lights in Europe, refrigerators in Mexico that are 25–40 percent less efficient compared to the United States, and office buildings in Thailand and irrigation systems in India that remain 50 percent less efficient than those in industrialized countries.[28]

---

[24] The Chairman of the Presidential Committee on Power Sector Reforms, Dr. Rilwanu Lukman, indicates that "the average age of all the transformers, generating stations and sub-stations in the country is twenty five years"; the aging infrastructure has been made worse again, he said, by a "poor maintenance culture." Dr. Lukman estimates that $85 billion dollars is needed to overhaul and fix the decrepit power sector, a sum that does not even include related gas infrastructure needs. "$85 Billion Needed for Stable Power; Supply Won't Improve till December," Daily Trust/All Africa Global Media, June 25, 2008.

[25] World Bank, *Project Paper Proposed Additional Financing Credit in the Amount of SDR $49.6 Million and a Proposed Additional Financing Grant in the Amount of SDR $10.5 Million to Nepal for the Power Development Project* (Washington, DC: World Bank Group, May 18, 2009, Report No. 48516-NP).

[26] Anthony D'Agostino and Benjamin Sovacool, "Energy Security: Introduction," *Asian Trends Monitoring Bulletin* 1 (February 2010), pp. 21–26.

[27] Gardiner Harris and Vikas Bajaj, "As Power Is Restored in India, the 'Blame Game' Over Blackouts Heats Up," *New York Times*, August 1, 2012.

[28] J.P. Painuly, H. Park, M.K. Lee, and J. Noh, "Promoting Energy Efficiency Financing and ESCOs in Developing Countries: Mechanisms and Barriers," *Journal of Cleaner Production* 11 (2003), pp. 659–665; Catherine Strickland and Russel Strum, "Energy Efficiency in World Bank Power Sector and Policy and Lending: New Opportunities," *Energy Policy* 26(11) (1998), pp. 873–883.

*Declining energy payback ratios*

A third type of inefficiency involves declining EPRs. As depletable fuels such as oil, coal, natural gas, and uranium get extracted, it gets harder – more energy-intensive – to explore, produce, and deliver them, meaning their overall carbon footprint increases. One useful technique for assessing the lifecycle efficiency of a given energy fuel chain is "energy payback," or EPR.[29] The EPR refers to the ratio of total energy produced by an energy system compared to the energy needed to build and operate that system. The higher the EPR, the better the fuel source, for it implies a given system produces vastly more energy than it consumes.

The Canadian energy consultant Luc Gagnon surveyed EPRs for a variety of energy systems in 2007 and found that those for coal, oil, and natural gas were strikingly low at between 1.6 and 5.1 (or a mean of 3.35), numbers illustrated in Figure 3.5. That is, for every one unit of energy put into these fossil-fueled energy systems, one got only 3.35 units out of them. That may sound good, but the EPR can be as high as 280 for hydroelectric power stations, 34 for onshore wind farms, 27 for biomass power, and 15 for nuclear power plants. This makes the most efficient hydro, wind, and biomass technologies between eighty-four and eight times better than fossil fuels from an energy payback perspective. Furthermore, Gagnon found that the EPR for fossil fuels is set to decline further.

Put in perspective, due to worsening EPRs, even energy sources that appear to be low carbon and efficient may not be for much longer. Consider the case of nuclear power. One peer-reviewed study on available uranium resources at ninety-three deposits and fields across the world noted that uranium miners have to go deeper and use more energy and water to extract uranium resources as the overall quality of ore declines.[30] In addition, researchers at the Oxford Research Group suggest that declining ore grades will eventually yield a net energy loss before the end of this century.[31] Even utilizing the richest ores available, a

---

[29] Luc Gagnon, "Civilization and Energy Payback," *Energy Policy* 36 (2008), pp. 3317–3322; Luc Gagnon, *Electricity Generation Options: Energy Payback Ratio* (Montreal: Hydro Quebec, July 2005, 2005G185-A).

[30] Gavin M. Mudd and Mark Disendorf, "Sustainability of Uranium Mining and Milling: Toward Quantifying Resources and Eco-Efficiency," *Environmental Science & Technology* 42 (2008), pp. 2624–2629.

[31] Oxford Research Group, "Energy Security and Uranium Reserves," *Secure Energy: Options for a Safer World Factsheet* 4 (2006).

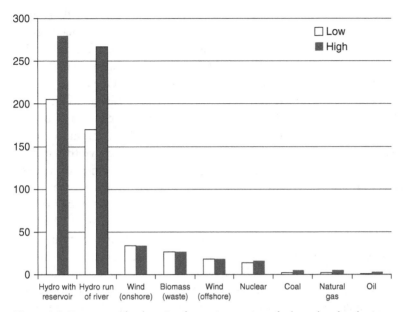

**Figure 3.5** Energy payback ratios for various energy fuels and technologies
*Source:* Adapted from Luc Gagnon, *Electricity Generation Options: Energy Payback Ratio* (Montreal: Hydro Quebec, July 2005, 2005G185-A).

nuclear power plant must operate for ten full load operating years before it has paid off its energy debts. Based on this estimation, several known facts can modify the model: not all plants use the richest ores, plants operate at full capacity for an average of only twenty years, most plants are decommissioned within thirty or forty years. Accordingly, a plant using average-quality uranium, operating at full capacity for twenty years out of a thirty-five year life span will only generate twice as much energy as consumed by the plant.

## Social barriers to energy-efficient behavior

One of the problems with making the energy system more efficient is that energy savings come in small pieces rather than concentrated in the large chunks that attract ribbon-cutters to energy-supply facilities; another substantial impediment is lack of information and awareness among energy users.

Indeed, misinformation concerning electricity and energy flourishes. A comprehensive study undertaken by Southern California Edison, surveying thousands of consumers, asked them, "Where does electricity come from?" Most people said, "Out of the plug in the wall," while others even said "lightning" and "static electricity." One of the authors of the study concluded that "people in this country have no idea how electricity is generated or transmitted."[32] Surveys conducted by the National Environmental Education and Training Foundation have consistently found that more than half of Americans believe that hydroelectricity, solar panels, and nuclear power were the "principal" sources of energy for the country, even though the correct answer was fossil fuels.[33] Almost half (41 percent) of respondents in a Kentucky survey identified "coal," oil," and "iron" as "renewable resources."[34] Another survey of American electricity consumers found that four-fifths were unable to name a single source of renewable energy (even including "dams" and "hydroelectric" generators).[35] A separate study found that nearly 70 percent of flexible fuel vehicle owners (people who purchased automobiles that could run on gasoline and/or ethanol) were unaware that they were driving one.[36]

Such gaps in awareness directly contribute to consumers making inefficient choices. For example, researchers from Vanderbilt University found that if people simply stopped idling their vehicles – keeping them "on" to get them "warmed up," while stopped at traffic signals, and during quick stops – the United States could save 10.6 *billion* gallons (40.1 billion liters) of fuel each year and displace 99 million tons of carbon dioxide, 1.6 percent of all national emissions.[37] Similarly, if

---

[32] Quoted in Sovacool, *The Dirty Energy Dilemma*.

[33] Michael P. Vandenbergh, "The Social Meaning of Environmental Command and Control," *Virginia Environmental Law Journal* 20 (2001), pp. 191–220.

[34] Kentucky Environmental Education Council, *The 2004 Survey of Kentuckians' Environmental Knowledge, Attitudes and Behaviors* (Frankfort, KY: Kentucky Environmental Education Council, January 2005).

[35] Suzanne Crofts Shelton, *The Consumer Pulse Survey on Energy Conservation* (Knoxville, TN: Shelton Group, 2006).

[36] Glenn Hess, "Bush Promotes Alternative Fuel," *Chemical and Engineering News* (March 6, 2006), pp. 50–58.

[37] See Jack N. Barkenbus, "Eco-Driving: An Overlooked Climate Change Initiative," *Energy Policy* 38(2) (February 2010), pp. 762–769; Amanda R. Carrico, Paul Padgett, Michael P. Vandenbergh, Jonathan Gilligan, and Kenneth A. Wallston, "Costly Myths: An Analysis of Idling Beliefs and Behavior in Personal Motor Vehicles," *Energy Policy* 37(8) (2009), pp. 2881–2888.

drivers in the United States learned to properly inflate their tires, they would save more crude oil than the maximum amount that could be annually produced from the Arctic National Wildlife Refuge in Alaska – more than 540,000 barrels of oil per day.[38]

Another major barrier to energy efficiency is the problem of "split incentives," something economists call the "principal-agent" problem because it "splits" the decisions made by principals (say, an investor in a company) from the agents (say, the factory workers in that company). The principal-agent problem comes in many different flavors relating to energy technologies:

- Architects, engineers, and builders design homes that they will not live in;
- Landlords purchase appliances and equipment for tenants;
- Industrial procurers select technology for plant operators;
- Specialists write product specifications for military purchases;
- Fleet managers select vehicles that others will drive;
- Automobile manufacturers will design less fuel-efficient vehicles because it is the owners and drivers that must pay for gasoline.[39]

For instance, architects, engineers, and builders select energy technologies that homeowners and dwellers use. Yet, the prevailing fee structures for building design are based on a percentage of capital cost of a project, penalizing engineers and architects for designing efficient but more expensive systems. The pressure to lower first-costs is reinforced by banks, lenders, and financers, since the builder is, in effect, building the house for them, and their criteria for selling a loan include

[38] B.K. Sovacool, "Solving the Oil Independence Problem: Is It Possible?," *Energy Policy* 35(11) (November 2007), pp. 5505–5514.

[39] See Vaclav Smil, *Energy Myths and Realities: Bringing Science to the Energy Policy Debate* (Washington, DC: Rowman and Littlefield, 2010); David J. Bjornstad and Marilyn A. Brown, *A Market Failures Framework for Defining the Government's Role in Energy Efficiency* (Knoxville, TN: Joint Institute for Energy and Environment, June 2004, JIEE 2004–02); Marilyn A. Brown, "Energy-Efficient Buildings: Does the Marketplace Work?," *Proceedings of the Annual Illinois Energy Conference* 24 (1997), pp. 233–255; Marilyn A. Brown, "The Effectiveness of Codes and Marketing in Promoting Energy-Efficient Home Construction," *Energy Policy* 21(4) (April 1993), pp. 391–402; Dennis Anderson, "Roundtable on Energy Efficiency and the Economists – An Assessment," *Annual Review of Energy and Environment* 20 (1995), pp. 562–573.

keeping the ratio of monthly payments to monthly income low enough to make the loan a reasonable risk.[40]

Therefore, the potential of energy efficiency – doing more with less, lowering levels of energy consumption by substituting fuels and technologies and educating consumers – remains hindered by a collection of pernicious obstacles. For instance, a study undertaken by one of the authors involved research interviews with more than 180 experts working for utilities, government agencies, and the national laboratories and identified thirty-eight nontechnical barriers to the deployment of distributed generation, renewable energy, and energy-efficiency technologies.[41] Another investigation of the barriers to energy-efficient technologies and energy-efficiency programs found eighty separate types of barriers.[42]

A few anecdotes put these types of barriers to energy efficiency into perspective. Tom Casten, who has almost four decades of experience selling cogeneration units to businesses, explains that both large and small manufacturing firms resist undertaking novel energy projects:

> The typical manufacturing enterprise focuses its intellectual and financial resources on core activities – making beer, or steel, or chemicals, etc. The vast bulk of industry will not invest in energy plants unless they are "broken" or, in the best case, when an energy efficiency project will pay back the capital investment in 12 to 18 months. Companies have a much higher investment hurdle rate for core activities than non-core activities, and they employ very few specialists in any non-core activity.[43]

Energy projects are often resisted by all levels of the business community because they perceive it as a "non-core activity" that distracts personnel from more profitable ventures. As a former researcher for the Alliance to Save Energy (ASE) explained:

> Facilities are thinly staffed, running flat out every day to meet production goals. Therefore distractions aren't welcome. For them, routine is a good thing, and their mantra becomes "that's the way we've always done it." So

---

[40] Amory Lovins, *Energy Efficient Buildings: Institutional Barriers and Opportunities* (Boulder: E-Source, 1992); US Office of Technology Assessment, *Building Energy Efficiency* (Washington, DC: USOTA, May 1992, OTA-E-518).

[41] B.K. Sovacool, "Rejecting Renewables: The Socio-Technical Impediments to Renewable Electricity in the United States," *Energy Policy* 37(11) (November 2009), pp. 4500–4513.

[42] Lovins, "Energy Myth Nine."

[43] Tom Casten, personal interview quoted in Sovacool, *The Dirty Energy Dilemma*.

when you propose energy [projects for] a facility, you are really proposing changes to the way they operate. You have people in operations, finance, procurement, and engineering – all of whom will be impacted by energy management, and all of whom usually have some reason to resist change ... Decision makers are continually making a tradeoff between risk, time, and money. If you propose an energy efficiency measure that saves X dollars, the facility manager wonders what the additional costs are in terms of risk and time. What labor hours are needed to support energy efficiency efforts? Should they allocate labor hours to making dollars, or saving dimes?[44]

Company employees may also be reluctant to admit the need for more efficient energy technologies because they believe such admissions become evidence of ineffective job performance.

Tragically, in the case of energy-efficiency practices and combined heat and power systems, the smaller the project, the *less* likely it will be undertaken. As one energy facility manager put it:

Size matters – not necessarily from a capital cost or efficiency standpoint, but it takes a lot of effort to do a small project as it does a large project, so the tendency is for an organization like ours to focus on the bigger projects because they can support the kinds of efforts needed to get the projects done. In contrast, getting smaller projects done requires such a disproportionate amount of senior management attention, legal attention, and other time and effort that it really burdens those projects with greater and greater costs so that people say it's not worth it.[45]

All the while, changing patterns of increased electricity consumption are occurring. Consumers have a growing appetite for new products and devices. The 42-inch plasma TV requires 250 Watts – a two-and-a-halffold increase from the 27-inch (now largely obsolete) cathode ray tube television. Incandescent lighting is another energy hog, costing four times as much to operate over its lifetime as fluorescent lighting (in this case, the newer technology), but incandescent bulbs are still purchased by consumers because their "up-front" cost is cheaper than alternatives.

Air conditioning is another important example. In the US the presence of air conditioning in new single-family homes jumped from 49 percent in 1973 to 89 percent in 2006.[46] In hot and humid places such as

---

[44] Quoted in *ibid.*    [45] Mark Hall, personal interview quoted in *ibid.*
[46] Jon Wellinghoff and David L. Morenoff, "Recognizing the Importance of Demand Response: The Second Half of the Wholesale Electric Market Function," *Energy Law Journal* 28(2) (2007), pp. 389–428, at p. 393.

Southern Florida, its use grew from 5 percent in 1950 to 95 percent in 1990. American motorists also use up 7 to 10 billion gallons of gas annually for air conditioning their cars. In aggregate, the United States on an annual basis now consumes more electricity for air conditioning than the entire continent of Africa consumes for all electricity uses.[47] Or, in other terms, the United States currently utilizes more energy (about 185 billion kWh) for air conditioning than all other countries' air-conditioning usage combined.[48] There is a trend for air conditioning to be used in developing countries in the tropics as well, with the number of air conditioners in rural Thailand expected to jump from 4 percent in 1995 to 100 percent by 2035 (when it will account for 40 percent of all electricity demand in the residential sector).[49] The percentage of urban Chinese households with an air conditioner jumped from less than 1 percent in 1990 to 62 percent in 2003, and in 2010, 50 million air-conditioning units were sold. India has also seen air-conditioning use grow at an annual rate of 20 percent per year.[50] More disturbingly, by 2100 worldwide energy demand for air conditioning could increase by 72 percent further as a result of warmer temperatures induced (ironically) by climate change.[51]

## Opportunity costs

Some energy systems, due to their longer lead times, capital intensity, need for research, and costly trial and error processes, involve substantial opportunity costs. Nuclear power, as one example, has higher costs than competitors per unit of net carbon dioxide displaced or unit of electricity delivered, meaning that every dollar invested in nuclear expansion buys less carbon reduction or energy than if that money was spent on other readily available solutions. Amory Lovins calculates that every 10 cents spent to buy a single kWh of nuclear electricity,

---

[47] Stan Cox, "Climate Risks Heat Up as World Switches on to Air Conditioning," *Guardian*, Tuesday July 10, 2012.

[48] Michael Sivak, "Will AC Put a Chill on the Global Energy Supply?," *American Scientist* 101(5) (September/October 2013), p. 330.

[49] Lawrence Agbemabiese, Kofi Berko, and Peter du Pont, "Air Conditioning in the Tropics: Cool Comfort or Cultural Conditioning?," *Proceedings of the 1996 ACEEE Summer Study on Energy Efficiency in Buildings* (Washington, DC, 1996), 8.1–8.9.

[50] Sivak, "Will AC Put a Chill on the Global Energy Supply?"    [51] *Ibid.*

assuming subsidies and regulation in the United States, could have purchased 10 kWh or more of energy efficiency.[52] As Lovins concluded, "[n]ew nuclear power buys you two to ten times less coal displacement per dollar than does micropower or improved end-use efficiency, and at a pace that is significantly slower."[53] Another study found that each dollar invested in energy efficiency displaces nearly seven times as much carbon dioxide as a dollar invested in nuclear power.[54]

Nuclear power is not the only technology involving opportunity costs. A study from Stanford Professor Mark Jacobson found that geothermal power plants, hydroelectric dams, nuclear facilities, and coal-fired power plants all involved substantial opportunity costs that added significantly to their carbon footprints – figures reflected in Table 3.1.

Table 3.1 *Lifecycle equivalent carbon dioxide emissions (grams of $CO_2$/kWh) for selected "clean" sources of modern energy*

| Technology | Lifecycle | Opportunity costs | Risk of leakage, accident, and disruption | Total | Mean |
|---|---|---|---|---|---|
| Wind | 2.8 to 7.4 | 0 | 0 | 2.8 to 7.4 | 5.1 |
| Concentrated solar power | 8.5 to 11.3 | 0 | 0 | 8.5 to 11.3 | 9.9 |
| Geothermal | 15.1 to 55 | 1 to 6 | 0 | 16.1 to 61 | 38.6 |
| Solar PV | 19 to 59 | 0 | 0 | 19 to 59 | 39 |
| Hydroelectric | 17 to 22 | 31 to 49 | 0 | 48 to 71 | 59.5 |
| Nuclear | 9 to 70 | 59 to 106 | 0 to 4.1 | 68 to 180 | 124 |
| Clean coal with CCS | 255 to 442 | 51 to 87 | 1.8 to 42 | 308 to 571 | 439 |

*Source:* Adapted from Mark Z. Jacobson, "Review of Solutions to Global Warming, Air Pollution, and Energy Security," *Energy & Environmental Science* 2 (2009), pp. 148–173.

[52] Amory B. Lovins, *Nuclear Power: Economics and Climate Protection Potential II* (Rocky Mountain Inst., E0508, 2005).
[53] *Ibid.*, p. 6.
[54] Bill Keepin and Gregory Kats, "Greenhouse Warming: Comparative Analysis of Nuclear and Efficiency Abatement Strategies," *Energy Policy* 16 (1988), pp. 538–552.

Table 3.2 *Carbon-to-cost ratio for "clean" sources of modern energy*

| | Mean | | Emissions saved | Cost/emissions saved | |
|---|---|---|---|---|---|
| | emissions (grams/kWh) | Mean cost (cents/kWh) | (grams/ kWh) | cents/grams | $/ton |
| Hydroelectricity | 59.5 | 2.8 | 940.5 | 0.00297714 | 29.8 |
| Wind | 5.1 | 5.6 | 994.9 | 0.00562871 | 56.3 |
| Geothermal | 38.6 | 6.4 | 961.4 | 0.00665696 | 66.6 |
| Concentrated solar power | 9.9 | 14.7 | 990.1 | 0.01484699 | 148.5 |
| Carbon capture and storage | 439 | 8.8 | 561 | 0.01568627 | 156.9 |
| Nuclear energy | 124 | 24 | 876 | 0.02739726 | 274 |
| Solar PV | 39 | 39 | 961 | 0.04058273 | 405.8 |

*Source:* Adapted from Benjamin K. Sovacool, "Exposing the Paradoxes of Climate and Energy Governance," *International Studies Review* 16(2) (June 2014), pp. 294–297.

Such figures correspond with the relatively poor carbon-cost ratios for some of these systems shown in Table 3.2.

Similarly, the private automobile involves a number of hidden opportunity costs. If we account for all of the personal expenses needed to own and operate a conventional automobile – that is, the time needed at work to pay for it, driving it, getting it repaired, cleaning it, etc. – a car owner spends 1,600 hours a year supporting their vehicle. Social critic Ivan Illich calculated that if one averages all car mileage in a given year by the time spent giving such support, they attain an average speed of 5 miles per hour, or the speed of a tricycle.[55]

## What is justice?

Given that most classical philosophy classes start with Plato and Aristotle, it may come as no surprise that they espoused one of the first conceptions of justice. Plato's (424 BC to 348 BC) work *The Republic* addresses a variety of topics ranging from abortion and carpentry to

[55] Quoted in P. Hawken, *The Ecology of Commerce: A Declaration of Sustainability* (New York: Harper Collins, 1994).

geometry and the afterlife, but it essentially explores one question: how should one live? Or, more relevant to justice theory, what is the essence of a just life? Aristotle (384 BC to 322 BC), Plato's student and mentor of Alexander the Great, refined many of Plato's arguments to create a *teleological* conception of justice, one that explores its essential nature, or ultimate purpose. More specifically, connections between ancient notions of virtue and energy occur in three places in the world of Plato and Aristotle: (1) the conception of an ideal state, (2) happiness, and (3) balance.

## An ideal state

To understand Platonic and Aristotelian notions of ideal states, it is useful to begin with Plato's Theory of the Forms (ἰδέαι), the idea that the material world as we know it is not the "real" world, and instead a copy of universal archetypes that exist in an unseen world.[56] The desk we may be reading this book on has a form that looks and feels a certain way to us, but its Form is a static blueprint that transcends both space and time, perfect and unchanging. Our entire world has been created, according to Plato, according to the patterns of the Forms. Basically, objects and items in our world are only imperfect and temporary representations of their true Form.

Following this logic, a human being can live a just life serving the good by trying to push the empirical world towards its ideal state. Or, as Plato writes, in "a state ordered with a view to the good of the whole we should be most likely to find justice."[57] Extended to the realm of energy, Plato would argue that there is such a thing as an ideal, perfect energy system that we should strive to create.[58]

---

[56] Yuji Kurihara, "Plato on the Ideal of Justice and Human Happiness: Return to the Cave (Republic 519e–521b)," in G. Anagnostopoulos (ed.), *Socratic, Platonic and Aristotelian Studies: Essays in Honor of Gerasimos Santas* (New York: Springer, 2011), pp. 271–279.

[57] Stephen Watt, "Introduction: The Theory of Forms (Books 5–7)," in *Plato: Republic* (London: Wordsworth Editions, 1997), pp. xiv–xvi.

[58] See John Cooper, "The Psychology of Justice in the Republic," *American Philosophical Quarterly* 15 (1977), pp. 151–157; Terence Irwin, *Plato's Moral Theory* (New York: Oxford University Press, 1977); Gregory Vlastos, *Platonic Studies* (Princeton University Press 1973); John Cooper, "Plato's Theory of Human Motivation," *History of Philosophy Quarterly* 1 (1984), pp. 3–21; Christine Korsgaard, "Self-Constitution in the Ethics of Plato and Kant," *Journal*

## Happiness

Plato and Aristotle advance a distinct notion of happiness and *telos*. In reference to the nature of objects, Aristotle speaks of the *telos*, or end, towards which things aim. Each thing, Aristotle claims, has an essential quality or property that makes that thing exactly what it is. The very first lines of Aristotle's inquiry in the *Nicomachean Ethics* states:

Every art and every inquiry, and similarly every action and choice, is thought to aim at some good; and for this reason the good has rightly been declared to be that at which all things aim ... Now there are many actions, arts and sciences, their ends also many; the end of the medical art is health, that of shipbuilding a vessel, that of strategy victory, that of economics wealth.[59]

The implications of what Aristotle means can be clearly understood from his example of the flute, as a flute is an object whose nature or aim or *telos* is to be "played well." Aristotle says that "When a number of flute-payers are equal in their art, there is no reason why those of them who are better born should have better flutes given to them; for they will not play any better on the flute, and the superior instrument should be reserved for him who is the superior artist."[60] It is, therefore, the purpose of the flute to be played by the best flute player, not the richest man or woman.

This line of thought leads to Aristotle's even more radical position that the purpose of giving the best flutes to the best flute players is *neither* to produce the best music, *nor* to obtain the result that listeners hear the best music.[61] The purpose is *not* to get something out of the object; instead, as justice theorist Michael Sandel clearly explains, Aristotle "thinks the best flutes should go to the best flute players because that's what flutes are *for* – to be played well."[62] Yet, as we noted at the beginning of this chapter, this assumes that we can reliably determine whether the true purpose of a flute is to be played, and not for such purposes as to earn money for its maker, or to decorate the wall of a palace.

of *Ethics* 3 (1999), pp. 1–29; and Gerasimos Santas, *Understanding Plato's Republic* (Oxford: Wiley–Blackwell, 2010).

[59] Aristotle, *The Politics*, in *The Complete Works of Aristotle*, vol. II, trans. Jonathan Barnes (Princeton University Press, 1984), p. 1729.

[60] *Ibid.*, p. 2036.    [61] Sandel, *Justice: What's the Right Thing to Do?*, p. 188.

[62] *Ibid.*

Essentially, though, Aristotle is telling us that "good" and "bad" are not subjective. They are absolute, and a good flute player is different from a bad one; a good state is also different from a bad state, and (taking the argument further) a good energy system would be distinct from a bad one.[63] Even Aristotle's conception of happiness, or εὐδαιμονία ("eudaimonia"), refers to achieving human potential by acting virtuously and reaching total fulfillment.[64] A virtuous energy system, then, would be one that achieves its end of delivering energy services the most efficiently and prudently. We can, of course, imagine other purposes for an energy system (such as returns on investment); however, if the purposes of that system are the betterment of society, then it is hard to see how it can justify receipt of a certificate to do business, or a right of eminent domain, or access to public research dollars or other vital supports based on the general good of all.

## Balance

A third connection involves Plato's and Aristotle's notions of balance, proportion, and restraint, the idea of "not doing too much." Aristotle states that some basic qualities are necessary for human beings to flourish and achieve happiness.[65] Of crucial importance to justice, though, these things need not be distributed on absolutely equal levels. Aristotle states that "What is just ... is what is proportionate, and what is unjust is what is counter-proportionate. Hence [in an unjust action] one term becomes more and the other less."[66] The implication is that human beings should approach things in moderation, never submitting themselves to vice or excess.[67] Applied to

---

[63] Aristotle, "Nicomachean Ethics," in Michael J. Sandel (ed.), *Justice: A Reader* (Oxford University Press, 2007), pp. 295–299.

[64] Bao Limin, "'Justice Is Happiness'? – An Analysis of Plato's Strategies in Response to Challenges from the Sophists," *Frontiers of Philosophy in China* 6(20) (2011), pp. 258–272.

[65] Richard Kraut, "Aristotle's Ethics," in Edward N. Zalta (ed.), *The Stanford Encyclopedia of Philosophy* (Summer 2010 edn.), found at http://plato.stanford.edu/archives/sum2010/entries/aristotle-ethics/, accessed July 9, 2010.

[66] Robert C. Solomon and Mark C. Murphy, *What Is Justice? Classic and Contemporary Readings*, 2nd edn. (New York: Oxford University Press, 2000), p. 40.

[67] Izhak Englard, *Corrective and Distributive Justice: From Aristotle to Modern Times* (Oxford University Press, 2009), p. 8.

energy, the implication is that we should take care to use it efficiently and with minimal waste.

In sum, Plato and Aristotle are arguing that justice requires us to think about the *telos*, or purpose, or the essential nature, of a thing or process. For Aristotle, justice is a matter of rewarding virtue, a measure of a just society is whether it produces virtuous citizens, and "justice consists in giving people what they deserve, and a just society is one that enables human beings to realize their highest nature, to attain the good life."[68] Ethics is not based on rules, but on character and how a given person or republic succumbs to its vices or supports its virtues. Ethical goodness is a state of being, an essential state.[69] A "good" electric utility system or refinery would be that which realizes its ultimate goal – the delivery of kWh or barrels of oil – efficiently. Finding a just energy system is one that requires understanding the fundamental nature, aim or purpose, of producing and delivering energy.

As odd or anachronistic as these ideas of virtue may sound, they have been incredibly influential in Western thought. The acclaimed philosopher Alfred North Whitehead went so far as to argue that the entire "European philosophical tradition" consists of "footnotes to Plato."[70] The ideas of perfection and virtue have also found their way into most religious traditions, with the Old Testament of the Christian Bible equating justice with "goodness and perfection as established by God's Law" and the "just person with the saint,"[71] ideas that have also influenced Buddhism, Judaism, and Islam. And, today, even in the most technical sense, our common regulatory statutes say that we should resolve disputes upon the basis of what is "just and reasonable."[72] Some of us have sworn to uphold and apply that standard professionally,

---

[68]  Michael J. Sandel, "Aristotle: Justice and Virtue," in Sandel (ed.), *Justice: A Reader*, p. 263.

[69]  Aristotle, "The Ethics of Virtue," in Louis P. Pojman (ed.), *Introduction to Philosophy: Classical and Contemporary Readings* (Belmont: Wadsworth Publishing, 1991), pp. 569–580; Aristotle, "Virtue and the Ethics of Perfectionism," in Mark Timmons (ed.), *Conduct and Character: Readings in Moral Theory* (Belmont: Wadsworth Publishing, 1999), pp. 233–244.

[70]  Alfred North Whitehead, *Process and Reality* (New York: Free Press, 1979), p. 39.

[71]  Jose Ambrozic, "Beyond Public Reason on Energy Justice: Solidarity and Catholic Social Teaching," *Colorado Journal of International Environmental Law and Policy* 21(2) (Spring 2010), pp. 381–398.

[72]  See, for one paradigmatic example, the 1935 Federal Power Act in the United States.

others have made it a moral choice for personal living. In either case, are there decisions to make and acts to take that will lead to more just and reasonable results? Our next section offers some thoughts about "what is to be done."

## What is to be done?

A series of different measures can make the global energy system more efficient. Energy-efficient behavior can include practices as diverse as switching from conventional coal power plants to combined heat and power units, lowering thermostats, better maintaining industrial boilers, and walking or cycling instead of driving. We briefly sample six such options in this section of the chapter. The implication is that such improvements in efficiency can bring homes and local energy systems closer to the virtuous ideal desired by Plato and Aristotle.

### Electricity demand-side management

In the electricity sector of industrialized countries such as the United States, studies have shown that cost-effective energy-efficiency measures could reduce consumption by an astounding 30 to 75 percent. These measures are cheaper to implement than purchasing any form of electricity supply and could save up to three-quarters of the power bill in the United States.[73] Another assessment looking at customer demand response to hourly market-based retail prices in the United Kingdom and United States found that it could reduce electricity loads by thousands of MW, lower summer peak prices by 19 percent, and produce energy cost savings from $300 million to $1.2 billion per year.[74] Put directly in the context of nuclear reactors, another study noted that cost-effective energy-efficiency resources could save the need to build more than 100 new nuclear power plants between 2010 and 2030.[75]

---

[73] B.K. Sovacool and A. D'Agostino, "Nuclear Renaissance: A Flawed Proposition," *Chemical Engineering Progress* 106(7) (July 2010), pp. 29–35.

[74] Wellinghoff and Morenoff, "Recognizing the Importance of Demand Response."

[75] Travis Madsen, Johanna Neumann, and Emily Rusch, *The High Cost of Nuclear Power: Why America Should Choose a Clean Energy Future over New Nuclear Reactors* (Baltimore: Maryland PIRG Foundation, March 2009).

Energy-efficiency projects also pay for themselves quite quickly. One assessment of forty-one energy-efficiency projects completed in the industrial sector of the United States found that they recovered the cost of implementation in slightly more than two years and then yielded an aggregate $7.4 million in savings every year thereafter. On a global scale, the International Energy Agency reviewed large-scale energy-efficiency programs and found that they saved electricity at an average cost of 3.2 cents/kWh, well below the cost of supplying electricity from *any* source.[76] A comprehensive report from the independent consulting firm McKinsey & Company looked at the maximum potential of an assortment of technological options to abate GHGs (presuming a tax of €60 per ton of $CO_2$ was in place), and found that a host of residential and industrial energy-efficiency options were far more cost effective than building power plants, even those running on natural gas or renewable fuels.[77] Its findings are depicted in Figure 3.6.

Indeed, countries and communities have recently put McKinsey's recommendations into practice, and shown how energy-efficiency measures can rapidly cut GHG emissions. The city of Woking, United Kingdom, a suburb of London, has adopted a comprehensive energy-efficiency approach to reducing emissions.[78] These include promoting the use of combined heat and power within the borough, deploying solar panels to meet peak electricity needs, and implementing a target of purchasing 20 percent of the entire city's energy from renewable resources. City planners incentivized walking, cycling, and working from home to minimize emissions associated with transport. The city has also introduced a local award to recognize outstanding projects that mitigated climate change, utilized irrigation systems that recycle storm water, and created wetlands near floodplains to reduce erosion. To minimize trash and waste, the city has ramped up its recycling efforts and aggressively promoted energy-efficiency efforts. Due to these combined

[76] International Energy Agency, *The Experience with Energy Efficiency Policies and Programs in IEA Countries: Learning from the Critics* (Paris: International Energy Agency, August 2005).

[77] McKinsey & Company, *Impact of the Financial Crisis on Carbon Economics: Version 2.1 of the Global Greenhouse Gas Abatement Cost Curve* (Boston, MA: McKinsey & Company, 2010), available at www.mckinsey.com/client_service/sustainability/latest_thinking/greenhouse_gas_abatement_cost_curves.

[78] Woking Borough Council, *Climate Change Strategy 2008 to 2013* (Woking: April 2008).

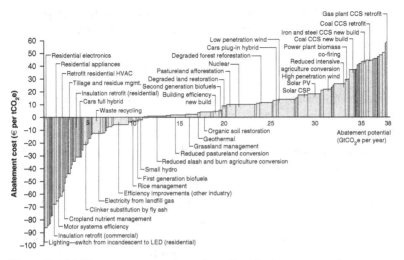

**Figure 3.6** McKinsey cost curve for carbon dioxide abatement options
*Note*: CSP: concentrated solar power.
*Source*: McKinsey & Company, *Impact of the Financial Crisis on Carbon Economics: Version 2.1 of the Global Greenhouse Gas Abatement Cost Curve* (Boston, MA: McKinsey & Company, 2010), available at www.mckinsey.com/client_service/sustainability/latest_thinking/greenhouse_gas_abatement_cost_curves.

efforts, the city has reduced energy consumption by 44 percent and carbon dioxide emissions by 72 percent between 1990 and 2005, and it intends to reduce emissions by 60 percent below 1990 levels by 2050 and 80 percent by 2100.[79]

In Beijing, city planners have implemented a series of programs relating to fuel substitution from coal to natural gas, the promotion of district heating, improved insulation in buildings, and energy-efficiency standards for appliances. A twenty member "energy-saving police team" even monitors office buildings, schools, and hotels to make sure their heating and cooling systems do not exceed government standards (which say a building cannot be colder than 79 degrees Fahrenheit in the summer or warmer than 68 degrees in the winter).[80] These efforts

[79] John Bailey, *Climate Neutral Bonding: Building Global Warming Solutions at the State and Local Level* (Minneapolis: Institute for Local Self-Reliance, February 2006), pp. 6–7.
[80] B.K. Sovacool and M.A. Brown, "Twelve Metropolitan Carbon Footprints: A Global Comparative Assessment," *Energy Policy* 38(9) (September 2010), pp. 4856–4869.

have ensured that while Beijing's economy grew more than 15 percent from 1985 to 1998, GHG emissions grew only 3.9 percent.[81]

## Transportation demand-side management

Less conventional, but still effective, is practicing demand-side management of automobiles – directly shaping consumer behavior, restricting the number of drivers' licenses or cars, and implementing congestion road pricing. Singapore, for example, has pursued a synergetic approach to urban transport policy.[82] Aspects have included restraint of vehicle ownership and vehicle moratoriums, steady improvement of public mass transit, road pricing schemes, and the provision of real-time information to drivers. "Supply-side" components have invested in train and bus infrastructure and constructed electronic road pricing schemes, whereas "demand-side" components attempt to alter behavior in favor of public mass transit by restricting the number of private vehicles through license quota systems, certificates of entitlement, and higher vehicle fees. One key element of Singaporean policies is that they rely on a mix of incentives and disincentives; so-called "sticks" raise the costs of driving a private automobile through purchase taxes and usage fees, whereas "carrots" encourage public transport and more efficient driving practices.[83] The Singaporean Ministry of Transport estimates that almost 5 million trips (about 60 percent) occur per day using mass rapid transit, light rail transit, and buses – impressive figures given that the country has a population of less than 5 million people. The cities of Minneapolis and St. Paul, Minnesota, have also implemented a toll system using priority lanes with differential pricing, dynamic instant messaging about traffic, and information about public transit options

---

[81] Shinji Kaneko and Shobhakar Dhakal, "Comparison of Urban Energy Use and Carbon Emission in Tokyo, Beijing, Seoul and Shanghai," presentation to the International Workshop on Urban Energy and Carbon Modeling, February 5–6, 2008 (AIT Centre, Asian Institute of Technology, Pathumthani, Thailand, 2008).

[82] Georgina Santos, Wai Wing Li, and Winston T.H. Koh, "Transport Policies in Singapore," in Georgina Santo (ed.), *Road Pricing: Theory and Evidence* (Oxford: Elsevier, 2004), pp. 209–235.

[83] Leo Tan Wee Hin and R. Subramaniam, "Congestion Control of Heavy Vehicles Using Electronic Road Pricing: The Singapore Experience," *International Journal of Heavy Vehicle Systems* 13(1/2) (2006), pp. 37–55.

and telecommuting, convincing hundreds of thousands of commuters to drive less.[84]

## Reductions in energy intensity

One of the most attractive ways to improve energy efficiency involves reducing energy intensity, the amount of energy (in BTUs) needed to produce one unit of GDP, through things like industrial retrofits, energy audits, and the hiring of energy service companies (ESCOs) with a dedicated mission of saving energy.[85] These types of activities have been so successful in the United States that total primary energy use per capita in 2000 was almost identical to energy use per capita in 1973. Over the same twenty-seven-year period, economic output (measured in terms of GDP per capita) increased 74 percent, yet national energy intensity fell 42 percent.[86] If the US had not dramatically reduced its energy intensity over the years, energy consumption would have risen 225 percent from 1973 to 2005, instead of increasing only by 30 percent, and consumers would have spent at least $700 billion more on energy purchases in 2012 (or more than $1.9 billion *every day*).[87] The difference in energy – about 75 EJ – is so much that its equivalent would be a freight train annually hauling nearly 18,000,000 railcars of coal, which would wrap around the earth seven times.[88]

When applied to the electricity industry, the gains made by energy efficiency outdo *every single source of electricity generation* today, including coal, natural gas, and nuclear energy. The trend holds true

[84] American Council for an Energy-Efficient Economy, "Major New US Energy Find Could Offset Nearly a Quarter of Nation's Power Use," News Release, June 5, 2012.

[85] See Ryoichi Komiyama and Chris Marnay, "Japan's Residential Energy Demand Outlook to 2030 Considering Energy Efficiency Standards 'Top Runner Approach'" (The Institute of Energy Economics, Japan, and Lawrence Berkeley National Laboratory, 2008), available at http://eetd.lbl.gov/ea/EMS/reports/lbnl-292e.pdf, as well as B.K. Sovacool, "Rising to the Challenge of Sustainability: Three Cases of Climate and Energy Governance," in Fereidoon P. Sioshansi (ed.), *Energy Sustainability and the Environment: Technology, Incentives, Behavior* (New York: Elsevier, 2011), pp. 551–570.

[86] The original figure was $438 billion in 2000, adjusted to $2007.

[87] Peter A. Seligmann and Michael Totten, "Pursuing Sustainable Planetary Prosperity," in *US–China 2022: US–China Economic Relations in the Next 10 Years* (Hong Kong: China–US Exchange Foundation, May 2013), p. 18.

[88] *Ibid.*

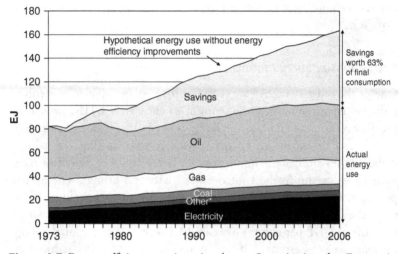

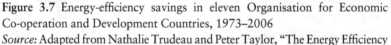

**Figure 3.7** Energy-efficiency savings in eleven Organisation for Economic Co-operation and Development Countries, 1973–2006
*Source:* Adapted from Nathalie Trudeau and Peter Taylor, "The Energy Efficiency Dimension of Energy Security," in B.K. Sovacool (ed.), *Routledge Handbook of Energy Security* (London: Routledge, 2010), pp. 218–238.

not just for the United States, but most industrialized countries. Figure 3.7 reveals findings from a comprehensive assessment of energy use in eleven Organisation for Economic Co-operation and Development countries which noted that energy-efficiency practices saved more energy, in exajoules, than any other source of energy.

### Energy-efficiency labeling and fuel economy standards

Mandatory energy-efficiency labels for electric appliances and automobiles, such as the Energy Star Program in the United States, can also drastically improve net efficiency. For example, Energy Star and other equipment standards established by the federal government in the early 1970s required the US Department of Energy to test and standardize the energy usage of appliances. These standards ordered manufacturers to improve the energy efficiency of gas furnaces by 25 percent between 1972 and 2001, central air conditioners by 40 percent, and refrigerators by 75 percent. From 2000 to 2015, adherence to these appliance standards will save consumers around $85 billion on a net present value basis.[89] In addition, setting higher corporate average fuel economy (CAFE) standards for cars can also push fuel economy up from its average of 27.5 miles per gallon (mpg) in the United States, Australia (30 mpg), China (30 mpg), the European Union (EU) (37.5 mpg), and Japan (46.5 mpg). Increasing fuel economy standards to 40 mpg in 2015 and 55 mpg in 2025 would save 4.9 million barrels of oil per day in the United States.[90]

## Smarter grids and electricity pricing

Conventional electric grids have simple or unsophisticated meters, flat or inflexible pricing, and are built according to a hub and spoke model of centralized supply. They offer little to no storage, cannot handle intermittent renewable sources well, and use only a minimal amount of information technology. Smart grids, illustrated by Table 3.3, have advanced net metering or smart meters, dynamic pricing that changes, and are built to accommodate distributed generation. They can incorporate various types of storage (batteries, appliances, cars), are friendlier to wind and solar, and utilize large-scale digital networking and feedback.[91]

Smarter grids can perhaps obviously improve efficiency in a variety of ways. One is by enabling the use of smart controls and communication technologies to enhance the efficiency of home appliances. Some of the newest products on the market, for example, are making use of variable speed compressors and fans that use sensors and controls to optimize operation to cut energy usage by 5 percent. So-called "smart" appliances such as refrigerators and air conditioners can also communicate directly with electric utilities, receiving real-time price signals and adjusting their operation in response.[92]

Another way to improve efficiency is by incorporating smarter electricity pricing, with options ranging from ascending block rate pricing,

---

[89] Steven Nadel, "National Energy Policy: Conservation and Energy Efficiency," hearing before the House Committee on Energy and Commerce (June 22, 2001), pp. 46–51.

[90] B.K. Sovacool, "Solving the Oil Independence Problem: Is It Possible?," *Energy Policy* 35(11) (November 2007), pp. 5505–5514.

[91] William J. Mitchell, Christopher E. Borroni-Bird, and Lawrence D. Burns, *Reinventing the Automobile: Personal Urban Mobility for the 21st Century* (Cambridge, MA: MIT Press, 2010), p. 126.

[92] American Council for an Energy-Efficient Economy, "Major New US Energy Find."

**Table 3.3** *Comparison between conventional electricity grids and "smart grids"*

| Goal | Current grid | Smart grid |
|---|---|---|
| Resilience and self-healing | Operators respond to prevent further damage, focus is on reaction and protection of assets following system faults | Automatically detects and responds to actual and emerging T&D problem, focus is on prevention |
| Information and involvement | Consumers are uninformed and nonparticipative in the power system | Consumers are informed, involved, and active |
| Quality of energy services | Focused on outages rather than power quality patterns | Quality of energy services is matched to energy end-user demands |
| Diversification | Relies on large centralized generating units with little opportunities for energy storage | Encourages large numbers of distributed generation deployed to complement storage options such as electric vehicles, with more focus on access and interconnection to renewables and V2G systems |
| Competitive markets | Limited wholesale markets still working to find the best operating models, not well suited to handling congestion or integrating with each other | More efficient wholesale market operations in place with integrated reliability coordinators and minimal transmission congestion and constraints |
| Optimization and efficiency | Minimal integration of limited operational data with asset management processes and technologies and time-based maintenance | Greatly expanded sensing and measurement of grid conditions, technologies deeply integrated with asset management processes and condition-based maintenance |

*Source:* Adapted from Table 7.9 from Cutler J. Cleveland and Christopher G. Morris, *Handbook of Energy Volume I: Diagrams, Charts, and Tables* (London: Elsevier Science, 2013).

real-time pricing, decoupling revenues from sales, and taxes. The promotion of inverse block rate pricing, where customers are charged higher rates for electricity the more they consume, encourages more rational use. At least three utility companies – Pacific Gas & Electric in California, the Arizona Public Service Company, and Idaho Power Company – have experimented with this type of approach for customers and exhibited substantial energy savings.[93] Similar programs exist abroad, such as Malaysia, where Figure 3.8 shows that the highest "block" tariff of 45.4 sens/kWh (13.5 cents/kWh) is more than *twice* the lowest tariff of 21.8 sens/kWh (6.5 cents/kWh).

Reflecting time of use through "real-time," "interval metering," "time-of-use," or "seasonal" rates also shows customers how electricity production and consumption varies according to the time of day, week, and month. The regulation of utilities has been based historically on average prices, set in rates revealed to customers in monthly bills. There are some markets where hourly electricity prices can vary by factors of 100 or more, but these prices are all always averaged, so consumers never see them. Most electricity bills combine charges for several appliances, lighting, water heating, space heating, and cooling all into a lump sum. It is impossible for consumers to tell, without careful monitoring and experimentation, how much of the bill results from the individual use of appliances or technologies, or how much the bill could be decreased by using more efficient models – flaws easily addressed by better metering and billing techniques.[94]

Another important policy innovation is decoupling the profits of electricity and natural gas utilities from their sales volumes. Some states in North America are adopting this policy, which allows electric utilities to keep a small share of the savings they achieve for their customers. In other words, the utilities are "rewarded for cutting your bill, not for selling you more energy."[95] The Natural Resources Defense Council has noted that decoupling ensures that utilities cannot make windfall profits by encouraging higher (and at times, unnecessary) sales and are

[93] Sheryl Carter, "Breaking the Consumption Habit: Ratemaking for Efficient Resource Decisions," *Electricity Journal* (December 2001), pp. 66–74.
[94] Paul C. Stern and Elliot Aronson, *Energy Use: The Human Dimension* (New York: Freeman & Company, 1984).
[95] Matt J. Hirschland, Jeremy M. Oppenheim, and Allan P. Webb, "Using Energy More Efficiently: An Interview with the Rocky Mountain Institute's Amory Lovins," *McKinsey Quarterly* (July 2008), online.

| | | BIL ELEKTRIK | | |
|---|---|---|---|---|
| ⚡ **TENAGA NASIONAL** ʙᴇʀʜᴀᴅ (200866-W) | | | JUMLAH | |
| NO. AKAUN PENGGUNA | KONTRAK | TARIF | CAGARAN | NO. BIL |
| 0121 00238942 10 | 8501036 | 013 | 500.00 | 46026136 RU 624 |

SILA KEMASKINI MAKLUMAT PENGGUNA SEPERTI DI BELAKANG BIL INI

‖‖‖‖‖‖‖‖‖‖‖‖‖‖‖‖‖‖ *0121002389421 0*   ‖‖‖‖‖‖‖‖‖‖‖ *46026136*

| KETERANGAN | TARIKH | JUMLAH | KOD | TARIKH KEMASKINI |
|---|---|---|---|---|
| BIL AKHIR | 17-08-2012 | 790.85 | E | 12-09-2012 |
| BAYARAN AKHIR | 08-08-2012 | 1087.20 | | |

| CAJ | UNIT | KADAR | | JUMLAH |
|---|---|---|---|---|
| BLOK KEGUNAAN ELEKTRIK | 420 | 0.218 | RM | 91.56 |
| | 210 | 0.334 | RM | 70.14 |
| | 210 | 0.400 | RM | 84.00 |
| | 210 | 0.402 | RM | 84.42 |
| | 210 | 0.416 | RM | 87.36 |
| | 210 | 0.426 | RM | 89.46 |
| | 210 | 0.437 | RM | 91.77 |
| | 210 | 0.453 | RM | 95.13 |
| | 3742 | 0.454 | RM | 1698.87 |
| KUMPULAN WANG TENAGA BOLEH BAHARU | | | RM | 16.10 |
| JUM. KEGUNAAN | | | RM | 2408.81 |
| JUM. ANGGARAN TERDAHULU | | | RM | -783.04 |

| PELBAGAI | : | | |
|---|---|---|---|
| PENALTI | : | JUMLAH BIL | : |
| TUNGGAKAN | : | PENGGENAPAN | : |
| CAGARAN TAMBAHAN: | | JUM. PERLU DIBAYAR: | |
| NO. JANGKA | DAHULU | KOD | SEMASA | KOD | KEGUNAAN | UNIT |

**Figure 3.8** Malaysian electricity bill showing ascending block-rate tariffs
*Source:* Photo taken by one of the authors.

not penalized when energy-efficiency programs and other efforts reduce consumption.[96] In the United States, for example, after decoupling, Idaho

---

[96] Natural Resources Defense Council, *Removing Disincentives to Utility Energy Efficiency Efforts* (Washington, DC: NRDC, May 2012).

Power's investments in demand-side management programs tripled between 2006 and 2009 and energy savings increased 220 percent (to 148 GWh per year); California utilities saw decoupling increase investments in energy efficiency by a factor of five from 1998 and 2008; and Utah saw about $50 million per year in savings of natural gas.[97]

Another pricing tool can be higher energy taxes. Denmark, for example, gives low-consuming households tax free fuel allowances, but taxes excessive use of energy. They have a progressive tax that charges only those that use more than 800 cubic meters of gas and 800 kWh of electricity per month.[98]

A final mechanism is integrating electric vehicles and plug-in hybrid electric vehicles with the electricity grid. An automobile capable of "vehicle-to-grid" (V2G) interaction, sometimes referred to as "mobile energy" or "smart charging," mates an automobile with the existing electric utility system. This intelligent, two-way communication between the electricity grid and the vehicle enables utilities to manage electricity resources better, and it empowers vehicle owners to earn money by selling power back to the grid. All in all, a shift to V2G technologies has the potential to displace 6.5 million barrels of oil per day, and a shocking 84 percent of electrically powered cars, light trucks, and sport utility vehicles in the United States could be supported by the existing electric infrastructure if they drew power from the grid at off-peak times.[99]

## Information and awareness campaigns

Thomas Jefferson used to say that "a democratic society depends upon an informed and educated citizenry," but that in order for education to occur, people had to be informed "even against their will." Electricity information and education campaigns are therefore warranted, and they could include grade-school classes on energy and the environment;

[97] Dylan Sullivan, Devra Wang, and Drew Bennett, "Essential to Energy Efficiency, but Easy to Explain: Frequently Asked Questions about Decoupling," *Electricity Journal* 24(8) (October 2011), pp. 56–70.

[98] Stephen Tindale and Chris Hewett, "Must the Poor Pay More? Sustainable Development, Social Justice, and Environmental Taxation," in Andrew Dobson (ed.), *Fairness and Futurity: Essays on Environmental Sustainability and Social Justice* (Oxford University Press, 1999), pp. 233–248.

[99] B.K. Sovacool and R.F. Hirsh, "Beyond Batteries: An Examination of the Benefits and Barriers to Plug-In Hybrid Electric Vehicles (PHEVs) and a Vehicle-to-Grid (V2G) Transition," *Energy Policy* 37(3) (March 2009), pp. 1095–1103.

public demonstrations and tours of clean power facilities; mandatory disclosure of electricity usage for the construction of new buildings and the renting and leasing of existing ones; free energy audits and training sessions for industrial, commercial, and residential electricity customers; improved labeling, rating, and certification programs for appliances and electricity-using devices; and national information "clearing house" consisting of websites, free books, indexing services, and libraries to help consumers gather and process information in order to make better choices about their electricity use.

Getting energy users to consume and act on this information, however, is tricky. Effective information programs must be carefully tailored. Information is less likely to be used if it requires effort or arrives when a household owner or business manager is busy with other things. Households and industries consume different fuels, in different kinds of buildings, and vary in their income, housing and facility tenure, and individual needs. To avoid creating information that is merely a distraction, "general" or "generic" distribution strategies must be avoided. Behavior that is perceived to be directly under the individual's control, that involves few barriers or adjustments, and includes built-in incentives (or has an absence of disincentives) tends to be the easiest to promote.[100] Psychologists Renee J. Bator and Robert B. Cialdini, for example, have found that public information campaigns can accomplish their goals if they (a) recognize saturation and realize that their message must compete with thousands of others, (b) set achievable goals that emphasize moderate and easy changes in behavior, and (c) target specific audiences and thoroughly understand the demographics, lifestyles, values, and habits of that audience.[101] When structured this way, public information campaigns have been proven to create norms and shift social attitudes, with specific programs relating to household hazardous waste disposal and littering reducing "undesirable" behavior by 10 to 20 percent.[102]

---

[100] Carrico, Padgett, Vandenbergh, Gilligan, and Wallston, "Costly Myths."
[101] Renee J. Bator and Robert B. Cialdini, "The Application of Persuasion Theory to the Development of Effective Proenvironmental Public Service Announcements," *Journal of Social Issues* 56(3) (2000), pp. 527–541.
[102] Michael P. Vandenbergh, "From Smokestack to SUV: The Individual as Regulated Entity in the New Era of Environmental Law," *Vanderbilt Law Review* 57 (2004), pp. 515–610.

# 4 | *Utility and energy externalities*

In 1945, planners in Orissa, India, faced a dilemma. The upper draining basin of the Mahanadi River passed through Orissa (later renamed the state of Odisha), causing massive floods in some years coupled with devastating droughts in others. Hydrological and engineering assessments concluded that a series of storage reservoirs, dykes, and dams could help regulate this uneven distribution of water. These assessments revealed that the best place to locate the largest of these projects would be 15 kilometers from Sambalpur, where a 5 kilometer long earthen dam could prevent the Mahanadi River from swelling during the monsoon season and regulate the drainage of 83,400 square kilometers of land, providing flood control to the districts of Cuttack and Puri. Such a dam could also help irrigate 75,000 square kilometers of crops throughout the districts of Sambalpur, Bargarh, Bolangir, and Subarnpu, in addition to providing 307.5 MW of hydroelectricity. At the time, in aggregate, these benefits would reach upwards of 3 million people.

However, achieving these benefits would come at the cost of flooding almost 150,000 acres (600 square kilometers) of land that would become a permanent reservoir. It would also require the forced relocation of more than 150,000 people from 22,000 families. In short, building the dam would necessitate "substantial mass agitation."[1]

If you were a planner in India, what decision would you make – would you sacrifice the wishes of the 150,000 people for the greater good of the 3 million? In 1946, Sir Howthrone Lewis, then Governor, decided to proceed with the project and laid the foundational stone of the Hirakud Dam. When the internally displaced communities complained to the national government, the Prime Minister himself visited Hirakud and spoke directly to the villagers. "If you are to suffer,"

[1] Balgovind Baboo, "Politics of Water: The Case of the Hirakud Dam in Orissa, India," *International Journal of Sociology and Anthropology* 1(8) (December 2009), pp. 139–144.

India's first Prime Minister Jawaharlal Nehru declared in 1948, "you should suffer in the interest of the country."[2] Such "suffering" for the greater benefit of humanity, the flagrant sacrificing of community interests for the greater national good, has been repeated around the world, from Three Gorges Dam in China and the Bakun Hydroelectric Project in Malaysia to the Itaipu Dam in Brazil and the Atatürk Dam in Turkey. And that is excluding other major energy and infrastructural projects such as highways, bridges, power plants, nuclear waste repositories, pipelines, transmission lines, refineries, landfills, and even wind farms.

As this chapter argues, utilitarians such as Jeremy Bentham, John Stuart Mill, and Henry Sidgwick would hold that these sacrifices make perfect sense, as long as the greater good is served, and so long as they result in a net gain of happiness. But they would also abhor the way that some energy systems bring with them suffering and misery. These utilitarian theorists would bemoan the way the global energy system imposes a host of social and environmental costs on society ranging from pollution from oil and gas drilling, coalmines, and uranium mines to nuclear waste and air pollution. They would denounce these things because they fly in the face of their principles that useful things in life are right insofar as they promote happiness and pleasure, but wrong insofar as they cause suffering and pain. Luckily for modern society, policy mechanisms such as a carbon tax, more accurate energy pricing, and environmental bonds could go a long way towards doing away with these negative externalities.

## What is reality?

In our current energy market, the rates and prices for energy fuels and services do not include "externalities" and therefore justify a significant amount of suffering and pain. Externalities are defined as "benefits or costs generated as an unintended product of an economic activity that do not accrue to the parties involved in the activity and where no compensation takes place."[3] "Think of externalities as a second price tag on every product we consume," notes Law Professor Noah Sachs,

---

[2] Peter Penz, "Development, Displacement and Ethics," *Forced Migration Review* 12 (January 2002), p. 5.

[3] Anthony D. Owen, "Environmental Externalities, Market Distortions, and the Economics of Renewable Energy Technologies," *Energy Journal* 25(3) (2004), pp. 127–152.

"representing the real costs of disposing the product and the environmental impacts directly flowing from the existence of that product. The price tag may be less than a cent for some products and several dollars for others, but because this price is never actually 'paid' by consumers or producers, the price becomes externalized as a social cost."[4]

For example, a pack of cigarettes would cost $3.43 more if it included the cost of lost wages, house fires, and greater healthcare expenditures associated with smoking,[5] and a hamburger at McDonald's would cost $2 to $3 more if its price included the risks associated with high cholesterol and heart disease.[6] Energy technologies are no different: most power plants and cars are like big cigarettes that spew toxic elements into our air, land, and water, emitting health-endangering GHGs similar to the fat in a hamburger, and imposing painful health risks at a later stage in life. Specific examples of externalities in the energy and climate sectors are striking. By far the largest is climate change, though this chapter will also discuss those from electricity generation, transportation, oil and gas production, mountaintop removal coalmining, uranium mining, nuclear waste, and IAP.

## Climate change

GHG emissions and the resulting changes in climate are an externality because they impose costs far away, temporally and geographically, from emitters. According to the IPCC, human sources emitted about 50 billion metric tons of carbon dioxide equivalent into the atmosphere in 2013 – the last time a global inventory was taken. Global GHG emissions grew 54 percent from 1990 to 2011,[7] and if trends continue could increase 130 percent by 2040.

---

[4] Noah Sachs, "Planning the Funeral at the Birth: Extended Producer Responsibility in the European Union and the US," *Harvard Environmental Law Review* 30 (2006), p. 56.

[5] Researchers at the University of California at San Francisco identified $7.6 billion in yearly expenses mainly in lost wages and higher healthcare costs from smoking in California. This amount worked out to the equivalent of $3.43 added on to every pack of cigarettes sold in the state. Paul Hawken, *The Ecology of Commerce: A Declaration of Sustainability* (New York: Harper Collins, 1994), p. 79.

[6] Steven D. Levitt and Stephen J. Dubner, *Freakonomics: A Rogue Economist Explores the Hidden Side of Everything* (New York: Penguin Books, 2006).

[7] IPCC, *Climate Change 2013: Summary for Policymakers* (Geneva: IPCC, 2013), SPM-7.

In aggregate, the damages from these emissions – something not currently factored into most energy markets – could be shockingly large, exceeding the expense of previous global threats such as AIDS, the Great Depression, and global terrorism. The Pew Center on Global Climate Change estimates that "waiting until the future" to address global climate change might bankrupt the US economy.[8] The Stern Report projected that the overall costs and risks of climate change will be equivalent to losing at least 5 percent of the world's GDP, or $3.2 trillion, every year, now and forever, and that these damages could exceed 20 percent of GDP ($13 trillion) if more severe scenarios unfold.[9] Stern's figures have since been critiqued for being too *conservative* and for underestimating the impacts from climate change.[10] Global economic damages from natural catastrophes, many of them climate related, have also doubled every ten years and reached about $1 trillion in total over the past fifteen years. Annual weather-related disasters have increased by a factor of four from forty years ago, and insurance payouts have increased by a factor of eleven over the same period, rising by $10 billion per *year* for most of the past decade.[11] The Center for American Progress estimates that every year the United States delays to cut emissions costs the country $500 billion of investment per year, a number that will balloon to $10 trillion by 2030 if the county does not change course.[12]

Unfortunately, as we will see in Chapter 9, the distribution of these negative impacts from climate change will be far from equitable. Developing countries, and those perversely least responsible for emissions, will be most at risk. Indonesia, the Philippines, Thailand, and

---

[8] Eileen Claussen and Janet Peace, "Energy Myth Twelve – Climate Policy Will Bankrupt the U.S. Economy," in B.K. Sovacool and M.A. Brown (eds.), *Energy and American Society – Thirteen Myths* (New York: Springer, 2007).

[9] Nicholas Stern, *The Economics of Climate Change: The Stern Review* (Cambridge University Press, 2007); IPCC, *Summary for Policymakers*.

[10] See Partha Dasgupta, "Comments on the Stern Review's Economics of Climate Change," University of Cambridge, November 11, 2006 (revised: December 12); Hal R. Varian, "Recalculating the Costs of Global Climate Change," *New York Times*, December 14, 2006.

[11] B. Sudhakara Reddy and Gaudenz B. Assenza, "The Great Climate Debate," *Energy Policy* 37 (2009), pp. 2997–3008.

[12] Jorge Madrid, Kate Gordon, and Tina Ramos, *America's Future under "Drill, Baby, Drill": Where We'll Be in 2030 if We Stay on Our Current Oil-Dependent Path* (Washington, DC: Center for American Progress, May 2012).

Vietnam are expected to lose 6.7 percent of their combined GDP by 2100, more than twice the global average, if climatic conditions follow IPCC forecasts.[13] China and India, among others, could exhaust between 1 and 12 percent of their GDP coping with climate refugees, changing disease vectors, and failing crops.[14] The situation reminds us that vulnerability to climate change is not only exposure to natural disasters and altered climates, but also sensitivity to change and the capacity (or lack thereof) to respond.

## Electricity generation

But serious as it is, climate change is not the only meaningful externality associated with energy production and use. In the electricity industry, the financial costs of generating supply may appear low, but they do not include the costs of coalmine dust that kills thousands of workers each year; black lung disease that has imposed at least $35 billion in health-care costs; and fossil-fuel emissions that cause acid deposition and smog, and also contribute to asthma, respiratory and cardiovascular disease, and premature mortality.[15] If put into monetary terms, the social and environmental damage from worldwide electricity genera-tion (excluding climate change) amounts to roughly 13 cents per kilowatt-hour (kWh), or $2.6 trillion in extra costs every year.[16] If the

[13] Asian Development Bank, *The Economics of Climate Change in Southeast Asia: A Regional Review* (Manila: Asian Development Bank, April 2009).

[14] Economics of Climate Adaptation Working Group, *Shaping Climate-Resilient Development: A Framework for Decision-Making* (Washington, DC: Global Environment Facility, European Commission, McKinsey & Company, The Rockefeller Foundation, Standard Chartered Bank, and Swiss Re, 2009); Arief Anshory Yusuf and Herminia A. Francisco, *Climate Change Vulnerability Mapping for Southeast Asia* (Singapore: International Development Research Centre, January 2009); Royal United Services Institute, *Socioeconomic and Security Implications of Climate Change in China* (Washington, DC: Center for Naval Analysis, November 4, 2009); Center for Naval Analysis, *Climate Change, State Resilience, and Global Security* (Center for Naval Analysis Conference Center, Alexandria, Virginia, November 4, 2009).

[15] Mark Z. Jacobson and Gilbert M. Masters, "Exploiting Wind Versus Coal," *Science* 293 (2001), pp. 1438–1439.

[16] In 2007, coal provided about 41 percent of 18,930 terawatt-hours (TWh) global electricity generation, natural gas 20.1 percent, hydroelectric 16 percent, nuclear 14.8 percent, oil 5.8 percent, and other renewables 2.3 percent. Every kWh of coal generation has 19.14 cents in negative externalities; every kWh of natural gas and oil 12 cents; nuclear 11.1 cents; hydroelectric 5 cents; other renewables

electricity industry were to remain in 2040 configured the way it was in the US in 2008, for example, the costs of power outages would exceed $412 billion, the industry would consume and withdraw more water than the agricultural sector (threatening widespread shortages), and more than 65,000 Americans would die prematurely from power plant pollution.[17]

## Automobiles and transport

In the transport sector, vehicle crashes are the leading cause of injury-related deaths in the US for people between the ages of one and sixty-five, causing 37,000 deaths, 2 million injuries, and $150 billion in related economic losses each year that are not reflected in the price of a new vehicle or its fuel. Gasoline is cheap because its price does not incorporate the cost of smog, acid rain, and their effects on health and the environment. Using some of the most recently available data, Table 4.1 shows that in the US deaths from PM pollution related to automobiles and power plants are comparable to those from Alzheimer's disease and influenza and greater than the deaths from nephritis, breast cancer, automobile accidents, prostate cancer, HIV-AIDS, and drunk driving.[18] One team of independent scientists calculated that the external costs for transportation in the United States surpassed $820 billion per year in 2010, inclusive of congestion delays, accidents, pollution, climate change, and noise.[19] In France, the Agency for Health and Environmental Safety projects that automobile emissions kill 9,513 people per year and result in 6 to 11 percent of all lung cancer cases identified in people above thirty years of

---

3 cents. Weighing these according to the percentage of global supply, every kWh of electricity has about 13.46 cents of negative externalities. 18,930 TWh multiplied by 13.46 cents equals $2,547,978,000,000. See International Energy Agency, *World Energy Outlook 2008* (Paris: OECD, 2008); and Benjamin K. Sovacool, *The Dirty Energy Dilemma: What's Blocking Clean Power in the United States* (Westport: Praeger, 2008).

[17] Sovacool, *The Dirty Energy Dilemma*, p. 221.

[18] Benjamin K. Sovacool, "A Transition to Plug-In Hybrid Electric Vehicles (PHEVs): Why Public Health Professionals Must Care," *Journal of Epidemiology and Community Health* 64(3) (March 2010), pp. 185–187.

[19] Amory Lovins and the Rocky Mountain Institute, *Reinventing Fire: Bold Business Solutions for the New Energy Era* (White River Junction: Chelsea Green Publishing Company, 2011), p. 43.

Table 4.1 *Approximate causes of death in the United States, 2011*

| Cause | Estimated annual deaths |
| --- | --- |
| Heart disease | 596,000 |
| Cancer | 575,000 |
| Stroke | 143,000 |
| Alzheimer's disease | 84,000 |
| PM pollution | 66,000 |
| Influenza and pneumonia | 54,000 |
| Nephritis | 46,000 |
| Breast cancer | 41,000 |
| Automobile fatalities | 37,000 |
| Prostate cancer | 30,000 |
| Parkinson's disease | 23,000 |
| HIV | 18,000 |
| Drunk driving | 17,000 |

*Source:* Adapted from the US Centers for Disease Control website, accessed October 2013.

age.[20] Another report from the WHO investigating automobile emissions in Austria, Switzerland, and France calculated 40,000 deaths per year.[21]

As the economist Charles Wheelan put it:

The problem is not that we like cars; the problem is that we do not have to pay the full cost of driving them. Yes, we buy the car and then pay for maintenance, insurance, and gasoline. But we don't have to pay for some of the other significant costs of driving: the emissions we leave behind, the congestion we cause, the wear and tear on public roads, the danger we pose to drivers in smaller cars. The effect is a bit like a night on the town with Dad's credit card: We do a lot of things we wouldn't do if we had to pay the whole bill. We drive huge cars, we avoid public transportation, we move to far-flung suburbs and then commute long distances. Individuals don't get the bill for this behavior, but society does – in the form of air pollution, global warming, and urban sprawl.[22]

---

[20] Julio Godoy, "Auto Emissions Killing Thousands," *Common Dreams News Release*, June 3, 2004, available at www.commondreams.org/headlines04/0603–08.htm.

[21] *Ibid.*

[22] Charles Wheelan, *Naked Economics: Undressing the Dismal Science* (New York: W.W. Norton & Company, 2003), p. xviii.

## Oil and gas production

As hinted at in Chapter 2 when describing energy "outputs," in the oil
and gas industry the average platform or well releases millions of liters of
produced water back into the ocean or sea every day. Produced water
contains lead, zinc, mercury, benzene, and toluene, making it highly toxic
and requiring operators to often treat it with chemicals, increasing its
salinity and making it fatal to many types of plants, before releasing it
into the environment. The ratio of waste to extracted oil is staggering:
every one gallon (3.78 liters) of oil brought to the surface yields 8 gallons
(30 liters) of contaminated water, cuttings, and drilling muds.[23] The next
stage, refining, involves boiling, vaporizing, and treating extracted crude
oil and gas with solvents to improve their quality. An ordinary refinery
processes 3.8 million gallons (14.4 million liters) of oil per day, and about
11,000 gallons (42,000 liters) of its product (0.3 percent of production)
escapes directly into the local environment every day of operation, where it
can contaminate land and pollute water.[24]

In Azerbaijan, a major producer of crude oil with a longer history of
development than the United States, about 30 percent of the entire coastal
area and half of the country's larger rivers have been so contaminated by
petroleum development officials deemed them unsafe for drinking and
agriculture.[25] About 90 percent of noxious pollutants emitted into the air
in Azerbaijan are connected to the oil industry, and Baku's oil refineries
release concentrations of hydrocarbons, sulfur dioxide, and nitrogen
oxides at levels considered unsafe by international standards.
Epidemiological studies have also confirmed an abnormally high percentage of children near oil-producing facilities in Azerbaijan that are
born premature, stillborn, or with genetic diseases – families living in
degraded landscapes like the one in Figure 4.1.[26] To put the findings

[23] David Waskow and Carol Welch, "The Environmental, Social, and Human
Rights Impacts of Oil Development," in Svetlana Tsalik and Anya Schiffrin (eds.),
*Covering Oil: A Reporter's Guide to Energy and Development* (New York: Open
Society Institute, 2005), pp. 101–123.

[24] *Ibid.*

[25] B.K. Sovacool, "Cursed by Crude: The Corporatist Resource Curse and the
Baku–Tbilisi–Ceyhan (BTC) Pipeline," *Environmental Policy and Governance*
21(1) (January/February 2011), pp. 42–57.

[26] J.E. Andruchow, C.L. Soskolne, F. Racioppi *et al.*, "Cancer Incidence and
Mortality in the Industrial City of Sumgayit, Azerbaijan," *International Journal of
Occupational Environmental Health* 12(3) (2006), pp. 234–241; J.W. Bickham,

**Figure 4.1** Oil and gas production near Baku, Azerbaijan
*Source:* Photo taken by one of the authors.

from these studies in perspective, average life expectancy for someone living near these oilfields is less than forty years compared to a global average above seventy years.

## Mountaintop removal coalmining

In the coalmining industry, activities can remove mountaintops in a process that clears forests and topsoil before it uses explosives to break up rocks, pushing mine spoils into adjacent streams and valleys. This can cause acid drainage into river systems. Of the more than 1 billion tons of coal mined in the United States annually, roughly 30 percent comes from mountaintop removal. The overall process has destroyed ecosystems, blighted landscapes, and diminished the water quality of rural communities – such as the one in Figure 4.2.

Tragically, one recent study noted that "there is, to date, no evidence to suggest that the extensive chemical and hydrologic alterations of streams by MTVF can be offset or reversed by currently required reclamation and mitigation practices."[27] Another survey of seventy-eight MTVF streams in the same region found that seventy-three of

C.W. Matson, A. Islamzadeh *et al.*, "The Unknown Environmental Tragedy in Sumgayit, Azerbaijan," *Ecotoxicology* 12 (2003), pp. 505–508.

[27] Emily S. Bernhardt and Margaret A. Palmer, "The Environmental Costs of Mountaintop Mining Valley Fill Operations for Aquatic Ecosystems of the

**Figure 4.2** Mountaintop removal coalmining near Kayford Mountain, West
Virginia
*Source:* Photo from Rodney Sobin, "Energy Myth Seven – Renewable Energy
Systems Could Never Meet Growing Electricity Demand in America," in B.K.
Sovacool and M.A. Brown (eds.), *Energy and American Society – Thirteen
Myths* (New York: Springer Publishing Company, 2007), pp. 171–200.

them had water pollution levels far past the threshold for toxic bioac-
cumulation.[28] As one of the authors of this study stated, "the scientific
evidence of the severe environmental and human impacts from mountaintop mining is strong and irrefutable. Its impacts are pervasive and
long lasting and there is no evidence that any mitigation practices
successfully reverse the damage it causes."[29] A separate study from a
team of economists estimated that the lifecycle impacts of coal and the

Central Appalachians," *Annals of the New York Academy of Sciences* 1223
(2001), 39–57.
[28] M.A. Palmer, E.S. Bernhardt, W.H. Schlesinger, K.N. Eshleman, E. Foufoula-
Georgiou, M.S. Hendryx, A.D. Lemly, G.E. Likens, O.L. Loucks, M.E. Power, P.
S. White, and P.R. Wilcock, "Mountaintop Mining Consequences," *Science* 327
(January 8, 2010), pp. 148–149.
[29] Quoted in Natural Resources Defense Council, Mountain Top Removal Coal
Mining, June 23, 2011.

waste stream generated cost the US public "a third to over one half a trillion dollars annually," meaning that "accounting for the damages conservatively doubles to triples the price of electricity from coal per kWh generated."[30]

## Uranium mining

In the uranium mining industry, to produce the 25 tons of uranium needed to keep a typical reactor working for one year, 500,000 tons of waste rock and 100,000 tons of mill tailings – toxic for hundreds of thousands of years – will be created, along with an extra 144 tons of solid waste and 1,343 $m^3$ of liquid waste.[31] Open-pit mining is prone to sudden emissions of radioactive gases and the degradation of land, as kilometer-wide craters are formed around uranium deposits, which then interfere with the flow of groundwater as far as 10 kilometers away.[32]

In Australia, the third largest producer of uranium in 2012, a detailed investigation of the environmental impacts from the Rum Jungle mine found that it has discharged acidic liquid wastes directly into creeks that flow into the Finniss River and has also gradually eroded the lowlands adjacent to the creeks. Land has been contaminated with radium-226, and "accounting for the radium has been extremely poor with very little focus on radium uptake in the environment or current levels leaching from the site."[33] The Roxby Downs mine has polluted the Arabunna people's traditional land with 80 million tons of annual dumped tailings, in addition to the mine's daily extraction of 30 million liters of water from the Great Artesian Basin. The Ranger mine has seen 120 documented leaks, spills, and breaches of its tailings waste, which has seeped into waterways and contaminated the Kakuda wetlands. The Beverley mine has been fined for dumping liquid radioactive waste into

---

[30] Nicholas Z. Muller, Robert Mendelsohn, and William Nordhaus, "Environmental Accounting for Pollution in the United States Economy," *American Economic Review*, 101(5) (August 2011), pp. 1649–1675.

[31] David Thorpe, "Extracting Disaster," *Guardian*, December 5, 2008.

[32] V.V. Shatalov, M.I. Fazlullin, R.I. Romashkevich, R.N. Smirnova, and G. M. Adosik, "Ecological Safety of Underground Leaching of Uranium," *Atomic Energy* 91(6) (2001), pp. 1009–1015.

[33] Gavin M. Mudd and Mark Disendorf, "Sustainability of Uranium Mining and Milling: Toward Quantifying Resources and Eco-Efficiency," *Environmental Science & Technology* 42 (2008), pp. 2624–2629.

groundwater.[34] The Olympic Dam mine, a vast open-pit mine, has generated windstorms carrying radioactive dust.[35] It also draws 15 million liters of water per day from the Great Artesian Basin, and has dumped 5 billion liters of toxic and acidic water from tailings into water sources. It may thus come as no surprise that the independent Senate References and Legislation Committee, part of the Australian federal government, documented a pattern at uranium mines where "short-term considerations have been given greater weight than the potential for permanent damage to the environment."[36] It is telling that the cleanup and decontamination of the Rum Jungle uranium mine will cost the Australian government far more than it ever earned from the mine.[37]

## Nuclear waste storage and decommissioning

Upstream, at nuclear reactors, the storage of nuclear waste is an externality because it imposes costs on future generations (for more about this topic, readers can skip ahead to Chapter 9, which has a section on "long-lived nuclear waste"); decommissioning is an externality because it imposes costs on taxpayers and those living near nuclear facilities who may not receive any nuclear electricity.

Generally, 1 ton of highly radioactive waste is generated for every 4 pounds of usable uranium, and each nuclear reactor consumes an average 32,000 fuel rods over the course of its lifetime. That means that a single nuclear plant will produce about 30 tons of high-level waste each year, and this waste can be radioactive for as long as 250,000 years. Assuming just one tenth of that time (25,000 years), and assuming the cost of storing the 30 tons of nuclear waste created per year was just $35,000 per ton, the lowest end of existing estimates,[38] each nuclear plant in the US assumes an additional undiscounted cost of $26.3 billion. Given that more than 430 nuclear power

[34] Friends of the Earth, *Uranium Mining for Belgian Nuclear Power Stations: Environmental and Human Rights Impacts* (Brussels: Friends of the Earth, 2008).

[35] Thorpe, "Extracting Disaster."     [36] *Ibid.*

[37] Michael Krockenberger, "Unclean, Unsafe, and Unwanted: The Nuclear Industry Nightmare," *Habitat* (Melbourne: Australian Conservation Foundation, June 1996).

[38] Allison Macfarlane, "The Problem of Used Nuclear Fuel: Lessons for Interim Solutions from a Comparative Cost Analysis," *Energy Policy* 29 (2001), pp. 1379–1389.

plants exist, the global undiscounted cost of storing their current waste surpasses $11.3 trillion dollars.

In terms of decommissioning, the price of energy inputs and environmental costs of every nuclear power plant continue long after the facility has finished generating its last useful kilowatt of electricity. While it will vary along with technique and reactor type, the total energy required for decommissioning can be as much as 50 percent more than the energy needed for original construction.[39] Indeed, every nuclear facility in operation now and every nuclear plant that will ever come online will eventually reach the end of its useful life and will begin the long and arduous task of decommissioning, or returning the facility, its parts and surrounding land to a safe enough level to be entrusted to other uses. This decommissioning process includes all of the administrative and technical actions associated with ceasing operations, removing spent or unused fuel, reprocessing or storing radioactive wastes, deconstructing and decontaminating structures and equipment, shipping contaminated equipment offsite, and remediating the land, air, and water around the reactor site. In most cases, the decommissioning process costs $300 million to $5.6 billion per power plant.[40] The Nuclear Decommissioning Authority in the United Kingdom has estimated total decommissioning costs with their units to be more than £73 billion in total.[41] When put into the context of how much this costs per unit of electricity delivered, after surveying decommissioning costs for twenty-six countries and a variety of reactor types and sizes, the World Energy Council (WEC) calculated that decommissioning adds the equivalent of 2.5 to 4.2 extra cents per kWh,[42] an amount greater than the levelized cost of actually generating that electricity at some facilities.

However, decommissioning at nuclear sites that have experienced a serious accident can be even greater. Three Mile Island Unit 2, which

[39] B.K. Sovacool and C. Cooper, "Nuclear Nonsense: Why Nuclear Power Is No Answer to Climate Change and the World's Post-Kyoto Energy Challenges," *William & Mary Environmental Law & Policy Review* 33(1) (Fall 2008), pp. 1–119.

[40] See United Kingdom Atomic Energy Authority, *Decommissioning Fact Sheet*, 2005, p. 2; Anibal Taboas, A. Alan Mohgissi, and Thomas S. LaGuardia, *The Decommissioning Handbook*, 2004, p. 140; Nuclear Energy Agency, *The Regulatory Challenges of Decommissioning Reactors* (2003), pp. 15 and 18.

[41] Sovacool and Cooper, "Nuclear Nonsense."

[42] WEC, *The Role of Nuclear Power in Europe* (London: WEC, January 2007).

shut down permanently after an accident in 1979, will not start the decommissioning process until 2014 and is estimated to cost an extra $918 million.[43] Fuel rods at Chernobyl, the site of the world's deadliest nuclear accident to date, are still being removed and operators expect it to take until at least 2038 to 2138 before the power plant is completely decommissioned; so far they have spent $2 billion simply stabilizing the structure and storing its fuel.[44] Conservative estimates of the cleanup operation in Fukushima, Japan, predict a dizzying price tag of at least $100 billion.[45]

Even other parts of the nuclear lifecycle such as enrichment facilities and reprocessing sites, perhaps surreptitiously, have their own substantial decommissioning costs. The West Valley plutonium processing facility in New York cost only $600 million to build in 1966 but cleanup costs were estimated in 2008 to surpass $5 billion.[46] The National Research Council (NRC) has similarly calculated that the decommissioning costs of three uranium enrichment facilities in the United States will likely cost $27.3 to $67.2 billion, with an additional $2 to $5.8 billion to cover disposal of a large inventory of depleted uranium hexafluoride.[47] One of the companies responsible for decommissioning uranium enrichment and processing plants in the United Kingdom, the state-owned British Nuclear Fuels Limited, reported £356 million of shareholder funds in 2001 but £35 billion in liabilities, underscoring the immensity of cleanup costs.[48] Likewise, France is expected to spend at

---

[43] "Three Mile Island decommission cost put at $918M," Associated Press, August 29, 2013, available at http://lancasteronline.com/news/three-mile-island-decommission-cost-put-at-m/article_6dbd62ec-3d19–5b07–87c4–8d7de3883731.html.

[44] European Bank for Reconstruction and Development, *Chernobyl 25 Years On: New Safe Confinement and Spent Fuel Storage Facility* (London: ERD, 2011), available at http://www.ebrd.com/downloads/research/factsheets/chernobyl25.pdf, mentioning "total costs" of $1.6 billion for the "Shelter Implementation Plan" and $300 million for the "Interim Storage Facility."

[45] Justin McCurry, "Fukushima Two Years On: The Largest Nuclear Decommissioning Finally Begins," *Guardian*, March 6, 2013.

[46] Dan Watkiss, "The Middle Ages of Our Energy Policy – Will the Renaissance be Nuclear?," *Electric Light and Power* (May 2008).

[47] Costs have been updated for inflation from the NRC Committee on Decontamination and Decommissioning of Uranium Enrichment Facilities, *Affordable Cleanup? Opportunities for Cost Reduction in the Decontamination and Decommissioning of the Nation's Uranium Enrichment Facilities* (Washington, DC: NRC, 1996), pp. 49–50.

[48] Sovacool and Cooper, "Nuclear Nonsense."

least €65 billion decommissioning its uranium enrichment facilities and some, such as Brennilis, will cost twenty times the original sum envisioned by developers.[49]

## Indoor air pollution

IAP from household cookstoves in the developing world – something explored more in Chapter 7 – is responsible for 4 *million* deaths each year, 3.5 million direct premature annual deaths and 500,000 from "secondhand cookfire smoke" outdoors.[50] As the Global Alliance for Clean Cookstoves provocatively asks in Figure 4.3, "What's one of the most dangerous activities for a woman in the developing world?" The answer is "cooking a meal for her family." IAP ranks *fourth* on the global burden of disease risk factors at almost 5 percent. This places it well ahead of physical inactivity and obesity, drug use, and unsafe sex. In India and all of South Asia, cookstove smoke is the *highest* health risk factor, beating out smoking and high blood pressure. It is second for Sub-Saharan Africa, third for Southeast Asia, and fifth in East Asia. In aggregate, such air pollution amounts to almost 11,000 deaths per day, or almost eight deaths per minute, most of them among women and children. The cost of this burden to national healthcare systems, not reflected in the price of fuelwood or energy, is $212 billion to $1.1 trillion.[51]

## What is justice?

In sum, like it or not, every kilowatt-hour (kWh) of conventional electricity generated, separative work unit of uranium produced, cubic meter of natural gas manufactured, barrel of oil delivered, or piece of firewood burnt inside a cookstove results in a sobering assortment of environmental and social damages. These damages may include an

---

[49] Greenpeace, *France's Nuclear Failures: The Great Illusion of Nuclear Energy* (Amsterdam: Greenpeace International, November 2008), p. 15.

[50] S.S. Lim *et al.*, "A Comparative Risk Assessment of Burden of Disease and Injury Attributable to 67 Risk Factors and Risk Factor Clusters in 21 Regions, 1990–2010: A Systematic Analysis for the Global Burden of Disease Study 2010," *Lancet*, 380 (2012), pp. 2224–2260.

[51] UNEP, *Natural Selection: Evolving Choices for Renewable Energy Technology and Policy* (New York: UN, 2000).

**Figure 4.3** The dangers of household cooking and indoor air pollution
*Source:* Image taken by one of the authors from materials from the Global Alliance for Clean Cookstoves.

altered global climate, radioactive waste and abandoned uranium mines and mills, acid rain and its damage to fisheries and crops, water degradation and excessive consumption, particle pollution, cumulative environmental damage to ecosystems and biodiversity through species loss and habitat destruction, and accelerated burdens of global disease.[52]

For utilitarians such as Bentham, Mill, and Sidgwick, however, justice is about maximizing utility, happiness, and welfare, meaning it provides strong reasons for trying to minimize or eliminate the extent of these externalities as much as possible.

## Jeremy Bentham

Jeremy Bentham (1748–1832) formulated his central idea simply enough: "the highest principle of morality is to maximize happiness, the overall balance of pleasure over pain."[53] Whereas the Aristotelian position was to order society according to essences therefore achieving an overall justice, Bentham is proposing that justice is to order things so as to gain happiness. According to Bentham's utilitarianism, we all desire pleasure and avoid pain, so the just society is the one that is able to avoid the most pain and create the most pleasure for the most individuals.

The utilitarian idea is sometimes expressed as "the greatest happiness for the greatest number." To arrive at such a state one must capitalize upon the "utility" of objects according to how they can maximize pleasure and minimize pain – hence, utilitarianism profits from the usefulness, or utility, of an object's potential for creating pleasure.[54] This form of "[u]tilitarianism assesses actions and institutions in terms of their effects on human happiness and enjoins us to perform actions and design institutions so that they promote – in one formulation, maximize – human happiness."[55]

For Bentham, then, government should enact laws and policies that will create the most happiness for the largest number of people. Bentham

[52] NRC, *Hidden Costs of Energy: Unpriced Consequences of Energy Production and Use* (Washington, DC: The National Academies Press, 2009).

[53] Michael J. Sandel, *Justice: What's the Right Thing to Do?* (New York: Farrar, Straus, and Giroux, 2009), p. 34.

[54] Jeremy Bentham, "Principles of Morals and Legislation," in Michael J. Sandel (ed.), *Justice: A Reader* (Oxford University Press, 2007), pp. 9–14.

[55] David Brink, "Mill's Moral and Political Philosophy," in Edward N. Zalta (ed.), *The Stanford Encyclopedia of Philosophy* (Fall 2008 edn.).

states that "The greatest happiness of the greatest number ought to be the object of every legislator: for accomplishing his purposes respecting this object, he possesses two instruments – Punishment and Reward. The theories of these two forces divide between them, although in unequal shares, the whole of legislation."[56] So Bentham's utilitarianism focuses on the sum whole of happiness in determining justice, and judges the success of an action or policy on the overall amount of happiness it creates for society (and perhaps the world). By using punishment and reward, utilitarianism offers "a science of morality, based on measuring, aggregating, and calculating happiness. It weighs preferences without judging them. Everyone's preferences count equally."[57]

Moreover, Bentham does not distinguish between pleasures. In fact, he gives what distinguished philosopher Alasdair MacIntyre called "fifty-eight synonyms for *pleasure*, and his logical sophistication about naming on other occasions does not prevent him from behaving as if *happiness*, *enjoyment*, and *pleasure* all name or characterize the same sensation."[58] What matters is the duration and intensity of a sensation, and when a decision-maker must choose between two alternative actions, the *only* thing that matters is the *quantity* of pleasure.[59]

Though deceptively simple, the practice of Bentham's utilitarianism does raise some ethical concerns. It does not determine how benefits and costs, pleasures and pain, are to be distributed throughout society. As long as total utility is increased, it would justify one person being blissfully happy even if it required ten people to be somewhat depressed. Or, as philosopher Julia Driver writes, "a utilitarian might well end up endorsing a system in which some members of society live in misery while others flourish at their expense, as long as that society has the best overall utility rating."[60] Maximum utility and collective happiness may also come at the cost of violating individual rights, such as a large

---

[56] Jeremy Bentham, *The Rationale of Reward* (London: R. Heward, 1830), p. 1.
[57] Sandel, *Justice*, p. 41.
[58] Alasdair MacIntyre, *A Short History of Ethics: A History of Moral Philosophy from the Homeric Age to the Twentieth Century* (New York: Macmillan Publishing Company, 1966), p. 234.
[59] *Ibid.*
[60] Julia Driver, "Ideal Decision Making and Green Virtues," in Walter Sinnott-Armstrong and Richard B. Howarth (eds.), *Perspectives on Climate Change: Science, Economics, Politics, Ethics* (Amsterdam: Elsevier, 2005), pp. 249–264.

majority opposing and then outlawing a minority religion.[61] And the development economist and ethicist Amartya Sen (discussed in detail in Chapter 7) has written that "the trouble with this approach is that maximizing the sum of individual utilities [pleasure, happiness, welfare] is supremely unconcerned with the interpersonal distribution of that sum. This should make it particularly unsuitable for measuring or judging inequality."[62]

## *John Stuart Mill*

Because of these sorts of difficulties, utilitarian advocates Mill and Sidgwick introduced notions of equality and impartiality to utilitarianism. John Stuart Mill (1806–1873) tells us that "human happiness is the sole end of human action, and the promotion of it the test by which to judge of all human conduct; by whence it necessarily follows that it must be the criterion of morality, since a part is included in the whole."[63] Mill's father, James Mill, collaborated professionally with Bentham, and trained the young Mill in utilitarian thinking.[64] In his famous "Proportionality Doctrine" or "Greatest Happiness Principle," Mill states that

> Actions are right in proportion as they tend to promote happiness, wrong as they tend to produce the reverse of happiness. By happiness is intended pleasure, and the absence of pain; by unhappiness, pain and the privation of pleasure ... For that standard is not the agent's own greatest happiness, but the greatest happiness altogether ... happiness secured to all mankind; and not for them only, but so far as the nature of things admits, to the whole sentient creation.[65]

Yet, Mill's utilitarianism differs slightly from Bentham's in the sense that all pleasures cannot be measured against one another. Whereas

---

[61] Michael J. Sandel, "Utilitarianism," in Sandel (ed.), *Justice: A Reader*, p. 9.

[62] Quoted in Stuart Corbridge, "Development as Freedom: The Spaces of Amartya Sen," *Progress in Development Studies* 2(3) (2002), pp. 183–217.

[63] J.S. Mill, *Essays on Ethics, Religion and Society*, ed. J.M. Robson (University of Toronto Press, 1969), p. 234.

[64] MacIntyre, *A Short History of Ethics*, p. 235.

[65] See David Brink, "Mill's Moral and Political Philosophy," in Zalta (ed.), *The Stanford Encyclopedia of Philosophy* (Fall 2008 edn.), Section 2.3; J.S. Mill, "Utilitarianism," in M.L. Morgan (ed.), *Classics of Moral and Political Theory* (Cambridge: Hackett Publishing Co., 1992); see also John Stuart Mill, "Utilitarianism," in Sandel (ed.), *Justice: A Reader*, pp. 14–47.

Bentham is basically a hedonist delegating all pleasures to one plane, Mill sees a hierarchy of pleasures where some are better than others.[66] Also, Mill's "first principle of morals" is articulated "as everyone counts as one and no one as more than one, the interests of all (in terms of pain and pleasure) should be seen as equal."[67] Thus, people count regardless of their race, wealth, or background, but they count only as one.[68]

Mill also distances himself from Bentham by focusing on freedom, and this is possibly Mill's biggest break from Bentham's utilitarianism. Defending each person's individual freedom, Mill's book *On Liberty* supports the thesis that each person "should be free to do whatever they want, provided they do no harm to others."[69] Mill states that "liberty is, of right, absolute. Over himself, over his own body and mind, the individual is sovereign."[70] Another essential aspect of Mill's utilitarian theory is that it incorporates the future into calculations of the present, believing that we ought to promote utility in the long run.[71]

## Henry Sidgwick

Henry Sidgwick (1838–1900) refined the arguments from Bentham and Mill in ways that consider justice and posterity. In his 1874 *Methods of Ethics*, Sidgwick espoused three key principles to achieving the "ultimate good" for society:

- A "principle of justice" which set constraints and limits on individual actions so that "whatever action any of us judges to be right for himself, he implicitly judges to be right for all similar persons in similar circumstances";[72]

---

[66] Brink, "Mill's Moral and Political Philosophy," in Zalta (ed.), *The Stanford Encyclopedia of Philosophy* (Fall 2008 edn.).

[67] Behnam Taebi, *Nuclear Power and Justice between Generations: A Moral Analysis of Fuel Cycles* (The Netherlands: Center for Ethics and Technology, 2010).

[68] Vivian Walsh, "Amartya Sen on Rationality and Freedom," *Science & Society* 71(1) (January 2007), pp. 59–83; Avner de-Shalit, *Why Posterity Matters: Environmental Policies and Future Generations* (London: Routledge, 1995).

[69] Sandel, *Justice: What's the Right Thing to Do?*, p. 49.

[70] John Stuart Mill, *On Liberty* (London: Longmans, Green, and Co., 1913), ch. 1.

[71] Sandel, *Justice: What's the Right Thing to Do?*, p. 50.

[72] Henry Sidgwick, *Methods of Ethics* (London: MacMillan, 1874), p. 379.

- A "principle of prudence" which argued that the goal of individual action should not be instantaneous or fleeting pleasure and happiness, but net happiness overall since "the mere difference of priority and posteriority in time is not a reasonable ground for having more regard to the consciousness of one moment than to that of another";[73]
- A "principle of rational benevolence" which stated that "the good of any one individual is of no more importance, from the point of view of the Universe, than the good of any other."[74]

These principles insert an element of impartiality and collective sociality to the utilitarian calculus: actions are right only as long as they treat individuals as equal in their worth. Sidgwick is also clear that, for him, utilitarianism is a matter of procedural justice, concerned with "the distribution of happiness, not the means of happiness."[75]

## What is to be done?

Although a variety of tools can be employed to address externalities and enhance utility, we strongly advocate three: placing a price on carbon through a tax, incorporating the cost of some types of externalities in retail products such as electricity and gasoline, and environmental bonds.

### Placing a price on carbon

Putting a price on carbon is a critical "core" policy because it addresses the principal market failure that has prevented individuals and firms from responding effectively to the damages precipitated by GHG emissions. One of the simplest actions countries and international institutions such as the UN could take to provide an equity-increasing and welfare-maximizing response to climate change is to provide a market price for GHG emissions and charge emitters for the cost of climate mitigation technologies. Currently, GHGs can be emitted into the atmosphere for free in many countries, but the impacts of these emissions impose real costs on society in other countries. Unlike many of the barriers that are specific to individual technologies or sectors, this single

---

[73] *Ibid.*, p. 381.    [74] *Ibid.*, p. 383.    [75] *Ibid.*, p. 47.

obstacle is economy-wide – and it could be overcome through either a tax or a cap-and-trade system.[76]

A graduated carbon tax would provide firms with an incentive to adopt lowest cost means of reducing their emissions, with the "payment" for additional reductions taking the form of tax savings. Just as firms subject to an emissions trading program could bank excess allowances, firms participating in a tax program could literally bank their tax savings from reduced emissions. An upstream tax, regarded as the most feasible and easiest to implement, would take the form of a tax on the carbon content of fuels sold into the energy system. It could be applied to a few thousand firms in each country that produce, refine, and market fuels such as oil, coal, and natural gas. Taxing these firms would lead to higher prices for carbon-intense fuels and therefore higher prices for electricity and gasoline, providing firms an incentive to mitigate emissions and consumers with incentives to switch fuels, increase efficiency, and reduce energy use.[77]

Indeed, in 2012 the Brookings Institute suggested that the United States should immediately implement a $20 tax per ton of carbon dioxide, steadily increase a "carbon excise fee" that would "discourage carbon dioxide emissions while shifting taxation onto pollution, financing energy efficiency and clean technology development, and providing opportunities to cut taxes or reduce the deficit."[78] This type of tax could take many different forms. One that might hold allure for conservatives would be "revenue neutral," meaning that the government would keep little of the tax revenues raised by cutting emissions, returning them instead to the public. The state of British Columbia in Canada has had such a tax since 2008, and it charges about $30 per ton.[79] MIT estimated that such a graduated carbon tax, starting at $20 per ton and rising at 4 percent annually, would raise about $150 billion per year

---

[76] Congressional Budget Office, *Limiting Carbon Dioxide Emissions: Prices Versus Caps*, Economic Budget Issue Brief (2005), p. 4, available at www.cbo.gov/doc. cfm?index=6148; Congressional Budget Office, *The Economic Effects of Legislation to Reduce Greenhouse Gas Emissions* (Washington, DC: Congressional Budget Office, 2009).

[77] See Richard N. Cooper, "Toward a Real Global Warming Treaty," *Foreign Affairs* 77(2) (March/April 1998), pp. 66–79.

[78] Patrick Parenteau and Abigail Barnes, "A Bridge Too Far: Building Off-Ramps on the Shale Gas Superhighway," *Idaho Law Review*, 49 (2013), pp.325–365.

[79] *Ibid.*

over a ten-year period and cut emissions in the United States 14 percent below 2006 levels by 2020.[80]

Cap-and-trade systems can also produce results. The Regional Greenhouse Gas Initiative (RGGI) in the Northeastern United States, for example, cut emissions from power plants in its nine participating states substantially during the first three years of the program. From January 1, 2009 to December 31, 2011, 206 of the 211 participating power plants met their compliance quotas and reduced emissions an average 126 million tons per year; pollution from the plants also declined by 33 percent over the same period.[81]

## Accurate price signals and tax shifting

A second, economy-wide solution is incorporating the price of externalities into energy products and services. Whatever type of price we are talking about for coal-generated electricity, it must include the money put into air quality, care of people with asthma and other respiratory problems, water shortages, and land reclamation. The cost of nuclear energy must include money for constructing and maintaining permanent waste storage sites, the risk of a catastrophic accident, and the price of decommissioning plants. The price of renewable sources of energy and biofuels must include the money that goes into R&D, construction, and maintenance. Not all things can be quantified; not all of those that can be are consistent; comparisons seldom assess costs and benefits across technologies; and most methods suffer from methodological shortcomings.

Nonetheless, there has been some synthetic scholarship looking comprehensively at the cost of externalities across a wide range of social and environmental impacts. For example, a host of academic studies have documented and quantified:[82]

---

[80] *Ibid.*

[81] Mireya Navarro, "Emissions Fell under Cap and Trade Program, Report Says," *New York Times*, June 4, 2012.

[82] See Godfrey Boyle, *Assessing the Environmental and Health Impacts of Energy Use, Energy Systems and Sustainability* (Oxford University Press, 2003), pp. 519–566; H. Scott Matthews and Lester B. Lave, "Applications of Environmental Valuation for Determining Externality Costs," *Environmental Science & Technology* 34 (2000), pp. 1390–1395; John P. Holdren and Kirk R. Smith, "Energy, the Environment, and Health," in Tord Kjellstrom, David Streets, and Xiadong Wang (eds.), *World Energy Assessment: Energy and*

- Catastrophic risks such as nuclear meltdowns, oil spills, coalmine collapses, natural gas wellhead explosions, and dam breaches;
- An increased probability of wars due to natural resource extraction or the securing of energy supply;
- Public health issues and chronic disease, morbidity, and mortality;
- Worker exposure to toxic substances and occupational accidents and hazards;
- Public deaths and injuries due to coal trucks, barges, and trains;
- Direct land use by power plants, pipelines, and upstream infrastructure;
- The destruction of land by mining operations including acid drainage and resettlement;
- Acid precipitation and its damage to fisheries, crops, forests, and livestock, especially the effects of $SO_2$ on wheat, barley, oats, rye, peas, and beans and the impacts of acid deposition on other high-value crops such as vegetables, fruit, and flowers;
- The effects of water pollution on fisheries and freshwater ecosystems, sensitive to water chemistry, as well as the release of radionuclides, drill cuttings, drilling muds, and oils;

*the Challenge of Sustainability* (New York: UN Development Program, 2000), pp. 61–110; W. Krewitt, P. Mayerhofer, R. Friedrich, A. Trukenmuller, N. Eyre, and M. Holland, "External Costs of Fossil Fuel Cycles," in Olav Hohmeyer, Richard L. Ottinger, and Klaus Rennings (eds.), *Social Costs and Sustainability: Valuation and Implementation in the Energy and Transport Sector* (New York: Springer, 1997), pp. 127–135; National Association of Regulatory Utility Commissioners, *Environmental Externalities and Electric Regulation* (Washington, DC: National Association of Regulatory Commissioners, September 1993, ORNL/Sub/95X-SH985C); Olav Hohmeyer, "Renewables and the Full Costs of Energy," *Energy Policy* 20(4) (1992), pp. 365–375; John P. Holdren, "Energy and Human Environment: The Generation and Definition of Environmental Problems," in G.T. Goodman, L. Kristoferson, and J. Hollander (eds.), *The European Transition from Oil: Societal Impacts and Constraints on Energy Policy* (London: Academic Press, 1981), pp. 100–101; Robert Stobaugh and Daniel Yergin, "Toward a Balanced Energy Program," in Robert Stobaugh and Daniel Yergin (eds.), *Energy Future: Report of the Energy Project at the Harvard Business School* (New York: Random House, 1979), pp. 216–227; William Ramsay, *Unpaid Costs of Electrical Energy: Health and Environmental Impacts from Coal and Nuclear Power* (Baltimore: Johns Hopkins University Press, 1979); Sam H. Schurr, Joel Darmstadter, Harry Perry, William Ramsay, and Milton Russell, *Energy in America's Future: The Choices before Us* (Baltimore: Johns Hopkins University Press, 1979), pp. 343–369; Robert J. Budnitz and John Holdren, "Social and Environmental Costs of Energy Systems," *Annual Review of Energy* 1 (1976), pp. 553–580.

Table 4.2 *Negative externalities associated with various energy systems (cents/kWh in 1998 dollars)*

| Statistic | Coal | Oil | Gas | Nuclear | Hydro | Wind | Solar | Biomass |
|---|---|---|---|---|---|---|---|---|
| Min. | 0.06 | 0.03 | 0.003 | 0.0003 | 0.02 | 0 | 0 | 0 |
| Max. | 72.42 | 39.93 | 13.22 | 64.45 | 26.26 | 0.80 | 1.69 | 22.09 |
| *Mean* | *14.87* | *13.57* | *5.02* | *8.63* | *3.84* | *0.29* | *0.69* | *5.20* |
| Std. Dev. | 16.89 | 12.51 | 4.73 | 18.62 | 8.40 | 0.20 | 0.57 | 6.11 |
| N | 29 | 15 | 24 | 16 | 11 | 14 | 7 | 16 |

N = number of estimates included.
*Source:* Adapted from Thomas Sundqvist, "What Causes the Disparity of Electricity Externality Estimates?," *Energy Policy* 32 (2004), pp. 1753–1766.

- Consumptive water use, with consequent impacts on agriculture and ecosystems where water is scarce;
- Degradation of cultural icons such as national parks, recreational opportunities, or activities such as fishing or swimming;
- Atmospheric damage to buildings, automobiles, and materials by corrosion and the increased maintenance costs for natural stone, mortar, rendering, zinc, galvanized steel, and paint;
- Continual maintenance of caches of spent nuclear fuel;
- Incidence of noise and reduced amenity, aesthetics, and visibility.

One excellent survey of 132 separate types of estimates of externalities conducted by econometricians Thomas Sundqvist and Patrik Soderholm found that, when averaged across studies and converted into a price per unit of electricity, these externalities added an additional 0.29 cents/kWh to 14.87 cents/kWh depending on the type of energy system.[83] Table 4.2 provides a full breakdown of their estimates.

Though these numbers may strike some readers as high, there are actually strong reasons they are conservative and underestimate damages. For instance, when surveying externalities, Sundqvist and Soderholm did not include any value for $CO_2$ and climate change. They explain that their meta-survey found a range of damages so

---

[83] Thomas Sundqvist and Patrik Soderholm, "Valuing the Environmental Impacts of Electricity Generation: A Critical Survey," *Journal of Energy Literature* 8(2) (2002), pp. 1–18; Thomas Sundqvist, "What Causes the Disparity of Electricity Externality Estimates?," *Energy Policy* 32 (2004), pp. 1753–1766.

large (from 1.4 cents/kWh to 700 cents/kWh) that they decided to exclude climate change externalities. In some cases individual estimates relied on a "willingness-to-pay" metric to assess damages, but many things (such as clear skies, the value of absolute silence, or a dead child) are practically impossible to quantify in dollars. Furthermore, virtually none of the studies accounted for the risk of irreversible damages – such as tipping points that are crossed as the earth's climate changes, unknown ecological thresholds that are passed, and species extinctions that are fundamentally final – impossible to recover from once they begin. Most of the estimates modeled damages associated with a single power plant, and not the combined or cumulative damages from a fleet of power plants or an entire utility system. Many estimates assumed reference, rather than representative, technologies; that is, they assumed benchmark and state-of-the art systems instead of those used by utilities in the real world where many are more than fifty years old. Almost no studies included the environmental damages associated with delivery of energy through pipelines and high-voltage transmission networks. These forms of infrastructure produce impacts ranging from land use conflicts, soil erosion, destruction of forests and natural habitat, as well as audible noise and interference with radio and television reception, deleterious effects on local birds, electrocutions, the use of chemical herbicides and vegetation management techniques along rights of way, and the human health effects of exposure to electric and magnetic fields (which some researchers claim may contribute to childhood cancer).[84]

Other respected studies have made similar estimates of the relative costs of various externalities. In one assessment, traditional coal boiler generation technology appeared to produce relatively cheap power – under 5 cents/kWh over the life of the equipment, which included capital, operating and maintenance costs, and fuel costs – while wind-turbine generators and biomass plants produced power that cost 7.4 cents/kWh and 8.9 cents/kWh, respectively (and tended to require larger amounts of land). But when analysts factored in a host of externality costs, coal boiler technology costs rose to almost 17 cents/kWh, while wind turbines and biomass plants yielded power costing around

---

[84] US Office of Technology Assessment, *Energy Efficiency: Challenges and Opportunities for Electric Utilities* (Washington, DC: US Government Printing Office, September 1993), pp. 31–32.

10 cents/kWh.[85] Researchers from the nonpartisan Alliance to Save Energy found that if damages to the environment in the form of noxious emissions and impacts on human health resulting from combustion of fossil fuels was included in electricity prices, coal would cost 261.8 percent more than it does. The researchers also found that if electricity was priced this way, fossil-fuel use would decrease 37.7 percent compared to projections; $CO_2$ emissions would decrease 44.1 percent; GDP would improve 7.7 percent; and household wealth would jump 5.5 percent, primarily as the result of improved health.[86]

The costs of these externalities can be factored into energy prices, or, similar to carbon dioxide, reflected in environmental taxes. One model here is the process of "tax shifting" in Europe, which involves "changing the composition of taxes but not the level" and "reducing income taxes and offsetting them with taxes on environmentally destructive activities."[87] No less than nine countries in the EU – shown in Table 4.3 – have undertaken tax shifting in this regard, beginning with Sweden's program to lower taxes on personal income but to raise them on carbon and sulfur emissions to disincentivize the burning of fossil fuels. Germany's four-year plan to reduce taxes on incomes and raise them on energy use from 1999 to 2003 shifted 2.1 percent of revenue generated and produced nearly $20 billion in taxes.[88]

Indeed, the idea of pricing externalities is not new. When the New England Power System was suddenly required to start burning low-sulfur oil in 1971, the new rules increased prices immediately from $1.67 per barrel of oil to $3.75, impacting customers with a cumulative bill of $15 to $20 million. Utility executives, seeking to soften the pain of the increase by communicating the reason for it to their customers, included a statement in their bills that the added cost was for "*Your Fair Share of Clean Air.*"[89] What we are suggesting is that society

[85] Ian F. Roth and Lawrence L. Ambs, "Incorporating Externalities into a Full Cost Approach to Electric Power Generation Life-Cycle Costing," *Energy* 29 (2004), pp. 2125–2144.

[86] Douglas L. Norland and Kim Y. Ninassi, *Price It Right: Energy Pricing and Fundamental Tax Reform* (Washington, DC: ASE, 1998).

[87] Lester R. Brown, *Eco-Economy: Building an Economy for the Earth* (New York: Norton and Company, 2001), pp. 236–237.

[88] *Ibid.*

[89] Gerald R. Browne, "A Utility View of Externalities: Evolution, Not Revolution," *Electricity Journal* 4(2) (March 1991), pp. 34–39.

Table 4.3 *Examples of environmental and energy tax shifting*

| Country, first year in effect | Taxes cut on | Taxes raised on | Revenue shifted (%) |
|---|---|---|---|
| Sweden, 1991 | personal income | carbon and sulfur emissions | 1.9 |
| Denmark, 1994 | personal income | motor fuel coal, electricity, and water sales; waste incineration and landfilling; motor vehicle ownership | 2.5 |
| Spain, 1995 | wages | motor fuel sales | 0.2 |
| Denmark, 1996 | wages, agricultural property | carbon emissions from industry; pesticide, chlorinated solvent, and battery sales | 0.5 |
| Netherlands, 1996 | personal income and wages | natural gas and electricity sales | 0.8 |
| United Kingdom, 1996 | wages | landfilling | 0.1 |
| Finland, 1996 | personal income and wages | energy sales, landfilling | 0.5 |
| Germany, 1999 | wages | energy sales | 2.1 |
| Italy, 1999 | wages | fossil-fuel sales | 0.2 |
| Netherlands, 1999 | personal income | energy sales, landfilling, household water sales | 0.9 |
| France, 2000 | wages | solid waste; air and water | 0.1 |

*Source:* Adapted from Lester R. Brown, *Eco-Economy: Building an Economy for the Earth* (New York: Norton and Company, 2001), pp. 236–237.

start paying for its fair shares of clean air, water, and land, and start recovering for the damages it has inflicted on communities and ecosystems around the world – that these "hidden" costs of energy become factored into its market, wholesale, and retail prices.

Doing so brings three massive advantages. First, pricing externalities would incentivize firms to quit polluting. The current energy system does the opposite. The more a company can externalize its cost of doing business, the greater return on capital it will receive in the short term. The more that firms externalize costs, the more difficult it is to attribute blame. The more power plants and refineries that pollute the air and water, the more liability is negated. The more liberally acceptable levels of pollution are set and the greater number of smokestacks and discharge points through which pollution is emitted, the lower the residual probability that a culprit or set of culprits can be identifiable and made responsible.[90]

Second, pricing externalities brings issues of utility and justice centrally into the marketplace. As they stand now, externalities are wholly undemocratic and exclusionary. The most affected parties – often the poor or disenfranchised – are under-represented in the marketplace, and have external costs imposed upon them,[91] particularly air pollution and toxics.[92] Yet, on a per capita basis, lower-income households consume less energy and hence contribute less to GHG emissions and other pollutants.

Third, pricing externalities properly aligns price signals. It is not that we do not pay for externalities as a society; we do through hospital admissions, lost worker days, higher taxes, blighted landscapes, death, pain, and suffering. Society and nature "pays" eventually, it is just those costs do not show up on our energy and gasoline bills. Put simply: energy's price does not match its cost.[93] Including externalities ensures that it starts to.

## Environmental bonds

A final way of mitigating externalities is to compensate communities marginalized or degraded by energy projects through an environmental bonding system. In the words of economists Laura Cornwell and

---

[90] Ulrich Beck, "From Industrial Society to the Risk Society: Questions of Survival, Social Structure and Ecological Enlightenment," *Theory, Culture, & Society* 9 (1992), pp. 97–123.

[91] Zachary A. Smith, *The Environmental Policy Paradox*, 5th edn. (Upper Saddle River: Prentice Hall, 2009).

[92] R.J. Brulle and D.N. Pellow, "Environmental Justice: Human Health and Environmental Inequalities," *Annual Review of Public Health* 27 (2006), pp. 103–124.

[93] David W. Orr, *Earth in Mind: On Education, Environment, and the Human Prospect* (Washington, DC: Island Press, 1994), p. 172.

Robert Costanza, environmental bonds "require those seeking to use society's resources to post a bond in advance of any potentially, environmentally damaging activity ... the most important aspect of the bond amount is that it provides the incentive to behave in an environmentally responsible manner."[94] Such a bond, kept in an interest-bearing escrow account by an independent third party, can be tied to either the value of the resources or the likely extent of environmental or social damage expected over the course of extraction and development. If resource users or energy companies can demonstrate that the damages to the environment were less than the amount of the bond, this difference and a portion of earned interest can be refunded; the bonding system thus ensures that the financial resources available for protecting the environment, or local communities, are roughly equal to the potential harm arising from the use of energy resources. If and when damages occur, the bond ensures that funds exist to rehabilitate or repair the environment and compensate injured parties. This, in practice, is almost more like environmental "bail" than a traditional interest-bearing "bond" since its punitive value is greater than its investment value.

Though the idea of environmental bonding may sound radical, it does already exist in various forms. Refundable deposits on glass bottles, for example, aim to encourage bottle users to dispose of the commodity in the most desirable way (by recycling) and to avoid its disposal in the least desirable way (as litter). By demanding that consumers pay in advance for the costs they might inflict on society if they adopted the most harmful method of disposal, such deposits reverse the usual presumption of innocence over guilt as applied to environmental damages. Another precedent for environmental bonds are producer-paid performance bonds frequently required for construction work. The 1935 Miller Act in the United States requires that contractors performing construction for the federal government secure performance bonds, a contractual guarantee that the principal (the entity which is doing the work or providing the service) will perform in a designated way. The

---

[94] Laura Cornwell and Robert Costanza, "Environmental Bonds: Implementing the Precautionary Principle in Environmental Policy," in Carolyn Raffensperger and Joel A. Tickner (eds.), *Protecting Public Health and the Environment: Implementing the Precautionary Principle* (Washington, DC: Island Press, 1999), pp. 220–240.

National Environmental Policy Act of 1969 further required the owners and operators of deepwater ports to "establish and maintain evidence of financial responsibility sufficient to meet the maximum liability to which the responsible party could be subjected."[95] The Surface Mining Control and Reclamation Act of 1977 stipulated the use of performance bonds to guarantee reclamation of mining sites for coal and other minerals.

Moreover, roughly a dozen states in the United States allow for the utilization of bonding instruments pertaining to environmental protection, and the federal government also requires the posting of a bond guaranteeing the complete and timely plugging of oil and gas leases on public lands as well as reclamation and restoration of any lands or surface waters affected by the lease operation. Additionally, the Nuclear Regulatory Commission stipulates regulations similar to bonds pertaining to the decommissioning of nuclear facilities and the storage and disposal of nuclear waste.[96]

Environmental bonds for the energy sector would work in a similar manner by providing a contractual guarantee that the principal of the bond performs in an environmentally benign, and socially responsible, manner, but would be levied for the current best estimate of the largest potential damages. Whereas insurance protects companies against loss, environmental bonds guarantee the fulfillment of an obligation. Responsibility for honoring the bond's conditions would fall both to the surety company and the principal.

There is some evidence that environmental bonds are starting to take off, though not precisely as Cornwell and Costanza, and we, advocate them. A more common, contemporary definition of a "green bond" or "environmental bond" is "where the proceeds of a bond go towards a climate change solution, which is a broad definition."[97] Under this definition, the World Bank has been offering "green bonds" for almost a decade, such bonds were authorized by the American Jobs Creation Act of 2004, and Berkshire Hathaway issued bonds in 2012 to finance a solar farm in California, raising $850 million.[98] In 2013, Massachusetts sold $130 million worth of "green bonds" to finance energy-efficiency

[95] 33 USc. § 2716(d).   [96] Cornwell and Costanza, "Environmental Bonds."
[97] Farah Khalique, "Could 'Green' Bonds Help Tackle Climate Change?," *Financial Times*, June 26, 2012.
[98] *Ibid.*

projects, the improvement of water quality, and more effective pollution control. According to Thomson Reuters, more than $1.7 billion of municipal bonds sold in 2013 had proceeds earmarked for environmental facilities.[99] The bonding that we advocate is more punitive, and narrow, than these types of instruments.

[99] Mike Cherney, "Massachusetts Goes 'Green,'" *Wall Street Journal*, June 4, 2013.

# 5 | Energy and human rights

The externalities and premature deaths associated with energy production and use elaborated on in Chapter 4 raise another interesting ethical dilemma: how are we to value human life when we weigh costs and benefits? Imagine that it is a quiet autumn afternoon in Washington, DC, and you are sitting in your office at the US EPA, preparing your memorandum to the Assistant Administrator for the Office of Air and Radiation. She has asked you to recommend a permissible level for toxic emissions coming from large electricity generating plants. You know that stricter standards will cost significantly more in terms of air pollution equipment (and result, ultimately, in higher energy prices), but you also know that tougher standards will save many lives from death or ruin by reducing the health effects of mercury and other heavy metals emissions.

Thus, there is an obvious tradeoff between protection of human health and costs of emissions control. How can you turn this from an abstract, "gut reaction," personal-values comparison to a quantifiable one of "deaths and dollars" that you can present for recommendations and debate? On the one hand, the electric utility industry asserts that stricter standards could result in the closure of sixty-eight coal-fired power plants – 8 percent of the country's entire fleet – risking blackouts and massive job layoffs.[1] The industry will also have to spend $11 billion by 2016 installing better scrubbers and pollution abatement equipment at their power plants, costs that will be passed onto households. On the other hand, EPA analyses and National Academies of Science studies suggest that stricter pollution controls will yield annual monetized benefits of $59 to $140 billion through 17,000 fewer annual deaths caused by PM and mercury pollution. As the EPA's own report concludes, "the

[1] Brad Plumer, "Will the EPA's Mercury Rule Cause a Wave of Blackouts?," *Washington Post*, December 24, 2011.

benefits outweigh costs by between 3 to 1 or 9 to 1 depending on the benefit estimate and discount rate used."[2]

How do you balance these competing arguments? Your predecessor and your peers tell you that the usual answer is to describe both deaths and emissions controls in a common unit of value – dollars. Central to these arguments is the belief that the value of an individual life is about $5 million. But is it? And what about differences in "life?" Are younger lives "worth" more than older lives, given that they have longer to live? Or, conversely, are the elderly "worth" more than the young, given their experiences and contributions to society? Are the sick "worth" less than the healthy, men less than women, minorities more, or less, than others?

This chapter demonstrates that philosophers such as Immanuel Kant would say that the mere act of assigning a dollar value on life – and attempting to differentiate whose life matters more – demeans the intrinsic worth of human beings. Put another way, Kant would argue that the value of human life is infinite, it is priceless. This means that if Kant could envision the way the world currently extracts coal, uranium, oil, and natural gas, he would likely be appalled at the way the global energy system uses people as a means to an end – that rather than treating indigenous communities and individuals with dignity, it pushes aside their basic human rights and civil liberties to maximize energy production. However, Kant might also be slightly pacified by the number of options available to planners to minimize and avoid these calamities: energy truth commissions, legal access to remedies for disenfranchised groups, improved impact assessments, and extractive industry transparency initiatives.

## What is reality?

Unfortunately, the global energy system places too little value on people in innumerable ways, including dangerous energy-related jobs, severely demeaned communities, contributions to corruption, and precipitating or worsening social and even armed military conflict.

---

[2] US EPA, *Regulatory Impact Analysis for the Final Mercury and Air Toxics Standards* (Washington, DC: EPA-452/R-11–011, December 2011).

## Occupational hazards and accidents

Perhaps the most direct way our energy systems violate Kant's categorical imperative (discussed below) is by using people as a means to an end to extract energy fuels in hazardous occupational settings. Coalmines, uranium mines, oil and gas facilities, and even power plants do this every day, to varying degrees. Indeed, the WHO reports that the burden of disease from occupational hazards is responsible for about 1.6 percent of the global total, a substantial proportion of which is attributable to the extractive and energy industries.[3]

Notwithstanding recently improved safety regulations and medical treatment, underground coalmining is still a very dangerous practice. Miners frequently encounter pockets of underground methane gas, which is highly explosive and produced in significant quantities when coal is removed. Shifting and unpredictable geologic conditions often make the roofs of mines unstable, and miners always face the ever-present risk of flooding and fire, hazards that have increased in recent years as miners dig deeper to reach seams.[4] Coalmining is so risky that in 2007 more than 3,300 accidents occurred in Chinese coalmines following 5,938 deaths in 2005, and 4,746 mining deaths in 2006, and an additional 163 deaths per year resulting from coal-related pneumoconiosis ("black lung disease") – which an estimated 800,000 Chinese coalminers in aggregate now suffer with.[5] This not just an issue in the developing world – though the numbers are not nearly as large, more than 700 coalminers have died in the United States over the past few decades[6] (see Table 5.1), and fatal accidents occur every few years in large coal-producing countries such as Australia.[7]

Even though the occupational hazards associated with mining are well known, and mitigation techniques for coalbed methane leaks have

---

[3] Paul Wilkinson, Kirk Smith, Michael Joffe, and Andrew Haines, "A Global Perspective on Energy: Health Effects and Injustices," *Lancet* 370 (September 15, 2007), pp. 965–977.

[4] US GAO, *Additional Guidance and Oversight of Mines' Emergency Response Plans Would Improve the Safety of Underground Coal Miners* (April 2008, GAO-08-424).

[5] World Wildlife Foundation, *Coming Clean: The Truth and Future of Coal in the Asia Pacific* (Washington, DC: World Wildlife Foundation, 2007).

[6] United States Mine Rescue Association, Historical Data on Mine Disasters in the United States, July 2013, available at www.usmra.com/saxsewell/historical.htm.

[7] Andrew Fraser, "Coalmining's Invisible Killer," *The Australian*, November 22, 2010.

Table 5.1 *Major coalmining accidents in the United States, 1940–2010*

| Year | Day | Mine | Location | Type | Deaths |
|---|---|---|---|---|---|
| 2010 | 04/05 | Upper Big Branch Mine, Massey Energy Company | Montcoal, WV | Explosion | 29 |
| 2007 | 08/06 08/16 | Crandall Canyon Mine, Genwal and Murray Energy Corporation | Huntington, UT | Collapse | 6 3 |
| 2006 | 05/20 | Darby Mine No. 1, Kentucky Darby LLC | Holmes Mill, KY | Explosion | 5 |
| 2006 | 01/02 | Sago Mine, International Mines Corp. | Tallmansville, WV | Explosion | 12 |
| 2001 | 09/23 | No. 5 Mine, Jim Walter Resources | Tuscaloosa County Brookwood, AL | Explosion | 13 |
| 1992 | 12/07 | No. 3 Mine, Southmountain Coal Co. | Wise County Norton, VA | Explosion | 8 |
| 1989 | 09/13 | William Station No. 9 Mine, Pyro Mining Co. | Union County Sullivan, KY | Explosion | 10 |
| 1986 | 02/06 | Loveridge No. 22, Consolidation Coal Co. | Marion County Fairview, WV | Suffocation (surface stockpile) | 5 |
| 1984 | 12/19 | Wilberg Mine, Emery Mining Corp. | Emery County Orangeville, UT | Fire | 27 |
| 1983 | 06/21 | McClure No. 1 Mine, Clinchfield Coal Co. | Dickinson County McClure, VA | Explosion | 7 |
| 1982 | 01/20 | No. 1 Mine, RFH Coal Co. | Floyd County Craynor, KY | Explosion | 7 |
| 1981 | 12/08 | No. 21 Mine, Grundy Mining Co. | Marion County Whitwell, TN | Explosion | 13 |
| 1981 | 12/07 | No. 11 Mine, Adkins Coal Co. | Knott County Kite, KY | Explosion | 8 |
| 1981 | 04/15 | Dutch Creek No. 1, Mid-Continent Resources, Inc. | Pitkin County Redstone, CO | Explosion | 15 |
| 1980 | 11/07 | Ferrell No. 17, Westmorland Coal Co. | Boone County Uneeda, WV | Explosion | 5 |

| Year | Date | Mine, Company | Location | Cause | Deaths |
|---|---|---|---|---|---|
| 1978 | 04/04 | Moss No. 3 Portal A, Clinchfield Coal Co. | Dickinson County Duty, VA | Suffocation (oxygen deficient air) | 5 |
| 1977 | 03/01 | Porter Tunnel, Kocher Coal Co. | Schuykill County Tower City, PA | Flood | 9 |
| 1976 | 03/9–11 | Scotia Mine, Blue Diamond Coal Co. | Letcher County Oven Fork, KY | Explosion | 26 |
| 1972 | 12/16 | Itmann No. 3 Mine, Itmann Coal Co. | Wyoming County Itmann, WV | Explosion | 5 |
| 1972 | 07/22 | Blacksville No. 1, Consolidation Coal Co. | Monongalia County Blacksville, WV | Fire | 9 |
| 1970 | 12/30 | Nos. 15 and 16 Mines, Finley Coal Co. | Leslie County Hyden, KY | Explosion | 38 |
| 1968 | 11/20 | Consol No. 9 | Farmington, WV | Explosion | 78 |
| 1951 | 12/21 | Orient No. 2 | West Frankfort, IL | Explosion | 119 |
| 1947 | 03/25 | Centralia No. 5 | Centralia, IL | Explosion | 111 |
| 1940 | 03/16 | Willow Grove No. 10 | St. Clairsville, OH | Explosion | 72 |
| 1940 | 01/10 | Pond Creek No. 1 | Bartley, WV | Explosion | 91 |

*Source:* Adapted from the United States Mine Rescue Association 2012.

been understood for two centuries now, studies have confirmed that as many as 12 percent of all coalminers develop one of several possibly fatal diseases – ranging from pneumoconiosis, progressive massive fibrosis, and emphysema to chronic bronchitis and accelerated loss of lung function – over the course of their work.[8] Advocates for the industry work hard to ensure that these deaths are treated as a "cost of doing business" rather than as a stimulus for social change, even in the face of major tragedies.[9]

Uranium mining operations present their own set of hazards. Underground mining presents a "significant danger" to workers since the radionuclides uranium-235, radium-226, radon, and strontium-21 accumulate in the soil and silts around uranium mines, often inhaled by miners in the form of radioactive dust.[10] At five separate mines in Australia – Nabarlek, Rum Jungle, Hunter's Hill, Rockhole, and Moline – gamma radiation levels have exceeded safety standards in some cases by 50 percent, leading to "chronic" exposure to miners and workers.[11]

As a result, uranium miners are exposed to excessively high levels of radon, and hundreds have died of lung cancer and thousands more had their lives shortened. According to reports by the International Commission on Radiological Protection, work-related deaths for uranium mining amount to 5,500–37,500 deaths per million workers per year, compared to 110 deaths for general manufacturing and 164 deaths for the construction industry.[12] Even more worrying is the evidence that there may be no "safe" level of exposure to the radionuclides at uranium

---

[8]  Anil Markandya and Paul Wilkinson, "Electricity Generation and Health," *Lancet* 370 (2007), pp. 979–990.

[9]  For instance, in the New Zealand Royal Commission on the Pike River Coal Mine Tragedy (October 30, 2012), the final report notes that "But, We declare that you are not, under this Our Commission, to inquire into and report upon the wider social, economic, or environmental issues, such as the following … the merits of coal mining, or any other mining, and related operations in New Zealand."

[10]  V.N. Mosinets, "Radioactive Wastes from Uranium Mining Enterprises and their Environmental Effects," *Atomic Energy* 70(5) (1991), pp. 348–354.

[11]  G.M. Mudd, "Uranium Mining in Australia: Environmental Impact, Radiation Releases and Rehabilitation," in International Atomic Energy Agency (IAEA) (ed.), *Protection of the Environment from Ionizing Radiation: The Development and Application of a System of Radiation Protection for the Environment* (Vienna: IAEA, 2003), pp. 179–189.

[12]  Roxby Action Collective and Friends of the Earth, *Uranium Mining: How It Affects You* (Sydney: Friends of the Earth, 2004).

mines. One longitudinal medical study found that low doses of radiation, spread over a number of years, are just as "dangerous" as acute exposure.[13]

To get a sense of how extremely lethal uranium mining was in the United States, consider the case of the Shiprock facility in New Mexico. Of the 150 miners working at the mine in the late 1950s and early 1960s, 38 died of radiation-induced cancer within twenty years and another 95 reported unusual serious respiratory ailments and cancers (meaning 89 percent of miners, in total, developed serious illnesses). That facility, once closed in 1968, left 70 acres of raw untreated tailings almost as radioactive as the ore itself. Other studies have shown higher rates of miscarriages, cleft palates, and birth defects among communities living near uranium mines, to say nothing of the psychological damage and guilt miners feel for infecting their families and loved ones with radioactive particles and resulting illnesses. One study recently argued that uranium mining creates "a health crisis of epidemic proportions" when done near communities.[14]

In Russia and the former Soviet Union, other countries with a legacy of mining, the milling and processing of uranium at Streltsovsk, Krasnokamensk, and Bambakai has discharged radioactive pollutants into local water sources and seen tailings seep into water tables. Indoor radon levels within both the mines and nearby homes are "dangerously high," and the new mine at Khiagdinskii no longer bothers to monitor radiation exposure to workers and residents at all.[15] In Kazakhstan, currently the world's largest producer of uranium, uranium mines have contaminated water wells and seeped millions of tons of radioactive sediment into the Koshkar-Ata Lake, which as it dries exposes residents of adjacent villages to radioactive dust.[16]

As a penultimate example, the oil and gas industry presents dire occupational risks. The Paul Scherrer Institute (PSI) collected data on major industrial accidents from 1945 to 1996 and recorded 13,914

---

[13] *Ibid.*

[14] Barbara Rose Johnston, Susan E. Dawson, and Gary E. Madsen, "Uranium Mining and Milling: Navajo Experiences in the American Southwest," in Laura Nader (ed.), *The Energy Reader* (London: Wiley–Blackwell, 2010), pp. 132–146.

[15] Friends of the Earth, *Uranium Mining for Belgian Nuclear Power Stations: Environmental and Human Rights Impacts* (Brussels: Friends of the Earth, 2008).

[16] *Ibid.*

incidents.[17] An astounding 31 percent of these accidents were related to the oil and gas industry – the highest of any individual sector.[18] The managers of the database found that the most significant immediate fatality rates were associated with liquid petroleum gas (LPG) followed by oil, coal, and natural gas. It noted that the "riskiest" stages for oil appeared to be when it was being distributed through regional pipelines and trucks, or transported to refineries. These two stages accounted for more than three-quarters of all oil-related accidents. It also noted that nearly three-quarters of all natural gas accidents were associated with pipelines, and about 21 percent of these accidents involved mechanical failure.

Lastly, power plants themselves pose some risks to human life. When fatalities associated with power plant accidents are compared independent from the amount of energy they produce, hydroelectric dams and nuclear power plants rank as the two most fatal sources of energy supply, far ahead of oil, coal, and natural gas systems.[19] Moreover, from 1907 to 2007 such sources of electricity supply, in total, were responsible for more than 180,000 deaths in addition to their $41 billion in property damages. When this is put into the context of fatalities per unit of energy produced, Figure 5.1 shows that nuclear power accidents result in almost fifty fatalities for every gigawatt-year of electricity generated compared to less than two fatalities per gigawatt-year for all other energy systems.[20]

---

[17] See Stefan Hirschberg, Gerard Spiekerman, and Roberto Dones, *Severe Accidents in the Energy Sector*, 1st edn., PSI Report No. 98–16 (Villigen, Switzerland: Paul Scherrer Institute, November 1998); Stefan Hirschberg and Andrej Strupczewski, "Comparison of Accident Risks in Different Energy Systems: How Acceptable?," *IAEA Bulletin* 41 (January 1999), pp. 25–30; Stefan Hirschberg, Peter Burgherr, Gerard Spiekerman, and Roberto Dones, "Severe Accidents in the Energy Sector: Comparative Perspective," *Journal of Hazardous Materials* 111 (2004), pp. 57–65.

[18] The architects of this database define a "severe accident" as one which involves one of the following: at least 5 fatalities, at least 10 injuries, 200 evacuees, 10,000 tons of hydrocarbons released, more than 25 square kilometers of cleanup, or more than $5 million in economic losses. Note that, interestingly, this valuation treats 5 deaths as the same as it treats 5 million dollars, implying that $1 million equals one human life.

[19] B.K. Sovacool, "The Costs of Failure: A Preliminary Assessment of Major Energy Accidents, 1907 to 2007," *Energy Policy* 36(5), pp. 1802–1820.

[20] Our argument should not be mistaken to mean that nuclear power is the most dangerous source of electricity generation. In aggregate, pollution from coal-fired power still remains the chief source of fatalities arising from energy production.

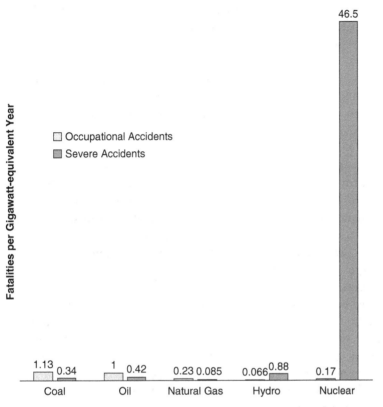

**Figure 5.1** Comparison of occupational and accident risks associated with various energy systems
*Source:* Adapted from S. Hirschberg and A. Strupczewski, "Comparison of Accident Risks in Different Energy Systems: How Acceptable?," *IAEA Bulletin* 41 (1999), pp. 25–30.

## Human rights abuses

Energy production and use contributes towards human rights abuses – which generally cut across the basic categories of civil, cultural, economic, political, and social rights and extend to cover issues of property, economic development, human health, safety, and the natural environment.[21]

However, it is clear that when nuclear power plants suffer extreme incidents they can cause a disproportionate amount of damage.

[21] Chris Ballard and Glenn Banks, "Resource Wars: The Anthropology of Mining," *Annual Review of Anthropology* 32 (2003), pp. 283–313, at p. 305.

As one example, large, international, conventional energy companies –
particularly oil and gas suppliers – have repeatedly employed private
security firms to protect their operations and suppress dissent. For
instance, the oil company Shell paid $15.5 million in a settlement
where it was accused of collaborating in the execution of eight activists
protesting Shell activities in Nigeria, including Ken Saro-Wiwa and
members of a grassroots organization called the Movement for the
Survival of the Ogoni People. When the group became popular, families
of the Ogoni Tribe alleged in their lawsuit that Shell conspired with the
Nigeria militia to capture and then hang the protesters. The families also
presented documents indicating that Shell worked with the Nigerian
army to bring about the torture of other protesters and that Shell
contributed information that resulted in the killing of dissidents. Shell
was also accused of providing the Nigerian army with vehicles, patrol
boats, and ammunition, as well as helping plan raids and military
campaigns against villages.[22]

In Myanmar/Burma, also, the Unocal Corporation, now Chevron, was
accused of authorizing the use of rape, murder, extermination, forced
relocation, and slavery to expedite the construction of oil and gas pipelines in Burma/Myanmar. In both the Karen and Mon states, the government was documented relying on forced labor to construct pipelines and
carrying out military attacks on civilians opposing such projects. Unocal,
one of the project partners, admitted in an American court to knowing
that the regime in Myanmar had a record of committing human rights
abuses, that the military forced villagers to work and entire villages to
relocate for the purposes of the project, and that the government committed various acts of violence in front of company employees. A pipeline
engineer with experience on dozens of projects around the world
remarked that "[in Myanmar, energy projects] are simply the *worst*
because they continue to directly endow a brutal regime with revenue."[23]

In Sudan, the government and companies such as Lundin Oil have relied
on a strategy of "preemptive repression" to secure oil and gas platforms
and pipelines. In one instance, the Sudanese Muslim government utilized
"aerial bombings and executions" to protect blocks at a reserve in Thar

---

[22] "Shell Pays Out $15.5m over Saro-Wiwa Killing," *Guardian*, June 9, 2009.
[23] Quoted in B.K. Sovacool, "Reassessing Energy Security and the Trans-ASEAN
    Natural Gas Pipeline Network in Southeast Asia," *Pacific Affairs* 82(3) (Fall
    2009), p. 482.

Jath. In another, the government created a "cordon sanitaire" around a 936-mile pipeline which involved displacing thousands of people.[24] In Afghanistan, the Talisman Oil Company has also been directly involved in the civil war, with evidence of the deployment of mujahedeen and child combatants to provide security around oil and gas blocks.[25]

Though less severe, energy companies and those advocating particular projects can violate basic civil liberties. As one example, the $4 billion Baku–Tbilisi–Ceyhan (BTC) oil pipeline now delivers more than 1 million barrels of oil per day from the Azeri–Chirag–Gunashli fields in the Caspian Sea off the coast of Baku, Azerbaijan, through Georgia, to the Turkish port of Ceyhan on the Mediterranean, traversing 1,768 kilometers. During construction, the Oil Workers Rights Protection Committee, a local Azeri NGO, awarded some oil executives involved with the BTC project the "torn shoe" award for violating local laws and labor protections, arguing that "their shoes must be torn from stepping on people all day long." One extensive, independent study conducted after all sections of the pipeline were built in Azerbaijan involved research visits to eighty-six communities along the pipeline corridor, interviews of 3,000 people, and the collection of 600 questionnaires. It found that more than three-quarters (76 percent) of those surveyed were unhappy with the BTC Project. The report noted that 7,500 internally displaced people were still living in tents and unlikely to relocate. It estimated that 90 percent of funds provided by the BTC Company and others for social relocation and community development went instead to foreign NGOs. It noted that roads in the Shamkir, Goranboy, Ujar, and Kurdamir regions sustained significant damage from construction but had not been repaired. It documented that at least fifty homes endured cracks and damage but received no compensation. And it found that many irrigation systems sustained damage from construction but were also never repaired.[26]

---

[24] Human Rights Watch, *Sudan, Oil and Human Rights* (Washington, DC: Human Rights Watch, 2003).

[25] Michael J. Watts, "Righteous Oil: Human Rights, the Oil Complex, and Corporate Social Responsibility," *Annual Review of Environment and Resources* 30 (2005), pp. 373–407.

[26] B.K. Sovacool, "Cursed by Crude: The Corporatist Resource Curse and the Baku–Tbilisi–Ceyhan (BTC) Pipeline," *Environmental Policy and Governance* 21(1) (January/February 2011), pp. 42–57; B.K. Sovacool, "Reconfiguring Territoriality and Energy Security: Global Production Networks and the Baku-Tbilisi-Ceyhan

In Australia, uranium mining at the Kakadu National Park in the Northern Territory has a long history utilizing coercive tactics to override opposition. Operators of both the Jabiluka Mine and the Ranger Mine have been documented intimidating, illegally imprisoning, bullying, and bribing the indigenous Mirrar people into signing over land rights. One academic assessment of these practices in Australia concluded that the mining industry there has taken a "'devil may care' attitude to the impacts of its operations: operating in areas without social legitimacy, causing major devastation, and then leaving when an area has been exhausted of all economically valuable resources."[27]

In Bangladesh, the government has ignored civil liberties as it has commenced building an open-pit mine (otherwise known as the Phulbari Coal Project) that would extract 15 million tons of coal from the Phulbari region, a key rice-producing area, that it would then ship on barges through the Sundarbans, one of the three largest mangrove forests in the world and a classified Biosphere Reserve by the UN. The project would involve the relocation of more than 40,000 people from 9,000 households spread across 5,200 hectares, in addition to causing water scarcity for 220,000 individuals who would lose access to water supplies.[28] The project proceeded without any consultation or consent from the affected communities. When community leaders and environmental groups attempted to peacefully but publicly protest the project in August 2006, state police and paramilitary forces physically beat hundreds of them, and then proceeded to indiscriminately fire their weapons into a crowd of 50,000, killing three people (including one fourteen-year-old boy) and injuring another hundred.[29]

(BTC) Pipeline," *Journal of Cleaner Production* 32(9) (September 2012), pp. 210–218.

27  Heledd Jenkins, "Corporate Social Responsibility and the Mining Industry: Conflicts and Constructs," *Corporate Social Responsibility and Environmental Management* 11 (2004), pp. 23–34.

28  Bank Information Center, ADB's Private Sector Arm considering Funding Controversial Coal Project in Northwest Bangladesh, April 2012, available at www.bicusa.org/en/Project.59.aspx.

29  International Accountability Project, *Open Letter to Financial Institutions Investing in Global Coal Management regarding the Phulbari Coal Project, Bangladesh* (Association for Sustainable Human Development *et al.*, August 2008), available at www.banktrack.org/download/open_letter_to_financial_institutions_investing_in_global_coal_management_regarding_the_phulbari_coal_project_bangladesh/0808_open_letter_phulbari_to_fis.pdf.

## Corruption

Various types of corruption – the looting of energy revenues by well-placed military and political representatives, kickbacks, bribes, illegal commissions, and illicit oil-for-arms deals – all too frequently occur regarding oil and gas production as well as the mining of coal.[30] In Iran, for example, $11 billion in oil revenues "vanished" over the course of nine months in 2010.[31] In Nigeria, an independent audit revealed $540 million "missing" from $1.6 billion in advance payments to oil companies to develop new fields in addition to 3.1 million barrels of oil that remain "unaccounted for" along with the disappearance of $3.8 billion in dividends from natural gas sales.[32] Collectively, since independence in 1960, it is estimated that between $300 and $400 *billion* of oil revenue has been stolen or misspent by corrupt Nigerian government officials – an amount of money approaching all the Western aid received by the entire African continent over the course of those years.[33] Even recently, fuel subsidies cost the Nigerian government $6.8 billion in theft over the course of 2010 to 2012, on top of "shady" deals worth $29 billion over the past decade, despite the fact that most Nigerians live on less than $1 per day.[34] In Angola, the second largest oil producer in Africa after Nigeria, investigators discovered in December 2000 that $4 billion in oil funds was missing and likely spent illegally on kickbacks to government officials and the purchase of military arms – these missing funds represented a staggering one third of all state income in Angola.[35] In March of 2012, the heads of state of Kenya, Ethiopia, and South Sudan met in Kenya to launch the construction of a $16 billion port and oil pipeline; they billed taxpayers $350,000 for the celebratory meal when it only cost them $4,000.[36] Table 5.2 depicts other

[30] Watts, "Righteous Oil."

[31] Cyrus Maximus, "Islamic Republic Corruption Scandal: $11 Billion in Oil Money Missing," March 28, 2011, available at http://iranchannel.org/archives/962.

[32] Joe Brock and Tim Cocks, "Nigeria Oil Corruption Highlighted by Audits," *Reuters News Service*, March 8, 2012.

[33] "Nigeria's Oil: A Desperate Need for Reform," *Economist*, October 20, 2012, p. 44.

[34] "Courage: Mon Brave," *Economist*, March 2, 2013, pp. 8–9.

[35] Shari Bryan and Barrie Hofmann, *Transparency and Accountability in Africa's Extractive Industries: The Role of the Legislature* (Washington, DC: National Democratic Institute for International Affairs, 2007), pp. 36–37.

[36] "Kenya, South Sudan, and Uganda: Pipeline Poker," *Economist*, May 25, 2013, pp. 47–48.

**Table 5.2** *Major cases of energy-related corruption, 1960–2010*

| Country | Period | Political leader | Amount looted (upper estimate) | Description |
|---|---|---|---|---|
| Libya | 1969 to 2011 | Muammar Qaddafi | $80 billion | Vast oil-related wealth enables Qaddafi and his family to acquire gold-plated pistols, infinity pools, and rare carpets |
| Egypt | 1987–2011 | Hosni Mubarak | $70 billion | Uses proceeds from state-controlled energy monopolies, among others, to purchase Spanish villas and other items |
| Tunisia | 1987–2011 | Zine el-Abidine Ben Ali | $5 billion | Puts state wealth to use buying personal luxury cars and a pet tiger |
| Nigeria | 1993–1998 | Sani Abacha | $5 billion | Uses state oil money to purchase dozens of luxury houses and cars |
| Indonesia | 1967–1998 | Suharto | $35 billion | Distributes 20 to 30 percent of the entire state budget to relatives in the form of licenses and monopolies on energy supply, roads, and agriculture |
| Zaire | 1965–1997 | Mobutu Sese Seko | $5 billion | Uses the country's mineral taxes and royalties to charter Concord flights and a white-marble retreat in the jungle village of Gbadolite |
| Philippines | 1965–1986 | Ferdinand Marcos | $10 billion | Utilizes state-owned assets, including electricity and water supply, to purchase 2,700 pairs of shoes, imported wine, and gold bricks |
| Haiti | 1971–1986 | Jean-Claude Duvalier | $800 million | Abuses government money to purchase Ferraris, Givenchy clothes, and Hermes children's horse saddles |

*Source:* Adapted from Transparency International and the International Centre for Asset Recovery. Estimates include wealth illicitly accrued by regime members and also assets frozen under UN sanctions.

notable instances of corruption across a range of countries, time periods, and sectors, many of them energy-related.[37] As one commentator quipped, oil has now become an "elixir of political dysfunction."[38]

It's not just "third world" governments and heads of state that are at risk to corruption. In the private sector, Gazprom, the world's largest natural gas producer, has repeatedly attempted to overcome "problems" related to oil and gas development by "drowning them with money." The Peterson Institute for International Economics estimated that Gazprom's profits were $46 billion in 2011, but that it lost $40 billion to corruption and inefficiency.[39] In Congo-Brazzaville, the head of its state-owned oil company, Société nationale des pétroles du Congo, was indicted for illegally taking as much as $4.2 million of company revenues per year and depositing them into his personal account.[40] In the United States, from 2009 to 2012 the Justice Department and Securities and Exchange Commission brought 185 corruption and fraud cases against electricity, oil, gas, and coal companies, charges that yielded more than $2 billion in penalties and settlements.[41] One of the settlements, levied against the oil giant Total in connection with its operations in Iran concerning bribes to officials to win the rights to gas fields, was worth $400 million, the fourth largest enforcement action of the US Foreign Corrupt Practices Act (FCPA) of all time.

Indeed, one study estimated that the energy sector accounts for almost 60 percent of all violations of the FCPA in the United States,[42] implying that it may be the single largest source of fraud, bribery, and corruption in the entire country. Most disturbingly, this study also noted dozens of cases of similar activity in Canada and the United Kingdom. It concluded that the energy sector was "particularly vulnerable" to corruption because it "operates worldwide and is constantly

---

[37] "Recovering Stolen Assets: Making a Hash of Finding the Cash," *Economist*, May 11, 2013, p. 63–64.
[38] Andrew Nikiforuk, "Oh Canada: How America's Friendly Northern Neighbor Became a Rogue, Reckless Petrostate," *Foreign Policy* (July/August 2013).
[39] "Gazprom: Russia's Wounded Giant," *Economist*, March 23, 2013, pp. 68–69.
[40] Bryan and Hofmann, *Transparency and Accountability in Africa's Extractive Industries*, pp. 36–37.
[41] Gordon Kaiser, "Corruption in the Energy Sector: Criminal Fines, Civil Judgments, and Lost Arbitrations," *Energy Law Journal* 34 (2013), pp. 195–259.
[42] *Ibid.*

negotiating leases with foreign governments and engaging in exploration and production on these properties through a wide variety of
subsidiaries, agents, and contractors, as well as joint venture partners."[43] Worldwide, about $200 million in annual taxes from the
mining sector go uncollected due to illicit negotiations and poor oversight. Whistleblowers attempting to challenge the system and expose
such corruption have faced "intimidation, prison, and even death."[44]

Even indubitable intergovernmental organizations charged with
fighting corruption and preserving human rights, such as the UN, are
susceptible to it. In 2002 and 2003, it was revealed that the UN Oil-for-
Food Program – established in 1995 to enable Iraq to sell oil on the
world market in exchange for food, medicine, and humanitarian aid to
offset the devastating effect of international sanctions – enabled
Saddam Hussein and the Iraqi regime to generate $10.1 billion in illegal
revenues, including $5.7 billion of smuggling proceeds and $4.4 billion
in illicit surcharges on oil products. An independent inquiry by the US
Government Accountability Office (GAO) documented more than
380 illegal contracts, with some of the revenues going directly into the
pockets of UN officials managing the program.[45]

## Social and military conflict

The revenues acquired from oil, gas, coal, and uranium production have
also been used to propagate low-intensity warfare, internal conflict,
geopolitical strife, and, in some cases, war – using people as a means
to an end in the very worst way. Oil revenue has endowed the regime in
Khartoum the means to expand its military and extend its campaign
in Darfur, Sudan. Oil and gas revenues have allowed General Than
Schwe to equip the Burmese military with light arms, helicopters, and
armored vehicles in Myanmar. Proceeds from the Chad–Cameroon oil
pipeline are allegedly helping fund conflicts in the Congo and Sudan,
and the oil and gas money from the BTC and South Caucasus Pipelines

---

[43] *Ibid.*
[44] International Rivers Network, *Congo's Energy Divide: Hydropower for Mines and Export, Not the Poor* (March 2011), pp. 1–4.
[45] Joseph A. Christoff, "Observations on the Oil for Food Program," *Testimony before the Committee on Foreign Relations, U.S. Senate* (Washington, DC: US GAO, April 7, 2004).

in Central Asia have enabled Azerbaijan to intensify its military campaign against Armenia.

Moreover, many terrorist groups receive funds indirectly from oil and gas revenues and then use those resources to plan attacks against oil and gas infrastructure. Saudi Arabia, for example, has used its oil wealth to offer more than $600 million in development and aid packages to Al Qaeda and the Taliban from 1993 to 2003, and has sent hundreds of thousands of barrels of oil to other groups in Afghanistan and Pakistan.[46]

These examples are not just anecdotal, and political scientist Shannon O'Leary has identified ten serious civil wars and conflicts from 1990 to 1999 directly fueled by natural resources: copper facilitated a secessionist revolt in Bougainville, Papua New Guinea; oil funded five separate civil wars in Angola, East Timor/Indonesia, the Kurkuk region of Iraq, Southern Sudan, and the Xinjiang province of China; natural gas enabled a conflict in Aceh, Indonesia; nickel a secessionist movement in New Caledonia, France; gold financed a war in West Papua, Indonesia; and phosphates contributed to conflict in the Western Sahara and Morocco.[47]

Similarly, Princeton academic Jeff D. Colgan has shown that "petrostates" where revenues from oil exports constitute at least 10 percent of GDP have an "above average propensity to engage in militarized interstate disputes."[48] He found that "petrostates" became embroiled in military conflict at a rate about 80 percent higher than nonpetrostates over the period of 1965 to 2001. His explanation was that revolutionary leaders are able to rely on oil export revenues to consolidate power and provoke international conflict. Thus the international trade of oil as currently structured places large amounts of money into a political system ill-equipped to use it responsibly.

[46] Robert Baer, "The Fall of the House of Saud," *Atlantic Monthly* (May 2003), pp. 34–48.

[47] Shannon O'Leary, "Resources and Conflict in the Caspian Sea," *Geopolitics* 9(1) (2004), pp. 161–175.

[48] Jeff D. Colgan, "Oil and Revolutionary Governments: A Toxic Mix," *Paper Presented to the 50th Annual Meeting of the International Studies Association*, New York, February 15–18, 2009; Jeff D. Colgan, "Oil and Revolutionary Governments: Fuel for International Conflict," *International Organization* 64 (Fall 2010), pp. 661–694.

Political scientist Michael L. Ross has also documented numerous cases of where oil revenues have exacerbated conflicts around the world.[49] He noted that raising money in petroleum-rich countries can be easy for insurgents and terrorist groups, who can steal and sell oil on the black market, as they did in Iraq and Nigeria. Such groups can extort money from oil companies working in remote areas, as they did in Colombia and Sudan. They can find business partners to fund them in exchange for future consideration if they seize power, which happened in Equatorial Guinea and the Republic of the Congo. As he concluded, "oil wealth often wreaks havoc on a country's economy and politics, makes it easier for insurgents to fund their rebellions, and aggravates ethnic grievances."[50]

Geographer Michael J. Watts has suggested that newfound oil wealth within OPEC has largely backed a global arms race – with countries in the Middle East spending roughly $45 billion a year on weapons and every 1 percent increase in oil revenues corresponding with a 3.3 increase in arms imports.[51] As he concluded, "the reconfiguration of the global oil industry has produced close alignments between oil, finance, and weapons of war, and it has resulted in a close association between oil security as a strategic concern and various types of conflict."[52]

## What is justice?

Theories of justice centered on human rights hold that certain interests of individual persons are more important than the interests of society – or, in other words, that a just society always respects and dignifies the individual. In the words of Georgetown Law Professor Dan Berkovitz, "under rights-based theories each person possesses an inviolability founded on justice that even the welfare of society cannot override."[53] Or, as the prominent justice theorist Ronald Dworkin noted, rights can be defined as "political trumps held by individuals. Individuals have

---

[49] Michael L. Ross, "Blood Barrels: Why Oil Wealth Fuels Conflict," *Foreign Affairs* 87(3) (May/June 2008), pp. 2–8.

[50] *Ibid.*, p. 2.    [51] Watts, "Righteous Oil."    [52] *Ibid.*, p. 378.

[53] Dan M. Berkovitz, "Pariahs and Prophets: Nuclear Energy, Global Warming, and Intergenerational Justice," *Columbia Journal of Environmental Law* 17(2) (1992), pp. 245–326.

rights when, for some reason, a collective goal is not a sufficient justification for denying them what they wish, as individuals, to have or to do, or not a sufficient justification for imposing some loss or injury upon them."[54]

Rights-centered notions of justice have a long history enshrined in all major religions, and dating all the way back to antiquity (and probably further). Hinduism, for example, addresses the necessity for good conduct toward others suffering in need; Judaism talks about the sacredness of the individual endowed with worth and equal value; Islam speaks of lifting the burdens of those less fortunate; Buddhism articulates a respect for all life and duties of compassion and charity; Confucianism argues in favor of treating human beings as having equal worth and recognizing that "within the four seas, all men are brothers"; and Christianity has its message of equality in that "there is neither Greek nor Jew, nor slave nor free, nor man nor woman, but we are all one in Christ" as well as the famous Golden Rule of "doing unto others as you would have them do unto you."[55] The Golden Rule especially "demands fairness or impartiality while requiring an attitude of solidarity toward others and readiness to carry it out in appropriate deeds."[56] Even the ancient civilization of Babylon had its "Code of Hammurabi" which established basic human rights principles such as equal protection of the law and remedies for mistreatment of prisoners.

## Immanuel Kant

One of the most influential advocates of rights-based notions of justice is the German philosopher Immanuel Kant (1724–1804). Kant proposed that each person has inherent, inalienable rights and dignity, that these rights cannot be taken away, and that all human beings, based upon this intrinsic dignity, are equal, a radical proposition in

---

[54] Ronald M. Dworkin, *Taking Rights Seriously* (Harvard University Press, 1978), p. xi.

[55] See Donald K. Anton and Dinah L. Shelton, *Environmental Protection and Human Rights* (New York: Cambridge University Press, 2011), pp. 151–182; Dinah L. Shelton, "An Introduction to the History of Human Rights Law," *GWU Law School Public Law Research Paper No. 346* (August 2007).

[56] Jose Ambrozic, "Beyond Public Reason on Energy Justice: Solidarity and Catholic Social Teaching," *Colorado Journal of International Environmental Law and Policy* 21(2) (Spring 2010), pp. 381–398.

his day.[57] Furthermore, different individuals desire different things and therefore each person possesses particular ideas concerning what happiness is for them.[58] As Berkovitz tells us, "Kantian ethics considers each person to be a rational, autonomous being, capable of continuously determining the ends of his or her life according to his or her own conception of what is good."[59] As it turns out, Kant believes that there is one universal law that all human beings, because they are rational, can give to themselves, and he calls this law the "categorical imperative." This law states that one should "Act only according to that maxim by which you can at the same time will that it should become a universal law." Practically, Kant argues, this amounts to the principle: "Act so that you treat humanity, whether in your own person or in that of another, always as an end and never as a means only."[60]

Kant's ethical theory, like John Stuart Mill's utilitarianism posited in Chapter 4, is rooted deeply within his notion of freedom. Kant argues thus: reason, or what Kant calls *pure practical reason*, is what separates human beings from the realm of animals. Because all human beings are rational beings, capable of pure practical reason, all human beings are worthy of respect. The ability to think and reason – free thought, so to speak – is intimately bound with the human capacity for freedom.[61]

However, Kant's notion of freedom is very different from Mill's. Kant distinguishes between two different types of freedom: negative freedom and positive freedom. Negative freedom is freedom from influences or constraints outside of oneself. Positive freedom is the "property of the Will to be a law to itself." This means that for Kant, the human will is self-legislating, and is thus the source of moral laws.[62] His theory is therefore somewhat similar to libertarianism, since human will and the individual ego are "good" independent of consequences. Or, as Kant wrote himself, "a good will is good not because of what it performs or

[57] John Ladd, in the Introduction to Immanuel Kant, *The Metaphysical Elements of Justice. Part I of the Metaphysics of Morals* (Indianapolis: Bobbs-Merrill Company, Inc., 1965), p. ix.
[58] Michael J. Sandel, *Justice: What's the Right Thing to Do?* (New York: Farrar, Straus, and Giroux, 2009), p. 138.
[59] Berkovitz, "Pariahs and Prophets."
[60] John Ladd, in the Introduction to Kant, *The Metaphysical Elements of Justice*, p. x.
[61] Sandel, *Justice: What's the Right Thing to Do?*, p. 108.
[62] Ladd, in the Introduction to Kant, *The Metaphysical Elements of Justice*, p. xi.

effects, not by its aptness for the attainment of some proposed end, but simply by virtue of the volition, that is, it is good in itself."[63]

Kant calls positive freedom "autonomy"[64] and juxtaposes it with pleasure and pain, and explicitly contrasts his conception to that of Bentham and utilitarian thinkers. For Kant, seeking pleasure and happiness and avoiding pain is deterministic living, and it is completely misguided to think that such natural inclinations could provide a foundation for justice and morality. The point is that when a human being desires happiness or pleasure, these traits are actually dependent upon factors that are extrinsic to who the individual really is – pleasure or pain are merely the results of deterministic dictates by either nature (biology) or social convention. As justice scholar Michael Sandel explains:

Suppose I'm trying to decide what flavor of ice cream to order: Should I go for chocolate, vanilla, or espresso toffee crunch? I may think of myself as exercising freedom of choice [in making this decision], but what I am really doing is trying to figure out which flavor will best satisfy my preferences – preferences I didn't choose in the first place. Kant doesn't say it's wrong to satisfy our preferences. His point is that, when we do so, we are not acting freely, but acting according to a determination given outside us. After all, I didn't choose my desire for espresso toffee crunch rather than vanilla. I just have it.[65]

Thus, according to Kant, what gives a person pleasure or pain is not determined by that person, because such determinations are given from outside of us, and therefore achieving pleasure and avoiding pain is merely a component within a deterministic system. Autonomy, though, is the free process of pure practical human reason, which is "to act according to a law I [freely and rationally] give myself."[66] The link via justice between the two types of freedom is that an individual must first be free from external causes in order to pursue positive freedom, and it is the goal of law and politics to insure freedom from external constraints to its citizens.[67] Basically, a just society reaches its status of

---

[63] Immanuel Kant, "The Moral Law and Autonomy of the Will," in Mark Timmons (ed.), *Conduct and Character: Readings in Moral Theory* (Belmont: Wadsworth Publishing, 1999), pp. 154–162.

[64] Ladd, in the Introduction to Kant, *The Metaphysical Elements of Justice*, p. xi.

[65] Sandel, *Justice: What's the Right Thing to Do?*, p. 108.      [66] *Ibid.*, p. 109.

[67] Ladd, in the Introduction to Kant, *The Metaphysical Elements of Justice*, p. xi.

"just" when it "harmonizes each individual's freedom with that of everyone else."[68]

As is perhaps obvious by now, Kant's thinking offers a strong critique of utilitarianism – and of the numerous examples of occupational injuries and deaths, human rights abuses, corruption, and conflict noted above. Scholars often refer to his categorical imperative as "deontological" since it does not depend on the desire for any particular consequence; it imposes on us law-abidingness for its own sake.[69] Stanford University philosopher Allen Wood explains that "consequentialist theories represent the fulfillment of our duties as bringing about desirable states of affairs; deontological ones represent it as obedience to an obligatory rule or commandment."[70] Oxford University philosopher H.J. Paton adds that according to Kant "A man is morally good not as seeking to satisfy his own desires or to attain his own happiness (though he may do both these things), but as seeking to obey a law valid for *all* men and to follow an objective standard not determined by his own desires."[71]

Because of this, Kant thinks that utilitarian thinking runs into problems trying to figure out which pleasure is better than another.[72] Five years after Bentham published his *Principles of Morals and Legislation*, Kant published a devastating critique of utilitarianism in his *Groundwork for the Metaphysics of Morals*.[73] Brown University Professor John Ladd provides a telling explanation of how Kant's theory is fundamentally at odds with utilitarianism:

In emphasizing the rights of the individual, Kant sets himself against every form of utilitarianism. He believes that neither morality nor law can be founded on social utility, the general happiness, or the common good; they are founded, rather, on the rights of individual man. Insofar as any course of action, private or public, conflicts with these rights, it is ipso facto wrong; and it is wrong regardless of the amount of good that may result from it. In this

---

[68] Sandel, *Justice: What's the Right Thing to Do?*, p. 138.

[69] Louis P. Pojman, "Kantian and Deontological Systems," in *Ethics: Discovering Right and Wrong* (Belmont: Wadsworth Publishing, 1995), pp. 133–159.

[70] Allen Wood, "Humanity as an End in Itself," in Paul Guyer (ed.), *Kant's Groundwork of the Metaphysics of Morals: Critical Essays* (New York: Rowman and Littlefield, 1998), pp. 165–187.

[71] H.J. Paton, *Immanuel Kant's Groundwork of the Metaphysic of Morals* (New York: Harper & Row, 1964), p. 22.

[72] Sandel, *Justice: What's the Right Thing to Do?*, p. 138.     [73] *Ibid.*, p. 105.

sense, he categorically repudiates the principle that the end justifies the means, however good and worthwhile the end may be.[74]

Kant also explicitly rejects the "happiness principles" espoused by Bentham and Mill because they "contribute nothing whatever toward establishing morality, since making a [person] happy is quite different from making [them] good."[75]

In sum, Kant and the rights-based theorists similar to him tell us that individual people need to be treated with dignity and respect. To be accorded proper dignity, each person must be permitted to pursue their own goals according to their own free will; people cannot be utilized as a means for some abstract notion of the good of others. For Kant in particular, actions are immoral if they involve people in something to which they cannot in principle consent. The two most common ways of doing this are (1) deceiving them or lying to them and (2) forcing or coercing them.[76] Modern notions of human rights extend these concerns globally, and argue that individual rights are grounded in a person's humanity, rather than their ethnicity, nation-state, or gender; that these rights are universal, protecting each and every person; and that they have a priority that takes precedence over other values.[77] Essentially, as Professor Wood summates, "the basic reason why it is wrong to harm people, or to fail to help them, is that we thereby show that we place too little value on them."[78]

## What is to be done?

The application of Kant's approach to rights and preserving human dignity requires treating all human beings as ends in themselves. But how do we go about such an application in practice to the realm of energy? We present a few options here: facilitating energy truth commissions and inspection panels, improving the process of undertaking

---

[74] Ladd, in the Introduction to Kant, *The Metaphysical Elements of Justice*, p. ix.
[75] Sandel, *Justice: What's the Right Thing to Do?*, p. 107.
[76] Onora O'Neil, "Kant on Treating People as Ends in Themselves," in Timmons (ed.), *Conduct and Character*, pp. 175–180.
[77] Simon Caney, "Climate Change, Human Rights, and Moral Thresholds," in Stephen M. Gardiner, Simon Caney, Dale Jamieson, and Henry Shue (eds.), *Climate Ethics: Essential Readings* (Oxford University Press, 2010), pp. 163–177.
[78] Wood, "Humanity as an End in Itself," p. 178.

environmental and social impact assessments, promoting transparency and accountability in the extractive industries, and providing communities access to legal remedies so that they can protect their rights.

### Energy truth commissions and inspection panels

The formulation and creation of truth commissions and inspection panels can go a long way towards spotlighting particular human rights abuses. Though they have not been applied to energy issues before, truth commissions have been successful at holding people accountable for human rights violations and genocides in places such as Rwanda and South Africa. Generally, such commissions are comprised of eminent citizens or regulators charged with investigating human rights violations and producing an official history of those abuses.

The creation of energy truth commissions would have at least five advantages. They would provide the mandate and authority to officially investigate abuses related to energy production and use in a given geographic area, bringing attention to them. They would enable a cathartic public airing of grievances, resulting in an official record of the truth that would help communities come to terms with what happened to them. They create a forum for victims and their relatives to tell their side of the story, providing a degree of acknowledgement of their loss, and leading to a formal record of events. They can establish the basis for legal action, including liability and lawsuits, compensation of victims, and the punishment of perpetrators. Finally, they are relatively quick and inexpensive, and can often begin holding hearings and collecting testimony in a matter of weeks at a cost in the thousands of dollars (rather than the hundreds of thousands or millions of dollars).[79]

Formal inspection panels offer another tool to document and remedy abuses and grievances. The exemplar here is the World Bank's Inspection Panel, which provides a forum for people to directly raise their concerns about *any* of the World Bank's projects to an independent group of experts. The World Bank created its Inspection Panel in 1993 after an independent review of its support for the Sardar Sarovar Dam on the Narmada River in India concluded that it "clearly

---

[79] Neil J. Kritz, "Coming to Terms with Atrocities: A Review of Accountability Mechanisms for Mass Violations of Human Rights," *Law and Contemporary Problems* 59(4) (Autumn 1996), pp. 127–152.

violated" Bank policies and had "devastating" human and environmental consequences, claims that were quickly substantiated.[80] The
World Bank thus established an Inspection Panel consisting of at least
three members nominated by the President of the Bank and approved by
their board of directors, serving for five-year terms, financed by the
Bank, but serving independently – with members disqualified if they had
worked for the Bank for at least two years and unable to work for the
World Bank after serving on the Panel.

Two or more local people can bring a claim to the Inspection Panel,
asking for an objective analysis of the World Bank's role in a project
and the degree to which it violated or failed to comply with any of its
policies and procedures. Claims are typically resolved within one year,
though some have taken as little as a few months.[81] Between 1993
and 2008, the Inspection Panel heard fifty-two complaints, finding
in favor of Requestors forty-five times, and they have succeeded at
blocking the construction of socially and environmentally destructive
dams in Nepal, coalmines in India, sewage treatment facilities in the
Philippines, and various attempts to unfairly resettle local people.[82]
So far such Inspection Panels have taken hold at most multilateral
development banks and a few other institutions, but we believe that
international bodies such as the UN and private companies, among
other actors, should begin to create and encourage their own inspection panels.

## Improved impact assessments

Most energy projects around the world today require the completion of
an Environmental Impact Assessment (EIA): an evaluation of the possible positive or negative impact the proposed project is expected to
have on the natural environment or on adjacent communities. Ordinary

---

[80] International Accountability Project, "World Bank Inspection Panel" (2012),
available at www.accountabilityproject.org/section.php?id=41.
[81] Enrique R. Carrasco and Alison K. Guernsey, "The World Bank's Inspection
Panel: Promoting True Accountability through Arbitration," *Cornell
International Law Journal* 41(30) (August 2008), pp. 577–626.
[82] See also World Bank, *The World Bank Inspection Panel: The First Four Years
(1994–1998)* (Washington, DC: World Bank Group); and World Bank,
*Accountability at the World Bank: The Inspection Panel 10 Years On*
(Washington, DC: World Bank Group).

EIAs, however, often fall short of comprehensive protection or are not adequately enforced. We believe they should be modified in at least four ways. They should be broadened to include human rights and other social issues, explicitly mention what happens if a project does *not* go forward in addition to projecting what would happen if a project *did* go forward, include worst-case scenarios in their assessments, and incorporate Impact-Benefit Agreements (IBAs) and Impact-Compensation Contracts.

First, EIAs need to encompass a broader set of impacts beyond the "ordinary" ones of environmental degradation and jobs, and they need to be better evaluated and monitored. More specifically, they should assess the likelihood that the impacts from a particular energy project will be:

- Extensive over space or time;
- Intensive in relation to assimilative capacity;
- Above or close to environmental standards or thresholds;
- Noncompliant with environmental policies, land use plans, and sustainability strategies;
- Likely to threaten public health or safety;
- Likely to limit agriculture, wood gathering or resource uses on which people rely for subsistence;
- Likely to deplete or damage resources that are commercially exploited;
- Likely to affect protected or ecologically sensitive areas, rare or endangered species or heritage resources; and
- Likely to disrupt the lifestyle of large numbers of people or that of vulnerable minorities.[83]

Such an approach would ensure that such assessments formally envelop human rights concerns alongside the more traditional impacts on land and resources. Furthermore, EIAs ought to provide better monitoring, auditing, and evaluation tools – say, from an independent board rather than project sponsors – to verify the accuracy of EIA predictions and review their effectiveness and performance.[84]

[83] Hussein Abaza, Ron Bisset, and Barry Sadler, *Environmental Impact Assessment and Strategic Environmental Assessment: Towards an Integrated Approach* (UNEP, 2004).
[84] *Ibid.*

Second, for those energy projects that have the potential to benefit communities, EIAs should state what would happen if the project would *not* go forward. It should declare not only the probable impacts for doing a project, but the impacts for not doing it in terms of lost jobs or deteriorating environmental quality. In the words of political scientist Aaron Wildavsky, this practice would entail identifying "those existing risks that will continue unabated by the choice to delay the introduction of new technology that could reduce them."[85] For example, a traditional EIA might show that building a particular wind farm would result in negative impacts on avian wildlife, convincing environmentalists not to support it. But if the EIA also presented evidence on what would occur without the wind farm – say, construction of a coal plant that would kill even more wildlife – the net, cumulative impact of the project on society would become clearer.

Third, EIAs should include assessments of what might happen in a worst-case scenario – if a project might catastrophically fail, such as a uranium mine polluting a waterway or a coalmine collapsing and burying hundreds of workers. Lloyds, an insurance company, and Chatham House, an independent policy institute based in London, recently made this case when they argued that

Full-scale exercises based on worst-case scenarios of environmental disaster should be run by companies with government involvement and oversight to provide a transparent account of the state of knowledge and capabilities, to foster expertise and to assuage legitimate public concerns. Integrated ecosystem-based management, incorporating the full range of economic factors, is needed in order to avoid one activity harming and displacing others and to take full account of the cumulative impacts of development. Long-term viability should be a key policy consideration for governments, business and other stakeholders.[86]

Such worst-case forecasting would ensure that communities and decision-makers better comprehend the full suite of risks involved in pursuing a particular energy technology or pathway.

Fourth, EIAs ought to include Impact-Benefit Agreements and Impact-Compensation Contracts, commonly known as "IBAs." IBAs ensure that

---

[85] Aaron Wildavsky, *Searching for Safety* (New Brunswick: Transaction Publishers, 1988), p. 191.
[86] Lloyds and Chatham House, *Arctic Opening: Opportunity and Risk in the High North* (London: Chatham House, 2012).

communities surrounding energy facilities and projects benefit from them and are compensated for negative impacts if they occur, especially vulnerable groups and indigenous peoples.[87] Some IBAs require employment by local people, revenue sharing, reclamation procedures, cross-cultural training, and dispute resolution. For instance, in the Canadian extractive industries sector, IBAs have required the involvement of Inuit businesses and communities in project contracts, established independent review boards, and funded social and educational programs. One IBA even mandates that the Inuit receive $14 million plus 4.5 percent of mining profits estimated at $60 million spread over fifteen years from a particular mine. In Saskatchewan, another IBA implemented through the Prince Albert Grand Council and the Athabasca Economic Development and Training Corporation requires uranium mining companies to enter into lease agreements and human resource development plans to ensure that indigenous communities are respected. Indeed, as of 2012, no less than seven IBAs were operating throughout Canada covering the production of oil, coal, and uranium, shown in Table 5.3.

## Extractive industry transparency initiatives

Another solution to energy-related human rights abuses involves better oversight, monitoring, and control over the activities of oil, gas, and coal companies. The most common application of this solution is known as "extractive industry transparency initiatives," or EITIs – voluntary, multistakeholder codes of conduct emerging from a collection of previous ad hoc efforts by companies, governments, and civil society. EITIs entered the international sphere in 2002, with support by the United Kingdom and leadership from former Prime Minister Tony Blair, and were formally presented at the World Summit on Sustainable Development in September 2002. The push for EITIs was also backed by an initial group of twenty governments, three industry associations, dozens of nongovernmental organizations including the Publish What You Pay Coalition and Global Witness, and a statement of support by

---

[87] Kevin O'Reilly and Erin Eacott, "Aboriginal Peoples and Impact and Benefit Agreement: Summary of the Report of a National Workshop," *Northern Perspectives* 25(4) (Fall–Winter 1999–2000), pp. 4–15.

Table 5.3 *Impact-benefit agreements in Canada, 2012*

| Project | Fuel | Province or territory | Year signed | Aboriginal signatory/signatories | Industry signatory/ signatories |
|---|---|---|---|---|---|
| Syncrude Oil Sands | Oil | Alberta | 1993–1998 | Athabasca Native Development Corp. | Syncrude Canada Ltd. |
| Morrison Project | Coke | British Columbia | 2008 | Lake Babine Nation | Pacific Booker Minerals Inc. |
| Mount Klappan | Anthracite | British Columbia | 2009 | Tahltan Central Council (Tahltan Nation) | Fortune Minerals Ltd. |
| Cluff Lake | Uranium | Saskatchewan | 1999 | Athabasca communities of Black Lake, Fond du Lac and Hatchet Lake Denesuline Nations along with Camsell Portage, Wollaston Lake, Uranium City, and Stony Rapids | Areva Resources Canada (Cameco Corp. and Cogema) |
| McClean Lake | Uranium | Saskatchewan | 1999 | Athabasca communities of Black Lake, Fond du Lac and Hatchet Lake Denesuline Nations along with Camsell Portage, Wollaston Lake, Uranium City, and Stony Rapids | Areva Resources Canada (Cameco Corp. and Cogema) |
| Black Lake | Uranium | Saskatchewan | 2006 | Black Lake Denesuline First Nation | CanAlaske Uranium Ltd. |
| Fond du Lac | Uranium | Saskatchewan | 2006 | Fond du Lac Denesuline First Nation | CanAlaske Uranium Ltd. |

*Source:* Adapted from Impact Benefits Assessment Research Network, "List of Known IBAs," May 2012, available at www.cbern.ca/impactandbenefit/IBA_Database_List/.

more than forty institutional investors and banks in the energy sector, including the World Bank.[88]

Though they vary in their implementation country to country, EITIs generally possess three core requirements:

- Energy companies must disclose everything they pay to the government;
- Institutions of the government must disclose everything they receive from energy companies;
- Independent auditors ensure the two sets of figures agree and produce a published report.

The general idea is that participating companies and governments publish all payments from the operators of oil, gas, and mining industries. EITIs are encouraged to subscribe to twelve formal criteria that revolve around a set of core principles, but these can be boiled down to independent verification of payments and receipts and the publication of the same; a process that must involve civil society and nongovernmental actors (it cannot be controlled by the government alone); and mandatory participation in the process for all extractive industry operators once the host country endorses its own EITI.[89] Its intent is to track the influence and interaction among energy companies and governments, protecting citizens, but also protecting governments and investors from "rotten apples" in the industry.[90] As of 2012, fourteen countries were in compliance with EITI standards (though Yemen was recently suspended) and a further twenty-one countries were considering their candidacy.[91]

---

[88] See Virginia Haufler, "Disclosure as Governance: The Extractive Industries Transparency Initiative and Resource Management in the Developing World," *Global Environmental Politics* 10(3) (August 2010), pp. 53–73; Bryan and Hofmann, *Transparency and Accountability in Africa's Extractive Industries*; and Cynthia A. Williams, "Civil Society Initiatives and 'Soft Law' in the Oil and Gas Industry," *New York University Journal of International Law and Policy* 36 (2003–2004), pp. 457–502.

[89] Paul D. Ocheje, "The Extractive Industries Transparency Initiative (EITI): Voluntary Codes of Conduct, Poverty, and Accountability in Africa," *Journal of Sustainable Development in Africa* 8(3) (Fall 2006), pp. 222–239.

[90] Peter Eigen, "Fighting Corruption in a Global Economy: Transparency Initiatives in the Oil and Gas Industry," *Houston Journal of International Law* 29 (2006–2007), pp. 327–354.

[91] The most up-to-date figures can be found at http://eiti.org/countries.

EITIs are not perfect. One obvious weakness is that they are voluntary – countries can elect whether to participate, and it is telling that only fourteen have signed on so far out of the more than 165 countries around the world involved in producing oil, gas, and/or coal. A second drawback is that most EITIs do not require individual company disclosures; they instead deal with aggregate data, allowing companies to pool their information, at times undercutting the transparency goals of the initiative.[92]

Nonetheless, EITIs have proven successful at improving the behavior and governance of energy companies. The Nigerian Extractive Industries Transparency Initiative (NEITI), for instance, effectively conducts and publishes independent audits of payments and revenues, and has been formally supported by the Nigerian President. NEITI publishes financial audits, including baseline analysis of financial flows out of the oil sector, and into the government, including transactions across upstream and downstream activities. It publishes physical audits including hydrocarbon volume balances at specific wells and refineries. It publishes process audits which explore revenues for marketing, licensing, expenditures, and accounting.[93] It requires that information is published in a disaggregated fashion, enabling auditors and the public to identify revenue disbursements by company, category, and oil well. Chad's EITI has similarly facilitated the creation of a petroleum revenue oversight committee consisting of members of parliament and civil society. São Tomé and Príncipe has also utilized its EITI to establish a Management and Investment Committee to supervise oil accounts, and a Petroleum Oversight Commission to oversee compliance of the oil sector with all aspects of state law.[94]

## Protect, respect, and remedy

Energy truth commissions, inspection panels, impact assessments, and EITIs, largely fact-finding in nature, should be coupled with the extension of access to legal remedies for individuals and communities

---

[92] Abdullah Al Faruque, "Transparency in Extractive Revenues in Developing Countries and Economies in Transition: A Review of Emerging Best Practices," *Journal of Energy and Natural Resources Law* 24 (2006), pp. 66–103.

[93] Bryan and Hofmann, *Transparency and Accountability in Africa's Extractive Industries.*

[94] Al Faruque, "Transparency in Extractive Revenues."

negatively impacted by energy projects. Harvard Professor John Ruggie, also Special Representative for Business and Human Rights to the UN Secretary-General, has encapsulated such an extension through his three principles of "protect, respect, and remedy." After analyzing about 400 public complaints and allegations against companies that violated the rights of citizens, as well as dozens of court cases, Ruggie tells us that his framework has three core elements:

First, the State duty to protect against human rights abuses by third parties, including business, through appropriate policies, regulation, and adjudication; second, the corporate responsibility to respect human rights, which in essence means to act with due diligence to avoid infringing on the rights of others; and third, greater access by victims to effective remedies.[95]

The first principle, "protect," calls on governments to extend civil rights protections beyond where they exist now to include things like trade and investment agreements, export credit guarantees, and bilateral treaties. The second principle, "respect," calls on companies and the private sector to "do no harm" and to comply with all applicable laws and social expectations. The third principle of "access to remedy" urges the creation of formal dispute resolution processes so that victims of abuses can seek redress.[96]

This third principle of "remedy" has significant room for expansion and improvement, especially in the area of nonjudicial grievance mechanisms which enable affected communities to address wrongdoing. Multilateral initiatives, including the Guidelines for Multinational Corporations and Principles of Corporate Governance from the Organisation for Economic Co-operation and Development, and the World Bank Policy on Indigenous Peoples and Draft Policy on Involuntary Resettlement, stipulate some protections, and the World Bank Group's Ombudsman and Inspection Panel have attempted to

---

[95] John Ruggie, "Human Rights and Transnational Corporations and Other Business Enterprises," *Statement before the 63rd Session of the General Assembly of the United Nations*, New York, October 27, 2008.

[96] See Cary Coglianese and Jennifer Nash, "Government Clubs: Theory and Evidence from Voluntary Environmental Programs," *Corporate Social Responsibility Initiative*, Working Paper No. 50 (Cambridge, MA: John F. Kennedy School of Government, Harvard University, 2008); John Ruggie, *Guiding Principles on Business and Human Rights: Implementing the United Nations "Protect, Respect and Remedy" Framework* (New York: UN, March 21, 2011).

increase the accountability of companies and projects being financed by the World Bank, but are naturally limited to those projects.

Other multistakeholder initiatives provide independent monitoring mechanisms, and some companies have set up independent hotlines that serve as a confidential contact point for aggrieved workers or community groups to register complaints.[97] The UN Global Compact, launched in 1999, urges companies, including those in the energy sector, to "support and respect the protection of internationally proclaimed human rights within their sphere of influence and make sure they are not complicit in human rights abuses." A joint United Kingdom and United States "Voluntary Principles on Security and Human Rights" was also signed in 2000, setting guidelines for how companies utilize private security agencies, and a slew of stakeholder initiatives have come from civil society, including Amnesty International's Human Rights Guidelines for Companies, the Global Sullivan Principles, the Australian Non-Government Organizations' Principles for the Conduct of Company Operations within the Minerals Industry, and the German NGO network's Principles for the Conduct of Company Operations within the Oil and Gas Industry.[98]

Such efforts can sometimes curtail human rights abuses when they result in negotiation and arbitration. Negotiation involves "direct dialogue between the parties to the grievance with the aim of resolving the grievance or dispute through mutual agreement," whereas arbitration is "the process by which neutral arbitrators selected by the parties to a dispute hear the positions of the parties, conduct some form of questioning or wider investigation and arrive at a judgment on the course of action to be taken in settling the grievance or dispute, often [but not necessarily] with binding effect on the parties."[99]

One innovative initiative focusing exclusively on energy has been the Mining Minerals and Sustainable Development (MMSD) project, a global effort funded by a consortium of large mining companies, and administered by the International Institute for Environment and Development in Canada from late 1999 to 2002. The MMSD relied on

---

[97] Cristina Cedillo, *Better Access to Remedy in Company–Community Conflicts in the Field of CSR: A Model for Company Based Grievance Mechanisms* (The Hague: Institute for Environmental Security, September 2011).

[98] Chris Ballard, *Human Rights and the Mining Sector in Indonesia: A Baseline Study* (International Institute for Environment and Development, October 2001).

[99] Cedillo, *Better Access.*

a process of stakeholder consultation and reviews of mining practices and the state of the industry to ensure that they protected human rights. The project grew to involve the International Union for Conservation of Nature (IUCN) and Conservation International (CI) and was formally presented at the Rio + 10 Earth Summit in Johannesburg, South Africa, in 2002.[100] The MMSD was intended to create a true "social license" for mining companies to operate, and to fully address the challenges of poverty alleviation, job creation, respect for human rights and sound governance, and stakeholder engagement.[101] Ten years after its completion, the International Institute for Environment and Development credited it in 2012 with being a "game-changer" for the mining sector by setting new industry standards and benchmarks, backed by the International Council on Mining and Metals, the World Bank, and the Intergovernmental Forum on Mining, Minerals, Metals, and Sustainable Development, which changed the practices of more than 700 private sector participants spread across twenty countries.[102]

[100] Ballard and Banks, "Resource Wars."

[101] Shirley M. Smith, Derek D. Shepherd, and Peter T. Dorward, "Perspectives on Community Representation within the Extractive Industries Transparency Initiative," *Resources Policy* 37(2) (2012), pp. 241–250.

[102] Abbi Buxton, *MMSD+10: Reflecting on a Decade of Mining and Sustainable Development* (International Institute for Environment and Development, 2012).

# 6 | *Energy and due process*

In 2000 and 2001, during the height of the California electricity crisis, the City of San Diego faced consistent rolling brownouts and electricity shortages. Fearing that the predicament was a taste of things to come, city planners, in association with the local utility San Diego Gas and Electric (SDG&E) and the California Independent Systems Operator, proposed creating a $130 million, 100-mile-long high-voltage (500 kV) above ground transmission line to connect the Valley Substation with the Rainbow Substation. Backed by these supporters, the Valley-Rainbow Interconnect Project had a number of large potential benefits. It would increase SDG&E's ability to import electricity into their service area by approximately 700 MW. The project would help interconnect SDG&E's network with that of Southern California Edison. It would improve system reliability, minimizing the risk of future blackouts, especially given that Riverside County, and the Project area as a whole, was at the time one of the fastest-growing places in the United States. It had "significant economic benefits to the State" in the form of "significant reductions in energy costs" and "substantial cost benefits to ratepayers" in the form of "avoided customer outage costs," ultimately benefiting about 3.4 million San Diego customers with improved connectivity and lower spot prices for electricity.

However, despite these possible gains, a collection of smaller cities, community groups, environmental nongovernmental organizations, and Indian tribes staunchly opposed the project. Much of the 100-mile corridor of land needed belonged not to the state, but to private owners and cities. The project required the state to "confiscate" more than 140 properties and roughly 638 acres of land from the cities of Temecula, De Luz, Glen Oaks, Redhawk, Vail Ranch, Oakridge Ranches, Winchester, Wine Country, French Valley, Sun City, Menifee, and Lake Skinner. The Southwest Association of Realtors and the Women's Council of Realtors protested against the line on the grounds that it would significantly lower property values across 4,600

191

residential units, 215 acres of commercial development, 167.2 acres of mixed-use development, three school sites, three parks, an eighteen-hole golf course and even a helicopter pilot training school. The Temecula Valley Wine Growers Association opposed it on the grounds that it would interfere with its vineyards. Civil society groups passionately argued that the line would "violate" twelve "pristine wilderness areas," including the Anza-Borrego Desert State Park, the second largest in the United States (after Adirondack Park in New York) and home to desert bighorn sheep and a variety of endangered species. Native Americans argued that the line would damage the sacred burial grounds of the Pechanga Band of Luiseno Mission.[1]

The Public Utilities Commission (PUC) in California had to decide whether to proceed with the line or not. At the core of their deliberation were two questions: When should the state be able to exercise eminent domain and expropriate land for energy projects? And, at what point do we as a society consciously and deliberately require individual interests and rights to suffer for a greater public good?

Ultimately, after three years of intense debate and $2.25 million in legal fees, the PUC in California decided *against* building the transmission line and in favor of the local interveners. In this case, community involvement was substantive and not only demonstrative or rhetorical. However, the picture gets more complicated when one looks a decade further. In September 2011, a massive blackout hit San Diego that clogged roads and caused traffic accidents, closed schools and businesses, grounded airplanes, trapped people in elevators, and left more than 4 million people across Southern California and Mexico without power. More than 200,000 of the county's poorest residents on food stamps saw the perishable items in their refrigerator expire, and two key water treatment facilities failed because they did not have working backup generators, sending millions of gallons of sewage into the ocean.[2] The National University System Institute for Policy

---

[1] Marc B. Mihaly, "Citizen Participation in the Making of Environmental Decisions: Evolving Obstacles and Potential Solutions through Partnership with Experts and Agents," *Pace Environmental Law Review* 27 (2009), pp. 151–226; San Diego Gas & Elec. Co. (U 902-E), Application 01–03–036 at 6 (Cal. Pub. Utils. Comm'n Mar. 23, 2001) (Application for Certificate of Public Convenience & Necessity); San Diego Gas & Elec. Co., Application No. 04–06–011.

[2] K. Hernandez, "Blackout: Food Stamps Recipients May've Been Hit Hard," *Voice of San Diego*, September 12, 2011.

Research estimated that the blackout cost $97 million to $118 million in food losses, government overtime, and lost productivity.[3] The primary cause – as perhaps readers may have guessed – was an oversubscribed high-voltage power line.[4]

Looking back, then, did the PUC make the right call placing the needs of these property owners and communities above those of the overall state? Regardless of your answer, this chapter demonstrates that all too often approaches to energy siting ignore or contravene the wishes of local communities. They violate notions of free, fair, and informed consent, and exclude important stakeholders from key energy decisions. In today's energy landscape, due process can be violated in a variety of ways by energy projects: with consent given after construction of a project begins (or at times, not at all), with communities not knowing about a project until after the fact or being excluded from hearings, and with the state or other actors coercing communities to participate, among others. Nonetheless, this chapter shows how tools such as community consultation and participatory technology assessment, among others, offer planners and people alike a way out of these injustices.

## What is reality?

The reality of the global energy system is far from the idyllic principles of due process and procedural justice. This section of the chapter focuses on four primary types of injustice: unfair negotiations involving energy and climate change, involuntary resettlement and lack of consent, improper licensing of energy facilities, and the marginalization of communities living near energy infrastructure.

### Unfair negotiations

Discussions and negotiations concerning energy and climate change are rarely representative and often asymmetrical and exclusionary. For instance, vulnerable developing countries are not equal partners in international negotiations and lack the ability to advance their own

---

[3] Dan Bauder, "Power Outage Cost Local Economy $100 Million," San Diego Reader, September 9, 2011.

[4] Mike Anton, Louis Sahagun, and Richard Marosi, "More than 4 Million Lose Power in Major Blackout," *Los Angeles Times*, September 8, 2011.

interests in processes such as the United Nations Framework Convention on Climate Change (UNFCCC).[5] Such countries have a very small market share of the global economy, are not members of the Organisation for Economic Co-operation and Development (meaning they are restricted from joining the International Energy Agency and other groups), and can only afford to send small delegations. The result is that industrialized countries such as the United States and industrializing countries such as Brazil, China, and India are able to wield disproportionate influence. At the fourth Conference of Parties (COP) in Buenos Aires, Argentina, in 1998, the delegation from the United States consisted of 83 people. The average delegation from Africa, by contrast, had between two and four people. Villanova Law Professor Ruth Gordon argues that therefore "African countries seemed to have no, or a weak, position and stance and have received few concessions."[6] At the fifteenth COP in Copenhagen, Denmark, in 2009, delegates from the US and EU boasted 1,200 limousines (one delegate had 42 vehicles to themselves) and 140 private jets; delegates from emerging economies in Asia and Africa, by contrast, arrived mostly by taxi and flew economy class.[7] As energy and climate scholars Stephen H. Schneider and Janica Lane lament, "the most marginalized groups tend to have little political and economic power and hence have little influence in the decision-making process."[8]

Philosopher Henry Shue argues that such lack of representation in negotiations is deplorable not only for being unfair, but also because it results in "dirty development" and higher rates of emissions. As he writes:

[5] See Jouni Paavola, W. Neil Adger, and Saleemul Huq, "Multifaceted Justice in Adaptation to Climate Change," in W. Neil Adger, Jouni Paavola, Saleemul Huq, and M.J. Mace (eds.), *Fairness in Adaptation to Climate Change* (Cambridge, MA: MIT Press, 2006), pp. 263–277; and J. Timmons Roberts and Bradley C. Parks, *A Climate of Injustice: Global Inequality, North–South Politics, and Climate Policy* (Cambridge, MA: MIT Press, 2007).

[6] Ruth Gordon, "Climate Change and the Poorest Nations: Further Reflections on Global Inequality," *University of Colorado Law Review* 78 (2007), pp. 1559–1624.

[7] Andrew Gilligan, "Copenhagen Climate Change Conference: Not the Science but the Vision," *Daily Telegraph* (London), December 7, 2009.

[8] Stephen H. Schneider and Janica Lane, "Dangers and Thresholds in Climate Change and the Implications for Justice," in Adger, Paavola, Huq, and Mace (eds.), *Fairness in Adaptation to Climate Change*, pp. 23–51.

Wealth provides bargaining strength because it constitutes resources that can be drawn upon in the absence of any agreement, making the wealthy bargainer willing to pay relatively less to reach agreement. The wealthy party can draw upon her wealth to survive non-agreement. In this case, however, non-agreement means dirty development rather than clean development ... the largest of the poor nations will presumably proceed with what they would have done anyway: the most cost-effective available development strategy in which the costs of, for example, emissions of greenhouse gases are ignored, as they were during the development of now wealthy countries.[9]

Even the preparation of key climate documents and the collection of data on climate change can be unintentionally elitist and exclusionary. National Adaptation Programs of Action (NAPAs) are documents registered with the UNFCCC on the urgent and immediate adaptation needs of least developed countries. They are intended to be peer-reviewed sources of information which provide an objective assessment of ranked climate change adaptation needs and vulnerabilities, as well as sector-specific costs and benefits.[10] However, such documents often include economists and scientists as well as government officials in their creation, but rarely representatives from the most vulnerable groups, their professional associations, and civil society organizations.[11]

## Involuntary resettlement

Millions of individuals are involuntary resettled every year due to energy projects. About 4 million people are currently displaced by activities relating to hydroelectricity construction or operation annually, and 80 million have been displaced in the past fifty years from the construction of 300 large dams.[12] Yet, total installed capacity and investments in hydropower dwarfed that of all other major renewable sources of energy in 2009 and 2010; China roughly doubled its

[9] Henry Shue, "The Unavoidability of Justice," in *The International Politics of the Environment: Actors, Interests, and Institutions* (Oxford University Press, 1992), pp. 373–397.

[10] UNFCCC, 2010, NAPAs, available at http://unfccc.int/national_reports/napa/items/2719.php.

[11] Saleem Huq and Mizan R. Khan, "Equity in National Adaptation Programs of Action: The Case of Bangladesh," in Adger, Paavola, Huq, and Mace (eds.), *Fairness in Adaptation to Climate Change*, pp. 181–200.

[12] World Commission on Dams, *The Report of the World Commission on Dams*, 2001.

hydroelectric capacity from 2004 to 2009 and significant expansion is expected in Brazil, India, Russia, Turkey, and Vietnam – necessitating the need to relocate millions more people.[13]

This relocation, however, often proceeds without true and meaningful consultation and consent. In Sarawak, the largest state of Malaysia, the Sarawak Corridor of Renewable Energy (SCORE) would build no less than twelve hydroelectric dams connected to industrial facilities along the coast of Borneo. The Corridor would extend for some 320 kilometers from Tanjung Manis to Samalajau, covering an area of 70,709 square kilometers, more than half the size of the state. The Master Plan calls for $105 billion worth of investment by 2030 with the goal of expanding the Sarawak economy by a factor of five, increasing the number of jobs in the state by a factor of 2.5, and doubling the population to 4.6 million.

Rather than provide electricity to the local population, the dams will instead supply all of their electricity to factories and smelters. The EIAs associated with the first of these dams, the Bakun Hydroelectric Project, were conducted only after construction commenced, and have been criticized for vastly underestimating the facility's negative effect on water quality, ecosystems, and communities. Key decisions to proceed occurred without the consent of affected communities, even though Bakun Dam necessitated the forceful removal of 10,000 indigenous people and Murum will require the resettlement of 3,400 people. Community leaders in opposition to the project have been reputedly beaten, tortured, and, in some cases, murdered.[14]

In China, the construction of the massive 17,680 MW Three Gorges Dam in Hubei Province – the largest hydroelectric dam in the world, shown in Figure 6.1 – inundated a stretch of land 632 kilometers long and flooded 19 cities and 632 towns, necessitating the relocation and

---

[13] B.K. Sovacool and L.C. Bulan, "Behind an Ambitious Megaproject in Asia: The History and Implications of the Bakun Hydroelectric Dam in Borneo," *Energy Policy* 39(9) (September 2011), pp. 4842–4859.

[14] B.K. Sovacool and L.C. Bulan, "Energy Security and Hydropower Development in Malaysia: The Drivers and Challenges Facing the Sarawak Corridor of Renewable Energy (SCORE)," *Renewable Energy* 40(1) (April 2012), pp. 113–129; B.K. Sovacool and L.C. Bulan, "Meeting Targets, Missing People: The Energy Security Implications of the Sarawak Corridor of Renewable Energy (SCORE) in Malaysia," *Contemporary Southeast Asia* 33(1) (April 2011), pp. 56–82; B.K. Sovacool and L.C. Bulan, "They'll Be Dammed: The Sustainability Implications of the Sarawak Corridor of Renewable Energy (SCORE) in Malaysia," *Sustainability Science* 8(1) (January 2013), pp. 121–133.

**Figure 6.1** The Three Gorges Dam in China
*Source:* Photo taken by authors for Xinhua News Agency.

evacuation of 2 million people.[15] In southern Chile, the construction of the 690 MW Ralco Dam on the Alto BioBio River has similarly "disrupted the semi-nomadic lifestyle and world view of the Mapuchel Pehuenche people," an indigenous group. The project sponsor, Endesa, was accused of relying on the use of "rumors," "false information," and "threats" to push its agenda, and of violating the country's Indigenous Peoples Law.[16] Similarly, in Turkey, the Southeastern Anatolia Project built 7,400 MW of hydroelectric capacity on the Euphrates and Tigris Rivers, effectively doubling the country's irrigable farmland, but only at the expense of inducing water shortages for farmers and indigenous peoples in Iraq and Syria.[17]

In Indonesia, the state-owned coalmining enterprises responsible for most production are poorly regulated and have extensively displaced

[15] Steven M. Hoffman, "Negotiating Eternity: Energy Policy, Environmental Justice, and the Politics of Nuclear Waste," *Bulletin of Science, Technology & Society* 21(6) (December 2001), pp. 456–472.
[16] Marcos A. Orellana, "Indigenous Peoples, Energy and Environmental Justice – The Pangue/Ralco Hydroelectric Project in Chile's Alto BioBio," *Journal of Energy & Natural Resources Law* 23(4) (November 2005), pp. 511–528.
[17] Güven Eken, "Turkish Dam Boom Threatens Anatolian Rivers," *World Rivers Review*, International Rivers Network, June 2012.

communities without consultation or consent. Part of this involuntary resettlement has to do with Indonesia's constitution, which states that the natural resources of the country are to be exploited under state control – with no need for informed consent – for the maximum benefit of the people. The Ombilin coalmine, with reserves of 109 million tons, has disregarded local land rights entirely and improperly managed acid rock drainage and sediment ponds to the point where sixty square kilometers of land had to be abandoned by indigenous communities.[18]

Indeed, one wide-ranging international survey estimated that at least 2.6 million people have been displaced due to mining in India from 1950 to 2009, and individual mines in Brazil, Ghana, Indonesia, and South Africa have involuntarily displaced between 15,000 and 37,000 people (each) from their homes.[19] That study noted two troubling conclusions. First, the impact of such displacement extends beyond loss of land, which represented only 10 to 20 percent of impoverishment impacts, to include joblessness, homelessness, marginalization, food insecurity, increased health risks, social disarticulation, and the loss of civil and human rights. Second, it found that compensation for resettlement rarely occurred, and that when it did, such compensation was insufficient to restore let alone improve quality of life for the displaced.

Even climate change adaptation projects being implemented under Reducing Emissions from Deforestation and Degradation (REDD) have proceeded, at times, without proper consent and inflicted damages on local communities. One independent assessment from the Center for People and Forests warned that some governments have seized indigenous lands in order to capitalize on forest carbon revenues, and have utilized exploitable contracts that convince communities to knowingly accept terms that sign away land use rights and set unfair liability standards, ultimately decreasing the production of local food and deepening poverty. In the highlands of Ecuador, voluntary carbon-offset plantations participating in REDD proceeded without informing local communities and without impact assessments, delayed their delivery of promised payments to villages, and dismissed complaints and questions about company

[18] Chris Ballard, *Human Rights and the Mining Sector in Indonesia: A Baseline Study* (International Institute for Environment and Development, October 2001).

[19] Theodore E. Downing, *Avoiding New Poverty: Mining-Inducted Displacement and Resettlement* (International Institute for Environment and Development, April 2002).

activities without independent review.[20] In Uganda, two Norwegian companies purchased thousands of hectares of land with a fifty-year lease from the government to plant fast-growing eucalyptus and pine trees. The companies will receive millions of dollars of revenue from selling credits but pay rents of only $21,800 each year to the government. The companies have hired only a handful of local workers to tend the plantations (which are low maintenance anyway) and evicted 8,000 people from thirteen villages to make room for their projects.[21]

## Improper licensing and deception

Improper licensing and dishonesty can afflict energy facilities as well, with examples from nuclear reactors and pipelines proving most illustrative. In the United States, India, France, the Soviet Union, and China, nuclear power licensing and siting have all, at times, violated the principles of due process and informed consent in various ways. Unable to legally bar the public from participating, the nuclear industry in the United States has been accused of relying on different tactics to resist or minimize public participation in licensing and permitting procedures. Some of their more common practices include:

- Setting the timing of hearings so that interveners and the public must gather information and present safety concerns before receiving the documents necessary to adequately evaluate the risks of a project;
- Interpreting rules narrowly to exclude unfavorable evidence and safety concerns;
- Attenuating inquiries into safety issues by prematurely ending proceedings.

Critics argue that these practices were designed to intentionally prevent the public from having significant influence over where nuclear facilities and infrastructure will go.[22]

---

[20] Patrick Anderson, *Free, Prior, and Informed Consent: Principles and Approaches for Policy and Project Development* (Bangkok: RECOFTC and GIZ, February 2011).

[21] Ann E. Prouty, "The Clean Development Mechanism and Its Implications for Climate Justice," *Columbia Journal of Environmental Law* 34(2) (2009), pp. 513–540.

[22] Steven L. Del Sesto, *Science, Politics, and Controversy: Civilian Nuclear Power in the United States, 1946–1974* (Boulder: Westview Press, 1979).

In India, nuclear power projects have also been exempt from public hearings so as to minimize involvement and expedite approval. As one study concluded:

Public hearings for nuclear projects have been always short and rushed affairs with insufficient time for all interested participants to seek information or clarifications ... Not only is public participation devalued, it often falls short in procedural terms. At a number of hearings, members of the public have complained that they have not managed to get copies of EIA reports. Authorities have not read out their summary (minutes) of the proceedings and sought the consent of those who participated.[23]

To compound the problem, industry representatives were under no legal obligation to release information regarding the true costs of facilities in addition to medical and safety risks.[24]

Similarly, in France, when the construction of the Superphoenix fast breeder reactor in Creys-Malville began in 1968, the government did not notify citizens of its existence, did not consult local groups, and ignored opinions voiced by those who caught wind of the project.[25] The state simply expropriated, ignored appeals, then responded to protests by deploying the CRS (Compagnies Républicaines de Sécurité) – special riot police – which killed one demonstrator and wounded 100 others through the use of tear gas and batons.[26] Purdue University Professor Daniel P. Aldrich has gone as far as to call the French government "highly coercive," relying on "hard social control tools" against opponents of nuclear power.[27]

In the Soviet Union, when the Mayak Industrial Reprocessing Complex in the Southern Urals suffered a devastating accident, the government evacuated the 272,000 people living around the facility but told them that it was only an exercise. After the Chernobyl accident in 1986, the Soviet government did not begin evacuations until April 28

---

[23] M.V. Ramana and Divya Badami Rao, "The Environmental Impact Assessment Process for Nuclear Facilities: An Examination of the Indian Experience," *Environmental Impact Assessment Review* 30 (2010), 268–271.

[24] *Ibid.*

[25] Charles de Saillan, "Disposal of Spent Nuclear Fuel in the United States and Europe: A Persistent Environmental Problem," *Harvard Environmental Law Review* 34 (2010), pp. 462–519.

[26] Daniel P. Aldrich, *Site Fights: Divisive Facilities and Civil Society in Japan and the West* (Ithaca: Cornell University Press, 2008).

[27] *Ibid.*

(two full days after the meltdown) because plant operators had delayed reporting the accident to Moscow out of fear it would spoil forthcoming May Day celebrations. Even after learning of the disaster, national officials had planned on covering up the extent of the damage until a Swedish radiation monitoring station 800 miles northwest of Chernobyl reported abnormally high radiation levels.[28]

In China, its policies on land acquisition, lack of judicial independence, and low levels of public environmental awareness accelerated the rapid siting of nuclear plants and subordinated attempts to stop facilities from being constructed. For much of the past century, the Chinese constitution actually banned private land transactions, meaning land was "neither considered as a commodity nor as an asset for producing economic wealth."[29] This enabled the state to distribute parcels of land for nuclear power plants and related facilities directly and with complete control.[30]

The nuclear power sector is not alone in its procedural impropriety. The construction of the BTC pipeline in Central Asia, mentioned in Chapter 5, has destroyed roads, small-scale wells and water distribution systems, farming land, and community buildings. What British Petroleum and the BTC Company termed as "consultation" with villagers amounted to little more than officials from these corporations giving lengthy presentations and instructions followed with one two-minute question and answer session (restricted further by some villages being permitted to ask only one question). Resettlement action plans were supposed to be in place sixty days before construction in each village, so that people would be informed about land acquisition and resettlement, but in practice some villagers were never notified at all. The result was that many Azerbaijanis and Georgians protested the project by lying down in front of bulldozers and filing thousands of complaints and dozens of lawsuits. In some cases, such as the village of Zayam in the Shemkir Region of Azerbaijan, communities received no consultation at all, and villagers claim that their documents had been

---

[28] B.K. Sovacool, *Contesting the Future of Nuclear Power: A Critical Global Assessment of Atomic Energy* (London: World Scientific, 2011).

[29] Chengri Ding, "Land Policy Reform in China: Assessment and Prospects," *Land Use Policy* 20 (2003), pp. 109–120.

[30] Chi-Jen Yang, "A Comparison of the Nuclear Options for Greenhouse Gas Mitigation in China and in the United States," *Energy Policy* 39(6) (June 2011), pp. 3025–3028.

falsified by an employee of the BTC Company who kept their relocation money for himself.[31]

## Community marginalization

Another challenge relates to institutions, procedures, and processes that result in the unequal distribution of energy burdens, eroding the vitality of communities surrounding energy facilities. For example, many forms of energy production can promote "environmental racism" or the "milk and cream" problem: both within and between communities, a certain proportion of society reaps the benefits of cleaner energy sources while another, often larger proportion becomes worse off, leaving them disorganized and polluted.[32] Dirty infrastructure can sometimes create "national sacrifice zones" that condemn poorer communities to suffer disproportionately.[33] Most of those working in energy-related jobs with greater occupational hazards (such as coalmines or refineries) tend to be near the poverty line; poorer families have less capital to invest in energy efficiency and thus live in homes and drive vehicles that consume more energy; and lower-income families live in neighborhoods in closer proximity to conventional power plants, high-voltage transmission lines, nuclear reactors, municipal landfills, trash incinerators, pipelines, abandoned toxic dumps, and nuclear waste repositories (and thus are more exposed to the life-endangering pollution that they bring).[34]

In Eastern Europe, the Roma have been displaced from so many countries and cities that they are forced to reside in settlements akin to "environmental time bombs." Roma communities in the Czech Republic and Slovakia, for example, reside in flats located above abandoned mines where they are prone to flooding, and susceptible to breathing methane

---

[31] B.K. Sovacool, "Cursed by Crude: The Corporatist Resource Curse and the Baku–Tbilisi–Ceyhan (BTC) Pipeline," *Environmental Policy and Governance* 21(1) (January/February 2011), pp. 42–57; B.K. Sovacool, "Reconfiguring Territoriality and Energy Security: Global Production Networks and the Baku–Tbilisi–Ceyhan (BTC) Pipeline," *Journal of Cleaner Production* 32(9) (September 2012), pp. 210–218.

[32] Elise Boulding and Kenneth E. Boulding, *The Future: Images and Processes* (London: Sage Publications, 1995).

[33] Robert D. Bullard, *Unequal Protection: Environmental Justice and Communities of Color* (San Francisco: Sierra Club Books, 1994).

[34] Dorothy K. Newman and Don Day, *The American Energy Consumer* (Cambridge, MA: Ballinger Publishing Company, 1975).

gas. Others live in abandoned factory sites surrounded by mining wastes where children are fully exposed to toxins and suffer long-term effects to their health.[35] The Roma living along the Upper Tisza River in Hungary also must confront the highest risks of floods in the entire country.[36] The situation with landfills in Scotland and nuclear waste storage facilities in Taiwan have also followed a similar trend, with studies confirming that the poor or marginalized suffer a "triple jeopardy" of being most exposed to higher levels of pollution, being more vulnerable and more likely to suffer health impacts, and being least responsible for generating environmental problems in the first place.[37]

One study concluded that current nuclear power and waste sites, as well as dumps, mines, and other energy facilities, express characteristics that make "peripheral communities" prone to accepting them set apart from vibrant (and often wealthier) urban communities.[38] These peripheral communities tend to be:

- *Remote*, either geographically separated from population centers or relatively inaccessible;
- *Economically marginal*, with most being homogeneous in terms of social and demographic background and dependent on the energy industry as a dominant employer;
- *Politically powerless*, with most key political decisions being made elsewhere, often in metropolitan centers;
- *Culturally defensive*, with residents expressing ambivalent or ambiguous attitudes towards nuclear energy combined with feelings of isolation and a fatalistic acceptance of nuclear activities;
- *Environmentally degraded*, meaning they tend to occupy previously polluted land or are close to places where environmental risks are already present.

---

[35] Tamara Steger, *Making the Case for Environmental Justice in Central and Eastern Europe* (Budapest: CEU Center for Environmental Law and Policy, March 2007).

[36] Joanne Linnerooth-Bayer and Anna Vari, "Extreme Weather and Burden Sharing in Hungary," in Adger, Paavola, Huq, and Mace (eds.), *Fairness in Adaptation to Climate Change*, pp. 239–259.

[37] Gordon Walker, *Environmental Justice: Concepts, Evidence, and Politics* (London: Routledge, 2012).

[38] A. Blowers and P. Leroy, "Power, Politics and Environmental Inequality: A Theoretical and Empirical Analysis of the Process of 'Peripheralisation,'" *Environmental Politics*, 3(2) (Summer 1994), pp. 197–228.

In essence, the researchers concluded that noxious energy facilities will invariably migrate to communities that lack the political, social, and economic strength to oppose them, especially indigenous peoples and tribes, often at the extreme social and geographical periphery of society.[39]

Consequently, people of color and minorities must bear a disproportionate share of the world's poisons and environmental hazards as the consequences of energy production move "from white, affluent suburbs to neighborhoods of those without clout."[40] One meta-analysis of studies documenting the spatial distribution of pollution found "clear and unequivocal evidence that income and racial biases in the distribution of environmental hazards exist."[41] A similar assessment of environmental pollution across 2,083 counties in the United States found that "toxic releases increase as a function of [minorities in] the population."[42] Sadly, the existing configuration of the energy industry reinforces these inequities since people living in poverty pay proportionally more for energy services, meaning they are less likely to accumulate the wealth needed to make investments to escape their poverty, and the deleterious health effects from energy-related pollution are more likely to impact household members. Readers should take note, too, that we're only talking here about the disproportionate effects of generating and producing energy; we are not discussing the adverse effects of having too little of it, something detailed in Chapter 7.

Even in the United States, injustices are apparent. African Americans consume more fish in larger portions than other Americans, meaning that they have a higher exposure to mercury poisoning from power plants and cars.[43] More than two-thirds of all African Americans live

---

[39] C. Michael Rasmussen, "Getting Access to Billions of Dollars and Having a Nuclear Waste Backyard," *Journal of Land Resources and Environmental Law* 18 (1998), pp. 335–367.

[40] Kimberlianne Podlas, "A New Sword to Slay the Dragon: Using New York Law to Combat Environmental Racism," *Fordham Urban Law Journal* 23 (Summer 1996), pp. 1283–1294.

[41] Paul Mohai and Bunyan Bryant, *Environmental Racism: Reviewing the Evidence* (Boulder: Westview Press, 1992), p. 174.

[42] David W. Allen, "Social Class, Race, and Toxic Releases in American Counties," *Social Science Journal* 38 (2001), pp. 13–25.

[43] Martha H. Keating and Felicia Davis, *Air of Injustice: African Americans and Power Plant Pollution* (Washington, DC: Clean Air Task Force, October 2002).

within 30 miles of a coal-fired power plant. They are rushed to the emergency room for asthma attacks at more than four times the national average, and have children three times as likely to be hospitalized for treatment of asthma.[44] About half of African American children have unacceptable levels of mercury and lead in the bloodstream compared to 16 percent of the general population, and nationwide studies demonstrate that the air in communities of color contain higher levels of PM, carbon monoxide, ozone, and $SO_2$.[45]

Energy burdens are also concentrated among certain locations and age groups. Ohio has the most polluted air of any state in the nation, and the 1.4 million people living there in Cuyahoga County face a cancer risk more than 100 times the goal established by the Clean Air Act.[46] One of the most comprehensive studies ever undertaken on environmental externalities, a $3 million, three year investigation by ORNL and Resources for the Future, found that power plant pollution was primarily responsible for increased mortality among the elderly, the very young, and individuals with preexisting respiratory disease.[47] It also found that the effects of airborne pollutants from power plants on human health were two orders of magnitude greater in the southeast. Analogously, heat waves, worsening because of climate change, unequally affect the old and homeless. Of the 2003 heat wave in France which caused 14,729 excess deaths, 11,731 of them were in those people over the age of seventy-five; the homeless and elderly have also borne a disproportionate number of heat-related deaths in the Netherlands and Spain.[48]

---

[44] Deanne M. Ottaviano, *Environmental Justice: New Clean Air Act Regulations and the Anticipated Impact on Minority Communities* (New York: Lawyer's Committee for Civil Rights Under Law, 2003).

[45] Adam Swartz, "Environmental Justice: A Survey of the Ailments of Environmental Racism," *Social Justice Law Review* 2 (Summer 1994), pp. 35–37.

[46] Ottaviano, *Environmental Justice*, pp. 5–8.

[47] US Department of Energy and the Commission of the European Communities, *US–EC Fuel Cycle Study: Background Document to the Approach and Issues* (Knoxville, TN: ORNL, November 1992, ORNL/M-2500); and US Department of Energy and the Commission of the European Communities, *Estimating Externalities of Coal Fuel Cycles* (Knoxville, TN: ORNL, September 1994, UDI-5119–94); Russell Lee, *Externalities and Electric Power: An Integrated Assessment Approach* (Oak Ridge, TN: ORNL, 1995).

[48] Walker, *Environmental Justice*, pp. 191–192.

## What is justice?

Like the concepts of human rights discussed in Chapter 5, notions of due process, fair treatment under the law, and procedural justice have a rich history.

### Due process

Law Professor Jacob G. Hornberger traces their foundation back to the year 1215, when English barons convinced King John to admit that his powers over subjects were limited by principles of fairness and justice.[49] This agreement came to be known as the *Magna Carta*, or Great Charter, and it stated that

No free man shall be seized or imprisoned, or stripped of his rights or possessions, or outlawed or exiled, or deprived of his standing in any other way, nor will we proceed with force against him, or send others to do so, except by the lawful judgment of his equals or by the law of the land.

Such protections became further strengthened in 1608 when the English scholar, parliamentarian, and Judge Edward Coke (1552–1634) convincingly argued that men should be governed not by the arbitrariness of rulers, but by *legem terrae*, or the "law of the land," that is, "by the common law, statute law, or custom of England ... by the due course, and process of law."[50]

---

[49]  Jacob G. Hornberger, *The Bill of Rights: Due Process of Law* (Fairfax, VA: Future of Freedom Foundation, 2005).

[50]  Coke argued that the "tree of liberty" was made up of nine essential branches: "(1) That no man be taken or imprisoned, but *Per legem terrae*, that is, by the Common Law, Statute Law, or Custom of England; for these words, *Per legem terrae*, being towards the end of this Chapter, doe refer to all the precedent matters in this Chapter, and this hath the first place, because the liberty of a man's person is more precious to him, then all the rest that follow, and therefore it is great reason, that he should by Law be relieved therein, if he be wronged, as hereafter shall be showed. (2) No man shall be disseized, that is, put out of session, or dispossessed of his free-hold (that is) lands, or livelihood, or of his liberties, or free customs, that is, of such franchises, and freedoms, and free customs, as belong to him by his free birth-right, unless it be by the lawful judgment, that is, verdict of his equals (that is, of men of his own condition) or by the Law of the Land (that is, to speak it once for all) by the due course, and process of Law. (3) No man shall be out-lawed, made an exlex, put out of the Law, that is, deprived of the benefit of the Law, unless he be out-lawed according to the Law of

Coke's ideas on due process and liberty became enshrined in the United States as well, both in the original Constitution and through various additions, especially the Fifth Amendment which states that "No person shall ... be deprived of life, liberty, or property, without due process of law." Indeed, in the Declaration of Independence on July 4, 1776, Thomas Jefferson (1743–1826) set forth a justification for the creation of government in society as securing a "fundamental, inherent, and preexisting right of the people." Jefferson reasoned that the government's monopoly on the use of force was needed to suppress murderers and thieves, but that in exchange it also had to subsume the responsibility of imposing justice and punishment on them.[51]

Writing more than a century later, German sociologist and philosopher Jürgen Habermas (1929–present) proposed his concept of "ideal speech communities" where "participation for all is possible" and "undistorted" communication can take place among all members of society.[52] Instead of emphasizing the achievement of only the rational, instrumentalist goals of the state, Habermas argued that communication must be used to build mutual trust, comprehension, and social capital. Key principles for achieving his harmonization of objectives through communication include recognition of all relevant stakeholders, spreading ownership, and appreciating diverse interests.[53] These Habermasian ideals contrast to "technocratic" methods of planning whereby public managers or experts possess all objective knowledge

---

the Land. (4) No man shall be exiled, or banished out of his Country, that is, *Nemo perdet patriam*, no man shall lose his Country, unless he be exiled according to the Law of the Land. (5) No man shall be in any sort destroyed (*Destruere. i. quod prius structum, & factum fuit, penitus evertere & diruere*) unless it be by the verdict of his equals, or according to the Law of the Land. (6) No man shall be condemned at the Kings suite, either before the King in his Bench, where the Pleas are Coram Rege, (and so are the words, *Nec super eum ibimus*, to be understood) nor before any other Commissioner, or Judge whatsoever, and so are the words, *Nec super eum mittemus*, to be understood, but by the judgment of his Peers, that is, equals, or according to the Law of the Land. (7) We shall sell to no man Justice or Right. (8) We shall deny to no man Justice or Right. (9) We shall defer to no man Justice or Right." See Edward Coke's *Liberty and Power*.

[51] Hornberger, *The Bill of Rights*.

[52] J. Habermas, *Legitimation Crisis*, trans. Thomas McCarthy (Boston, MA: Beacon Press, 1976).

[53] N. Harris, "Collaborative Planning: From Theoretical Foundations to Practical Forms," in P. Allemendinger and M. Tewdwr-Jones (eds.), *Planning Futures: New Directions for Planning Theory* (London: Routledge, 2002).

and make decisions on the basis of maximizing social welfare. Instead, Habermas is arguing that justice and due process involve "collaborative" methods of planning that regard knowledge as socially situated and entirely within the domain of ordinary people. Habermas suggested that when technocratic and exclusionary methods of planning prevail, a "legitimation crisis" occurs for those in power, who are distant from their electorate and make decisions without involving them or accepting their forms of knowledge.

## Procedural justice

Contemporary justice theorists and advocates have built upon these earlier ideas to build a more elaborate array of protections often known as "procedural justice," "procedural rights," "retributive justice," "compensation for injuries and unfair exchange," "justice as participation," "fundamental justice," and "representative justice."[54] Generally, these protections center on these interrelated justice issues:

- Who gets to decide and set rules and laws? Which parties and interests are recognized in decision-making?
- By what process do they make such decisions?
- How impartial or fair are the institutions, instruments, and objectives involved?

As geographers John Farrington and Conor Farrington put it:

A just society is one that *inter alia* grants the opportunity of participation in society to all of its members, and a society will certainly be unjust if it does not grant this opportunity to all of its members. Thus, a just society is *inter alia* a socially inclusive one, and a society is unjust if it is a socially exclusive one.[55]

---

[54] John Ash, "New Nuclear Energy, Risk, and Justice: Regulatory Strategies for an Era of Limited Trust," *Politics & Policy* 38(2) (2010), pp. 255–284; W. Neil Adger, Jouni Paavola, and Saleemul Huq, "Toward Justice in Adaptation to Climate Change," in Adger, Paavola, Huq, and Mace (eds.), *Fairness in Adaptation to Climate Change*, pp. 1–19; Brian Barry, *Justice as Impartiality* (Oxford University Press, 1995); Debra J. Salazar and Donald K. Alper, "Justice and Environmentalisms in the British Columbia and US Pacific Northwest Environmental Movements," *Society & Natural Resources* 24(8) (2011), pp. 767–784.

[55] John Farrington and Conor Farrington, "Rural Accessibility, Social Inclusion and Social Justice: Towards Conceptualization," *Journal of Transport Geography* 13 (2005), pp. 1–12.

Unlike the rights- and virtue-based notions of justice espoused in the earlier chapters, procedural theories of justice are all oriented with process – with the fairness and transparency of decisions, the adequacy of legal protections, and the legitimacy and inclusivity of institutions involved in decision-making.[56] Procedural justice deals with recognition (who is recognized), participation (who gets to participate), and power (how power is distributed in decision-making forums).[57] New Zealand philosopher Gillian Brock argues that such procedures are an instrumental part of preserving basic fundamental liberties, such as the ability to be informed about what is happening to one's environment, the opportunity to have meaningful input into social affairs and decisions that affect one's community or well-being, and the ability to seek justice through an independent judiciary when such liberties are violated.[58]

Though procedural justice may strike some as dry and unimportant, fair procedures matter because they tend to promote better – more equitable but also more efficient and effective – outcomes, decisions, and investments.[59] Sociologist Claire Haggett compellingly argues that there are strong *pragmatic* reasons for ensuring due process.[60] Public involvement can increase the likelihood of support, and therefore ultimate approval, for the siting of energy projects. As she writes, "while fiscal regulations and subsidies, technical efficiency and political deliberations all affect the deployment of renewables, the stark fact remains that all of this matters little if there is no public support for a development."

---

[56] Burns H. Weston, "Climate Change and Intergenerational Justice: Foundational Reflections," *Vermont Journal of Environmental Law* 9 (2008), pp. 375–430; see also Burns H. Weston and Tracy Bach, *Climate Change and Intergenerational Justice: Present Law, Future Law* (South Royalton: Vermont Law School, 2008).

[57] Paavola, Adger, and Huq, "Multifaceted Justice in Adaptation to Climate Change."

[58] Gillian Brock, *Global Justice: A Cosmopolitan Account* (Oxford University Press, 2009).

[59] Paul Dolan, Richard Edlin, Aki Tsuchiya, and Allan Wailoo, "It Ain't What You Do, It's the Way that You Do It: Characteristics of Procedural Justice and Their Importance in Social Decision-Making," *Journal of Economic Behavior & Organization* 64 (2007), pp. 157–170.

[60] Claire Haggett, "Public Engagement in Planning for Renewable Energy," in Simin Davoudi, Jenny Crawford, and Abid Mehmood (eds.), *Planning for Climate Change: Strategies for Mitigation and Adaptation for Spatial Planners* (London: Earthscan, 2009), pp. 297–307.

Public involvement can also provide new knowledge, and identify new goals, with a discussion of merits and impacts contributing to the determination of what a good outcome even is or should be for a particular energy project. Yale Professor Ian G. Barbour writes that "citizen participation is a source of information about public attitudes and perceptions of which assessors might otherwise be unaware" and that "later protests and opposition might be reduced if potential objectives were anticipated and alternatives were developed to take them into account."[61] Fair processes and public involvement can rehabilitate eroded trust in authorities and institutions. Legal scholar Sanford Lewis adds that public involvement, open information and deliberation can help to counter corporate cover-ups, false advertising campaigns, biased research, and the manipulation of public relations.[62]

One assessment of case studies across Europe, Latin America and Asia even found that "low-cost, high-quality" delivery of electricity, water, and natural gas rested on "democratic regulation" which involved complete open public access to information and full public participation in setting prices and standards of service.[63] Conversely, "closed" decision-making and limited public involvement was correlated with higher prices, less reliable service, industry job losses, and hardships for the poor.

Because of its intrinsic and pragmatic value, notions of due process related to energy and the environment have become enshrined in various facets of international law. Principle 10 of the 1992 Rio Declaration on Environment and Development, proclaimed at the same time the UNFCCC was signed, stated the global right to due process as follows:

Environmental issues are best handled with the participation of all concerned citizens ... At the national level, each individual shall have appropriate access to information concerning the environment that is held by public authorities, including information on hazardous materials and activities in their communities, and the opportunity to participate in decision-making processes. States

---

[61] Ian G. Barbour, *Technology, Environment, and Human Values* (Westport: Praeger, 1980), p. 204.

[62] Sanford Lewis, "The Precautionary Principle and Corporate Disclosure," in Carolyn Raffensperger and Joel A. Tickner (eds.), *Protecting Public Health and the Environment: Implementing the Precautionary Principle* (Washington, DC: Island Press, 1999), pp. 241–251.

[63] Greg Palast, Jerrold Oppenheim, and Theo MacGregor, *Democracy and Regulation: How the Public Can Govern Essential Services* (London: Pluto Press, 2003).

shall facilitate and encourage public awareness and participation by making information widely available. Effective access to judicial and administrative proceedings, including redress and remedy, shall be provided.[64]

Some of the unanimous conclusions adopted by the International Labor Office in 1999 concerning the provision of water, gas, and electricity supplies mention that "transparency in information and procedures should be taken into consideration so that there can be positive results for all," that "social dialogue should take place at all appropriate stages of the decision-making process," and that "utility and government information and methods must be open for review by industry, workers' representatives and the public."[65] Article 7 of the Aarhus Convention, which entered into force in October 2001, states that "Each Party shall make appropriate practical and/or other provisions for the public to participate during the preparation of plans and programs relating to the environment, within a transparent and fair framework, having provided the necessary information to the public."[66] Similar statutes and claims supporting public involvement in decision-making appear in the 1993 North American Agreement on Environmental Cooperation, the 1994 UN Convention to Combat Desertification, and a series of bilateral treaties.

The next logical question is, of course, who represents the public, or who counts as a stakeholder? In most cases, typical stakeholders and representatives of the public would include:

- Local people (individuals) and communities (for example, villages) likely to be affected by a project. Traditional leaders or representatives on community-level bodies such as ward councils can be consulted to obtain a community viewpoint, as can nonresident social groups who may use local resources such as pastoralists;
- Selected social categories, for example women, the elderly, or the poorest in society;
- Religious leaders;
- Politicians;

[64] International Council on Human Rights Policy, *Climate Change and Human Rights: A Rough Guide* (Versoix, Switzerland: International Council on Human Rights Policy, 2008).

[65] Palast, Oppenheim, and MacGregor, *Democracy and Regulation.*

[66] International Council on Human Rights Policy, *Climate Change and Human Rights.*

- NGOs and voluntary organizations such as local community development or resource users' groups, gender-based groups, labor unions and cooperatives;
- Private sector bodies such as professional societies, trade associations and chambers of commerce;
- The different media (newspapers, radio, television); and
- National and local government ministries, departments, and statutory agencies whose remit and responsibilities includes areas and sectors likely to be affected (such as health, natural resources, and land use).

Consultation and involvement can also take a variety of forms. It can include public meetings without restrictions on access and attendance, or advisory panels chosen to represent stakeholder groups. It can include open houses – a staffed facility in an accessible location which contains information on a proposed project – or interviews and questionnaires with selected community representatives. It can also include some of the participatory appraisal techniques discussed in the next section.

Regardless of the stakeholders and type of involvement, general principles exist regarding how meetings ought to be conducted. Relevant information must be offered in a way that is easily understood by non-experts. Sufficient time must be given for individuals to read and digest information and its implication. Mechanisms to incorporate feedback must be offered so that concerns can be addressed. The place and date of meetings must encourage maximum attendance and free exchange of views, including those that may wish to oppose a project.[67]

Actual engagement with the public can take a variety of forms. One type is "engagement as information provision," attempting to inform and even educate the public on energy issues. This keeps in line with the traditional "decide, announce, defend" mentality of informing people of plans that have been made, and distributing emails, leaflets, advertising, and providing exhibitions and displays. One type is "engagement as consultation," which seeks not only to provide information to a passive public, but also to actively solicit feedback from them. Another type is "engagement as deliberation," where the public are not just permitted to discuss plans, but are thoroughly involved in their development. This shifts the public's role from participation to consultation, and though it

---

[67] Hussein Abaza, Ron Bisset, and Barry Sadler, *Environmental Impact Assessment and Strategic Environmental Assessment: Towards an Integrated Approach* (UNEP, 2004).

is rarer, common examples include citizens' juries, interactive panels, and workshops.[68]

In sum, when aggregated and applied to the domain of energy, a procedurally just world would provide meaningful involvement and access to the decision-making process. It would ensure the availability of information about energy, a condition of participation and informed consent. It would seek to include and represent minorities and all stakeholders in decision-making, at all stages of the energy process, from agenda setting and formulation to siting and evaluation. It would also provide access to legal processes for challenging violations of energy rights, something touched upon in Chapter 5.[69]

## What is to be done?

As this section argues, a rich mosaic of interrelated tools – including better information disclosure and auditing, community consultation and stakeholder involvement, participatory technology assessment, and the practice of free prior informed consent (FPIC) – are available to justice advocates wishing to ensure due process and fair and impartial procedures throughout the energy sector.

### Better information disclosure and auditing

One relatively simple way to enhance due process is to provide information about energy, climate change, environmental pollution, and other related topics to the public. For instance, in the United States, access to information is one of five key principles for setting electric utility tariffs (the other four are just and reasonable rates, prices that match costs, minimizing conflicts of interest, and protecting utility investments). As a general rule, "rights of transparency and participation" must be observed to the degree that "utility prices are set in a glass bowl."[70] As a result, to justify their prices electricity, water, gas, and other utilities typically file 300 to 3,000 pages of explanation, calculations, and documentation. If requested by *any* customer, the utility company must also provide documentation to back up its initial filing

---

[68] Haggett, "Public Engagement in Planning for Renewable Energy."
[69] Walker, *Environmental Justice.*
[70] Palast, Oppenheim, and MacGregor, *Democracy and Regulation.*

and answer all questions relating to costs and operations. In total, a typical price review can exceed 100,000 pages of information, all of it public. As governance scholars Greg Palast, Jerrold Oppenheim, and Theo MacGregor surmise, in such a process "Who is excluded? No one. The whole point of democracy is that it is open."[71]

Sometimes information to the public can take the form of environmental audits or inventories. Institutions, both public and private, can be given an "affirmative duty to study" the risks or environmental hazards involved in their activities, as with an oil company being required to give citizens access to company studies of contamination, dioxin, and other toxic chemical emissions, and evaluations of pollution prevention opportunities. Institutions can also be assigned an "obligation of rapid disclosure and transparency" where they disclose all of their data concerning pollution or even social and economic damage.[72] The paradigmatic example here is also from the United States, and it relates to the country's Toxics Release Inventory (TRI), a freely accessible database that provides information on about 650 chemicals released into the environment. In its latest and most up-to-date incarnation, the TRI contained data on how nearly 22,000 industrial and government facilities – including many electric utilities, wastewater treatment sites, and oil and gas systems – used, managed, disposed, and recycled their hazardous wastes. From the start of the program in 1988 to 2007, facilities decreased their onsite and offsite releases of TRI listed chemicals by 61 percent, a reduction amounting to almost 2 billion pounds (one million metric tons) of chemical pollution per year.[73]

## Broader public involvement and participatory energy decision-making

By itself, information may be necessary, but insufficient, to guarantee due process. There are numerous other ways in which community participation and involvement can enhance procedural energy justice through community-based research, consultations, debates, conferences, and referendums.

---

[71] *Ibid.*   [72] Lewis, "The Precautionary Principle and Corporate Disclosure."
[73] M.A. Brown and B.K. Sovacool, "The Toxics Release Inventory in the United States, 1988–2007," in *Climate Change and Global Energy Security: Technology and Policy Options* (Cambridge, MA: MIT Press, 2011), pp. 307–316.

### Community-based energy research

Contrasting "traditional" methods of conducting research, where experts often drive research agendas, community-based research serves a local group and encourages participation of community members at all levels. Democracy scholar Richard Sclove argues that "community based research offers a tested and relatively economical means for addressing a wide variety of social, economic, and environmental problems."[74]

Fruitful examples of community-based research related to energy abound. The Jacksonville Community Council Incorporation, a broad-based civic organization dedicated to improving the quality of life in northeast Florida, has utilized research from human service institutions, labor leaders, and the public at large to set guidelines for preventing the flooding and enhancing the drainage of streets. The Neighborhood Planning for Community Revitalization, a consortium of colleges and universities in Minneapolis and St. Paul, Minnesota, funds research by local community groups to assist the city and state with setting air and water quality standards. One spinoff from this work has the city of Minneapolis, Minnesota and CenterPoint Energy operating a series of innovative neighborhood energy workshops. Staff working for the city identify and train local volunteers to serve as block captains who then invite their neighbors to energy training sessions. These workshops emphasize providing information about energy use habits, the energy efficiency and consumption of domestic appliances, and techniques that could be implemented quickly to save energy such as caulking or adding insulation. In Massachusetts, the Childhood Cancer Research Institute specializes in epidemiological studies of radiation – such as those from nuclear power plants – conducted jointly by experts and the public.

### Participatory technology assessment and consensus conferences

Another tool to improve the transparency and accountability of energy decisions is participatory technology assessment (PTA) – involving the public through committees and panels concerning decisions about science and technology. PTA offers at least three benefits compared to decision-making done only by experts. First, it increases democracy, satisfying the "democratic right" of citizens to be entitled to direct

[74] Richard B. Sclove and Madeleine L. Scammell, "Practicing the Principle," in Raffensperger and Tickner (eds.), *Protecting Public Health*, pp. 252–265.

participation and effective representation in technological decisions. Second, experience with PTAs over the past decade have shown that laypeople tend to excel at articulating previously unforeseen ethical and moral concerns that experts might have "missed." Third, PTAs can reduce costs by avoiding and reducing controversy and public disapproval proactively. As one study concluded, "when science and technology decisions are demonstrably responsive to the concerns of a wider range of citizens, the public is more likely to accept those decisions."[75]

One type of PTA is a "consensus conference." Developed throughout the 1980s by the Danish Board of Technology, consensus conferences are designed to "stimulate broad and intelligent social debate on policy issues involving technical complexity and scientific uncertainty."[76] Such conferences elevate ordinary laypeople to positions of influence and prominence, and also create a forum open to the public that ensures they become better informed about salient issues. Both the conference itself and its judgment, usually written in a formal report, become a focal point for media attention, typically at a time when the issue at hand is due for debate in parliament.[77] Since 1987, the Danish Board of Technology has organized twenty consensus conferences on topics ranging from genetic engineering to educational technology, food irradiation, air pollution, human infertility, sustainable agriculture, telecommuting, and the future of private automobiles. Moreover, no less than seven other countries – France, Japan, the Netherlands, Norway, Switzerland, the United Kingdom, the United States – have held their own consensus conferences. Table 6.1 shows seven successful PTA experiences spanning the last decade – though it also shows that the PTA process can become costly. Regardless, one such conference, held by Landscape Design Associates in the United Kingdom in 2000, helped build "consensus" over wind energy by incorporating the concerns of the rural public, leading to the more efficient siting of wind turbines.[78]

[75] Richard Sclove, *Reinventing Technology Assessment: A Twenty-First Century Model* (Washington, DC: Woodrow Wilson International Center for Scholars, April 2010).

[76] Sclove and Scammell, "Practicing the Principle."

[77] See *ibid.*; Richard E. Sclove, "Town Meetings on Technology: Consensus Conferences as Democratic Participation," in Daniel Lee Kleinman (ed.), *Science, Technology, and Democracy* (State University of New York Press, 2000), pp. 33–48.

[78] Haggett, "Public Engagement in Planning for Renewable Energy."

**Table 6.1 Participatory technology assessments undertaken from 2005 to 2009**

| Project | Description | Year | Total cost (USD) | Cost per participant (USD) |
|---|---|---|---|---|
| Worldwide views on global warming | 4,000 citizens from 38 nations on 6 continents deliberate at 44 sites for one day | 2009 | $3.5 million | $900 |
| European citizens' consultations | 1,600 citizens from 27 EU nations deliberate for 3 weekends in national meetings | 2009 | $2.9 million | $1,800 |
| EuroPolis Project – Europewide deliberative poll | 348 citizens from 27 EU nations deliberate in Brussels for 3 days | 2009 | $3.6 million | $10,400 |
| US National Citizens' Technology Forum on nanotechnology and human enhancement | 74 US citizens and residents at 6 sites meet for 6 days face-to-face and hold 9 2-hour sessions | 2008 | $500,000 | $6,700 |
| Tomorrow's Europe – Europewide deliberative poll | 362 citizens from 27 EU nations deliberate in Brussels for 3 days | 2007 | $2.2 million | $6,000 |
| Meeting of Minds | 126 multilingual citizens from 9 EU nations hold 6 days of national meetings and 4 days of pan-European meetings | 2005–2006 | $2.6 million | $23,000 |
| Typical national consensus conference in Europe | 16 participants from 1 nation meet for 8 days | – | $290,000 | $18,000 |

*Source:* Adapted from Claire Haggett, "Public Engagement in Planning for Renewable Energy," in Simin Davoudi, Jenny Crawford, and Abid Mehmood (eds.), *Planning for Climate Change: Strategies for Mitigation and Adaptation for Spatial Planners* (London: Earthscan, 2009), pp. 297–307.

## Debates, referendums, review boards, and consultation

Still other ways to involve the public include debates, referendums, review boards, and mandated consultation. In January of 1974, for instance, the Swedish government started a campaign of study groups, organized not only by political parties but also by companies, labor unions, and community institutions, to debate national policy on nuclear power. All in all, 80,000 people participated representing 1 percent of the population at that time. They influenced the government's change in energy policy in 1975 when it committed to decreasing energy growth by 2 percent, placing higher taxes on energy, and reducing deployment plans for nuclear power.[79] Similar processes occurred in Germany in November 1978, Austria in 1980, and the Soviet Union in 1986 and 1987, when public involvement, in part, convinced governments to change their stances on nuclear power.[80]

Moving to contemporary examples, the government of Saskatchewan has created a Saskatchewan Rate Review Panel (SRRP) to advise on proposed tariff increases proposed by energy providers such as SaskEnergy, SaskPower, and the Saskatchewan Government Insurance Auto Fund. The SRRP reviews each rate application based on the criteria of reasonableness and fairness, and explicitly calls for public input and formal comments to be submitted via email, letters, and telephone messages. The SRRP then produces a transparent report and media release summarizing their views and recommendations to appropriate government ministers.[81]

In Nepal, the government currently requires that all commercial energy projects adhere to a "participatory approach" stipulated by the country's Water Resources, Electricity, and Environmental Protection Acts. An Environmental Core Group consists of 110 government members from seventeen ministries and departments as well as ten nongovernmental organizations and seven organizations representing consumers and the private sector. It is responsible for setting

---

[79] David W. Orr, "U.S. Energy Policy and the Political Economy of Participation," *Journal of Politics* 41 (1979), pp. 1027–1056.

[80] *Ibid.*, as well as B.K. Sovacool and S.V. Valentine. *The National Politics of Nuclear Power: Economics, Security, and Governance* (London: Routledge, 2012).

[81] SRRP, Fairness in Utility Rate Setting, May 2012, available at www.saskratereview.ca/.

national impact assessment guidelines so that they are "tailored to local needs and conditions."[82]

Similarly, Mexico's General Law of Ecological Balance and Environmental Protection, reformed in the 1990s, calls for "extensive public consultations" to "reflect the general trend toward greater public participation." The result has been a series of meetings with public officials and community leaders precipitating reforms implemented in the late 1990s and early 2000s. These reforms improved the accountability and transparency of how EIAs were done in the energy and infrastructure sectors, transferred some decision-making powers to state and local governments, and institutionalized citizen participation in the impact assessment process.[83]

The Akassa Project in the Nigerian state of Bayesla, funded by Statoil, British Petroleum, and Chevron-Texaco, offers a final example of effective consultation and stakeholder involvement. Though the Akassa Project was formally implemented by a Nigerian development NGO called ProNatura, it was driven entirely by the priorities of the local community. In contrast to the relatively superficial exercises previously undertaken by oil companies, ProNatura conducted in-depth appraisals of community needs involving extensive consultations over a long period of time – including ProNatura staff living in the community for more than a year, holding hundreds of meetings, and adhering to a planning process that involved not just chiefs but also women and youths. Based on this feedback, the Akassa Project focused on building the capacity of the community to set up new institutions, such as a development foundation and a community development council, that have since benefited more than 30,000 people from the Akassa clan.[84]

Another productive way of involving communities is to incentivize their ownership of actual energy infrastructure such as wind farms, solar panels, and rural mini-grids. This tends to democratize energy production and use by placing more of it in direct "control" of people and communities themselves, and it also cultivates environments with more trust and accountability and less social opposition to projects. Germany's feed-in tariff (FIT), passed in 1990, forced utilities to accept

---

[82] Abaza, Bisset, and Sadler, *Environmental Impact Assessment.*    [83] *Ibid.*

[84] Jedrzej George Frynas, "The False Development Promise of Corporate Social Responsibility: Evidence from Multinational Oil Companies," *International Affairs* 81(3) (2005), pp. 581–598.

solar energy from decentralized suppliers, meaning that most solar panels are now owned by residents, with more than 90 percent of panels operated by homeowners, cooperatives, and communities. Similarly, in Denmark, many communities own and operate wind turbines themselves and many entrepreneurs are "do-it-yourself" builders. More than 85 percent of wind farms there are owned by individuals and cooperatives.[85] In Nepal, community-led schemes tend to be more efficient and save money, with locally owned and operated mini-grids serving households for $94 per month compared to twice as much for grid electricity and $455 for diesel generators. Community cooperatives reduce electricity pilferage and system losses because networks are owned in part by the community, meaning people are ashamed to steal and waste electricity. Electricity theft and inefficiency across the entire Nepal Electricity Authority network averages 25 percent and, in some specific communities, surpasses 50 percent, yet community-owned grids report losses below 15 percent. They also report fewer unpaid bills, lower costs for meter reading and maintenance, and quicker connections to the grid.[86]

## Free prior informed consent

Going even further than information and involvement is FPIC, which refers to "a consultative process whereby a potentially affected community engages in an open and informed dialogue with individuals or other persons interested in pursuing activities in the area or areas occupied or traditionally used by the affected community."[87] The Center for People and Forests describes it as "the establishment of conditions under which people exercise their fundamental right to negotiate the terms of externally imposed policies, programs, and activities that directly affect their livelihoods or wellbeing, and to give or withhold their consent to them,"[88] making it distinct from mere negotiations and consultation.

---

[85] B.K. Sovacool and P. Ratan, "Conceptualizing the Acceptance of Wind and Solar Electricity," *Renewable and Sustainable Energy Reviews* 16(7) (September 2012), pp. 5268–5279.

[86] Annabel Yadoo and Heather Cruickshank, "The Value of Cooperatives in Rural Electrification," *Energy Policy* 38 (2010), pp. 2941–2947.

[87] Donald K. Anton and Dinah L. Shelton, *Environmental Protection and Human Rights* (New York: Cambridge University Press, 2011), p. 431.

[88] Anderson, *Free, Prior, and Informed Consent*.

Each of the four words in "FPIC" is meaningful.[89] "Freely given" implies that no coercion, intimidation, or manipulation has occurred: that potentially affected people freely offer their consent. "Prior" implies that consent has been sought sufficiently in advance of any meaningful decision to proceed with a project, before things like financing or impact assessments begin. "Fully informed" means that information about the project is provided that covers its nature, size, pace, reversibility, and scope; expected costs and benefits; the locality of areas to be affected; personnel and revenues likely to be involved; and procedures for resolving conflicts, should they occur. In other words, affected communities must understand their own rights, and the true implications of the project as best as they can be known, so that opponents and proponents can negotiate with equality of information. Lastly, "consent" means "harmonious, voluntary agreement with the measures designed to make the proposed project acceptable."[90] It does not necessarily mean absolute consensus: a majority of 51 percent suffices some of the time, and it does not always mean direct involvement; consensus can occur through representatives, through plebiscites (direct single issue votes) and referendums. It is, however, distinct from consultation – the act of merely discussing a project with a community – because it gives communities the ability to "say no."[91]

Though the concept of FPIC is remarkably new compared to other instruments of international law, it has been honed under stress by a flurry of agreements. One of its earliest codifications was the Nuremburg Code of 1947 concerning the conditions under which medical experiments could be carried out on human beings, and various iterations of consent have been stated by the 1966 International Bill of Rights, 1966 International Covenant on Economic, Social and Cultural Rights, and 1966 International Covenant on Political and Civil Rights, which all entered into force in 1976. The 1989 International Labor

---

[89] Robert Goodland, "Free, Prior and Informed Consent and the World Bank Group," *Sustainable Development Law & Policy* 4(2) (Summer 2004), pp. 66–74; United Nations Permanent Forum on Indigenous Issues (UNPFII), *Report of the International Workshop on Methodologies Regarding Free Prior and Informed Consent and Indigenous Peoples*, Document E/C.19/2005/3, submitted to the Fourth Session of UNPFII, May 16–17, 2005.

[90] Goodland, "Free, Prior and Informed Consent."

[91] Matt Finer, Clinton N. Jenkins, Stuart L. Pimm, Brian Keane, and Carl Ross, "Oil and Gas Projects in the Western Amazon: Threats to Wilderness, Biodiversity, and Indigenous Peoples," *PLoS One* 3(8) (August 2008), pp. 1–9.

Organization Indigenous and Tribal Peoples Convention states that indigenous peoples must be consulted about development projects on their territories, and the UN Food and Agricultural Organization established a 1989 "Code of Conduct" making consent mandatory. The 1992 Convention on Biological Biodiversity acknowledges that indigenous knowledge may only be used with prior approval and requires governments to protect indigenous cultures, and annexes to both the 1994 UNFCCC and 2009 REDD+ set safeguards detailing how vulnerable communities ought to be protected from energy projects. The 1989 Basel Convention, 1998 Rotterdam Convention on Free Prior Informed Consent, 2001 Stockholm Convention on Persistent Organic Pollutants, World Bank's Forest Carbon Partnership Facility and Forest Investment Program, Voluntary Carbon Standard practiced by some institutions trading credits under the 1998 Kyoto Protocol, and the Community Climate Biodiversity Alliance (a consortium of international NGOs) also all refer to FPIC as an important "right."[92]

---

[92] Goodland, "Free, Prior and Informed Consent."

# 7 | *Energy poverty, access, and welfare*

It starts as a good week. Despite the snow and cold, you celebrate your twenty-fifth birthday and first year on the job as the service engineer for an electric utility in Kazakhstan. You deposit a reasonable paycheck and are proud of bringing energy services to the households, enterprises, and industries that need it. This week, too, you have a new assignment: five houses within 10 miles of your service center have failed to pay their electric bills for the past two months. Your work orders are simple: disconnect those five homes from the electric grid.

How do you feel about this task? What do you ask yourself before you either implement the disconnection, or defer it? Does your company have any hard rules or soft policies to guide you? Does it matter whether a storm is coming in, or if a cold snap is expected? Or if you know the age, health, wealth, or merit of the people living in those homes? Does it matter if the cost of keeping "deadbeats" on the system will be paid by the utility's investors, or by surcharges from other homeowners who do pay their bills on time?

These are not abstract questions. Indeed, around the world, they come up literally millions of times per month throughout the year. Not surprisingly, different companies, different states, and different nations have different rules. One state in the United States, for example, provides that residential customers can, indeed should, be disconnected for nonpayment except between November 1 and March 31 – i.e. the winter months; or if a physician's certificate is provided indicating that a resident would suffer "an immediate and serious health hazard by the disconnection."[1] Even in such cases, use of a physician's certificate to prevent disconnection is limited to two

---

[1] State of Vermont, "The Vermont Statutes Online," Title 24 Municipal and City Government.

consecutive months and no more than three thirty-day periods in any
calendar year.[2]

Is this the proper standard? Should other customers bear the burden
of providing electricity to those who do not pay for it? Alternatively,
should we send out people like you, as a service engineer, to disconnect sick old people in freezing winter months when they are most
vulnerable? Or when there is a terrible drought or heat wave during
the blistering summer months? What is the "just and reasonable" in
such cases?

This chapter holds that eminent justice scholars John Rawls,
Amartya Sen, and Martha Nussbaum would be troubled by the
way the global energy system does not benefit the least-well-off, the
way it constrains people's capabilities and freedoms, the way it keeps
them literally in the dark and cold. They might be appalled by
how lack of access to electricity, dependence on traditional solid
fuels for cooking, and the incidence of fuel poverty create substantial burdens for billions of women and children. They would
argue that we ought to design justice principles based on a social
contract and a veil of ignorance. For if we imagine we will be transported into a future society without knowing our place in it, we want
the highest probability of having electricity and modern energy
ourselves in that future world, and that path is the one with the
most ubiquitous penetration of the grid and other modern energy
systems. Rawls, Sen, and Nussbaum, moreover, might be appeased
by the ability for a suite of technologies and public private partnerships to overcome and alleviate many of the constraints to modern
energy access, and to meet the ideals of welfare, difference, and
equality.

## What is reality?

The inaccessibility of modern forms of energy, the prevalence of fuel
poverty, and restrictions on intellectual property and technology are all
situations where the global energy system does not fairly or fully promote welfare.

---

[2] Vermont Public Service Board Rule 3.300: Disconnection of Residential Gas,
Electric, and Water Service.

## Accessibility, energy poverty, and drudgery

Perhaps the most obvious, and calamitous, aspect of the global energy system is energy poverty, a term that refers to lack of access to modern energy services. The most common way of conceptualizing energy poverty relates to two metrics: lack of access to electricity and dependence on solid biomass fuels for cooking and heating. According to the most recent data available, approximately 1.4 billion people still live without electricity, and an additional 2.7 billion people depend entirely on wood, charcoal, and dung for their domestic energy needs – figures reflected in Table 7.1.[3] Of about 7 billion people in the world:

- 500 million consume a yearly average of 10,000 kWh/household;
- 2.5 billion average 5,000 kWh/household;
- 2.5 billion average 1,000 kWh/household;
- 1.4 billion live without electricity at all.

There are other situations where modern energy systems literally bypass those most in need – like in the Congo, where the world's longest transmission line carries electrons past millions of households without access so that it can feed aluminum smelters and copper mines,[4] or in southern Israel, where the high-voltage wires depicted in Figure 7.1 do not enable connections from "unrecognized Bedouin villages" just south of Be'er Sheva in the Negev desert. This energy deprivation for the bottom of the pyramid results in four interrelated sets of negative consequences: poverty, death, gender inequality, and environmental degradation.

Poverty and energy deprivation go hand-in-hand, with energy expenses accounting for a significant proportion of household incomes in many developing countries. Generally, 20 to 30 percent of annual income in poor households is directly expended on energy fuels, and an additional 20 to 40 percent is expended on indirect costs associated with collecting and using that energy, such as healthcare expenses, injury, or loss of time. In other words, the poor pay on average eight times more

---

[3] International Energy Agency, UN Development Program, UN Industrial Development Organization, *Energy Poverty: How to Make Modern Energy Access Universal?* (Paris: OECD, 2010).

[4] International Rivers Network, *Congo's Energy Divide: Hydropower for Mines and Export, Not the Poor* (March 2011), pp. 1–4.

Table 7.1 *Number and share of population without access to modern energy services, 2009*

| | Without access to electricity | | Dependence on traditional solid fuels for cooking | |
|---|---|---|---|---|
| | Population (million) | Share of population (%) | Population (million) | Share of population (%) |
| Africa | 587 | 58 | 657 | 65 |
| Nigeria | 76 | 49 | 104 | 67 |
| Ethiopia | 69 | 83 | 77 | 93 |
| Congo | 59 | 89 | 62 | 94 |
| Tanzania | 38 | 86 | 41 | 94 |
| Kenya | 33 | 84 | 33 | 83 |
| Other Sub-Saharan Africa | 310 | 68 | 335 | 74 |
| North Africa | 2 | 1 | 4 | 3 |
| Asia | 675 | 19 | 1,921 | 54 |
| India | 289 | 25 | 836 | 72 |
| Bangladesh | 96 | 59 | 143 | 88 |
| Indonesia | 82 | 36 | 124 | 54 |
| Pakistan | 64 | 38 | 122 | 72 |
| Myanmar | 44 | 87 | 48 | 95 |
| Rest of developing Asia | 102 | 6 | 648 | 36 |
| Latin America | 31 | 7 | 85 | 19 |
| Middle East | 21 | 11 | 0 | 0 |
| Developing countries | 1,314 | 25 | 2,662 | 51 |
| World | 1,417 | 19 | 2,662 | 39 |

*Source:* Adapted from the International Energy Agency website in October 2012.

Figure 7.1 Bedouin villages in Southern Israel without access to the electricity grid that surrounds them
*Source:* Photo courtesy of Jenny Thomas from Vermont Law School.

for the same unit of energy than other income groups.[5] In extreme cases, some of the poorest households directly spend 80 percent of their income obtaining cooking fuels.[6]

In Africa, twenty-five of the forty-four poorest countries in the Sub-Saharan region face "crippling electricity shortages." Lawrence Musaba, the manager of the Southern African Power Pool, states that "we've had no significant capital injection into generation and transmission, from either the private or public sectors, for 15, maybe 20 years." Excluding South Africa, the most developed country in the region, the remaining

---

[5] F. Hussain, "Challenges and Opportunities for Investments in Rural Energy," presentation to the United Nations Economic and Social Commission for Asia and the Pacific (UNESCAP) and International Fund for Agricultural Development Inception Workshop on Leveraging Pro-Poor Public-Private-Partnerships (5Ps) for Rural Development, UN Convention Center, Bangkok, Thailand, September 26, 2011.

[6] Jamil Masud, Diwesh Sharan, and Bindu N. Lohani, *Energy for All: Addressing the Energy, Environment, and Poverty Nexus in Asia* (Manila: Asian Development Bank, April 2007).

700 million citizens have access to roughly as much energy as do the 38 million citizens of Poland. Some grids are so poorly maintained that suppliers get paid for only 60 percent of what they generate; and in Nigeria, only nineteen of seventy-nine power plants work and blackouts cost the economy $1 billion per year.[7]

More seriously, energy poverty literally kills people. It has grave and growing public health concerns related to IAP, physical injury during fuelwood collection, and lack of refrigeration and medical care in areas that lack modern energy services. The most severe of these is IAP, where burning firewood, dung, and charcoal is as physiologically damaging as residing inside a giant, constantly smoking cigarette. Put in perspective, Figure 7.2 exhibits that deaths from IAP are already greater than those from malaria, tuberculosis, and HIV/AIDS, and will likely remain that way beyond 2030.

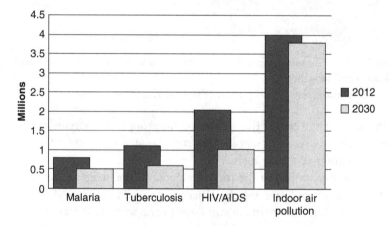

**Figure 7.2** Annual deaths worldwide by cause, 2012 and 2030
*Source:* Adapted from International Energy Agency, *World Energy Outlook 2006* (Paris: OECD, 2006); International Energy Agency, UN Development Program, UN Industrial Development Organization, *Energy Poverty: How to Make Modern Energy Access Universal?* (Paris: OECD, 2010), p. 7; and S.S. Lim *et al.*, "A Comparative Risk Assessment of Burden of Disease and Injury Attributable to 67 Risk Factors and Risk Factor Clusters in 21 Regions, 1990–2010: A Systematic Analysis for the Global Burden of Disease Study 2010," *Lancet*, 380 (2012), pp. 2224–2260.

---

[7] Michael Wines, "Toiling in the Dark: Africa's Power Crisis," *New York Times*, July 29, 2007.

The IAP statistics for some particular countries are frightening. In Gambia, girls under the age of five carried by their mothers while cooking have a six times greater risk of lung cancer than if their parents smoked cigarettes and were not exposed to IAP from cooking.[8] From 2005 to 2030, at least 10 million women and children in Sub-Saharan Africa will die from the smoke produced by cooking stoves.[9] One investigation of four provinces in China found that IAP affected every person in a rural home, and also that inefficient combustion of fuel was not the only problem; so was food drying and storage.[10]

Unfortunately, IAP is not the only health consequence of energy poverty. Women and children face exposure to health related risks during the burdensome and time-intensive process of collecting fuel. Common injuries include back and foot damage, wounds, cuts, sexual assaults, and exposure to extreme weather. The large number of daily hours women need to collect and use solid fuel leaves them with no other option than to take young children along, in essence exposing both to the same health impacts.[11] In Addis Ababa, Ethiopia, 10,000 fuelwood carriers supply one third of the wood consumed by the city and suffer frequent falls, bone fractures, eye problems, headaches, anemia, internal body disorders, and miscarriages from carrying loads often equal to their body weights. Fuel collection also places women in areas of physical or psychological violence. Hundreds of documented cases revealed Somalian women being raped while collecting fuel, and women in Sarajevo faced sniper fire to collect biomass.[12] In India, for instance, the typical woman spends forty hours collecting fuel per month during fifteen separate trips, many walking more than 6 kilometers round trip.[13] This amounts to 30 billion hours spent

[8] A. Gaye, "Access to Energy and Human Development," *Human Development Report 2007/2008*, UN Development Program Human Development Report Office Occasional Paper, 2007.

[9] *Ibid.*

[10] Y. Jin, "Exposure to Indoor Air Pollution from Household Energy Use in Rural China: The Interactions of Technology, Behavior, and Knowledge in Health Risk Management," *Social Science & Medicine* 62 (2006), pp. 3161–3176.

[11] Masud, Sharan, and Lohani, *Energy for All.*

[12] UN Development Program, *Energy after Rio: Prospects and Challenges* (Geneva: UN, 1997).

[13] K. Sangeeta, "Energy Access and its Implication for Women: A Case Study of Himachal Pradesh, India," presentation to the 31st IAEE International Conference Pre-Conference Workshop on Clean Cooking Fuels, Istanbul, 16–17 June, 2008.

annually (82 million hours per day) collecting fuelwood, with an economic burden (including time invested and illnesses) of $6.7 billion (300 billion rupees) per year.[14]

Countries without access to modern energy also tend to have more dilapidated health systems. Compared to developing countries, infant mortality rates are more than five times higher in energy-poor countries, as is the proportion of children below the age of five who are malnourished (eight times higher), the maternal mortality rate (fourteen times higher), and proportion of births not attended by trained health personnel (thirty-seven times higher).[15] In Papua New Guinea, for example, many doctors in rural areas without electricity perform births while holding a flaming torch in one hand for light, and operating with the other, often subjecting pregnant women to severe burns. In Sri Lanka, midwives and those assisting women with giving birth sometimes knock over kerosene lanterns, resulting in serious fires.

In terms of wealthier countries, a disparity between the energy rich and poor can be expressed through a Gini coefficient or Lorenz curve, a tool that describes the degree of income concentration related to energy consumption (varying between zero for perfect equality and one for maximum inequality). One study appraised the equity of energy use in El Salvador, Kenya, Norway, Thailand, and the United States.[16] Even the most equitable country, Norway, saw half of residential electricity being used by only 38 percent of customers; in the United States half of electricity was used by 25 percent of households; in El Salvador, 15 percent; Thailand, 13 percent; Kenya, 6 percent. A separate study found that in Sri Lanka, the poorest income group (by decile) spends almost 12 percent of their income on transportation, whereas the wealthiest group (by decile) spends less than 3 percent, and even then the *type* of transport differs, with the poor relying on bicycles, buses, and scooters and the rich relying on private motor cars and vans.[17] In this

---

[14] B. S. Reddy, P. Balachandra, and H. S. K. Nathan, "Universalization of Access to Modern Energy Services in Indian Households – Economic and Policy Analysis," *Energy Policy* 37 (2009), pp. 4645–4657.

[15] UN Development Program, *Energy after Rio*.

[16] Arne Jacobson and Daniel Kammen, "Letting the (Energy) Gini out of the Bottle: Lorenz Curves of Cumulative Electricity Consumption and Gini Coefficients as Metric of Energy Distribution and Equity," *Energy Policy* 33(14), pp. 1825–1832.

[17] Battam Fattouh, "Dynamics of Global Demand: Implications for Middle Eastern Producers," in *The Oil Era: Emerging Challenges* (Abu Dhabi: Emirates Center for Strategic Studies and Research, 2011), pp. 39–76.

way, energy poverty and access is an issue of distributional injustice, linked to "wider established concerns over inequality, poverty and the interests of the least advantaged."[18]

## Fuel poverty, health, and excess winter deaths

Switching away from equity and access to another dimension – affordability – millions of people around the world suffer "fuel poverty," a condition where they must spend more than 10 or 15 percent of their monthly income on energy bills. More often than not, these "fuel poor" households cannot afford to pay at all, and thus endure with cold homes during the freezing temperatures of winter. Mary O'Brien, Specialty Registrar in Public Health at the Wessex Deanery in the United Kingdom, has found that fuel poverty results in "inadequately heated housing" and, as a result, higher rates of mortality among the elderly, a greater prevalence of circulatory and respiratory diseases in adults, reduced physical and emotional well-being, and an increased risk of falls, mental illness, social isolation, and hospital admissions.[19] Other studies have confirmed the connection between homelessness and the inability to pay utility bills, the loss of central heat and increased heart disease, between malnutrition and the heating season, and between utility disconnections and children placed in foster care.[20] As Greg Palast and his colleagues write, "Even in the US, every day, poor people must choose between heating their houses and feeding their children, between electricity and medicine, even with relatively low regulated prices ... A sickly poor child is put at risk by a system that requires a parent to choose between nutrition and electricity for refrigeration."[21]

More severely, fuel poverty quite literally kills people who go without essential heat and then suffer "excess winter mortalities." One epidemiological study looked at eleven industrialized countries in both the

---

[18] Gordon Walker and Rosie Day, "Fuel Poverty as Injustice: Integrating Distribution, Recognition and Procedure in the Struggle for Affordable Warmth," *Energy Policy* 49 (October 2012), pp. 69–75.

[19] Mary O'Brien, "Policy Summary: Fuel Poverty in England," *Lancet* (December 2011), available at http://ukpolicymatters.thelancet.com/?p=1603.

[20] Greg Palast, Jerrold Oppenheim, and Theo MacGregor, *Democracy and Regulation: How the Public Can Govern Essential Services* (London: Pluto Press, 2003).

[21] *Ibid.*, p. 73.

Table 7.2 *Average excess winter mortality in twelve countries, 2008*

| Country | Population (millions) | Average excess winter mortality |
|---|---|---|
| Australia | 19.5 | 6,973 |
| Canada | 30.3 | 8,113 |
| Cyprus | 0.8 | 317 |
| France | 59.5 | 24,938 |
| Greece | 9.5 | 5,820 |
| Italy | 54.4 | 37,498 |
| Japan | 127.9 | 50,887 |
| New Zealand | 3.5 | 1,600 |
| Spain | 37.5 | 23,645 |
| Sweden | 8.8 | 4,034 |
| United Kingdom | 60.9 | 36,700 |
| United States | 287.3 | 77,884 |
| Total | | 278,409 |

*Source:* Data for all countries but the UK adapted from M.E. Falagas, D.E. Karageorgopoulos, L.I. Moraitis, E.K. Vouloumanou, N. Roussos, G. Peppas, and P.I. Rafailidis, "Seasonality of Mortality: The September Phenomenon in Mediterranean Countries," *Canadian Medical Association Journal* 181 (2009), pp. 484–486. UK data is adapted from Rosie Day and Russell Hitchings, "'Only Old Ladies Would Do That': Age Stigma and Older People's Strategies for Dealing with Winter Cold," *Health & Place* 17 (2011), pp. 885–894.

Northern and Southern Hemispheres and found a clear correlation between the winter months and unusually high rates of mortality.[22] Shockingly, Table 7.2 shows the average excess winter deaths – defined as the extra deaths in the four winter months in comparison with the previous and succeeding four months – across a dozen countries and calculates that these amount to 278,409, exceeding the global number of deaths (about 166,000) attributed by the WHO to climate change (though these latter deaths will certainly increase over the next few

[22] M. E. Falagas, D. E. Karageorgopoulos, L. I. Moraitis, E. K. Vouloumanou, N. Roussos, G. Peppas, and P. I. Rafailidis, "Seasonality of Mortality: The September Phenomenon in Mediterranean Countries," *Canadian Medical Association Journal* 181 (2009), pp. 484–486.

decades). For now, however, this makes fuel poverty as urgent a health issue as climate change, given that a 2006 WHO review of ten countries projected that the attributable fraction of excess winter deaths due to housing conditions was 40 percent.[23] According to this logic, increasing electricity generation and heat supply are perhaps as important as carbon dioxide control.[24] Put another way, as we face the overwhelming challenge of climate change, it will also be essential to deal with the extra deaths caused by fuel poverty. Indeed, in New Zealand, the health benefits of better insulated homes are ten times greater than the other economic benefits.[25]

## Intellectual property

It is not only energy services that some poor (and even comparatively rich) communities lack access to, but also technologies and intellectual property. Most developing countries lack the capacity and technology to shift to more sustainable and affordable supplies of energy. One survey of the twenty-four least developed countries in the world found that due to the "tyranny of terrain" twenty-two of them each had less than 1 percent of their region's total energy resources.[26] With scarce energy resources of their own, these countries must rely on either the global trading system or bilateral donations, but international donors remain mostly focused on fossil fuels for commercial energy use, not helping the poor. Although much financing for energy development goes through private sector hands, various agencies of the UN system and the multilateral development banks, and in particular the World Bank, play a key role in setting the terms of the debate and in providing funding. By far the lion's share of World Bank funding on energy

---

[23] Philippa Howden-Chapman, Helen Viggers, Ralph Chapman, Kimberley O'Sullivan, Lucy Telfar Barnard, and Bob Lloyd, "Tackling Cold Housing and Fuel Poverty in New Zealand: A Review of Policies, Research, and Health Impacts," *Energy Policy*, 49 (October 2012), pp. 134–142.

[24] Fortunately, some of the most important cures for each of these problems of fuel poverty and climate change help with the other.

[25] Barry Barton *et al.*, *Energy Cultures: Implications for Policymakers* (University of Otago Center for Sustainability, Energy Cultures Research Project, February 2012, available at www.csafe.org.nz/energy_).

[26] UNESCAP, *Energy Security and Sustainable Development in Asia and the Pacific* (Geneva: UNESCAP, ST/ESCAP/2494, April 2008), p. 185.

continues to support traditional centralized fossil-fuel or hydroelectric plants.[27]

In addition, the lending strategy behind multilateral development banks such as the World Bank Group and the Asian Development Bank is controversial. These banks often tie their loans to particular reforms in the energy sector such as market restructuring, liberalization, and privatization. One survey of more than fifty empirical studies, however, found that privatized service deliveries could be more efficient and lower costs in water provision, trash collection, street cleaning, ship maintenance, housing construction, bus operation and railroad repair, but not with energy and electricity supply, which appear to be different because of their relative inelasticity of demand and lack of available substitutes.[28] In some countries in Asia, the restructuring of natural gas and electricity markets has enabled private elites to "capture" formerly public resources and consolidate their wealth, with little independent regulation or competition.[29]

Sociologist Michael Goldman has gone so far as to attack the World Bank's overly technocratic approach to development, arguing that, for every $1 invested by the Bank in developing countries, somewhere between $10 and $13 goes back to its members. A greater amount of capital therefore flows *out* of borrowing countries rather than *in*. And, since the World Bank always has more capital than it can lend, to survive Goldman argues that it must continually grow its investment portfolio and create demand for its services. Put in this light, the Bank's primary task is not to be held accountable for its projects, or to help poor people, but to make money as a business.[30]

---

[27] See Howard Schneider, "World Bank Turns to Hydropower to Square Development with Climate Change," *Washington Post*, May 8, 2013; Douglas F. Barnes, Bipul Singh, and Xiaoyu Shi, "Modernizing Energy Services for the Poor: A World Bank Investment Review-FY2000–2008," *World Bank Energy Sector Management Assistance Program Report*, December 2010; World Bank, "What Is the Status of the Bank's Energy Strategy?," 2013, available at http://go.worldbank.org/6ITD8WA1A0.

[28] James Q. Wilson, *Bureaucracy: What Government Agencies Do and Why They Do It* (New York: Basic Books, 1989), at pp. 349–350.

[29] Chuenchom Greacen and Chris Greacen, "Thailand's Electricity Reforms: Privatization of Benefits and Socialization of Costs and Risks," *Pacific Affairs* 77(3) (2004), pp. 517–541.

[30] M. Goldman, "Imperial Science, Imperial Nature: Environmental Knowledge for the World (Bank)," in S. Jasanoff and M. Long Martello (eds.), *Earthly Politics:*

The UN has also warned that the liberalization and deregulation of energy markets can result in privatized enterprises refusing to sufficiently invest in maintenance and reserve capacity to meet rising demand so that prices become inflated. Privatized entities tend to default to the cheapest and dirtiest fuels to keep costs low, increasing damage to the environment and human health. They also tend to be less concerned about serving the poor. Whereas governments tend to use energy pricing and subsidies to promote social development, the UN suggested that these goals are not always in the interests of a privatized market.[31]

Some technology firms have used patents as intentional tools to impede innovation and competition in the energy sector. For example, some companies will collect patents on products that they never intend to manufacture or produce. This technique, called warehousing, happens when companies "warehouse" patent rights in order to extract cash from entities that are found to be infringing such rights.[32] A "submarine" patent occurs when an inventor or firm files an application with broad or incomplete claims, and then files continuing applications to keep the patent submerged in the patent office. Once someone else innocently decides to use the patented idea, the inventor surfaces the application through its issuance to demand royalties and payment.[33] The technique, also called "trolling," is an ingenious if not predatory abuse of the patent continuation process.[34] Another anticompetitive

*Local and Global in Environmental Governance* (Cambridge, MA: MIT Press, 2004), pp. 55–80; see also M. Goldman, *Imperial Nature: The World Bank and Struggles for Social Justice in the Age of Globalization* (New Haven, CT: Yale University Press, 2005).

[31] UNESCAP, *Energy Security*.

[32] See Ted Sabety, "Nanotechnology Innovation and the Patent Thicket: Which IP Policies Promote Growth?," *Albany Law Journal of Science & Technology* 15 (2005), pp. 477–515; and Uche Ewelukwa, "Patent Wars in the Valley of the Shadow of Death: The Pharmaceutical Industry, Ethics, and Global Trade," *University of Miami Law Review* 59 (January 2005), pp. 203–293.

[33] Steve Blount, "The Use of Delaying Tactics to Obtain Submarine Patents and Amend Around a Patent that a Competitor Has Designed Around," *Journal of the Patent and Trademark Office Society* 81 (January 1999), pp. 11–39.

[34] Carl Shapiro, "Navigating the Patent Thicket: Cross Licenses, Patent Pools, and Standard Setting," in Adam B. Jaffe, Josh Lerner, and Scott Stern (eds.), *Innovation and the Economy* (Cambridge, MA: MIT Press, 2000); Carl Shapiro, "Patent System Reform: Economic Analysis and Critique," *Berkeley Technology Law Journal* 19 (Summer 2004), pp. 1017–1047.

patent technique concerns "suppression." Some energy companies have suppressed new and innovative technologies that threaten to disrupt profits in a market. As one study noted, "economic markets will always encourage and reward suppression (whether patented or not) if the technology could displace established markets or reduce profit margins."[35] Patent "blocking," a final practice, enables multiple owners of a single patent to exclude others from privilege of use.[36]

These four practices – patent warehousing, submarine patents, suppression, and blocking – have limited the diffusion of innovative energy techniques and technologies, often to the developing world. The Automobile Manufacturers Association has used them to suppress air pollution control equipment.[37] General Electric has utilized them to suppress more efficient lamps.[38] Ford Motor Company has employed them to suppress higher-quality and more fuel-efficient internal combustion engines with longer lifetimes, which would have eaten into profits related to maintenance.[39]

Similarly, a survey of 1,478 R&D laboratories in the US found that a majority of firms are starting to rely on patent blocking, especially when numerous, separately patentable inventions need to be combined to produce a single product. The study found that blocking patents was frequently used to extract licensing revenue or to force inclusion in cross-licensing negotiations.[40] The Ford Motor Company has resisted purchasing Toyota's technology for hybrid vehicles because of hefty licensing fees, and Honda has not been able to successfully negotiate a

---

[35] Charles Allen Black, "The Cure for Deadly Patent Practices: Preventing Technology Suppression and Patent Shelving in the Life Sciences," *Albany Law Journal of Science & Technology* 14 (2004), p. 398.

[36] Michael A. Heller and Rebecca S. Eisenberg, "Can Patents Deter Innovation? The Anticommons in Biomedical Research," *Science* 280(5364) (May 1, 1998), pp. 698–701.

[37] Black, "The Cure for Deadly Patent Practices."

[38] Kurt M. Saunders, "Patent Nonuse and the Role of Public Interest as a Deterrent to Technology Suppression," *Harvard Journal of Law & Technology* 15 (Spring 2002), pp. 389–451.

[39] See *ibid.*; Kurt M. Saunders and Linda Levine, "Better, Faster Cheaper – Later: What Happens When Technologies Are Suppressed," *Michigan Telecommunications and Technology Law Review* 11 (Fall 2004), pp. 23–69.

[40] Wesley M. Cohen, Richard R. Nelson, and John P. Walsh, "Protecting their Intellectual Assets: Appropriability Conditions and Why U.S. Manufacturing Firms Patent (Or Not)," *National Bureau of Economic Research Working Paper* 7552 (February 2000).

license to use nickel metal halide batteries in their hybrid vehicles.[41] And a 1992 patent on variable speed technology for wind turbines has prevented firms in Asia from accessing more efficient wind energy components in North America.[42]

## What is justice?

A "contractionist" theory of justice, one based on the idea of a social contract, provides us with a novel way of responding to these types of injustices. This concept is an intellectual response to Thomas Hobbes' famous notion that without social order, society would devolve into anarchy and lives that were "solitary, poor, nasty, brutish, and short." The idea is that people make a contract with one another and agree to give up the private use of force and other social ills, such as thievery or murder, in exchange for peace, security, and mutual advantage; a society in which all people surrender some power before the law and due process.[43] As one study noted, "contract-theory states that only free and rational agreements that are reached in social cooperation can generate moral norms."[44] Iowa Professor Clark Wolf explains that

according to contractarian theories, the concept of justice is essentially associated with a companion concept of free and rational agreement: one simple contractarian conception of justice holds that all and only those social arrangements are just that either are or could be the object of a free and rational agreement on the part of all who participate in or are affected by them.[45]

---

[41] B. K. Sovacool, "Placing a Glove on the Invisible Hand: How Intellectual Property Rights May Impede Innovation in Energy Research and Development (R&D)," *Albany Law Journal of Science & Technology* 18(2) (Fall 2008), pp. 381–440.

[42] Benjamin K. Sovacool, *The Dirty Energy Dilemma: What's Blocking Clean Power in the United States* (Westport: Praeger, 2008).

[43] John Rawls, "Justice as Fairness," in Wilfried Sellars and John Hospers (eds.), *Readings in Ethical Theory* (Englewood Cliffs: Prentice Hall, 1970), pp. 578–595.

[44] Behnam Taebi, *Nuclear Power and Justice between Generations: A Moral Analysis of Fuel Cycles* (The Netherlands: Center for Ethics and Technology, 2010).

[45] Clark Wolf, "Intergenerational Justice," in R. G. Frey and Christopher Heath Wellman (eds.), *A Companion to Applied Ethics* (London: Blackwell Publishing, 2003), pp. 279–294.

The idea also shows that if we divest human beings from the artificial advantages they hold – wealth, rank, social class, education, musical ability, athleticism – they will agree to a contract of a certain sort.[46] Or as John Rawls himself writes, we should take as a starting point that "reasonable principles of justice are those everyone would accept and agree to from a fair position."[47]

## John Rawls

Anyone who has read the late Harvard Professor John Rawls' (1921–2002) most influential work, *A Theory of Justice*, already knows it is long and complex: the updated edition we worked with has 535 pages, to say nothing of his other books and contributions to the field. Thus, for the purposes of energy justice, we focus on only the most relevant concepts: his "equality of opportunity principle," his "difference principle," and the notions of "primary goods" and the "veil of ignorance."

To begin to understand Rawls, it is useful to start with his assumption that people in society face what he termed "circumstances of justice": circumstances that matter whenever "mutually disinterested persons put forward conflicting claims to the division of social advantages under conditions of moderate scarcity." The problem is that different communities disagree in their values, and conflicts between them can lead to social instability and even bloody conflict. One possible outcome, the one that Rawls takes, is to presume that each community attempts to realize its own values as nearly as possible in isolation from the others.[48] Put another way, Rawls conception of justice is "utopian" because it conceives of the proper moral and ethical values society should have so that it is to be called reasonable and just.

Rawls also has a very particular notion of freedom. If the libertarian aims at freedom, and defines justice by the amount that an individual

---

[46] Martha C. Nussbaum, *Frontiers of Justice: Disability, Nationality, Species Membership* (Cambridge, MA: Belknap Press, 2006), pp. 9–10.

[47] John Rawls, *A Theory of Justice: Revised Edition* (Cambridge, MA: Belknap Press, 1999), p. 12.

[48] John A. Edgren, "On the Relevance of John Rawls's Theory of Justice to Welfare Economics," *Review of Social Economy* 55(3) (1995), pp. 332–349; K. J. Arrow, "Some Ordinalist-Utilitarian Notes on Rawls's Theory of Justice," *Journal of Philosophy* 82(4) (May 1975), pp. 345–363; D. Gauthier, "Bargaining and Justice," in E. Paul, J. Paul, and F. Miller, Jr. (eds.), *Ethics and Economics* (Oxford: Basil Blackwell, 1985).

can achieve in society, Rawls does almost the opposite: instead of freedom, he focuses on the lack of freedom people have in choosing their natural talents like, for instance, intelligence or beauty. According to Rawls, such natural talents (or lack thereof), along with the social (and economic) birthplace that each of us has landed, are not free and have been determined by forces outside of us.

This finding has tremendous ramifications for Rawls. If we cannot choose our talents and social and economic birthplace, then the parts of success based upon these factors is unfounded, and so is any reward coming out of such success. As Wisconsin philosopher Harry Brighouse says, "If factors which we did not deserve play such a powerful role in explaining our achievements, then the rewards for our achievements must, in large part, be undeserved."[49] This means that the libertarian idea of justice, according to Rawls, is just that: ideal. The place each human being really starts is determined.

Rawls extrapolates, and offers a thought experiment now widely known as the "veil of ignorance" getting at his theory of justice. The idea, basically, is that since we do not choose our talents or lot in life, then we must imagine, from behind a "veil of ignorance," what principles we would choose for governing life. In the context of our work, we might ask "not knowing whether you will be the engineer that disconnects people from electricity, or the person that is disconnected, what disconnection rules do you think a society should apply across the board?"

As Rawls writes:

The parties do not know to which generation they belong or what comes to the same thing the stage of civilization of their society. They have no way of telling whether it is poor or relatively wealthy, largely agricultural or already industrialized, and so on. The veil of ignorance is complete in these respects. Thus the persons in the original position are to ask themselves how much they would be willing to save at each stage on the assumption that all other generations are to save at the same rates. That is they are to consider their willingness to save at any given phase of civilization with the understanding that the rates they propose are to regulate the whole span of accumulation. In effect, then, they must choose a just savings principle that assigns an appropriate rate of accumulation to each level of advance.[50]

---

[49] Harry Brighouse, *Justice* (Cambridge: Polity Press, 2004), p. 31.
[50] Rawls, *A Theory of Justice*, p. 287.

So what would people choose? According to Rawls, people would not want utilitarianism because they might end up being in a minority that could in some way be sacrificed for the overall pleasure and happiness of the majority. Similarly, individuals would not choose libertarianism because, although we might end up being extremely rich, there is also a good chance that we would end up poor or even homeless. They would not choose feudal and caste systems since these have a fixed hierarchy based on birth; one might end up either the prince or the pauper.

Behind the veil of ignorance, Rawls states that human beings would choose two things: "equal basic liberties for all citizens, such as freedom of speech and religion" and social and economic benefits that offer security to the least-well-off members of society.[51] Or, as he put it:

First: each person is to have an equal right to the most extensive scheme of equal basic liberties compatible with a similar scheme of liberties for others;

Second: social and economic inequalities are to be arranged so that they are both (a) reasonably expected to be to everyone's advantage, and (b) attached to positions and offices open to all.[52]

The "first" has come to be known as the "equality of opportunity" or "liberty" principle, and the "second" the "difference" principle.

In erecting these two cornerstones of his theory of justice, Rawls comments that the equality of opportunity principle is "lexically prior" to the difference principle; it must be satisfied prior to any consideration of the difference principle. The two cannot be balanced against each other; they are not equal, and the liberty principle must be satisfied regardless of the extent to which the difference principle is realized.[53] The difference principle, justifying social and economic inequalities only if they are to the greatest benefit of the least advantaged, also has its own, internal lexical priority: "Injustice is tolerable only when it is necessary to avoid an even greater injustice," as Rawls put it.[54]

---

[51] Michael J. Sandel, *Justice: What's the Right Thing to Do?* (New York: Farrar, Straus, and Giroux, 2009), p. 142.

[52] Rawls, *A Theory of Justice*, revised edn. (Cambridge, MA: Belknap Press, 1999), p. 53.

[53] Dan M. Berkovitz, "Pariahs and Prophets: Nuclear Energy, Global Warming, and Intergenerational Justice," *Columbia Journal of Environmental Law* 17(2) (1992), pp. 245–326.

[54] Rawls, *A Theory of Justice*, revised edn., p. 4.

The difference principle ensures that society is endowed with a minimum set of "primary goods," or "goods every rational man is presumed to want," including basic liberties such as freedom of thought, freedom of movement, and freedom of choice, powers and prerogatives of offices and positions of responsibility, income, and wealth, and self-respect and confidence.[55] The difference principle provides a "social minimum" and kicks in to correct for unequal distribution of talent by rewarding only attributes that benefit society as a whole. For Rawls, naturally talented and gifted people should be allowed to use resources to excel and make use of their talents, but only to the degree that their training, schooling, and benefits are used to help the less fortunate. Rawls says:

> The difference principle represents, in effect, an agreement to regard the distribution of natural talents as a common asset and to share in the benefits of this distribution whatever it turns out to be. Those who have been favored by nature, whoever they are, may gain from their good fortune only on terms that improve the situation of those who have lost out. The naturally advantaged are not to gain merely because they are more gifted, but only to cover the costs of training and education and for using their endowments in ways that help the less fortunate as well. No one deserves his greater natural capacity nor merits a more favorable starting place in society. But it does not follow that one should eliminate these distinctions. There is another way to deal with them. The basic structure of society can be arranged so that these contingencies work for the good of the least fortunate.[56]

Although egalitarian in nature, Rawls' position is not strictly egalitarian in the sense that all income, wealth, goods and services should be distributed at exactly the same levels to all members of a society.[57] Rawls instead supports the position that some inequality can actually benefit society as a whole more.

Rawls' work has been criticized. First, his principles of justice provide no commitment to substantial improvement in socioeconomic equality,

---

[55] See John Rawls, "The Basic Liberties and their Priority," in Sterling M. McMurrin (ed.), *Liberty, Equality, and Law: Selected Tanner Lectures on Moral Philosophy* (Cambridge University Press, 1987), pp. 1–88; see also Edgren, "On the Relevance of John Rawls's Theory of Justice to Welfare Economics"; and Frank I. Michelman, "In Pursuit of Constitutional Welfare Rights: One View of Rawls' Theory of Justice," *University of Pennsylvania Law Review* 121(5) (May 1973), pp. 962–1019.

[56] Sandel, *Justice: What's the Right Thing to Do?*, pp. 158–159.

[57] Brighouse, *Justice*, pp. 52–53.

only a minimum requirement; how far communities go beyond that minimum is up to them, but not compulsory. Justice, according to Rawls, is also not necessarily what is due to each person, but is instead what competing preferences negotiate in a fair process – making justice limited by what everyone will accept, a pragmatic compromise rather than a virtuous and absolute ideal.[58] Furthermore, Rawls is reluctant to apply his theory across cultures, essentially arguing that it is inappropriate to thrust liberal ideals on nonliberal peoples.[59] Additionally, his veil of ignorance experiment used to construct a single society is imagined as self-sufficient and independent; in truth, we have hugely different societies and are very interdependent.[60] Moreover, Rawls was explicit in not applying his framework to nonhuman species or future generations; in essence, his critique boiled down to "we can do something for posterity but posterity can do nothing for us," meaning the "question of justice does not arise."[61] Lastly, the classical theorists that Rawls based his theory on all assumed that contracting agents were equal in capacity and capable of productive economic activity. This conception implicitly excludes children, elderly people, and those with physical and mental impairments and disabilities.[62]

## Amartya Kumar Sen

Despite these criticisms, the theory of justice enumerated by Rawls has been formative in influencing two other great justice thinkers. The Nobel Prize winning economist Amartya Kumar Sen (1933–present) argues that the notion of "primary goods" iterated by Rawls is a nice starting point, but is less useful than the notion of "capabilities" for

[58] Jose Ambrozic, "Beyond Public Reason on Energy Justice: Solidarity and Catholic Social Teaching," *Colorado Journal of International Environmental Law and Policy* 21(2) (Spring 2010), pp. 381–398; Darrel Mollendorf, *Cosmopolitan Justice* (Boulder: Westview Press, 2002).

[59] Louis Kaplow and Steven Shavell, "Fairness versus Welfare: Notes on the Pareto Principle, Preferences, and Distributive Justice," *Journal of Legal Studies* 32 (January 2003), pp. 331–362; Gillian Brock, *Global Justice: A Cosmopolitan Account* (Oxford University Press, 2009).

[60] Brock, *Global Justice*; and Mollendorf, *Cosmopolitan Justice*.

[61] Anita Margrethe Halvorssen, *Equality among Unequals in International Environmental Law: Differential Treatment for Developing Countries* (Boulder: Westview Press, 1999), p. 56.

[62] Nussbaum, *Frontiers of Justice*.

securing substantive human freedoms. The focus for Sen lies on what people can achieve with their life, something he calls "functionings," or "the various things a person may value doing," such as being well fed, or receiving proper medical care, or being loved and safe, almost akin to states of mind, "doings," or "beings." Accordingly, functions go beyond income and economic goods; what counts is what people put those goods and services towards achieving.

His notion of "capabilities" refers to the substantial freedoms people ought to have to enjoy the various combination of functionings that they can realize. To the degree that poverty, or poor environmental conditions, or physical disabilities impede a person from experiencing the capacity or freedom to achieve the same level of functionings as others, then an injustice results.[63] For Sen, justice involves, first, the removal of various types of un-freedoms that leave people with little choice, and secondly, opportunity for exercising their reasoned agency.[64]

## Martha C. Nussbaum

Martha C. Nussbaum (1947–present), Distinguished Professor of Law and Ethics at the University of Chicago and a colleague of Sen, extends and builds upon the notion of capabilities in her own work on justice. Her starting point is the fact that most ways of calculating the quality of life tend to distort human experience for the "poor" of the developing world because they assume living standards always improve as GDP does. This "crude approach" encourages many planners to work for economic growth without attending to the actual living conditions of poorer citizens. She develops what she calls the "Human Development" or "Capabilities" approach, which asks: "What are people actually able to do and to be?" and "What real opportunities are available to

---

[63] See A. Sen, *Resources, Values and Development* (Oxford: Basil Blackwell, 1984); A. Sen, "Capability and 'Well-Being,'" in M. Nussbaum and A. Sen (eds.), *The Quality of Life* (Oxford University Press, 1993), pp. 30–53; A. Sen, *Development as Freedom* (Oxford University Press, 1999). See also Vivian Walsh, "Amartya Sen on Rationality and Freedom," *Science & Society* 71(1) (January 2007), pp. 59–83; Edward A. Page, "Intergenerational Justice of What: Welfare, Resources or Capabilities?," *Environmental Politics* 16(3) (June 2007), pp. 453–469; Barbara Muraca, "Towards a Fair Degrowth-Society: Justice and the Right to a 'Good Life' beyond Growth," *Futures* 44(6) (August 2012), pp. 535–545.

[64] Stuart Corbridge, "Development as Freedom: The Spaces of Amartya Sen," *Progress in Development Studies* 2(3) (2002), pp. 183–217.

them?"[65] She uses the term "capabilities" to "emphasize that the most important elements of a people's quality of life are plural and qualitatively distinct: health, bodily integrity, education, and other aspects of individual lives cannot be reduced to a single metric without distortion."[66]

The core of her theory of justice is a more concrete elaboration of the key capabilities people need to achieve their functionings. Whereas Sen offers many examples and anecdotes in his work, he never creates a systematic listing of capabilities. Nussbaum therefore defends a list of ten "central human functional capabilities":[67]

1. Life.
2. Bodily health.
3. Bodily integrity.
4. Senses, imagination and thought.
5. Emotions.
6. Practical reason.
7. Affiliation.
8. (A relationship with) Other species.
9. Play.
10. Political and material control over one's environment, including political participation, freedom of speech, and the ability to hold property on an equal basis with others.

Nussbaum does admit that "justice" does not provide any concrete guarantee that all people remain healthy or that they will have satisfying lives over most of their adulthood, but rather that all persons have the capability to realize these valuable functionings if they behave properly. Moreover, according to Nussbaum, a person lacking *any* of the ten capabilities fails to lead a fully human and dignified life. Similarly, deficiencies in any one capability do not offset or enhance the provision of others.[68] As she puts it, "the capabilities approach is fully universal: the capabilities in question are held to be important for each and every citizen, in each and every nation, and each person is to be treated as an end."[69]

---

[65] Martha C. Nussbaum, *Creating Capabilities: The Human Development Approach* (Cambridge: Belknap Press, 2011).

[66] *Ibid.*, p. 18.

[67] Nussbaum's list is similar to that of the psychologist Abraham Maslow, who proposed a "hierarchy of needs." See A. Maslow, *Motivation and Personality*, 3rd revised edn. (New York: Harper & Row, 1987; orig. edn., 1954).

[68] Page, "Intergenerational Justice of What."      [69] Nussbaum, *Frontiers of Justice.*

Note here that the contributions of Sen and Nussbaum respond to some of the most pernicious criticisms of Rawls. In many ways, Rawls' theory of justice is about procedure rather than outcomes. It does not examine the outputs of the global economic system as a characteristic of moral adequacy, and instead designs a procedure that encourages features of fairness and impartiality, the so-called "social contract" and the "veil of ignorance." But for Sen and Nussbaum, outcomes matter just as much. Rawls' theory is akin to designing a procedure to divide slices of cake, but not figuring out how big each slice ought to be. The notions of capabilities and functionings rectify this gap and start by explicitly determining what the outcomes of a just society ought to be – the size of each slice of cake – and work backwards at achieving it.

What does all this mean for energy justice, readers may rightly ask at this point? First, it means that energy systems ought to maximize welfare – not necessarily in the narrow utilitarian way explained in Chapter 4, but also in the ability to enable persons to realize functionings and capabilities.[70] Second, it means that energy planners ought to direct most of their effort to benefiting the *least-well-off*, adhering to a global application of the difference principle.[71] As one group of scholars put it, "a society is just only if it is arranged in such a way that the position of the least advantaged is optimized."[72] Third, it implies that every person has the right to a "social minimum" of energy or electricity so that they can enjoy a modern, healthy lifestyle. As ethicist Simon Caney puts it, "global equality of opportunity requires that people of equal talent have equal access to positions of an equal standard of living (where the standard of living is assessed in terms of their contribution to well-being)."[73]

---

[70] Sven Ove Hansson, "Welfare, Justice, and Pareto Efficiency," *Ethical Theory and Moral Practice* 7(4) (August 2004), pp. 361–380.

[71] Thomas C. Grey, "Property and Need: The Welfare State and Theories of Distributive Justice," *Stanford Law Review* 28(5) (May 1976), pp. 877–902.

[72] Kirstin Dow, Roger E. Kasperson, and Maria Bohn, "Exploring the Social Justice Implications of Adaptation and Vulnerability," in W. Neil Adger, Jouni Paavola, Saleemul Huq, and M. J. Mace (eds.), *Fairness in Adaptation to Climate Change* (Cambridge, MA: MIT Press, 2006), p. 81.

[73] Simon Caney, "Cosmopolitan Justice and Equalizing Opportunities," *Metaphilosophy* 32 (2001), pp. 113–34. See also Elizabeth Anderson, "What Is the Point of Equality?," *Ethics* 109 (1999), pp. 287–337.

## What is to be done?

In sum, global energy patterns are unjust under the theories offered to us by Rawls, Sen, and Nussbaum. As clergyman Jose Ambrozic has written:

It is unjust and inhumane that there are billions who do not have their basic needs met, such as access to water, food, energy, and education, which would allow them to live with dignity. It is also unjust and inhumane that millions who have more resources are unwilling to share with those in need. It demeans their own dignity to neglect or deny their vocation to love and to fail to serve and give generously to those in need when they can. When so-called developed societies deny their peoples' duty to virtue and duty to help those in need in the name of freedom, they betray their human nature and frustrate their own fulfillment.[74]

We must then ask whether there are, or reasonably could be, energy systems that would meet a test like that of "the veil of ignorance." Are there policies that are so widely beneficial that they seem attractive regardless of whether we might be a small residential user or a large industrial customer? Luckily, policymakers, communities and households do have various options they can use to expand access to energy and combat fuel poverty: investments in small-scale renewable energy systems, pro-poor public private partnerships (5Ps), "social pricing," low-income assistance, and weatherization programs.

### Investing in small-scale renewable energy

Planners and energy users can utilize biogas digesters, solar PV panels, small wind energy systems, microhydro dams, and improved cookstoves – relatively simple technologies without major intellectual property restrictions – to provide light and energy services without connecting to a fossil-fueled electric grid, and to use energy resources more efficiently.[75] For example, Tuvalu, a low-lying nation between Hawaii and Australia, announced plans to rely 100 percent on these types of

---

[74] Ambrozic, "Beyond Public Reason on Energy Justice."
[75] R. Pode, "Solution to Enhance the Acceptability of Solar-Powered LED Lighting Technology," *Renewable and Sustainable Energy Reviews* 14 (2010), pp. 1096–1103.

renewables by 2020 and already uses solar panels to reduce diesel use by 17,000 liters over fourteen months and lessen the number of diesel spills in surrounding seas.[76] Brazil was able to increase use of lique-fied petroleum gas for cooking fuels from 16 percent in 1960 to 100 percent in 2004, and China, Morocco, and Tunisia provided electricity for more than 70 percent of their respective populations by 2001.[77] Denmark was able to install more than 6,200 commercial scale wind turbines in less than ten years, Germany 430,000 residen-tial solar panels in nine years. Grameen Shakti in Bangladesh has installed 250,000 solar home systems, 40,000 cookstoves, and 7,000 biogas plants in fifteen years benefiting more than 1 million people. The Chinese installed a whopping 185 million cleaner burning cook-stoves in about a decade.[78]

One assessment compared the economic costs of investing in new cookstoves – including the expense of fuel, program costs, and capital costs for technology – to their corresponding benefits, such as reduced healthcare expenses, productivity gains, time savings, and improve-ment of the environment.[79] It studied these costs and benefits in eleven developing countries from 2005 to 2015, and found that if these countries switched to 50 percent coverage of improved stoves, the results would be:

- Substantial reduction of acute lower respiratory infections, chronic obstructive pulmonary diseases, and lung cancer;
- Increased numbers of illness free days and deaths avoided;
- Time savings from reduced needs to survey fuel areas and collect fuel, as well as quicker cooking times;
- Avoided deforestation; and
- Avoided carbon dioxide and methane emissions.

---

[76] Moises Velasquez-Manoff, "A Pacific Island Chain with a Real Energy Incentive," *Christian Science Monitor*, August 7, 2009.

[77] V. Modi, S. McDade, D. Lallement, and J. Saghir, *Energy Services for the Millennium Development Goals* (Washington and New York: International Bank for Reconstruction and Development/The World Bank and the UN Development Program, 2005), pp. 13–14.

[78] M. A. Brown and B. K. Sovacool, *Climate Change and Global Energy Security: Technology and Policy Options* (Cambridge, MA: MIT Press, 2011).

[79] G. Hutton, E. Rehfuess, and F. Tediosi, "Evaluation of the Costs and Benefits of Household Energy and Health Interventions," presentation to the Clean Cooking Fuels & Technologies Workshop, June 16–17, 2008, Istanbul, Turkey.

The study concluded that the benefit-to-cost ratio of investing in cook-stoves was extremely high, with an investment of $650 million producing $105 billion in benefits per year. Similarly, the IEA noted that switching to LPG stoves at the global scale would cost about $13.6 billion but would produce annual benefits exceeding $91 billion.[80]

The provision of mechanical power from diesel generators and hydro-electric systems also increases the efficiency and effectiveness of productive activities supporting sustainable development, as well as physical processes fundamental to meeting basic human needs. Mechanical services have great potential to tremendously reduce time spent on fuelwood gathering, to improve air quality in homes, and to raise household and community incomes. Mechanical power enables activities such as pumping, transporting, and lifting water, irrigating fields, processing crops, small-scale manufacturing, and natural resource extraction. As one recent study concluded:

> Experiences show that mechanical power helps alleviate drudgery, increase work rate and substantially reduce the level of human strength needed to achieve an outcome, thus increasing efficiency and output productivity, producing a wider range of improved products, and saving time and production costs ... In this regard, financing of mechanical power is often one of the most cost effective ways to support poor people.[81]

These examples strongly suggest that some of the most fundamental services required for reducing poverty and promoting human development involve mechanical energy and increasing the productivity of human labor. A phrase as old as the Bible refers to the roles of most human laborers as "hewers of wood and drawers of water."[82] In a very real sense, that is still the status of hundreds of millions of people that live in energy poverty. Fortunately, emerging energy solutions offer a chance for humanity to escape that status, with a ubiquity widespread enough to satisfy Rawls' test.

---

[80] International Energy Agency, *World Energy Outlook 2006* (Paris: OECD, 2006).

[81] L. Bates *et al.*, "Expanding Energy Access in Developing Countries: The Role of Mechanical Power," *Practical Action Report* (Washington, DC: UN Development Program, 2009).

[82] See www.biblestudytools.com/asv/joshua/9–27.html; Alexander Hamilton is reputed to have said that "those who do not industrialize become hewers of wood and haulers of water."

## Harnessing the "pro-poor public private partnership" approach

How ought these energy poverty fighting technologies be promoted? A number of distinct financing models have emerged within the past decade. A "cash model" refers to when customers purchase the product paying the full cost. A "credit model" refers to when local dealers sell their products to rural clients on credit against collateral or personal guarantees, with payment made in installments. A "mixed finance model" is when governments provide a fixed subsidy and the balance is borne by villagers or private firms. A "donation model" is one where the technology is transferred to the community as a gift, usually from a private entity (part of their corporate social responsibility program) or a development donor. A "fee for service" model is one where the energy system is owned, operated, and maintained by a supplying company, but the customer pays regular fees for using it. Other models include a "technology improvement and market development" model which attempts to improve performance and lower cost by conducting research on new technologies; a "community mobilization fund" which funnels revenues into local community development; a "cooperative model" where communities own part of the energy system themselves; and hybrid arrangements that combine some of the preceding types.[83]

By far the most innovative, and perhaps effective, of these models is known as the "5P" or "pro-poor public private partnership" approach. The 5P method explicitly targets the provision of services to poor communities, which are often ignored by traditional partnerships since supplying the poor can involve substantial business risk. The 5P model views the poor not only as consumers that receive benefits, but also as partners in business ventures, something illustrated by Figure 7.3. It expands beyond the private sector to include partners from development banks, equipment manufacturers, rural ESCOs, philanthropic organizations, community-based organizations, cooperatives, and households themselves.[84]

---

[83] M. Bazilian, P. Nussbaumer, C. E. Singer, A. Brew-Hammond, V. Modi, B. K. Sovacool, V. Ramana, and P. K. Aqrawi, "Improving Access to Modern Energy Services: Insights from Case Studies," *Electricity Journal* 25(1) (January 2012), pp. 93–114.

[84] A. Chaurey, P. R. Krithika, D. Palit, S. Rakesh, and B. K. Sovacool, "New Partnerships and Business Models for Facilitating Energy Access," *Energy Policy* 47(1) (June 2012), pp. 48–55.

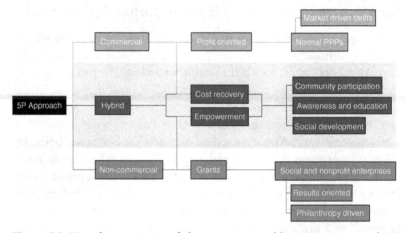

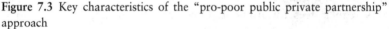

**Figure 7.3** Key characteristics of the "pro-poor public private partnership" approach
*Source:* Adapted from B.K. Sovacool, "Expanding Renewable Energy Access with Pro-Poor Public Private Partnerships in the Developing World," *Energy Strategy Reviews* 1(3) (March 2013), pp. 181–192.

One excellent example of a 5P project in action is the 210 kW Cinta Mekar Microhydro Project in West Java, Indonesia. The facility was built through a partnership between public, private, and community organizations where energy has been used to electrify village homes and produce revenue through exports to the national grid. Profits from the project are divided equally between a private company, Hidropiranti Inti Bakti Swadaya, and the community itself, represented by a village cooperative.

Because of its innovative 5P structure, and its focus on community empowerment, the benefits of the Cinta Mekar Project have been manifold. The community itself now has a reliable source of revenue, an ambitious social development plan has been implemented, standards of living for the poorest members of the village have improved, and the village has seen the continual betterment of infrastructure such as roads and better schooling. The most direct benefit has been the complete electrification of the village, with all homes now receiving affordable electricity that they use for lighting, cooking, and other productive uses – freeing them from the "slavery" of hewing wood and water. Such electrification has occurred with no disruption of water needed for irrigation and no recorded pollution of the local river. A secondary benefit has been the extra revenue from the electricity exported to the Indonesian energy utility, Perusahaan Gas Negra, grid. About 72,000 kWh are exported every month creating $3,780 of extra income.

Based on a democratic voting process and survey with the villagers themselves, the cooperative disbursed their share of this income according to the following priorities:

- Power connections to the poorest households;
- Microcredit loans for income-generating activities;
- Sponsorship for children's education and adult skills training;
- Healthcare;
- Infrastructural improvement to roads, buildings, and telecommunications.

After the cooperative met all of these targets during the first seventeen months of operation, Table 7.3 shows they slightly shifted expenditures to focus more on education and healthcare. As of 2008, the cooperative had paid the connection installation fees for all poor households in the village, granted scholarships to 156 children, generated seed capital for local enterprises, rehabilitated irrigation canals, and built a health clinic, a community radio station, and a village telephone network.[85]

Another example of a successful 5P approach, this time implemented internationally, is the Renewable Energy and Energy-Efficiency Partnership (REEEP). REEEP is a 5P fund that funnels investment into clean energy projects in the developing world. Established in 2002 by a collection of regulators, businesses, banks, and nongovernmental organizations, REEEP's mission centers on reducing emissions, improving the access to reliable and clean forms of energy in developing countries, and promoting energy efficiency.

REEEP funds energy-efficiency and renewable energy projects with the potential to be widely replicated in many different regulatory frameworks and a variety of countries and energy markets. The 2012 program year, the organization's ninth funding cycle, saw REEEP partnering with 44 governments, 180 private organizations (such as banks, businesses, and other nongovernmental organizations), and 6 multilateral organizations (such as the UN). The organization managed a €3.95 million annual operating budget distributed

---

[85] Fabby Tumiwa, Henriette Imelda Rambitan, and Olivia Tanujaya, *Cinta Mekar Micro-Hydro Power Plant: Giving Power to the People* (Jakarta: Institute for Essential Services Reform, 2009).

Table 7.3 *Community improvement from the Cinta Mekar Microhydro Project, 2004–2008*

| Category | Percentage of revenue (2004–2005) | Percentage of revenue (2005–2008) | Target beneficiaries |
|---|---|---|---|
| Electrification | 62.5 | 0 | 122 households |
| Community cooperative costs | 10 | 5 | All members of the cooperative |
| Education | 8 | 65 | Training for 4 groups of villagers, scholarship for 30 children (first 17 months) and then 156 children (as of 2008) |
| Seed capital for income-generating activities | 8 | 7.5 | 15 local enterprises |
| Infrastructure | 5 | 4 | Improved roads, rehabilitated irrigation canals, a community radio station, and a village telephone network |
| Health | 4 | 16 | Health cards for 142 households, a new village health center, treatment of 5 villagers for chronic illnesses |
| Administration costs | 2.5 | 2.5 | – |

*Source:* Adapted from Fabby Tumiwa, Henriette Imelda Rambitan, and Olivia Tanujaya, *Cinta Mekar Micro-Hydro Power Plant: Giving Power to the People* (Jakarta: Institute for Essential Services Reform, 2009).

among dozens of projects worth a total cumulative investment of €9.62 million, most of this leveraged from REEEP partners through equity financing. Some of REEEP's newest projects included the promotion of solar energy systems at textile factories in China, small-scale off-grid renewable energy in Cambodia, energy-efficient lighting in South Africa, and assessing the regulatory framework for renewable energy in Namibia and Tonga.[86]

## Social pricing and assistance programs

Social pricing programs refer to an array of tools to enhance affordability for poorer customers and more vulnerable energy consumers. One is concessionary tariffs and affordability programs. Many states, municipalities, and electric utilities offer a range of concessions (including a percentage reduction in energy bills, special loans, and extra rebates) to the unemployed, elderly, disabled, and low-income households to offset rising energy prices. Some even offer "direct assistance" in paying utility bills, usually as either a fixed dollar amount or a fixed percentage of the bill. One survey noted that such programs have discounts ranging from 7 to 40 percent, depending on the state and utility company (e.g. California provides a 20 percent discount on electricity prices; Massachusetts discounts reach up to 40 percent for natural gas).[87] One national program called Low Income Home Energy Assistance Program (LIHEAP), known commonly as "Fuel Assistance," provides eligible households with help in paying a portion of winter heating bills (and summer air-conditioning bills) in the United States. Evaluations from the Department of Health and Human Services have noted that the program saves most households $380 to $411 per year, and that the average LIHEAP recipient sees their home energy burden reduced by 52 percent (from 8 percent of income to 3.8 percent of income).[88]

Consumer protections are a second option, involving things like common collection practices and installment billing requirements, making it easier for customers to pay their bills on time. In the United States, most states and municipalities prohibit or restrict late payment penalties and reconnection fees for energy, set limits on the size of deposits, mandate levelized billing plans, encourage debt forgiveness, and protect the most vulnerable customers from service disconnection. In most cold

[86] REEEP, *Annual Report 2012/13: An Overview of REEEP Activities & Achievements*, April 1, 2012 – March 31, 2013.

[87] Palast, Oppenheim, and MacGregor, *Democracy and Regulation.*

[88] Division of Energy Assistance, Office of Community Services, Administration for Children and Families, US Department of Health and Human Services, *LIHEAP Energy Burden Evaluation Study* (July 2005).

northern states, as in the Vermont example with which we began this chapter, utilities cannot unconditionally be shut off during the winter.[89]

A third solution is education programs that "teach consumers about prudent energy use and counsel them about budgeting."[90] In Connecticut, as one example, when a contractor installs a new refrigerator in a poor household, they also explain how to use all of their energy-using appliances in the most efficient manner possible. Other utility companies may have community relations personnel on staff that can provide budget counseling and educational outreach to communities and neighborhoods in need.[91]

A fourth solution is energy-efficiency, weatherization, and low-income assistance programs that help consumers control their energy bills by reducing their demand for energy. These programs usually start with an energy audit of households to determine which energy-saving measures will work the best. The Massachusetts Electric Company manages one low-income baseload efficiency program (the Appliance Management Program), which includes replacing refrigerators to reduce household energy use as much as 15 percent. More often than not, total budgets for these programs are based on a small percentage (0.3 or 0.4 percent) of the utility's total revenues, or through small surcharges made on all customers. Similarly, the Solar and Energy Loan Fund, a community-based lending organization that focuses on improving the quality of life of underserved populations in Florida, has completed 810 energy audits and helped more than 200 families finance nearly $2 million of energy retrofit projects. Clients are reducing average household energy consumption by 20 percent, and redirecting dollars toward home improvements.[92]

The US DOE currently runs a Weatherization Assistance Program that provides households below the poverty line with free energy-efficiency improvements. These improvements are not just traditional "weatherizing" (such as caulking, leak plugging, and adding weather stripping to doors and windows to save energy) but also a wide variety of energy-efficiency measures that encompass the building envelope, home heating and cooling systems, electricity, and electrical appliances. The basic premise is to make multifamily and low-income homes the most energy-efficient to permanently reduce energy bills. From 1976 to 2009, the program provided weatherization services to more than

[89] Palast, Oppenheim, and MacGregor, *Democracy and Regulation.*    [90] *Ibid.*
[91] *Ibid.*    [92] Personal correspondence with Samantha Ruiz, July 26, 2013.

6.4 million families.[93] Instead of distributing one-time dispensations of aid, the program helps minimize dependency by lowering heating bills an average of 31 percent and overall energy bills by $437 per year.[94] Because weatherization enhances the infrastructure of homes and buildings, it also increases the value of housing stock. Local industry is stimulated as well, and the DOE estimates that the national weatherization program already supports 8,000 technical jobs in low-income communities.[95] One evaluation of weatherization programs in the United States found an average 23 percent reduction in natural gas consumption for space heating per participating household.[96]

Similarly, the "Warm Front" program in England saw 2.3 million "fuel-poor" British homes receive energy-efficiency upgrades to save them money and improve their overall health over its duration from 2000 to 2013. Warm Front not only lessened the prevalence of fuel poverty; it also significantly cut GHG emissions, produced an average extra annual income of £1,894.79 per participating household, and reported exceptional customer satisfaction, with more than 90 percent of its customers praising the scheme.[97]

In aggregate, these four measures – (1) affordability programs, (2) consumer protections, (3) education and counseling, and (4) low-income assistance – not only reduce the severity of energy and fuel poverty. They can also help energy companies and, thus, all other customers, an important point under Rawls' concerns. Studies have shown that such efforts minimize carrying costs on late payments (arrearages), reconnection costs, and the expense of collection notices, termination notices, collection calls, and related activities. They lessen administrative and regulatory expenditures related to disputed bills and other complaints, and reduce theft of service. They, lastly, have lower incidences of uncollectibles and bad debt.[98] The implication is that justice can benefit both ordinary people and businesses simultaneously.

[93] Sovacool, *The Dirty Energy Dilemma*, p. 214.
[94] US Department of Energy, "Weatherization Assistance Program," January 30, 2012.
[95] Sovacool, *The Dirty Energy Dilemma*, p. 214.
[96] Palast, Oppenheim, and MacGregor, *Democracy and Regulation*.
[97] Benjamin K. Sovacool, *Energy and Ethics: Justice and the Global Energy Challenge* (New York: Palgrave, 2013).
[98] Palast, Oppenheim, and MacGregor, *Democracy and Regulation*.

# 8 | Energy subsidies and freedom

In 1954, US President Dwight Eisenhower faced a difficult situation. Under the Atoms for Peace Program, announced in December 1953 to the UN General Assembly, he had pledged to "strip the atom's military casing and adapt it to the art of peace."[1] The central theme behind Atoms for Peace was to demonstrate that the power of the atom could be converted from a terrifying military force into a benign commodity. A secondary driver, less obvious but still salient, was competition with the Soviet Union. Developments outside the nuclear industry during the 1940s and 1950s, such as the Alger Hiss case, the pro-Soviet coup in Czechoslovakia, the Soviet blockage of West Germany, the Chinese revolution, and Soviet progress developing atom bombs, hydrogen bombs, and nuclear reactors convinced many American planners that they were in a "race to save the world from communism."[2] Atomic energy was one key component of winning this race, and the reason for choosing to go forward was not necessarily to produce a "cost competitive" nuclear power plant but to demonstrate to the world the superiority of American engineering prowess.[3] The role of the government, in other words, was to be an entrepreneurial custodian of atoms.[4] Yet, atomic energy was then far from technically or economically feasible.

How, then, were Eisenhower and his planners to, first, decide whether his program should be done by the government as opposed

---

[1] Richard Munson, *From Edison to Enron: The Business of Power and What It Means for the Future of Electricity* (London: Praeger, 2005), p. 80.

[2] B.K. Sovacool and S.V. Valentine, *The National Politics of Nuclear Power: Economics, Security, and Governance* (London: Routledge, 2012).

[3] Lee Clarke, "The Origins of Nuclear Power: A Case of Institutional Conflict," *Social Problems* 32(5) (June 1985), pp. 474–487.

[4] Shelia Jasanoff and Sang-Hyun Kim, "Containing the Atom: Sociotechnical Imaginaries and Nuclear Power in the United States and South Korea," *Minerva* 47(2) (2009), pp. 119–146.

to private industry? Secondly, if it was to be government sponsored, how was he to convince investors, vendors, and taxpayers to participate? The Eisenhower Administration's answer was a program of lavish public subsidies, earmarking billions of tax dollars for research, development, demonstration projects, and offering limited liability guarantees for nuclear accidents. In the American case, government created a market for nuclear power, rather than seeing one emerge organically.

The strategy worked, at least to some degree. The United States leads the world in the generation of nuclear electricity, accounting for close to one third of all total output. Its 104 nuclear reactors generated about 20 percent of the country's electricity in 2011, although inauspiciously, almost all of its operational power plants were built between 1967 and 1990.[5] But this nuclear push came at an incredible economic cost. During its first twenty-five years of development in the United States, nuclear power enjoyed several *billion* historical dollars in energy research spending compared to only *millions* of dollars for fossil-fueled and renewable energy systems. Nuclear power operators received subsidies of $15.30 per kWh during the first fifteen years of the launch of the technology (1947 to 1961) while solar power and wind power providers received only $7.19 per kWh and $0.46 per kWh, respectively, during the first fifteen years when those technologies came into more widespread use (1975–1989).[6]

The industry is also, today, almost completely dependent on subsidies. The Energy Policy Act of 2005 elevated government commitment by covering up to 80 percent of the cost of a new nuclear plant. These subsidies were additional to numerous other benefits the nuclear industry has traditionally enjoyed: government funded security, use of actual or implied eminent domain to acquire sites for generation and transmission of nuclear power, and disposal facilities for radioactive waste. Indeed, Douglas Koplow looked at five decades' worth of subsidies data and concluded that "subsidies to the nuclear fuel cycle have often exceeded the value of the power produced. This means that buying

---

[5] Sovacool and Valentine, *The National Politics of Nuclear Power.*
[6] Marshall Goldberg, Federal Energy Subsidies: Not All Technologies Are Created Equal (Washington, DC: Renewable Energy Policy Project, July 2000).

power on the open market and giving it away for free would have been less costly than subsidizing the construction and operation of nuclear power plants."[7]

Did Eisenhower make the right call? And was he right or wrong for subsidizing this particular energy source, or merely for the idea of subsidizing – intervening in the market – as a concept? This chapter illustrates that the situation with nuclear power – and, indeed, many other energy technologies that receive subsidies – would have some "libertarians" objecting. For example, Robert Nozick, whose thoughts we will discuss in more detail below, would look at our subsidized energy landscape, and quickly conclude that it was an affront to individual liberty. He would point out that it involves an involuntary wealth transfer to recipients, essentially raiding the pocket books of the unwilling. Nozick would argue that freedom refers to liberty, and to people possessing the free will to make their own choices, or at least to not have energy subsidies imposed on them without consent. Luckily for all that agree with Nozick, those seeking energy justice need not live in a perpetually subsidized energy world. Instead, they can rely on the elimination of inappropriate subsidies, subsidy impact assessments, sunset clauses, and adjustment packages to (in part or whole) restore liberty and individual autonomy.

## What is reality?

Though there are other forms of government intervention in energy markets, perhaps the most significant threat to freedom is energy subsidies, which receive their funding from taxes that a libertarian would consider an involuntary transfer of public wealth to select industries and producers.

### Defining subsidies

The UN and International Energy Agency define an energy subsidy as "any measure that keeps prices for consumers below market levels, or for producers above market levels, or that reduces costs for consumers

---

[7] D. Koplow, *Nuclear Power: Still Not Viable without Subsidies* (Washington, DC: Union of Concerned Scientists, February 2011).

and producers."[8] As Table 8.1 reveals, at least seventeen different types of subsidies are on the books for many countries around the world, and most of these were oriented towards lowering the cost of energy production.[9]

Table 8.1 *Types of global energy subsidies*

| | | How it works | | |
| --- | --- | --- | --- | --- |
| Type of subsidy | Example(s) | Lowers cost of production | Raises price to disfavored producer | Lowers price to consumer |
| Direct financial transfer | Grants to producers | X | | |
| | Grants to consumers | | | X |
| | Low-interest or preferential loans | X | | |
| Preferential tax treatment | Rebates or exemptions on royalties, sales taxes, producer levies and tariffs | X | | |
| | Investment tax credits | X | | |
| | Production tax credits | X | | |

[8] UN Environment Program Division of Technology, Industry and Economics and the International Energy Agency, *Reforming Energy Subsidies: An Explanatory Summary of the Issues and Challenges in Removing or Modifying Subsidies on Energy that Undermine the Pursuit of Sustainable Development* (New York and Paris: UNEP and IEA, 2002); and UN Environment Program Division of Technology, Industry and Economics, *Reforming Energy Subsidies: Opportunities to Contribute to the Climate Change Agenda* (New York: UNEP, 2008).
[9] Douglas N. Koplow, *Federal Energy Subsidies: Energy, Environmental, and Fiscal Impacts* (Washington, DC: ASE, April 1993); Doug Koplow and John Dernbach, "Federal Fossil Fuel Subsidies and Greenhouse Gas Emissions: A Case Study of Increasing Transparency for Fiscal Policy," *Annual Review of Energy & Environment* 26 (2001), pp. 361–389; Doug Koplow, "Subsidies to Energy Industries," *Encyclopedia of Energy* 5 (2004), pp. 749–765.

Table 8.1 (*cont.*)

| | | How it works | | |
| | | Lowers cost of production | Raises price to disfavored producer | Lowers price to consumer |
| Type of subsidy | Example(s) | | | |
|---|---|---|---|---|
| | Accelerated depreciation | X | | |
| | State-sponsored loan guarantees | X | | |
| Trade restrictions | Quotas, technical restrictions, and trade embargoes | | X | |
| | Import duties and tariffs | | X | |
| Energy-related services provided by government at less than full cost | Direct investment in energy infrastructure | X | | |
| | Publicly sponsored R&D | X | | |
| | Liability insurance | X | | |
| | Free storage of waste or fuel | X | | |
| | Free transport | X | | |
| Regulation of the energy sector | Demand guarantees and mandated deployment rates | X | X | |
| | Price controls and rate caps | | X | X |
| | Market-access restrictions and standards | | X | |

*Source:* Adapted from Trevor Morgan, *Energy Subsidies: Their Magnitude, How They Affect Energy Investment and Greenhouse Gas Emissions, and Prospects for Reform* (Geneva: UNFCCC Secretariat Financial and Technical Support Program, June 2007).

Energy subsidies can be pervasive, yet difficult to identify. Consider the example of one small subsector, transport of energy fuels. Inland waterway maintenance for the delivery of coal barges is often provided by national and local governments, rather than user fees. Coastal ports and harbors receiving oil, natural gas, and coal are subsidized by federal and other government entities. Most roadways used to deliver various energy fuels are owned, operated, and maintained by municipalities, funded through local tax dollars, and the interstate highway system in the United States received gargantuan federal subsidies in the 1950s and 1960s. Many rail lines receive state subsidies for labor and fuel, many pipeline rights of way are government backed, and transmission extensions to rural areas are often priced below cost because of a "duty to serve" customers.[10] Because they are indirect and hidden, these types of subsidies rarely "count" in official government audits and documents.

Practically every energy system has been subsidized at some point: oil wells were given free licenses in the 1860s, coalmines received tax breaks in the 1880s and 1890s, natural gas turbines benefited from military research on jet engines and rocket boosters, solar panels received some of their earliest support from NASA for their ability to provide electricity in outer space, and nuclear power has long been backed by steep contributions from the defense industry.[11] Even today, renewable energy sources such as wind turbines and geothermal power plants receive a production tax credit in many countries, coal receives special tax treatment and black lung benefits paid by government, oil and gas receives huge tax shelters as well as research subsidies.[12]

Some of these subsidies, notably low-income assistance to poor households (under the LIHEAP, discussed more in Chapter 7), or those funding the early efforts of the Rural Electrification Administration, have served a social purpose in the United States. Today, however, many, if not most, serve almost no discernible public good – and, in some ways,

---

[10] Koplow, "Subsidies to Energy Industries."
[11] Vicki Norberg-Bohm, "Creating Incentives for Environmentally Enhancing Technological Change: Lessons from 30 Years of U.S. Energy Technology Policy," *Technological Forecasting and Social Change* 65 (2000), pp. 125–148.
[12] Mark Z. Jacobson and Gilbert M. Masters, "Letters and Responses: The Real Cost of Wind Energy," *Science* 294(5544) (November 2, 2001), pp. 1000–1003.

they do considerable bad. As Kiyo Akasaka, Deputy Secretary-General of the Organisation for Economic Co-operation and Development (OECD), has noted, "Subsidies often introduce economic, environmental, and social distortions with unintended consequences. They are expensive for governments and may not achieve their objectives while also inducing harmful environmental and social outcomes."[13]

Interestingly, the nonpartisan US Energy Information Administration (US EIA) conducted an in-depth exploration of energy subsidies in the United States, and noted two salient trends.[14] First, the level of subsidies has actually gotten worse over the past decade; the US EIA estimated that direct energy subsidies have *doubled* from 1999 to 2007 and indirect tax expenditures have *tripled* over the same period. Second, and oddly, the US EIA concluded that the subsidies did not really do anything at the national scale. They had no net result on energy production, which the US EIA called "virtually unchanged." One explanation might be that this is because some types of subsidies cancel others out – some, say, encourage energy efficiency, convincing customers to save energy, whereas others encourage production and lower prices, convincing customers to use more energy. They certainly helped particular industries, but resulted in no net positive change for the country.

Despite their pervasiveness and (at times) invisibility, such subsidies cultivate a long list of negative social and environmental impacts, including larger budget deficits for governments, artificially increased consumption and reduced efficiency, inhibited competition and trade, distorted price signals, energy shortages, the exacerbation of poverty, inflated GHG emissions, and self-replication.

## Government deficits

The most obvious impact is that subsidies create larger budget deficits and higher taxes, diverting funds from potentially better options for fiscal support and programs such as healthcare and education. One

---

[13] Kiyo Akasaka, "Preface," *Subsidy Reform and Sustainable Development: Political Economy Aspects* (Paris: OECD, 2007), pp. 7–8.

[14] US EIA Office of Coal, Nuclear, Electric, and Alternate Fuels, *Federal Financial Interventions and Subsidies in Energy Markets 2007* (Washington, DC: US Department of Energy, April 2008, R/CNEAF/2008–01).

international survey of 171 countries found that in 29 of them, refined gasoline and diesel prices were lower per unit than the international price of crude oil and below the minimum retail level in competitive markets in 52 additional countries – implying the existence of significant subsidies.[15] Figure 8.1 shows some of the results of this survey. An extreme example of such subsidies is Venezuela, where the price for gasoline was a mere 6 cents per gallon (or 1.6 cents per liter) – less than one fiftieth of what somebody in California pays – perhaps explaining why gasoline consumption there is 40 percent greater than in any other Latin American country and three times the average for the region.[16]

Though difficult to estimate, one independent review from Myers and Kent calculated that energy subsidies in 1999 amounted to a whopping 21.1 percent of all energy prices, in essence subsidizing – for libertarians, unjustly interfering with – more than one fifth of global consumption. They calculated that subsidies for fossil fuels and energy exceeded $331 billion in 2000 and that subsidies for road transportation amounted to $1,180 billion – a total of $1.5 trillion, or $1.9 trillion updated to today's dollars.[17] They mused that these subsidies, among other things, made gasoline cheaper than bottled water.

Their numbers may sound high, but a second independent study from the International Center for Technology Assessment calculated global energy subsidies at between $627.2 billion and $1.9 trillion in 2004.[18] More recently, the International Monetary Fund (IMF) projected in 2013 that fossil-fuel subsidies amounted to $1.9 trillion on a "post-tax basis" globally, equivalent to 8 percent of all government revenue for that year.[19] If the estimates that energy-related subsidies amounting

[15] Trevor Morgan, *Energy Subsidies: Their Magnitude, How They Affect Energy Investment and Greenhouse Gas Emissions, and Prospects for Reform* (Geneva: UNFCCC Secretariat Financial and Technical Support Program, June 2007).

[16] Lucas Davis, *The Economic Cost of Fossil Fuel Subsidies* (Berkeley: Haas Energy Institute, 2013).

[17] Norman Myers and Jennifer Kent, *Perverse Subsidies: How Tax Dollars Can Undercut the Environment and the Economy* (Washington, DC: Island Press, 2001).

[18] World Institute of Sustainable Energy, *Power Drain: Hidden Subsidies to Conventional Power in India* (Pune, India: World Institute of Sustainable Energy, 2008), p. 15.

[19] Robert Howse, "Energy Subsidies: The Ball Is Now in the WTO's Court," *Globe and Mail*, April 2, 2013. See also IMF, *Energy Subsidy Reform: Lessons and Implications* (New York: IMF, January 2013).

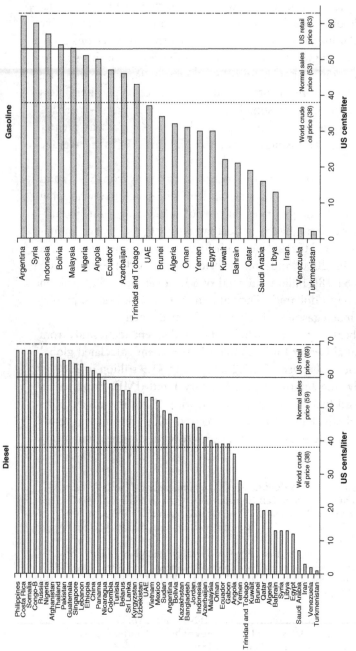

**Figure 8.1** Subsidies for gasoline and diesel in selected countries

*Source:* Adapted from Trevor Morgan, *Energy Subsidies: Their Magnitude, How They Affect Energy Investment and Greenhouse Gas Emissions, and Prospects for Reform* (Geneva: UNFCCC Secretariat Financial and Technical Support Program, June 2007).

to more than $1 trillion per year are accurate, then they are equivalent to the GDP of all low-income countries in the world per year.[20]

Think of what these billions (and possibly trillions) of dollars could otherwise be spent on. Independent of where the money would go, every incremental reduction of a country's debt strengthens their local currency, decreases inflation, increases employment, and decreases the amount of interest on foreign loans – and in the United States, the federal government spends $197 billion per year on such interest alone, an amount expected to rise to $800 billion by 2020.[21] Furthermore, the UN projects that $40 to $50 billion is enough to achieve universal energy access (think about all of the great things that would do, given the discussion in Chapter 7). Nineteen billion dollars is enough for a campaign to eliminate global hunger and malnutrition; $12 billion, enough for reproductive healthcare for all women; $10 billion enough for clean drinking water for all; $5 billion for universal literacy; $1.3 billion for immunizing every child, if the numbers from the UN are accurate.[22] One statistic bears repeating: though a libertarian would never say a government should necessarily do it, if the world's potential $1.9 trillion in energy subsidies were repealed tomorrow, that would provide enough money to eliminate worldwide hunger and malnutrition one *hundred* times over.

## Increased consumption and reduced efficiency

Depending on the type of subsidy, most generally increase levels of consumption far beyond where they would otherwise be. By lowering the end price of energy, subsidies therefore lead to higher energy use, and they also reduce the economically rational incentives to properly maintain or meter energy systems and products.

For example, in the former Soviet Union district heating was often provided far below cost – sometimes for free – leading people to "waste" heat in a variety of ways, including keeping windows open in the winter

---

[20] Cees van Beers and André de Moor, *Public Subsidies and Policy Failures: How Subsidies Distort the Natural Environment, Equity, and Trade, and How to Reform Them* (Cheltenham: Edward Elgar, 2001).

[21] Congressional Budget Office, Federal Debt and Interest Costs, December 14, 2010, available at www.cbo.gov/publication/21960.

[22] David Held, "Global Challenges: Accountability and Effectiveness," in Colin Hay (ed.), *New Directions in Political Science: Responding to the Challenges of an Interdependent World* (London: Palgrave Macmillan, 2010), pp. 211–230.

and growing tropical flowers.[23] Iran spends an annual $66 billion or 20 percent of the country's GDP in energy subsidies, mostly oil, to keep prices low and encourage consumption. Saudi Arabia, Venezuela, and Egypt each provided oil subsidies of $10–$20 billion in that same year. Oil subsidies are even offered in China ($24 billion) and India ($13 billion), major oil-importing nations, despite the fact that they encourage excessive consumption that requires more imports.[24] India subsidizes total fossil energy consumption by $21 billion or some $16 per person every year – a substantial amount given that 500 million of its people live on less than $2 per day. In India, subsidies for electricity encourage so much waste that the UN calculated that removing them would cut demand by 34 percent.[25]

Subsidies, by inflating the cost of energy, also erode motivations to promote energy efficiency or to conserve energy. Subsidies on coal production in Europe, for instance, hamper efforts to improve productivity and capture methane from empty coalmines. In the United Kingdom, coal subsidies have slowed the transition to better, safer mines and also discouraged producers from developing advanced coal pollution equipment. In the Czech Republic and the Slovak Republic, subsidies have held back innovation in the oil and gas sectors. Guaranteed profits meant operators did not invest in upgrades or, at times, maintenance. Similarly, in Russia, the large subsidies for district heating mentioned above meant that operators had no incentives to fix leaking steam pipes, did not improve their metering and billing practices, and did not invest in insulation and better building envelopes, leading to "extreme" inefficiency.[26] In the Middle East, governments such as Kuwait, Oman, Qatar, Saudi Arabia, and the United Arab Emirates are so heavily dependent on oil subsidies that they need at least $80 per barrel to remain profitable – and some, such as Saudi Arabia, are still expected to encounter budget deficits in 2014 – whereas

---

[23] UN Environment Program Division of Technology, Industry and Economics and the International Energy Agency, *Reforming Energy Subsidies: An Explanatory Summary*; and UN Environment Program Division of Technology, Industry and Economics, *Reforming Energy Subsidies: Opportunities to Contribute.*

[24] IEA, *World Energy Outlook 2008* (Paris: OECD, 2008).

[25] UNEP, *Energy Subsidies: Lessons Learned in Assessing their Impact and Designing Policy Reforms* (New York: UN Foundation, 2004).

[26] *Ibid.*

private companies such as ExxonMobil and British Petroleum can reputedly turn a profit with oil at $20 per barrel.[27]

## Anticompetitive behavior and poor investment

Energy subsidies hurt competition, and distort price signals by lowering the costs of innovation in mature industries and increasing barriers to entry for newer, cleaner, and emerging technologies. In India, a study from the World Institute of Sustainable Energy looked at nineteen coal-fired, natural gas, and hydroelectric power plants and calculated that cumulative subsidies amounted to 150 percent of the cost of the original investment – meaning the subsidies enabled the industry to operate at a collective loss to taxpayers and Indian society.[28] It is telling in India that fuel subsidies for kerosene and liquid propane gas are of the same magnitude as those for education.[29] In the United States, subsidies have done the same – enabled an industry to operate at a net, cumulative loss – for the country's fleet of nuclear power plants[30] and uranium enrichment facilities (see Chapter 4's discussion of "nuclear waste storage and decommissioning" for more on those costs).[31] Subsidies also contribute to smuggling: Canadians purchase cheap gasoline in the United States, Tunisians consume cheaper (illegal) fuel from Algeria, Yemeni oil is smuggled into Djibouti, and black market Nigerian fuel is illicitly distributed into many West African countries.[32]

Most of the time, energy subsidies explicitly pick "winners" and can entrench dirtier, less efficient forms of energy supply such as fossil-fueled power plants, nuclear reactors, and crude oil refineries. Looking closely at

---

[27] See Suzanne Maloney, "The Gulf's Renewed Oil Wealth: Getting it Right this Time?," *Survival* 50(6) (December 2008/January 2009), pp. 129–150; Sean L. Yom and F. Gregory Gause, "Resilient Royals: How Arab Monarchies Hang On," *Journal of Democracy* 23(4) (October 2012), pp. 74–88; and personal correspondence with Salman Shaikh, Director of the Brookings Doha Center and fellow at the Saban Center for Middle East Policy.

[28] World Institute of Sustainable Energy, *Power Drain.*

[29] Evan Mills, "The Specter of Fuel-Based Lighting," *Science* 308 (May 27, 2005), pp. 1263–1264.

[30] Koplow, *Nuclear Power.*

[31] B.K. Sovacool, *Contesting the Future of Nuclear Power: A Critical Global Assessment of Atomic Energy* (London: World Scientific, 2011).

[32] IMF, *Energy Subsidy Reform*, pp. 16–17.

the numbers in the United States, conventional sources have received almost 90 percent of all subsidies for the past six decades.[33] In 1973, before the energy crisis, the federal government awarded 93 percent of its subsidies to conventional technologies but only 6 percent to energy efficiency, renewable electricity, and other alternatives. Even in fiscal year 1979, when subsidies for renewable energy peaked at $1.5 billion, subsidies for fossil fuels were greater at $1.9 billion and more than 58 percent of the DOE research budget was directed at nuclear power.[34] Another longitudinal study of US energy subsidies going all the way back to the 1800s estimated that nuclear subsidies amounted to more than 1 percent of the entire federal budget, that oil and gas subsidies made up one half to 1 percent of the total budget, but that support for cleaner systems such as renewables and energy efficiency have constituted only one tenth of 1 percent.[35]

What about recently, astute readers may inquire? The GAO notes that during the last decade, not much has changed, with fossil energy receiving 86 percent of government subsidies, nuclear energy 8 percent, and renewables and energy efficiency only 6 percent.[36] An examination of current federal electricity subsidies over the past six years shows that government policymakers remain heavily committed to supporting conventional sources. These large financial outlays convinced the *Economist* magazine to recently conclude that "however you measure the full cost of a gallon of gas, pollution and all, Americans are nowhere close to paying it. Indeed, their whole energy industry – from subsidies for corn ethanol to limited liability for nuclear power – is a pool of preferences and restrictions, without peer."[37]

---

[33] Koplow, *Federal Energy Subsidies*. From 1943 to 1999, for instance, direct federal subsidies for nuclear power totaled $144.5 billion, more than twenty-five times the cumulative spending on wind and solar ($4.4 billion for solar thermal and PV and only $1.3 billion for wind).

[34] David W. Orr, "Problems, Dilemmas, and the Energy Crisis," in Karen M. Gentemann (ed.), *Social and Political Perspectives on Energy Policy* (New York: Praeger, 1981), pp. 1–17.

[35] Nancy Pfund and Ben Healey, *What Would Jefferson Do? The Historical Role of Federal Subsidies in Shaping America's Energy Future* (DBL Investors, September 2011).

[36] US GAO, *Department of Energy: Key Challenges Remain for Developing and Deploying Advanced Energy Technologies to Meet Future Needs* (Washington, DC: US GAO, December 2006, GAO-07–106).

[37] "Deep Trouble," *Economist*, May 8, 2010, p. 11.

Subsidies hurting competition and inhibiting the entry of newer and cleaner technologies exist around the world, not just in the United States. When disaggregated by technology, petroleum products received the bulk of global energy subsidies in 2012 ($879 billion, or 46.2 percent) followed by coal ($539 billion, 29.4 percent), natural gas ($299 billion, 15.7 percent), and electricity ($179 billion, 9.4 percent).[38] The International Institute for Sustainable Development (IISD) similarly estimated that three-quarters of energy subsidies go towards conventional systems such as fossil fuels and nuclear power.[39] In the OECD as a whole, the bulk of research subsidies also goes (again) towards fossil fuels and nuclear power. Technologies and processes such as Generation IV nuclear reactors, combined cycle natural gas turbines and clean coal technologies such as carbon sequestration, fluidized gas combustion, and integrated coal gasification combined cycle systems have received $417 billion dollars in research funds from industrialized countries, more than nine times the $45 billion spent on the entire class renewables, figures reflected in Figure 8.2.[40]

## Energy shortages and exacerbation of poverty

Ironically, in some cases subsidies can cause energy shortages and, in others, contribute to poverty. Caps and ceilings on prices clearing particular market levels have led to physical shortages of energy (such as that of natural gas in the 1970s and 1980s in the United States[41]) and, at times, government rationing programs. In India, crude oil and oil products are strictly rationed for precisely these reasons, and the below-market price delivery of small liquefied petroleum gas cylinders has led to "large distortions" in prices and shortages among some 42 million households.[42] Similarly, in Myanmar, fixed prices for electricity, diesel,

---

[38] IMF, *Energy Subsidy Reform.*
[39] IISD, *Achieving the G-20 Call to Phase Out Subsidies to Fossil Fuels* (Canada: IISD, October 2009).
[40] International Energy Agency, *Energy Technology RD&D 2008 Edition* (Paris: International Energy Agency, 2009).
[41] Joseph P. Tomain and Richard D. Cudahy, *Energy Law in a Nutshell* (New York: West Publishing Company, 2011).
[42] UN Environment Program Division of Technology, Industry and Economics and the International Energy Agency, *Reforming Energy Subsidies: An Explanatory Summary*; and UN Environment Program Division of Technology, Industry and Economics, *Reforming Energy Subsidies: Opportunities to Contribute.*

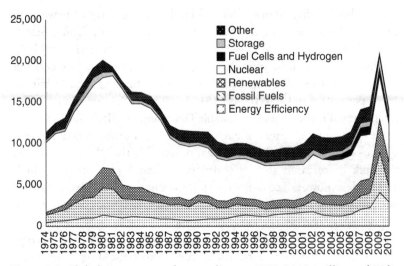

**Figure 8.2** Global energy research expenditures, 1974–2010 (millions of US$)
*Source:* Adapted from the International Energy Agency website, accessed November 2012.

and gasoline have resulted in shortages when those prices fall below international market levels – convincing suppliers to focus on exports to China and Thailand rather than domestic use.[43]

Subsidies for some fuels such as kerosene, liquefied petroleum gas, natural gas, and electricity can worsen levels and intensities of poverty. In many developing countries, modern energy carriers are subsidized for an apparent purpose of improving household living conditions by making energy more affordable. The UN warns that, instead, most of these subsidies benefit energy companies, equipment suppliers, and wealthier households in towns and cities; *not* the urban poor and *not* communities living in rural villages. As a result, "many energy-subsidy programs intended to boost poor households' purchasing power or rural communities' access to modern energy through lower prices can, paradoxically, leave the poor worse off, since the costs are shared by the entire population including the poor." The explanation is threefold: poorest households are often unable to afford even subsidized energy; the poor have

---

[43] B.K. Sovacool, *Review of Rural Energy Access and Environmental Conservation Challenges and Approaches in Myanmar* (Yangon: UN Development Program-Myanmar, March 2012).

lower consumption levels, meaning on a per-unit basis subsidies benefit those with higher incomes; and wealthier homes have been known to hoard, smuggle, and export energy fuels and services abroad.[44]

## Externalities and emissions

Because subsidies generally inflate production and consumption, they also produce more externalities (see Chapter 4) and contribute to climate change (see Chapter 10). United Nations Environment Program (UNEP) subsidy expert Trevor Morgan explained it this way:

Energy subsidies deliberately distort price signals and, therefore, investment in infrastructure to supply different fuels and in the capital stock that transform or consume energy. Because the bulk of energy subsidies worldwide result in a lower price for fossil fuels to end users, they cause more of those fuels to be consumed, increasing carbon-dioxide and other greenhouse-gas emissions and contributing to climate change.[45]

As just one example, subsidies for coal in the EU and Japan are responsible for 50 to 100 million extra tons of carbon dioxide emissions per year.[46] In Australia, cheap subsidies for coal-fired electricity have resulted in a smelting industry that produces 2.5 times as many GHG emissions per ton of manufactured aluminum as the world average.[47] The World Bank has estimated that the removal of subsidies for oil, coal, and natural gas would immediately reduce global GHG emissions by 9 percent[48] – more than any single national source of annual emissions except for China and the United States. The IMF similarly calculated in 2013 that fossil-fuel subsidies result in an extra 4.5 *billion* tons of carbon dioxide emissions from additional energy consumption.[49]

[44] UN Environment Program Division of Technology, Industry and Economics and the International Energy Agency, *Reforming Energy Subsidies: An Explanatory Summary*; and UN Environment Program Division of Technology, Industry and Economics, *Reforming Energy Subsidies: Opportunities to Contribute.*

[45] Morgan, *Energy Subsidies.*

[46] European Commission, *Reforming Environmentally Harmful Subsidies* (UK: Institute for European Environmental Policy, March 2007).

[47] H. Turton, *The Aluminum Smelting Industry: Structure, Market Power, Subsidies, and Greenhouse Gas Emissions* (Canberra: Australia Institute Discussion Paper, January 2002).

[48] Bjorn Larsen and Anwar Shah, *World Fossil Fuel Subsidies and Global Carbon Emissions* (World Bank, October 1992, WPS 1002).

[49] Howse, "Energy Subsidies."

## Subsidy "lock-in" and "addiction"

Importantly, subsidies become self-replicating because, once enacted, they continue to shape energy choices through the long-lived infrastructure and capital stock they create. This justifies further expenditures to operate, maintain, and improve those subsidised technologies. Coal and nuclear plants built forty years ago, for example, still receive subsidies for coalmining and uranium enrichment.[50] Subsidies also have a degree of infectiousness, given that once one country starts subsidizing a particular energy fuel or system, others are motivated to respond with their own subsidies to compete.

The federal government in the United States subsidizes fossil fuels so much that among the thirty industrialized nations forming the OECD – including the EU, Japan, Australia, and Korea – it is responsible for 70 percent of all subsidies for coal worldwide.[51] This subsidization creates higher demand for fossil-fuel imports globally, forcing other counties to subsidize their own energy sectors.[52] Cees van Beers, Associate Professor of Economics at Delft University of Technology, and André de Moor, Deputy Head of International Environmental Assessment Division at the National Institute of Public Health and Environment (RIVM) in the Netherlands, argue that subsidies create something very close to addiction.[53] Governments initially favor dispensation of privileges in exchange for political support, but grow more dependent on that support over time.

This trend of subsidy "lock-in" and "dependency" is nicely illustrated with an example of subsidies for crude oil in developing countries. In 2004, crude oil prices climbed to historic highs, increasing in price sevenfold only to lose all of their previous gains over the preceding five years in a few months. The World Bank assessed the responses of forty-nine developing countries to these oil price increases, with a sample of governments spread across Africa, Asia, Latin America, and the Middle

---

[50] Koplow, *Federal Energy Subsidies.*
[51] Sadeq Z. Bigdeli, "Will the Friends of Climate Emerge in the WTO? The Prospects of Applying the Fisheries Subsidy Model to Energy Subsidies," *Carbon & Climate Law Review* 2(1) (2008), pp. 78–88.
[52] Andrew Simms, *The Price of Power: Poverty, Climate Change, the Coming Energy Crisis, and the Renewable Revolution* (London: New Economics Foundation, 2004).
[53] Van Beers and de Moor, *Public Subsidies.*

East.[54] The Bank study found that many governments resorted to subsidies in the face of rising prices in an attempt to keep consumers protected. These new subsidies included credits for the exploration and production of oil, tax reductions, agricultural exemptions, discounts for passenger transport, price controls for fuel for fisheries, and partial compensation for domestic refineries. China, India, and Mexico alone had $67 billion worth of these new subsidies. However, the study noted that when prices for oil receded, the subsidies remained: powerful constituencies had become dependent on them, and consumers resented the option of suddenly paying more for energy. The implication is that enacting subsidies is far easier than scaling them back.

## What is justice?

Despite the clear problems with subsidies, they are, and have been, common across many nations and over many decades. Can justice theory help us judge how to respond to arguments for prolonging or expanding such support schemes? One group of justice theorists, "libertarians," favors free markets and criticizes most government regulation. What does their thinking offer us in making decisions about energy subsidies?

Libertarian theorists begin with the idea that each of us has an individual, fundamental right to liberty, a right to do whatever we want with what we own, provided we do not violate other people's right to do the same. Only a minimal state is justified morally, one that enforces contracts, protects property, and keeps the peace. We own ourselves and the fruits of our labor, and thus have a right to decide what to do with ourselves and our assets.[55] For libertarians, the notion of individual free will, and the "self," is sacrosanct.[56] The libertarian position holds that human freedom is, and should be, the only concern

---

[54] Masami Kojima, *Government Responses to Oil Price Volatility* (Washington, DC: World Series Report #2, July 2009); Masami Kojima, *Changes in End-User Petroleum Product Prices* (Washington, DC: World Bank, Extractive Industries for Development Series #2, July 2009).

[55] Michael J. Sandel, "Libertarianism," in Michael J. Sandel (ed.), *Justice: A Reader* (Oxford University Press, 2007), p. 49.

[56] C.A. Campbell, "Libertarianism: The Self Has Free Will," in Louis P. Pojman (ed.), *Introduction to Philosophy: Classical and Contemporary Readings* (Belmont: Wadsworth Publishing, 1991), pp. 391–398.

of social institutions.[57] Governments should protect their citizens, and citizens should not be able to impose upon other citizens' freedom.[58]

## Robert Nozick

One of the most influential libertarian theorists is the late philosopher and Harvard Professor Robert Nozick (1938–2002). Nozick begins by arguing that people are free and people have rights and entitlements. As he stated unequivocally: "Individuals have rights, and there are things no person or group may do to them (without violating their rights). So strong and far-reaching are those rights that they raise the question of what, if anything, the state and its officials may do,"[59] and: "Things come into the world already attached to people having entitlements over them."[60] These rights and entitlements cannot be diminished by the power of government (or other individuals) because to do so would be to limit the freedom of the individual. Furthermore, people have money, and the money that each person has belongs to him or her alone. Money, therefore, is a possession, which entails a personal right of ownership. To take this money for any reason, except to provide basic policing powers – the only legitimate governmental power, according to the libertarian – is to limit a person's rights and freedom. This is true even if the money would be used for a "good cause," or social welfare. For the libertarian position, "prominent among the things that no one should be forced to do is help other people."[61]

Each individual has certain rights, and impingement upon these rights by anyone, including the government, is unjust. Nozick then continues:

Our main conclusions about the state are that a minimal state, limited to the narrow functions of protection against force, theft, fraud, enforcement of contract, and so on, is justified; that any more extensive state will violate persons' rights not to be forced to do certain things, and is unjustified; and that the minimal state is inspiring as well as right. Two noteworthy implications are that the state may not use its coercive apparatus for the purpose of

---

[57] Jan Narveson, *The Libertarian Idea* (Canada: Temple University Press, 2001), Preface.

[58] Michael J. Sandel, *Justice: What's the Right Thing to Do?* (New York: Farrar, Straus, and Giroux, 2009), p. 60.

[59] Robert Nozick, *Anarchy, State, and Utopia* (New York: Basic Books, 1974), p. ix.

[60] *Ibid.*, p. 151.    [61] Sandel, *Justice: What's the Right Thing to Do?*

getting some citizens to aid others, or in order to prohibit activities to people for their own good or protection.[62]

For Nozick, there is no central distribution, institution, person, or group entitled to control resources or other people's property.[63]

Nozick also developed his own theory of "distributive justice."[64] For him, a valid theory of justice encompassed three parts, or principles: acquisition, transfer, and rectification. The principle of acquisition described how people legitimately acquire holdings. The principle of transfer described how people transfer holdings; it means that acquisition from a previous owner must be by voluntary agreement, i.e. a gift or an exchange.[65] The principle of rectification described how past injustices should be rectified. His answer to what enables just acquisition and transfer is, unsurprisingly, respect for private property and the free market. As he wrote, "a distribution is just if it arises from another (just) distribution by legitimate means"[66] and "whoever makes something, having bought or contracted for all other held resources used in the process (transferring some of his holdings for these competing factors), is entitled to it."[67] The free market increases the means of production by placing it directly in the hands of laborers; it enables people to decide on the patterns and types of risks they want to personally bear; it protects even future generations by "leading some to hold back resources from current consumption for future markets." Most important here, for us, is how Nozick proposes to rectify unjust distribution, to undo something the government has done wrongly to us. His answer is that if an injustice has occurred, we must determine what the expected outcome would be if that injustice had not occurred – we must undo it.

## Milton Friedman

This basic libertarian philosophy is the foundation of the free market theories of the economist, professor, and public intellectual Milton

---

[62] Nozick, *Anarchy, State, and Utopia*, p. ix.

[63] Thomas C. Grey, "Property and Need: The Welfare State and Theories of Distributive Justice," *Stanford Law Review* 28(5) (May 1976), pp. 877–902.

[64] Robert Nozick, "Distributive Justice," *Philosophy and Public Affairs* 3 (1973), pp. 45–61.

[65] James A. Caporaso and David P. Levine, *Theories of Political Economy* (Cambridge University Press, 1992).

[66] Nozick, "Distributive Justice," p. 47.    [67] *Ibid.*, p. 160.

Friedman (1912–2006). As one of his biographers put it, "Friedman is best known as an advocate of libertarianism, the free market, and capitalism."[68] Friedman's theories about government encroachment were fairly radical at the time. He believed that social security was an infringement of individual freedom, arguing that people should be able to live for today, and not save, if they desire.[69] He also claimed that employers should be able to pay employees whatever they want, no matter how little, and that the minimum wage is an unjust use of government power. Moreover, the free market, and therefore justice, is not achieved by antidiscrimination laws. As justice expert Michael Sandel explains: "If employers want to discriminate on the basis of race, religion, or any other factor, the state has no right to prevent them from doing so. In Friedman's view, such legislation clearly involves interference with the freedom of individuals to enter into voluntary contracts with another."[70] The crux of Friedman's claim was that personal freedom "can only be achieved in systems of economic freedom."[71]

## *Libertarian theory in a nutshell*

Taken together, the libertarian theory of justice rejects three philosophic tenants that often form the foundation of many modern governments. First, "no paternalism." Libertarians oppose laws to protect people from harming themselves. Paternalism, or the idea that the government, standing in the role of a father, knows what is best for you even if you do not know it or do not agree, is the antitheses of libertarianism. Under the libertarian ideal, no person or authority can decide what is right for the individual because to do so would be an imposition on a person's rights.

Second, no "morals legislation." Libertarians oppose using the coercive force of law to promote notions of virtue or to express the moral convictions of the majority. Prostitution may be morally objectionable to many people, but that does not justify laws that prevent consenting adults from engaging in it. According to the libertarian, unless an action or way of life threatens another person's freedom or rights, it is unjust to force morality on the populace, or upon individuals.

---

[68] Lanny Ebenstein, *Milton Friedman: A Biography* (New York: Palgrave Macmillan, 2007), Introduction.

[69] Sandel, *Justice: What's the Right Thing to Do?*, p. 61.    [70] *Ibid.*, p. 62.

[71] Harry Brighouse, *Justice* (Cambridge: Polity Press, 2004), p. 86.

Third, "no redistribution of income." The libertarian theory of rights rules out any law that requires some people to help others, including taxation for redistribution of wealth. Desirable though it may be for the affluent to support the less fortunate – by subsidizing their healthcare, housing, or education – such help should be left up to the individual to undertake, not mandated by the government. According to the libertarian, redistributive taxes are a form of coercion, even theft.[72]

As is perhaps obvious, libertarianism is open to some basic criticisms. It does nothing to enable the poor or minorities to escape their current predicaments, and it naturalizes existing patterns of wealth. Even worse, Berkeley economist Hal R. Varian notes that "the private ownership, laissez-faire society Nozick describes does indeed tend to generate extreme distributions of wealth."[73] Libertarians believe that taxing the rich to help the poor is tantamount to coercion and violates their right to do what they want with what they own.[74] Furthermore, libertarians implicitly believe in the Pareto optimality of exchanges within the marketplace, and that the market economy will, by itself, equitably, efficiently, and fairly produce positive outcomes.[75] Yet, Pareto efficiency and perfect markets have *never* existed, and may not be theoretically possible.[76] As the Nobel Prize winning economist Joseph Stiglitz pointed out, there is only one way markets can be perfect, but a virtually infinite number of ways they can be imperfect, so we

---

[72] Sandel, *Justice: What's the Right Thing to Do?*, p. 60.

[73] Hal R. Varian, "Distributive Justice, Welfare Economics, and the Theory of Fairness," *Philosophy & Public Affairs* 4(3) (Spring 1975), pp. 223–247.

[74] Clark Wolf, "Intergenerational Justice," in R.G. Frey and Christopher Heath Wellman (eds.), *A Companion to Applied Ethics* (London: Blackwell Publishing, 2003), pp. 279–294.

[75] A Pareto optimum, named after the economist Vilfredo Pareto, is regarded as a situation where all possible gains from the voluntary exchange of goods and services has been exhausted, and no participant is willing to make further exchanges at the terms of trade that currently exist. Under these conditions, an exchange takes place only when both parties feel they benefit from it. When no more beneficial exchanges can be made, the economy has reached a situation where each individual cannot improve their economic welfare without damaging that of another. When no one can be better off without someone being worse off, Pareto optimality has been achieved. In economic parlance, an efficient balance has been obtained. See Allen V. Kneese, "Natural Resources Policy, 1975–1985," *Journal of Environmental Economics and Management* 3 (1976), pp. 253–288.

[76] Guido Calabresi and A. Douglas Melamed, "Property Rules, Liability Rules, and Inalienability: One View of the Cathedral," *Harvard Law Review* 85(6) (April 1972), pp. 1089–1128.

should expect the latter, not the former.[77] Additionally, the Nozick position, like other libertarian positions, focuses on the dangers of "the state" to a degree that seems to blind them to the dangers of other entities such as big businesses, tribes, or theocracies. As such, it misses the argument of John Kenneth Galbraith (and others) that the powers of the state are "needed" as a "countervailing" force to protect individuals against powerful nonstate actors, not just to coerce them.[78] Lastly, libertarians refuse to enable laws and rules that would actually protect people from harming themselves – think of no laws requiring seatbelts, no laws prohibiting prostitution or speeding, no laws stopping drunk driving or heroin use.

A personal story may help illustrate the significance of this last point. One of us is the parent of a child who was once in an automobile accident when the car in front of her lost control and crashed head-on into her vehicle. Amazingly, none of the seven passengers in the two cars were seriously injured. Why not? The motors would have crushed the bodies of the front seat passengers were it not for the invention of crumple zones. The windshields, which shattered, would have lacerated and possibly blinded the passengers, were it not for standards requiring beaded glass fragments instead of splintered shards. Seatbelts prevented the passengers from being thrown against the car's metal frame. Airbags kept them from being smashed against the front of each car. These and other mandatory safety measures allowed seven people to survive, battered but healthy, after a crash that would have otherwise killed or crippled them. Yet, none of these safety features arose from unregulated free market economics or consumer choices; they each required regulation, and government intervention.[79] Thus, there is something to be said for governmental "paternalism" requiring that cars be built to be safe enough to protect us against the poor decisions of other drivers.

---

[77] Joseph E. Stiglitz, "Information and the Change in the Paradigm of Economics," *American Economic Review* 92(3) (June 2002), pp. 460–501.

[78] John Kenneth Galbraith, *The New Industrial State* (New York: Basic Books, 1967).

[79] The case also demonstrates how many decisions are not based upon economic rationality. The driver of the other car in this case was an unlicensed youngster joyriding in his older brother's vehicle. Perhaps the speed of the oncoming car in the wrong lane was driven as much by teenage hormones as by an economically rational calculus of risk.

More generally, there may be a role for government to protect citizens against harms when markets fail to do so.

Still, despite these shortcomings, the libertarian ethic makes a strong case for individual freedom, and applied to energy it clearly argues that the government *not* intervene in the marketplace concerning particular energy technologies and fuels. Georgia Tech Philosophy Professor Bryan Norton notes that because libertarianism is about freedom, freedom is about choices, and "choices require options. So options are a prerequisite of true freedom; if I control the options you choose among, I control the range – and substance – of your free choice."[80] As Nozick himself wrote:

No state more extensive than the minimal state can be justified ... The minimal state treats us as inviolate individuals, who may not be used in certain ways by others as means or tools or instruments or resources; it treats us as persons having individual rights with the dignity this constitutes. Treating us with respect by respecting our rights, it allows us, individually or with whom we choose, to choose our life and realize our ends and our conception of ourselves, insofar as we can, aided by the voluntary cooperation of other individuals possessing the same dignity. How dare any state or group of individuals do more. Or less.[81]

Freedom here can only be the absence of interfering in the actions of others; it therefore demands the absence of subsidies for particular energy systems and fuels.[82]

## What is to be done?

Are there tools that would meet some (if not all) of the libertarian ideal for less government intervention in the energy sector? Let us consider four policy shifts that might be strong contenders: the elimination of inappropriate energy subsidies, the sponsoring of subsidy impact studies, sunset clauses for subsidies, and adjustment packages.

---

[80] Bryan Norton, "Ecology and Opportunity: Intergenerational Equity and Sustainable Options," in Andrew Dobson (ed.), *Fairness and Futurity: Essays on Environmental Sustainability and Social Justice* (Oxford University Press, 1999), pp. 118–150.

[81] Nozick, *Anarchy, State, and Utopia*, pp. 297, 333–334.

[82] Jan Narveson, "Welfare and Wealth, Poverty and Justice in Today's World," *Journal of Ethics* 8 (2004), pp. 305–348.

*Eliminating inappropriate subsidies*

Elimination of subsidies could follow the true libertarian ideal and be complete, meaning a government would abolish every type of subsidy, across the board. A second variant would be more targeted, removing subsidies only for "conventional," "dirty," or "undesirable" energy systems such as oil, coal, natural gas, and possibly nuclear power. A third variant would be to remove what energy scholars Norman Myers and Jennifer Kent call "perverse subsidies." These are subsidies that harm both the economy and the environment. Examples include those that:

- Maintain production processes that would otherwise be uneconomic, such as subsidies to grow corn for ethanol in arid areas;
- Artificially reduce costs, such as fuel subsidies that make gasoline cheaper than water in the United States;
- Produce un-usable surpluses, such as the "lakes" of butter, milk, and wheat commonly discarded in the 1980s;
- Deter efforts at sustainability, such as subsidies for the harvesting of old-growth forests for heating fuel instead of a shift towards plantation forestry;
- Stimulate activity that degrades natural resources underpinning agriculture and economic growth, such as subsidies for electric irrigation systems in places that otherwise should not grow crops.[83]

Removing all, some, or only the most "perverse" subsidies has the potential to rapidly change energy markets for the better. Myers and Kent estimate the removal of "perverse" subsidies would immediately cut energy consumption by 3.5 percent and reduce emissions by 4.6 percent per year, and also increase global welfare by $35 billion and increase real income for the world by 0.7 percent.[84] One group of economists calculated that by merely cutting fuel subsidies for gasoline by 80 percent, global demand for oil would immediately drop by 5 percent – the equivalent of removing 2.5 million barrels of oil a day from the market (at that time).[85]

---

[83] Norman Myers and Jennifer Kent, *Perverse Subsidies: How Tax Dollars Can Undercut the Environment and the Economy* (Washington, DC: Island Press, 2001).

[84] *Ibid.*, pp. 52–53, 77.

[85] Tony Regan, "Relations between Producers and Consumers of Energy" (seminar on Sustainable Development and Energy Security, Institute of Southeast Asian Studies, Singapore, April 22 and 23, 2008).

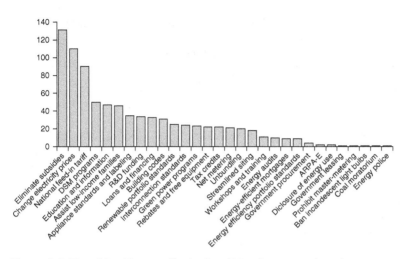

**Figure 8.3** Top thirty "most effective" policies for promoting clean energy (n = 181)
*Note*: ARPA–E: Advanced Research Projects Agency – Energy.
*Source*: B.K. Sovacool, "The Importance of Comprehensiveness in Renewable Electricity and Energy Efficiency Policy," *Energy Policy* 37(4) (April 2009), pp. 1529–1541.

The International Energy Agency's estimates suggest that the removal of subsidies for energy consumption in a group of eight developing economies would reduce energy use by 13 percent, reduce carbon dioxide emissions 16 percent, and raise incomes by 1 percent in aggregate.[86] The IMF correspondingly estimated that removing fossil-fuel subsidies would cut global emissions of carbon dioxide, and other health-damaging pollutants such as $SO_2$, by 13 percent.[87] These estimates may be why one recent survey of energy experts concluded that "removing subsidies" was the single most preferred, and effective, policy option for promoting cleaner forms of energy supply, compared to dozens of other types of mechanisms – results shown in Figure 8.3.

Though rare, energy subsidy removal has been done successfully before. Several European states depicted in Table 8.2 repealed reduced value added tax (VAT) rates to coal, fuel oil, natural gas, and electricity providers over the past three decades. These artificially low VAT rates had been implemented to benefit poor households – similar to low

[86] Morgan, *Energy Subsidies*.    [87] Howse, "Energy Subsidies."

Table 8.2 *VAT energy subsidies removed in Europe, 1983–2005*

| | Type of subsidy removed | | | | |
|---|---|---|---|---|---|
| Country | Coal | Fuel Oil | Natural Gas | Electricity | Year(s) |
| Austria | X | X | X | X | 1983 |
| Belgium | | X | X | X | 1980–1983 |
| Czech Republic | X | X | X | X | 1994–1997 |
| Greece | X | X | X | | 1992–1998 |
| Hungary | | X | X | X | 2003–2005 |
| Italy | | X | X | | 1984–1988 |
| Poland | X | X | X | X | 1998 |
| Portugal | | X | | | 1996–2001 |
| Slovakia | X | X | X | X | 2003 |

*Source:* Adapted from European Commission, *Reforming Environmentally Harmful Subsidies* (UK: Institute for European Environmental Policy, March 2007).

VAT rates on other "basic needs" such as food. However, the VAT subsidies were eliminated when it was discovered that most of their benefits went to the rich, rather than the poor, since the wealthy tended to consume more energy, and that removal had only a negligible impact on energy market prices but saved drastic amounts of tax revenue for the governments involved.[88] The IMF has in parallel documented at least twenty examples of successful energy subsidy reform across eighteen countries over the past sixty years, summarized by Table 8.3, with some of them having substantial impacts on energy prices and/or national GDP.

## Subsidy impact studies

Rather than repealing subsidies, governments and communities could conduct subsidy impact studies to better determine the costs and benefits of particular subsidies, and which ones could be revised or repealed. As the UNEP clarifies: "Transparency is essential. The financial costs and the channels through which [subsidies] are made must be fully transparent, to

[88] European Commission, *Reforming Environmentally Harmful Subsidies*.

Table 8.3 *Successful examples of national subsidy reform, 1952– 2012*

| Country | Year(s) | Energy source | Description/result |
|---------|---------|---------------|--------------------|
| Armenia | 1994 | Electricity | Scaled back electricity subsidies by 22 percent from 1994 to 2004 |
| Brazil | 1990–2002 | Oil and gas | Lowered subsidies for oil and gas from 0.8 percent of GDP to revenue generating in 2002 |
| Brazil | 1993–2003 | Electricity | Lowered subsidies equivalent to 0.7 percent of GDP |
| Chile | 1995 | Coal | Removed its subsidies after it became apparent that coal production prices were extraordinarily high ($95 per ton) compared to other countries ($54 in Brazil, $52 for the United States); the removal actually raised incomes by almost 1 percent among all Chilean households and cut emissions of carbon dioxide and PM by nearly 8 percent |
| Ghana | 2005 | Oil and gas | Removed subsidies to the degree that they realigned the price of energy by 50 percent |
| Indonesia | 2005–2009 | Oil and gas | Subsidies declined from 3.5 percent of GDP in 2005 to 0.8 percent in 2009 |
| Iran | 2010 | Oil and gas | Reduced annual growth in the national consumption of petroleum products to zero |
| Kenya | 2001–2008 | Electricity | Subsidies dropped from 1.5 percent of GDP in 2001 to 0 percent in 2008 |
| Mauritania | 2011 | Oil and gas | Subsidies declined from 2 percent of GDP to close to zero in one year |
| Namibia | 1997 | Oil and gas | Removed subsidies equal to about 0.1 percent of GDP |
| Niger | 2011 | Oil and gas | Removed subsidies equivalent to 0.9 percent of GDP |
| Nigeria | 2011–2012 | Oil and gas | Subsidies declined from 4.7 percent of GDP to 3.6 percent of GDP |

Table 8.3 (*cont.*)

| Country | Year(s) | Energy source | Description/result |
|---------|---------|---------------|--------------------|
| Peru | 2010 | Oil and gas | Lowered subsidies for petroleum equivalent to 0.1 percent of GDP |
| Philippines | 1996 | Oil and gas | Government successfully removed energy subsidies equivalent to 0.1 percent of national GDP |
| Philippines | 2001–2006 | Electricity | Subsidies dropped from 1.5 percent of national GDP to 0 percent |
| Poland | 1998 | Coal | Forced the coal sector to improve its efficiency and substantially reduced fiscal transfers |
| South Africa | 1952–1957 | Oil and gas | Successfully avoided subsidies and still secured energy supply |
| Turkey | 1998 | Electricity | Removal of fossil-fuel subsidies put competitive pressure on electricity suppliers and turned their net losses into profitability |
| Uganda | 1999 | Electricity | Subsidies declined equivalent to the amount of 2.1 percent of GDP |
| Yemen | 2005–2010 | Oil and gas | Subsidies dropped from 8.7 percent of GDP in 2005 to 7.4 percent in 2011 |

*Source:* Adapted from IMF, *Energy Subsidy Reform: Lessons and Implications* (New York: IMF, January 2013); UNEP, *Energy Subsidies: Lessons Learned in Assessing their Impact and Designing Policy Reforms* (New York: UN Foundation, 2004).

prevent abuse and enable the authorities and the public to monitor whether the [subsidy] should be continued or not. On-budget costs should be properly accounted for and the results made available to the public."[89] Such subsidy studies, apart from revealing financial flows, could include standardized ways of defining subsidies, tracking them and publishing data about them, and creating an international

---

[89] UN Environment Program Division of Technology, Industry and Economics and the International Energy Agency, *Reforming Energy Subsidies: An Explanatory Summary.*

framework of independent monitors to continuously evaluate them.[90] Subsidy impact studies could even be published visibly in places such as the *Federal Register* in the United States, where they would be subject to public commenting.[91] Such studies may show that rather than removing subsidies entirely, they instead need tweaked: perhaps given to households or poor customers themselves, rather through intermediaries such as oil and gas companies or utilities, or shifted from dirtier or less efficient energy systems to cleaner and more efficient ones.

One innovative option is a Public Registry of Basic Information about Subsidies.[92] This registry, managed by local and national governments, could track and evaluate the manner in which subsidies are implemented, who has jurisdiction over them, their annual cost, and citations to relevant legal authorities. Regulators could consider subsidies that do not appear on the registry null and void after a certain period, forcing all departments and ministries to reveal a complete set of costs.[93] In parallel would be Subsidy Justification Analyses defending any subsidies on the registry deemed beneficial enough to be considered for renewal.[94]

## Sunset clauses

The insertion of sunset clauses into regulation would set an explicit expiration date and prevent subsidies from operating indefinitely; it would also give stakeholders a clear expectation about when a subsidy

---

[90] IISD, *Achieving the G-20 Call to Phase Out Subsidies to Fossil Fuels*.

[91] Doug Koplow, "Energy," in *Subsidy Reform and Sustainable Development: Political Economy Aspects* (Paris: OECD, 2007), pp. 93–110.

[92] This concept bears some similarity to the Public Registry of Natural Resource Stock Depletion (and other forms of natural resource accounting) advocated as an improvement to Gross National Product calculations. See R. Repetto and W.B. Magrath, *Natural Resources* Accounting (Washington, DC: World Resources Institute, 1988); Robert Repetto *et al.*, *Wasting Assets: Natural Resources in the National Income Accounts* (Washington, DC: World Resources Institute, 1989); NRC, *Nature's Number: Expanding the National Economic Accounts to Include the Environment*, ed. William D. Nordhaus and Edward C. Kokkelenberg (Washington, DC: National Academy Press, 1999); Glenn-Marie Lange, *Policy Applications of Environmental Accounting*, World Bank Environment Department Papers, Environmental Economics Series (January 2003).

[93] Koplow and Dernbach, "Federal Fossil Fuel Subsidies."    [94] *Ibid.*

would end, reducing the risk of dependency and lock-in.[95] The United Kingdom placed a sunset clause on their reintroduction of coal subsidies in 2000 – intended to bolster the competitiveness of the mining industry – explicitly stating that those subsidies would expire in 2002.[96] Similar sunset clauses and explicit expiration dates have existed for production tax credits for both nuclear power and renewable energy, for better or for worse, in the United States, implemented under the Energy Policy Acts of 1992 and 2005. A libertarian view might be that sunset provisions could be an early step towards complete elimination of such supports; but it is hard to see why such a view would not also insist upon setting termination dates for energy subsidies that are currently open-ended, such as those for fossil-fuel extraction.

## Adjustment packages

Though it would violate the libertarian ideal, another pragmatic solution is to provide adjustment packages for those most harmed from subsidy removal – an action that undercuts some of the political opposition against the elimination of subsidies. For instance, if one is cutting back a subsidy for offshore deepwater oil and gas platforms, the funds gained could be used to help train the soon-to-be-unemployed workers in other skills, or provide them with medical insurance or unemployment benefits for an extended period of time. The Australian dairy industry, for example, relied on an adjustment package funded by subsidy removal which gave technical assistance to farmers wishing to leave the industry, and grants to communities where dairy was central to local economies.[97]

---

[95] Stephen Barg, Aaron Cosbey, and Ronald Steenblik, "A Sustainable Development Framework for Assessing the Benefits of Subsidy Reform," in *Subsidy Reform and Sustainable Development: Political Economy Aspects* (Paris: OECD, 2007), pp. 31–60.

[96] UN Environment Program Division of Technology, Industry and Economics and the International Energy Agency, *Reforming Energy Subsidies: An Explanatory Summary*; and UN Environment Program Division of Technology, Industry and Economics, *Reforming Energy Subsidies: Opportunities to Contribute.*

[97] Anthony Cox, "Easing Subsidy Reform for Producers, Consumers, and Communities," in *Subsidy Reform and Sustainable Development: Political Economy Aspects* (Paris: OECD, 2007), pp. 61–70.

Similarly, the German federal government and the state of North Rhine-Westphalia removed their subsidies for coal exports over a twelve-year period of 1997 to 2008, phasing in reductions slowly so that subsidies shrunk from €4.73 billion to €2.38 billion with a complete removal scheduled for 2018. Proceeds from some of the saved revenues were put into an adjustment package for miners who had lost their jobs. The result of the removal included a reduction in operating mines from nineteen to eight, a reduction in production from 46 million tons to 26 million tons, and the number of mining jobs reduced from 78,100 to 38,500, though for most the retraining was successful and they were able to find employment in other sectors.[98] Subsidy reform packages introduced by Iran, Namibia, the Philippines, and Turkey also had similar "compensating measures" to affected stakeholders, and eight other national instances of reform relied on "targeted cash transfers" to vulnerable groups.[99]

In extreme cases, adjustment packages could prevent mass rioting and social conflict, sometimes the situation in developing countries where poor customers depend on subsidies to keep energy prices affordable. In an understandable effort to reduce government deficits, the Myanmar government removed state subsidies on natural gas and diesel in 2007, leading to a doubling of domestic prices for bus fares and automobile fuel and spilling over into an increase in the price of basic commodities such as rice, beef, fish, milk, and eggs – hitting rural and poor households the hardest, and eventually leading to popular protest and a reactive state crackdown involving an "unknown" number of violent deaths.[100] Plans to raise electricity prices in India in 2000 were later abandoned after they provoked mass demonstrations and rioting. Adjustment packages could have, in theory, lessened these dire consequences.

---

[98] European Commission, *Reforming Environmentally Harmful Subsidies.*
[99] IMF, *Energy Subsidy Reform.*
[100] Matthew F. Smith and Naing Htoo, "Energy Security: Security for Whom?," *Yale Human Rights and Development Law Journal* 11 (2008), pp. 217–258.

# 9 | Energy resources and future generations

In 2001, President Fradique Menezes of the Democratic Republic of São Tomé e Príncipe was in trouble. São Tomé is an archipelago of roughly 1,000 square kilometers in the Gulf of Guinea. With a population of 160,000, it is West Africa's smallest democracy, Africa's second smallest country after the Seychelles, and the third smallest economy in the world. To put its size in perspective, the country is about five times the area of Washington, DC.

During this time, President Menezes' country was almost entirely dependent on foreign aid, notorious for somewhat humorous cases of petty corruption and, due to lack of money, government neglect and a highly undiversified economy. For instance, throughout the 1990s, foreign aid represented 97 percent of government revenue, making it the largest recipient of donor aid per capita in the world. São Tomé also had the highest debt to GDP ratio of any country in the world.[1] São Tomé had to import everything – every light bulb, car battery, computer, sock, fork, plate, curtain, shoe, and so on – from vast distances, since neighboring countries also produced little and imported almost everything from Europe.[2] The national economy was dependent on cocoa production as the main commercial crop which produced less than $4 million per year, and income from tourism was marginal. Due to its sheer lack of resources and high rates of debt, the São Tomé economy featured numerous "creative" state-sponsored enterprises such as offering black

---

[1] See P. Conti-Brown, "Increasing the Capacity for Corruption? Law and Development in the Burgeoning Petro-State of Sao Tome e Principe," *Berkeley Journal of African American Law and Policy* 12 (2010), pp. 33–65; as well as R. Soares de Oliveira, *Oil and Politics in the Gulf of Guinea* (London: Hurst and Company, 2007).

[2] J.G. Frynas, G. Wood, and R. M. S. Soares de Oliveira, "Business and Politics in São Tomé e Príncipe," *African Affairs* 102 (2003), pp. 51–80.

market passports, licensing flags of convenience for international shipping companies, producing commemorative postal stamps featuring Marilyn Monroe and the Beatles, and even government-endorsed X-rated telephone calling centers.[3]

However, President Menezes envisioned a way out of this trap: in an offshore Joint Development Zone (JDZ) shared with Nigeria, geologists discovered upwards of one *billion* barrels of oil. This potential oil "bonanza" catapulted the São Tomé government and the entire Gulf of Guinea "from strategic neglect into geopolitical stardom."[4] How best to develop these oil resources, though? Transnational oil companies were renowned, in previous dealings, for "swooping in" and "controlling negotiations with the unsophisticated Sao Tomeans."[5] The World Bank described the contractual terms between oil companies and the São Tomé government in the 1990s as "unprecedented" in the amount of resources they awarded foreign entities. In both a tragic and a comic act of exploitation, Nigeria actually impounded and refused to release São Tomé's entire navy in order to gain more favorable oil contracts.

What was the President to do? Leave the oil in the ground, and continue to promote São Tomé's "creative" enterprise? Or partner with foreign entities, but run the risk of the "resource curse" and of getting taken advantage of by international actors?

Cognizant of this state of affairs, President Fradique Menezes took a third – and surprising, yet innovative – path. He called the Columbia University sustainable development expert Jeffrey Sachs, saying that "we've found some oil and the sharks are swimming around us now … I'd like some help to manage this properly."[6] At that time, President Menezes knew his country had neither the expertise to deal with the oil companies nor a potential oil economy. He wanted to ensure that São Tomé did not go the way of practically every other developing country that had acquired sudden natural resource wealth, such as its neighbors Nigeria, Gabon, Angola, and Equatorial Guinea, which earned billions of dollars each year but whose people continued to live in squalor. Sachs agreed, and then began the task of designing a

---

[3] *Ibid.*
[4] G. Weszkalnys, "The Curse of Oil in the Gulf of Guinea: A View from Sao Tome and Principe," *African Affairs* 108 (2009), pp. 679–689.
[5] Conti-Brown, "Increasing the Capacity for Corruption?"
[6] Quoted in Benjamin K. Sovacool, *Energy and Ethics: Justice and the Global Energy Challenge* (New York: Palgrave, 2013), at p. 123.

series of regulations and policies with input from specialists from Mexico, India, Ethiopia, Brazil, Portugal, the United Kingdom, Norway, and the United States, as well as the Open Society Institute, a nongovernmental organization concerned with transparaency and accountability.

The end result of this collaboration and discussion was São Tomé's Oil Revenue Management Law (ORML), a groundbreaking decree that regulates the "payments, management, use, and oversight" of revenues arising from oil operations throughout São Tomé and within the JDZ. Wary of the potential for oil revenues to encourage corruption, the ORML created a "National Oil Account" held by an international and independent custodial bank, the New York Federal Reserve. The ORML mandated that all oil payments be made directly into the fund, bypassing senior ministers and politicians. Outflows of oil cannot legally exceed the highest amount of oil production that can be sustained in perpetuity (except for a beginning transitional period).[7] The ORML required competitive tenders for all oil and gas contracts and also made those contracts public.[8] To avoid inflation, all oil revenues were held in foreign-denominated currencies; to mitigate corruption, revenues had to match deposits precisely.

Moreover, the ORML also set limits on withdrawals from the National Oil Account so that a significant amount of revenues accrue to a sub-account known as the "Permanent Fund for Future Generations" or the "Permanent Oil Fund," which cannot be spent now and forms a "national endowment" to "foster development even after oil resources have been exhausted."[9] Furthermore, annual spending amounts from the National Oil Account had to be expended in accordance with the priorities enshrined within the country's Poverty Reduction Strategy, and 10 percent given directly to local governments.

In sum, the São Tomé oil laws were designed to deal with intergenerational equity by turning a depletable asset into an ongoing and sustainable resource. As such, they rejected the depletion incentives inherent in the "first to claim" concepts of the traditional "rule of capture" and

---

[7] A. Heuty, *Can Natural Resource Funds Address the Fiscal Challenges of Resource-Rich Developing Countries?* (Washington, DC: Revenue Watch Institute, 2010).

[8] J.C. Bell and T.M. Faria, "Sao Tome and Principe Enacts Oil Revenue Law, Sets New Transparency, Accountability, and Governance Standards," *Oil, Gas & Energy Law Intelligence* 3(1) (2005), pp. 1–8.

[9] Quoted in Sovacool, *Energy and Ethics*, at p. 125.

they explicitly recognized the interests of future generations. It remains to be seen whether those aspirations can be achieved and sustained but the goal is clear, the effort seems serious, the resources seem large enough to satisfy both current and future populations and the inherent justice of the project gives it a strength that may endure.

In this chapter, we note that philosophers and justice theorists such as Ronald Dworkin, Brian Barry, and Edith Brown Weiss would likely praise the ORML (at least for its concepts and goals, while perhaps waiting to see how it plays out in practice.) They would look at the way our energy systems harness depletable resources such as fossil fuels, and would point out that such depletion violates principles of posterity and common patrimony. The global energy system relies predominately on exhaustible fuels to meet its current energy needs, essentially spending billions of years' worth of energy in the span of a few centuries. Nonetheless, a series of solutions to this depletion exist including investment in new research and energy efficiency, a shift to nondepletable, renewable resources, and the establishment of national resource funds that explicitly state a duty to conserve for future generations.

## What is reality?

Our energy reality is far from the ideals of egalitarianism, reciprocity, and duty to future generations – as both the examples of nuclear waste and the depletion of fossil fuels clearly illustrate.

### Long-lived nuclear waste

Nuclear reactors create more than 100 dangerously radioactive chemicals, including strontium-90, iodine-131, and cesium-137, the same toxins found in the fallout from nuclear weapons. Some of these contaminants, such as strontium-90, remain radioactive for 600 years, concentrate in the food chain, are tasteless, odorless, and invisible, and have been found in the teeth of young children living near nuclear facilities.[10]

---

[10] Helen Caldicott, "Nuclear Power Isn't Clean, It's Dangerous," *Sydney Morning Herald*, August 27, 2001; see also Helen Caldicott, *Nuclear Madness* (New York: Norton and Norton, 1994).

Because nothing is burned or oxidized during the fission process, nuclear plants convert almost all of their fuel to waste with little reduction in mass. Typically, a single nuclear reactor will consume an average of 32,000 fuel rods over the course of its lifetime, and it will also produce 20–30 tons of spent nuclear fuel per year – an average of about 2,200 metric tons annually for the entire US nuclear fleet.[11] As already mentioned in Chapter 4, which discusses nuclear waste and decommissioning as an externality, the global nuclear fleet creates almost five times that amount – 10,000 metric tons of high-level spent nuclear fuel – each year. About 85 percent of this waste is not reprocessed, and most of it is stored onsite in special facilities at nuclear power plants.

Yet determining where this waste will go – technically, and even economically and socially – is a pernicious problem. In the United States, the amount of waste generated by the industry could potentially increase to between 150,000 and 200,000 metric tons by mid-century, and plans to build the nation's first permanent underground repository at Yucca Mountain have been indefinitely suspended.[12] France is also running out of storage space, and existing sites will likely be full by 2015. A law from 1991 requiring the creation of a geologic storage facility underground was never implemented due to public opposition.[13] In South Korea, an underground repository for the permanent disposal of spent nuclear fuel will not be ready until 2041, but interim storage pools will likely reach maximum capacity by 2024.[14] All the onsite research for the permanent waste repositories in Finland and Sweden has been conducted by the companies themselves with no independent review; and the bedrock in both sites is believed to be less stable and full of more cracks than originally believed, with new

---

[11] See A. Funk and B.K. Sovacool, "Wasted Opportunities: Resolving the Impasse in United States Nuclear Waste Policy," *Energy Law Journal* 34(1) (May 2013), pp. 113–147; as well as B.K. Sovacool and A. Funk, "Wrestling with the Hydra of Nuclear Waste Storage in the United States," *Electricity Journal* 26(2) (March 2013), pp. 67–78.

[12] Blue Ribbon Commission on America's Nuclear Future, *Report to the Secretary of Energy* (Washington, DC: January 2012), p. 14.

[13] Yves Marignac, Benjamin Dessus, Helene Gassin, and Bernard Laponche, *Nuclear Power: The Great Illusion* (Paris: Global Chance, October 2008).

[14] Chang Min Lee and Kun-Jai Lee, "A Study on Operation Time Periods of Spent Fuel Interim Storage Facilities in South Korea," *Progress in Nuclear Energy* 49 (2007), pp. 323–333.

evidence revealing that copper canisters could be corroded at the site within a century.[15] As one study concluded,

the management and disposal of irradiated fuel from nuclear power reactors is an issue that burdens all nations that have nuclear power programs. None has implemented a permanent solution to the problem of disposing of high-level nuclear waste, and many are wrestling with solutions to the short-term problem of where to put the spent, or irradiated, fuel as their cooling pools fill.[16]

The issue of waste provoked the nuclear physicist Alvin M. Weinberg to conclude that nuclear power, temporally speaking, was a "Faustian bargain." It fosters an unbreakable commitment whereby society benefits from electricity generation for a few decades, but in return has to bear the costs of managing nuclear waste for astonishingly long periods of time often measured in millennia. Plutonium, not found in nature and a byproduct of nuclear power generation, takes 240,000 years to become stable. Stonehenge is slightly more than 4,000 years old; *Homo sapiens* migrated to Europe and Australia 40,000 years ago; and our species has been on earth for only 230,000 years.[17] With nuclear energy, society stakes everything on "the remarkable belief that it can devise social institutions that are stable for periods equivalent to geologic ages."[18] In other words, nuclear reactors will produce waste that will persist longer than our civilization has practiced Catholicism, longer than humans have cultivated crops, and longer than our species has existed.

This creates at least three pesky problems for future generations. First, it introduces the "cost" problem already discussed in Chapter 4. Even if the waste will not leak and technical standards ensure it is safe and protection remains at present levels, the costs of maintaining that waste are unfair, since only the present generation receives the benefits of nuclear electricity, and they do not have to bear the full financial burden of the waste. Second, it introduces a problem of "capability," as it potentially erodes the ability of future generations to retain present levels of technological and managerial capacity that might be lost

[15] "Further Nuclear Reactor Construction Delays," *Helsingin Sanomat*, August 11, 2007, p. 11.

[16] Allison Macfarlane, "Interim Storage of Spent Fuel in the United States," *Annual Review of Energy and Environment* 26 (2001), pp. 201–235.

[17] Greenpeace, *Nuclear Power: A Dangerous Waste of Time* (Amsterdam: Greenpeace International, 2009).

[18] Alvin M. Weinberg, "Social Institutions and Nuclear Energy," *Energy and the Way We Live* 305 (1980), pp. 311–312.

somehow due to social or even armed conflicts over nuclear waste sites. Third, it introduces the problem of "mistakes," a situation where future generations face the risk of some type of accident, earthquake, or natural disaster that results in a catastrophic release of radiation.[19]

## Resource depletion

A second issue – perhaps equally serious – concerns the depletion of fossil fuels. As the economist Herman E. Daly explains, because "future people cannot bid in present markets," the market "is of necessity temporally parochial and tends to undervalue depletable resources."[20] The world's four primary energy fuels – coal, oil, natural gas, and uranium – are concentrated in a dramatically low number of countries, creating significant patterns of import dependence, and these reserves are running out. The world's known 1.2 trillion barrels of oil reserves are concentrated in volatile regions of the world, as are the world's largest petroleum companies. The three biggest of these – Saudi Arabian Oil Company, National Iranian Oil Company, and Qatar Petroleum – own more crude oil than the next forty largest oil companies combined. The twelve largest oil companies control roughly four-fifths of petroleum reserves and are all state owned (an inconvenient truth that is often ignored in ideological claims that petroleum policy can be based on assumptions about free markets). The distribution of other conventional energy resources, such as coal, natural gas, and uranium, is almost consolidated to an equal degree.

Figure 9.1 provides a graphic illustration of energy reserves by country, even including formally unconventional resources such as shale gas. The fundamental point is that energy resources and energy needs are distributed very differently. As one striking example, 80 percent of the world's oil can be found in nine countries that have only 5 percent of the world population and 5 percent of the world's GDP. Similarly, 80 percent of the world's natural gas is in thirteen countries with only 12 percent of world population and just 26 percent of world GDP. In addition, 80 percent of the world's coal is in six countries (though these

[19] David L. Bodde, "A Neutrality Criterion for Radioactive Waste Management," in Douglas MacLean and Peter G. Brown (eds.), *Energy and the Future* (Totowa, NJ: Rowman and Littlefield, 1983), pp. 120–128.

[20] Herman E. Daly, *Steady-State Economics* (Washington, DC: Island Press, 1991), p. 231.

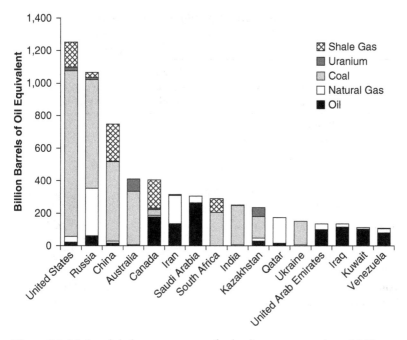

**Figure 9.1** Major global energy reserves for leading energy nations, 2012
*Source:* B.K. Sovacool and S.V. Valentine, "Sounding the Alarm: Global Energy Security in the 21st Century," in B.K. Sovacool (ed.), *Energy Security* (London: Sage Library of International Security, 2013), pp. xxxv–lxxviii.

countries have 45 percent of world population and 46 percent of world GDP). Indeed, many of the same countries are among the six that control more than 80 percent of global uranium resources. Thus, a mismatch between energy need and resource locations is highly stressful in "spatial" terms.

A "temporal" mismatch is at least as significant, though less often recognized. To date, the world has consumed about 1 trillion barrels of oil. Although commercial oil production has occurred since the nineteenth century, 99.5 percent has happened within the last sixty years. Today we consume 30 *billion* barrels of oil per year, and future demand for oil is projected to grow at more than twice the historic rate since 1980.

Though these reserves may seem vast, a growing worldwide demand for electricity and mobility threatens to exhaust them relatively soon. Projections of world energy demand vary greatly, of course, but some estimates based on historic growth expect demand to expand by

Table 9.1 *Life expectancy of proven fossil-fuel and uranium resources, 2012*

| | | | Life expectancy (years) | | |
|---|---|---|---|---|---|
| | Proven reserves | Current production | 0% Annual production growth rate | 1.6% Production growth rate | 2.5% Production growth rate |
| Coal | 930,400 million short tons | 6,807 million short tons | 137 | 85 | 61 |
| Natural gas | 6,189 trillion cubic feet | 104 trillion cubic feet | 60 | 42 | 37 |
| Petroleum | 1,317 billion barrels | 30.56 billion barrels | 43 | 33 | 30 |
| Uranium | 4,743,000 tons (at $130/kg of uranium) | 40,260 tons | 118 | 67 | 56 |

*Source:* Adapted from B.K. Sovacool and S.V. Valentine, "Sounding the Alarm: Global Energy Security in the 21st Century," in B.K. Sovacool (ed.), *Energy Security* (London: Sage Library of International Security, 2013), pp. xxxv–lxxviii.

45 percent between now and 2030, and by more than 300 percent by the end of the century (though, again, these estimates are far from certain).[21] This last estimate functionally means that we may have to build three *times* the amount of today's energy infrastructure by the end of our century – think of tripling every power plant, refinery, pipeline, oil tanker, gasoline station, and so on between then and now. Still, if levels of production were to remain constant worldwide, Table 9.1 illustrates that known coal reserves will become exhausted within 137 years, and petroleum and natural gas reserves would become exhausted in the next half century or so. If rates of production increase to keep up with growing demand particularly in the rapidly developing economies of Brazil, Russia, India, and China, known fossil-fuel reserves would be depleted much more rapidly. Essentially, we in the present are using the lion's share of Earth's energy resources.

    M. King Hubbert, a geophysicist, often remarked that it would be rather difficult for people living now, accustomed to exponential growth

---

[21] M.A. Brown and B.K. Sovacool, *Climate Change and Global Energy Security: Technology and Policy Options* (Cambridge, MA: MIT Press, 2011).

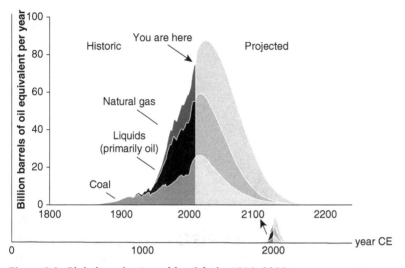

**Figure 9.2** Global production of fossil fuels, 1800–2200
*Source:* Adapted from Amory B. Lovins and the Rocky Mountain Institute, *Reinventing Fire: Bold Business Solutions for the New Energy Era* (White River Junction: Chelsea Green Publishing Company, 2011).

in energy consumption, to assess the transitory nature of fossil fuels – to comprehend just how fast we are using up resources that have taken millions of years to form. Hubbert argued that proper reflection could happen only if one looked at a time scale of millennia.[22] On such a scale, Hubbert thought that the complete cycle of the world's exploitation of fossil fuels would encompass perhaps little more than 1,000 years, with the principal segment of this cycle covering about 300 years shown in Figure 9.2. As Engineering Professor David J.C. MacKay muses, "given that fossil fuels are a valuable resource, useful for manufacture of plastics and all sorts of other creative stuff, perhaps we should save them for better uses than simply setting fire to them."[23]

This resource concentration and depletion results in two sets of impacts to *present* generations in addition to deleterious consequences for future generations: transfers of wealth, and unpredictable and often

[22] Adapted from M. King Hubbert, "Energy Resources of the Earth," *Scientific American* 225 (September 1971), p. 61.
[23] David J. C. MacKay, *Sustainable Energy – Without the Hot Air* (Cambridge: UIT, 2008), p. 5.

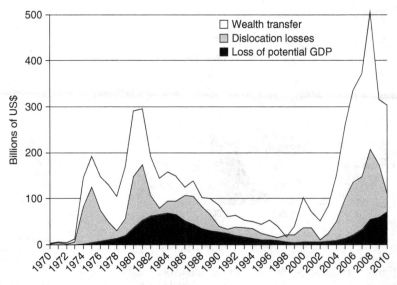

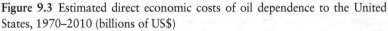

**Figure 9.3** Estimated direct economic costs of oil dependence to the United States, 1970–2010 (billions of US$)
*Source:* Adapted from David L. Greene, Roderick Lee, and Janet L. Hopson, *OPEC and the Costs to the US Economy of Oil Dependence: 1970–2010* (Oak Ridge, TN: ORNL, 2011).

rising prices, both violating (as we will see) the notion of "conservation of access." Reliance on crude oil to fuel most vehicles has transferred immense wealth to petroleum producers. Researchers from ORNL estimated that from 1970 to 2010 American dependence on foreign supplies of oil has cost the country $5.6 trillion, or more than the financial costs of all wars fought by the country going back to the Revolutionary War including both World Wars, as Figure 9.3 painfully illustrates.[24] This is not the cost of the oil itself, but the direct economic costs of macroeconomic shocks and transfers of wealth.

The issue of oil dependence can be even harsher for many developing countries. Rises in the cost of crude oil and gasoline mean that the foreign exchange required for oil imports create a heavy burden on their balance of trade. While developed countries spend just 1 or 2 percent of their

[24] David L. Greene, Roderick Lee, and Janet L. Hopson, *OPEC and the Costs to the U.S. Economy of Oil Dependence: 1970–2010* (Oak Ridge: ORNL, 2011).

GDP on imported oil, those in the developing world spend an average of 4.5 to 9 percent of their GDP. Higher prices for oil also hit developing countries twice: once for costlier barrels of oil, and again for inflated transportation costs that reflect the increase in fuel prices.[25] One study looked at the world average price of crude oil for 161 countries from 1996 to 2006, when prices increased by a factor of seven, and concluded that lower-middle-income countries were the most vulnerable followed by low-income countries, even though these countries consumed less oil per capita than industrialized or high-income countries.[26]

Two other impacts from the concentration of energy fuels noted above (as well as their rapid rates of depletion) are disruptions in supply and volatile prices. To cite a few prominent examples of unexpected alterations in supply, oil transit supplies were disrupted in Latvia in 1998, natural gas pipelines shut off between Russia and Ukraine in 2005 and 2006, shortages of coal occurred in China in 2007, lack of rain and snow caused hydropower shortfalls in California, Brazil, and Fiji, blackouts hit North America in 2003 and Europe in 2005, and Hurricane Katrina caused a substantial number of refinery shutdowns.[27] A multitude of serious oil supply shocks averaging eight months in duration and affecting almost 4 percent of global supply have occurred from 1950 to 2003.[28] One study identified five major disruptions in the global oil market in the two decades *after* the famed oil shocks of the 1970s:

- The Gulf War of 1990 and 1991, which removed 4.3 million barrels per day (mbd) of oil production from the market;
- Suspension of Iraqi oil exports in 2001, which removed 2.1 mbd;
- A Venezuelan strike in 2003 and 2004, which removed 2.6 mbd;

---

[25] Benjamin K. Sovacool, "Sound Climate, Energy, and Transport Policy for a Carbon Constrained World," *Policy & Society* 27(4) (2009), pp. 273–283.

[26] R. Bacon and M. Kojima, *Vulnerability to Oil Price Increases: A Decomposition Analysis of 161 Countries* (Washington, DC: World Bank, Extractive Industries for Development Series, 2008).

[27] Hans-Holger Rogner, Lucille M. Langlois, Alan McDonald, Daniel Weisser, and Mark Howells, *The Costs of Energy Supply Security* (Vienna: IAEA, December 27, 2006).

[28] P.N. Leiby, D.W. Jones, T.R. Curlee, and R. Lee, *Oil Imports: An Assessment of Benefits and Costs* (Oak Ridge: ORNL ORNL-6851, 1997); D.W. Jones, P. N. Leiby, and I.K. Paik, "Oil Price Shocks and the Macroeconomy: What Has Been Learned Since 1996?," *Energy Journal* 25(2) (2004), pp. 1–32.

- The Gulf War of 2003, which removed 2.3 mbd;
- Hurricane Katrina in 2005, which removed 1.5 mbd.[29]

In November 2007, an accidental explosion at the Enbridge Pipeline in Minnesota spilled 15,000 gallons of oil, killed two employees, shut down one fifth of US oil imports for days and resulted in an increase in global oil prices of $4 per barrel.[30] Political instability in Northern Africa during the "Arab Spring" of 2011, creating speculation about the safety of the Suez Canal in Egypt, caused prices to rise more than 5 percent to $101 a barrel.[31] In the electricity sector, another study identified seventeen major disruptions in supply in North America alone from 1965 to 2003, or an average number of 700,000 customers per year that suffered disruptions in service.[32]

## What is justice?

Advocating justice for future generations means supporting the sentiments of the great Irish playwright George Bernard Shaw (1856–1950), who wrote that "life is no brief candle to me. It is a sort of splendid torch which I have got a hold of for the moment, and I want to make it burn as brightly as possible before handing it on to future generations."[33] The idea of equal sharing of natural resources for those future generations dates to and beyond John Locke (1632–1704). Locke himself argued that people may justly use resources provided that they (a) exploit the resources productively, and do not waste them and (b) leave "enough and as good for others."[34] His thinking inspired the mathematical economist Leon Walras (1834–1910), who proclaimed that land and rent should be socialized so as to provide an equal distribution of their benefits for current and future generations. The utilitarian Henry

---

[29] Andreas Loschel, Ulf Moslener, and Dirk Rubbelke, "Indicators of Energy Security in Industrialized Countries," *Energy Policy* 38 (2010), pp. 1665–1671.

[30] John Wilen, "Oil Rises Slightly on Pipeline Fire," Associated Press, November 29, 2007.

[31] "The World this Week," *Economist*, February 5, 2011, pp. 6–7.

[32] Massoud Amin, "North America's Electricity Infrastructure," *IEEE Security and Privacy* (September/October 2003), pp. 19–25.

[33] Quoted in Pierre Bertaux, "The Future of Man," in William R. Ewald (ed.), *Environment and Change: The Next Fifty Years* (Bloomington: Indiana University Press, 1968), pp. 13–20.

[34] Joanna Pasek, "Obligations to Future Generations: A Philosophical Note," *World Development* 20(4) (1992), pp. 513–521.

Sidgwick (see Chapter 4) stated that same century that the welfare of all persons must be weighted equally, including the yet unborn.[35] Immanuel Kant (see Chapter 5) passionately argued that "human nature is such that it cannot be indifferent even to the most remote epoch which may eventually affect our species, so long as this epoch can be expected with certainty."[36] John Rawls (see Chapter 7) advanced his "savings principle" to suggest that contemporary people have an obligation to compensate future generations for the damage they inflict on the world, meaning they must set a social minimum of "savings" that transcends generations.[37] Notions of responsibility to future generations also appear in many major religious traditions including Buddhism, Christianity, and Judaism. The Hebrew phrase *tikkun olam* can be translated as "repairing the world" for tomorrow's citizens.[38]

Amongst this abundance of thought, some of the most coherent and influential thinking on futurity and posterity comes from three modern theorists: Ronald Dworkin and his notion of equality of resources, Brian Barry's notions of reciprocity and consent, and Edith Brown Weiss' ideas of conservation of options, conservation of quality, and conservation of access.

## Ronald Dworkin

New York University Professor Ronald Dworkin (1931–2013) starts his argument in favor of equality by discussing a theory of markets. Dworkin notes that, on the one hand, economic markets serve as an efficient device for setting prices for a variety of goods and services, but

---

[35] Scott Gordon, *Welfare, Justice, and Freedom* (New York: Columbia University Press, 1980).

[36] Burns H. Weston, "Climate Change and Intergenerational Justice: Foundational Reflections," *Vermont Journal of Environmental Law* 9 (2008), pp. 375–430.

[37] For Rawls, "just savings" implies that societies should save enough so that succeeding generations are able to live in a just society. They need not pass on any more than that and certainly need not seek to maximize the condition of the least advantaged persons who will ever live. As he wrote, "in arriving at a just saving principle ... the parties are to ask themselves how much they would be willing to save ... on the assumption that all other generations have saved, or will save, in accordance with the same criterion." See John Rawls, *A Theory of Justice*, revised edn. (Cambridge, MA: Belknap Press, 1999), p. 255.

[38] William Antholis and Strobe Talbott, *Fast Forward: Ethics and Politics in the Age of Global Warming* (Washington, DC: Brookings Institution Press, 2010), p. 116.

on the other hand, markets are not sensitive to the distribution of assets and liabilities; they are, instead, amoral. To rectify this amorality, Dworkin proposes his concept of "equality of resources," arguing that people must decide what sorts of lives they wish to live based on the total stock of resources that may be fairly used by them.[39] His stance, sometimes called "resource egalitarianism," holds that a just scheme treats people as equals when it distributes or transfers assets so that no further transfer would leave their shares of total resources less equal.[40] We would add that markets inevitably function only *after* rights to possession of resources are allocated and recognized by society. Thus, an oil developer may corner the market on drilled fuel that she "captures" from subsoil because resource law grants a right of possession to the first captor of the resource; but she may not corner the market on air, wind, or clouds because the Federal Air Transport Act of 1958 denies any private property right in the atmosphere that would deter or inhibit air travel.

Essentially, Dworkin is concerned with equality or "equal concern" and "ethical individualism." His two maxims backing his "equality of resources" argument are the principle of equal importance and the principle of special responsibility. The principle of equal importance tells us that each person has equal importance as a human life, regardless of their ethnicity, or wealth, or gender. It requires that governments adopt laws and policies that ensure their citizens' fates are insensitive to who they are, their economic backgrounds, or the particular skills and handicaps they have. The principle of special responsibility insists that "so far as choices are to be made about the kind of life a person lives, within whatever range of choice is permitted by resource and culture, she is responsible for making those choices herself."[41] It demands that governments work to make people's fates sensitive to the choices that they actually make.[42]

---

[39] Ronald Dworkin, "What Is Equality? Part 1: Equality of Welfare," *Philosophy & Public Affairs* 10(3) (Summer 1981), pp. 185–246; Ronald Dworkin, "What Is Equality? Part 2: Equality of Resources," *Philosophy & Public Affairs* 10(4) (Autumn 1981), pp. 283–345. See also R. Dworkin, *Sovereign Virtue: The Theory and Practice of Equality* (Cambridge, MA: Harvard University Press, 2000).

[40] Dworkin, "What Is Equality? Part 2."    [41] Dworkin, *Sovereign Virtue*, p. 6.
[42] *Ibid.*

One vital part of Dworkin's concept of resource egalitarianism is the notion of "envy elimination." Someone envies another when they prefer to own that person's bundle of resources. As Philosophy Professor Edward Page explains:

> To the extent that future generations inherit a damaged environment within which to pursue their life plans, intergenerational justice of impersonal resources regards these people as deserving of compensation. We could say that [Dworkin's] theory endorses the test that no generation should be put in the position where they have reason to envy the impersonal resources enjoyed by earlier generations ... It is likely that future generations will have ample reason to envy the personal resources enjoyed by their predecessors. Because their envy arises from the adoption of policies for which they cannot be held responsible, future generations will have a clear complaint that additional measures should have been undertaken by their predecessors.[43]

Essentially, according to Dworkin consuming depletable resources is unfair because it both erodes the resource base for achieving equality and leads to envy between generations.

## Brian Barry

Oxford University moral and political philosopher Brian Barry (1936–2009) builds upon the work of both Dworkin and Rawls to argue that "from a temporal perspective, no one generation has a better or worse claim than any other to enjoy the earth's resources" and that "the minimal claim of equal opportunity is an equal claim on the earth's natural resources."[44] Basically, Barry constructs his theory of intergenerational justice by arguing that whatever we decide a nice life is, say we collectively value it as "10," its value as we enjoy it today should be sustained into the future so that future generations do not fall below our level of "10."[45]

---

[43] Edward A. Page, "Intergenerational Justice of What: Welfare, Resources or Capabilities?," *Environmental Politics* 16(3) (June 2007), pp. 453–469.

[44] Brian Barry, "Justice as Reciprocity," in *Democracy, Power and Justice: Essays in Political Theory* (Oxford: Clarendon Press, 1989), pp. 463–494.

[45] Brian Barry, "Sustainability and Intergenerational Justice," *Theoria* 45(89), pp. 43–65; Brian Barry, "Sustainability and Intergenerational Justice," in Andrew Dobson (ed.), *Fairness and Futurity: Essays on Environmental Sustainability and Social Justice* (Oxford University Press, 1999), pp. 93–117.

To make this point, Barry advances three interrelated reasons. The first is an argument from reciprocity.[46] The present generation cannot claim that it is entitled to a larger share of goods supplied by nature, because most of our technology and capital stock are not the sole creation of the present. We cannot claim exclusive credit to it, as resources are inherited, and therefore fall outside any special claims based on the present generation "deserving them." As Barry writes, "since we have received benefits from our predecessors some notion of equity requires us to provide benefit for our successors."[47] This means we should preserve those resources out of a sense of reciprocity. As the Bible puts it, each of us "drinks from wells we did not dig; we are each warmed by fires we did not light."[48] What we have been given from the past, we owe to the future.

Barry's second argument rises from the principle of consent. When we do things now that impose risks on future people, we do so without their consent, violating their freedom and autonomy as individuals. Future generations cannot consent to the risks that present people coerce upon them.[49]

Third, doing harm is not canceled out by doing good. If we do future generations harm and limit their choices without consent, it is not "undone" with whatever good we achieve by putting our resources to use today. Similarly, if somebody saved two lives by building a safer car, it would not entitle them to shoot one motorist and reckon that in the end they came out morally ahead.

Barry believes that these justifications for posterity are supported on both utilitarian and contractarian grounds. For utilitarians, we have the notion of "offsetting," that we should do what we can to provide future generations with the same level of utility as they would have had if we had not depleted their resources. For contractarian theorists such as Rawls, Sen, and Nussbaum (see Chapter 7), we have the notion

---

[46] Brian Barry, "Circumstances of Justice and Future Generations," in Richard Sikora and B.M. Barry (eds.), *Obligations to Future Generations* (Philadelphia: Temple University Press, 1978), pp. 205–248.

[47] Brian Barry, *Theories of Justice* (Los Angeles: University of California Press, 1989), p. 403.

[48] Deut. 6.11.

[49] Brian Barry, "Circumstances of Justice and Future Generations," in Sikora and Barry (eds.), *Obligations to Future Generations.*

of capabilities and opportunities, calling on us to provide future generations with productive opportunities to make up for the destruction we have caused. We have a "strong presumption in favor of arranging things so that, as far as possible, each generation faces the same range of opportunities with respect to natural resources."[50] The fact that we happen to be alive today with current energy resource constraints, rather than in the future when resources may be gone or in the past when they were plentiful, is a historical accident; it is essentially tantamount to "luck." Since we should not claim credit or responsibility for our existence now, we have no moral basis to treat these resource "gifts" as our property; we have no moral right to do with them as we please. As ethicist Douglas MacLean writes, "to the extent that future generations have an equal interest in natural resources, they have an equal claim to them."[51]

In the end, Barry notes that "justice requires us to compensate future generations for depleted resources, so that they have as much productive potential as they would have inherited had the resources not been depleted."[52] He also argues that "the exploitation of non-renewable natural resources raises a special problem in intergenerational equity [because] ... any resources we use will not be available in the future ... non-renewable energy resources – fossil fuels – cannot be recycled. Once they have been burned, they have gone forever, as far as any use to human beings is concerned."[53]

## Edith Brown Weiss

Georgetown Law Professor Edith Brown Weiss (1942– present) extends the arguments from Dworkin and Barry further. She argues that the imperative to protect the future has strong roots in social biology and anthropology; it is not just a matter of being just, but a matter of protecting our young and ensuring the future survival of the human race. She states that energy activities are immoral to future generations in three

[50] Barry, *Theories of Justice*, p. 515.
[51] Brian Barry, "Intergenerational Justice in Energy Policy," in MacLean and Brown (eds.), *Energy and the Future*, pp. 15–30.
[52] Barry, *Theories of Justice*, p. 517.
[53] Brian Barry, "The Ethics of Resource Depletion," in *Democracy, Power and Justice*, pp. 511–525.

ways.[54] First, they deplete scarce resources. The consumption of higher-quality resources leads to higher real prices for those resources for future generations. It can also deplete resources not yet identified as valuable, in ignorance of their potential importance, an example being the common flaring of natural gas in the oil industry before it was realized that gas had value; another example, the rapid extinction of species which can narrow the options future generations have for using biomimicry to design technologies or new crop strains for biofuels. Second, they degrade environmental and social quality by contaminating the air, water, soils, and the vibrancy of communities – Chapters 4 and 5 set out these implications more comprehensively. Third, they involve discriminatory access and use of resources, something elaborated on in Chapter 7. Yet, according to Brown Weiss, "each generation has an equitable right to use and benefit from the planetary resources."[55]

The way towards a socially just future involves her three principles of intergenerational equity. (1) "Conservation of options": each generation should be required to conserve the diversity of the natural and cultural resource base, so it does not restrict options for future generations, their ability to solve their problems, and their capacity to satisfy their own values. (2) "Conservation of quality": each generation should maintain the quality of the planet passed on in no worse condition than they received it, matching Barry's notion of reciprocity. (3) "Conservation of access": each generation should provide its members equitable access to the legacy from past generations, conserving this access to future generations, passing it along in a sort of intergenerational "trust." Thus, Brown Weiss' "tripartite definition of intergenerational equity" comprises both rights and duties, and it encompasses intragenerational and intergenerational factors.[56]

An obligation to future generations along these grounds has faced a series of objections. The ethicist Bryan Norton has identified three challenges to considering future generations: (1) a "distance problem" making it uncertain how far into the future obligations extend; (2) an "ignorance" problem since we do not know who they will be or how to identify future people, making it difficult to know what they want or

---

[54] Edith Brown Weiss, *In Fairness to Future Generations: International Law, Common Patrimony, and Intergenerational Equity* (Dobbs Ferry, NY: Transnational Publishers, 1989).
[55] *Ibid.*, p. 13.   [56] Weston, "Climate Change and Intergenerational Justice."

need; and (3) a "typology of effects problem" which makes it difficult to determine which of our actions will reach that far into the future.[57] Others have critiqued resource egalitarianism for the simple reason that it does not tell us which goods and conditions should count as resources, nor does it tell us how we should distribute resource shares given that people have very different tastes and preferences.[58]

Put another way, people derive different amounts of satisfaction from any given resource. Australian Professor Robert E. Goodin writes that "some individuals are superefficient pleasure machines, deriving a big bang from any given buck; others (e.g. the handicapped) require lots more dollars to achieve the same level of accomplishment."[59] Another issue is what to do about resources that cannot be transferred[60] – say, a large geothermal power plant that will only work in one part of the world. Yet another issue is whether it is superfluous to give resources to those already at their satiation. A classical economist might phrase this as "decreasing personal utility per unit of consumption"; a Little League coach might note that each child's happiness per post-game milkshake declines rapidly after the first quart of vanilla frappe. A final critique suggests that we might want to consider populating the globe to the limit of our capability, so as to bring in many more people that would otherwise not exist.[61]

Some of these objections, such as the "ignorance" and "distance problem," do have compelling responses. We do not necessarily need to know precisely what future individuals want to realize that they ought to have the widest range of choices possible available to them – in other words, Dworkin, Barry, and Brown Weiss are not really focused on

---

[57] Derek Parfit, "Future Generations: Further Problems," *Philosophy and Public Affairs* 11(2) (Spring 1982), pp. 113–172; Bryan Norton, "Ecology and Opportunity," in Dobson (ed.), *Fairness and Futurity*, pp. 118–150.

[58] T.M. Scanlon, "Equality of Resources and Equality of Welfare," *Ethics* 97(1) (October 1986), pp. 111–118. See also Andrew Williams, "Resource Egalitarianism and the Limits to Basic Income," *Economics and Philosophy* 15(1) (1999), pp. 85–107.

[59] Robert E. Goodin, "Egalitarianism, Fetishistic and Otherwise," *Ethics* 98(1) (October 1987), pp. 44–49.

[60] Tomas Schwartz, "Obligations to Posterity," in Sikora and Barry (eds.), *Obligations to Future Generations*, pp. 3–13; D. Parfit, *Reasons and Persons* (New York: Oxford University Press, 1984); John E. Roemer, "Equality of Resources Implies Equality of Welfare," *Quarterly Journal of Economics* 101(4) (November 1986), pp. 751–784.

[61] Douglas MacLean, "Introduction," in MacLean and Brown (eds.), *Energy and the Future*, pp. 1–14.

identifying what will make people happy, but a system that provides them the capability and opportunity to achieve their own happiness. In this sense, they imply that markets do not make choices about how people should live; markets only provide mechanisms to allow people to make their own choices about whether more joy comes from watching a football game or giving your spouse a good massage, or from going for a bike ride or drinking a glass of wine. Moreover, the Israeli philosopher Avner de-Shalit argues that we have an obligation to future generations for our own selfish reasons. The extent that they carry on projects that are meaningful to us gives our contemporary lives more depth and meaning.[62]

In terms of the "distance problem," the sociologist Elise M. Boulding and Iroquois Nation leader Daisaku Ikeda propose the concept of the "two-hundred-year-present." As they write:

We propose ... thinking in a time-span which we call the "two-hundred-year-present." It begins one hundred years ago today, on the day of the birth of those among us who are centenarians, celebrating their one hundredth birthday today. The other boundary of this present moment is the hundredth birthday of the babies being born today. It is a continuously moving moment, always reaching out one hundred years in either direction from the day we are in. We are linked with both boundaries of this moment by the people among us whose lives began or will end at one of those boundaries, three and a half generations each way in time.[63]

This conception of a "two-hundred-year-present" overcomes multiple objections at once. It helps demystify the notion of "past" and "future" generations by signaling not far-off abstracted people but those around us: our parents, our great-grandparents, our children, our great-grandchildren. It helps personalize our understanding of what we have inherited from the past, therefore reminding us that all futures have pasts. The outer boundary of 100 years also moves with each generation so that unborn persons become "drawn into the framework" as its temporal bubble or envelope passes over them.[64]

Despite these complexities, obligations to future generations have been codified in a number of general laws and practices. Long-term ground leases, for instance, allow landowners to retain ownership of a

[62] Avner de-Shalit, *Why Posterity Matters: Environmental Policies and Future Generations* (London: Routledge, 1995).
[63] Quoted in Weston, "Climate Change and Intergenerational Justice."     [64] *Ibid.*

property to capture its appreciation in value over time, and short-term leases require the return of property in good condition for use by future (and possibly unborn) tenants. Private and public trusts impose duties on trustees to protect the trust for future (and possibly unborn) beneficiaries. Legislation can direct visitors of public parks not to despoil them for future use. The preamble of the 1972 Stockholm Declaration several times states the "goal" of defending and improving the human environment "for present and future generations," and its Principle 1 expresses "the common conviction" that humanity "bears a solemn responsibility to protect and improve the environment for present and future generations."[65] The "equitable utilization of shared resources" is recognized in international law and is a "widely accepted principle" applied in fisheries and forestry management.[66] Similar stipulations for future generations or equitable resource use appear in the 1972 London Ocean Dumping Convention, the 1972 World Cultural and Natural Heritage Convention, the 1973 Endangered Species Convention, the 1974 Charter of Economic Rights and Duties of States, the 1976 Barcelona Mediterranean Sea Convention, the 1982 UN World Charter for Nature, the 1987 report of the UN World Commission on Environment and Development, and the 1997 UNESCO Declaration on Responsibilities towards Future Generations, among others.[67]

Even in the energy sector, intergenerational equity is sometimes acknowledged. The electric utility industry can defer costs that are presently incurred, such as construction, to the generation that realizes the benefits of a project. Nuclear power plant decommissioning can accelerate the future costs of a project so that the present generation, reaping its benefits, pays for them. The same rationale supports incurring pollution control costs to prevent emissions in the future.[68]

In sum, the concepts from Dworkin, Barry, and Brown Weiss, along with the implicit assumption behind a collection of international agreements and common practices, imply that we have an obligation not to diminish the opportunities of future generations to achieve well-being

---

[65] *Ibid.*
[66] Donald K. Anton and Dinah L. Shelton, *Environmental Protection and Human Rights* (New York: Cambridge University Press, 2011), p. 96.
[67] Weston, "Climate Change and Intergenerational Justice."
[68] Burns H. Weston and Tracy Bach, *Climate Change and Intergenerational Justice: Present Law, Future Law* (South Royalton: Vermont Law School, 2008).

at least equal to those that came before them.[69] Our current choice to consume, our failure to preserve and conserve, makes many depletable resources forever inaccessible.[70] As Law Professor Burns H. Weston emphatically writes:

> At a minimum, each of us has a moral responsibility to ensure that today's children and future generations inherit a global environment at least no worse than the one we received from our predecessors ... What parent, grandparent, or great-grandparent would disavow a climate legacy beneficial to their descendants? What child, grandchild, or great-grandchild will not feel at least a little resentful if such a legacy is denied them? Somewhere deep inside, all of us know that life is an energetic concurrence of the past, present, and future; that we are a temporary part of it; and that, whatever our past failings, we must reach beyond our egoistic selves to ensure its continuity with fairness to today's children and communities of the future. It is axiomatic – a "no-brainer," as we say.[71]

Or, as one commentator put it, "Whatever my attitude toward foreigners, it would be wrong of me to send one a letter-bomb. Would it also not be wrong to send posterity a time-bomb?"[72]

## What is to be done?

In her work *In Fairness to Future Generations*, Brown Weiss concludes that "as an initial step in formulating planetary rights, we need to consider drafting a Declaration of Planetary Obligations and Rights."[73] Others have proposed amending the US Constitution to create a "Court of Generations" to judge whether society is "in contempt of intolerably threatening the security of the blessings of liberty to our Posterity."[74] We do not go that far, but we do argue that one path to a more just and equitable future lies in energy efficiency and conservation of existing resources coupled with investments in research, development and

[69] Norton, "Ecology and Opportunity."
[70] Clark Wolf, "Intergenerational Justice," in R.G. Frey and Christopher Heath Wellman (eds.), *A Companion to Applied Ethics* (London: Blackwell Publishing, 2003), pp. 279–294.
[71] Weston, "Climate Change and Intergenerational Justice," p. 376.
[72] De-Shalit, *Why Posterity Matters*, p. 6.
[73] Brown Weiss, *In Fairness to Future Generations*, p. 443.
[74] Bruce E. Tonn, "The Court of Generations: A Proposed Amendment to the US Constitution," *Futures* (June 1991), pp. 482–498.

innovation, and rapid adoption of technologies relying on nondepletable fuels. Brown Weiss goes one step further and advocates restoration, restoring the damage we have done, when she argues that "if one generation fails to conserve the planet at the level of quality received, succeeding generations have an obligation to repair this damage, even if it is costly to do so."[75] This option is certainly defensible, but we elaborate more on it in the next chapter (Chapter 10) where we discuss adaptive capacity and building resilience to climate change.

## Efficiency and innovation

According to the justice theorists in this chapter, we have a duty to use nonrenewable resources as judiciously as we can – extracting them and using them most efficiently. Barry notes, for instance, that his concept of reciprocity does not mean that current generations simply cannot use energy resources. Such cessation would imply that our economic activity would grind to a halt, and our living standards – and those of future generations affected by our loss of infrastructure – might plummet as a result. Instead, he argues that we must come up with better extraction methods now and plans to compensate future generations for current use. We must stipulate, in other words, that future generations are owed compensation in other ways for reducing their access. As he argues, a "combination of improved technology and increased capital investment should be such as to offset the effects of depletion."[76]

The best starting place for achieving such a scenario lies with energy efficiency (see Chapter 3). If we draw down an oil well by 10 percent, but develop new technology that makes it possible to extract 10 percent more oil from a given deposit, we have in fact met our obligation to future generations. Alternatively, if we draw down an oilfield by 10 percent, but install home insulation or develop transportation systems that reduce the need (the "demand") for oil by a larger amount, then we may be passing forward more than we take. If we consume one third of the world's natural gas reserves, but develop a natural gas combined cycle turbine that produces one third more energy per unit of fuel, or we have better designed homes so that they need one third less heat from natural gas, we have similarly met our obligation to future

[75] Brown Weiss, *In Fairness to Future Generations*, p. 24.
[76] Barry, *Theories of Justice*, p. 512.

generations. Barry's conception of justice also means if a resource is exhausted, we research the development of substitutes to it – think here of biodiesel, cellulosic ethanol, or algal fuels as "substitutes" for oil and gasoline, or liquefied petroleum gas and electricity as more efficient substitutes for fuelwood or dung.

To be sure, history is full of examples where we have drastically improved the efficiency of various energy technologies, sometimes in the timespan of a few decades. In practice, we have not seen efficiency gains dwindling as "low hanging fruit" is consumed; instead, we have seen new paths to greater efficiency developing as technologies improve. The best example is the history of lighting, as human beings transitioned from open fires to candles up to incandescent lamps, through compact fluorescent bulbs and, now, LEDs – for more about this, see the "Prime movers" section of Chapter 2.

The historian Roger Fouquet makes an equally convincing point in his study of the history of heating, power, transport, and lighting in the United Kingdom from 1300 to 2000.[77] Table 9.2 presents his findings which indicate that since 1750, due mostly to improvements in efficiency, the cost of lighting has fallen by a factor of a thousand, transport by a factor of forty, heating by a factor of ten.

Ordinary refrigerators offer a paradigmatic third example. A 20.9 cubic foot refrigerator purchased at Sears in January 2012 is 59 percent cheaper, uses 77 percent less energy, and is 24 percent larger by volume

Table 9.2 *Prices of end-use energy in Britain, 1300–2000 (1900 = 100)*

|           | 1300 | 1500 | 1700  | 1750  | 1800 | 1850 | 1900 | 1950 | 2000 |
|-----------|------|------|-------|-------|------|------|------|------|------|
| Heat      |      | 225  | 275   | 300   | 140  | 110  | 100  | 80   | 28   |
| Power     | 85   | 155  | 160   | 165   | 185  | 150  | 100  | 50   | 12   |
| Transport | 390  | 360  | 690   | 790   | 330  | 260  | 100  | 75   | 20   |
| Lighting  |      | 950  | 1,115 | 1,170 | 570  | 300  | 100  | 6    | 1    |

*Source:* Adapted from Roger Fouquet, *Heat, Power and Light: Revolutions in Energy Services* (Cheltenham: Edward Elgar, 2008).

[77] Roger Fouquet, *Heat, Power and Light: Revolutions in Energy Services* (Cheltenham: Edward Elgar, 2008).

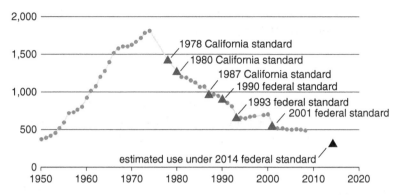

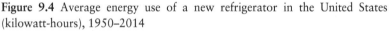

**Figure 9.4** Average energy use of a new refrigerator in the United States (kilowatt-hours), 1950–2014
*Source:* Adapted from US Department of Energy, Office of Energy Efficiency and Renewable Energy, Building Technologies Office.

compared to units in the 1970s.[78] Figure 9.4 shows improvements in efficiency across all refrigerators in the United States from 1950 to 2014, driven largely by national programs such as Energy Star and state standards from California.

Still other examples abound. From 1985 to 2005, Danish research enabled wind turbines to produce 180 times more electricity at 20 percent the cost. Over the same period, commercial turbine output grew 100-fold, from 30 kW in the 1980s to 3.0 MW in 2006.[79] In an open fire, less than 5 percent of the energy embodied in wood ends up as useful heat that cooks the food. A simple cookstove improves the performance to 15 to 20 percent, and today's most efficient household furnaces for space heating convert 94 to 97 percent of energy in natural gas to heat. Similarly, an early Newcomen steam engine transferred less than 1 percent of the energy in coal into reciprocating motion, the compound steam engines of the 1900s had efficiencies of 20 percent, and steam locomotives rarely passed 10 percent, whereas today's best

[78] Richard F. Hirsh, "America's Energy Crisis: Thinking like a Social Scientist," presentation at Vermont Law School, June 22, 2012.
[79] B.K. Sovacool, H.H. Lindboe, and O. Odgaard, "Is the Danish Wind Energy Model Replicable for Other Countries?," *Electricity Journal* 21(2) (March 2008), pp. 27–38.

combined cycle natural gas turbines have conversion efficiencies greater than 60 percent.[80]

## Natural resource funds

Another tool to promote posterity and reciprocity, besides innovation and efficiency, is natural resource funds which state a duty to conserve resources for future generations. These funds usually entrust revenues from current oil and gas production into a pool of money available for the benefits of citizens and future generations as "trustees."[81] The ORML in the introduction is one example of such a fund, but not the only one. Chad passed a Petroleum Revenue Management Law in 1999, known as "Law 001." The law requires that funds from its oil reserves are distributed according to the following arrangement:

- 72 percent go towards five priority sectors: education, healthcare, rural development, infrastructure, and water and environmental resources;
- 13.5 percent are allocated to recurrent government expenditures;
- 10 percent are placed in a "Future Generations Fund" to be used when oil reserves are exhausted;
- 4.5 percent are allocated to communities living in oil-producing areas.[82]

Though the law has been modified to enable Chadian policymakers to spend more on national security in the midst of internal conflicts (and an attempted military coup), its "Future Generations Fund" offers a model for how to simultaneously meet Brown Weiss' notion of conservation of options and conservation of access.[83]

Similarly, the National Fund of the Republic of Kazakhstan is entrusted with preserving revenue as savings for the welfare of

---

[80] Vaclav Smil, *Energy Transitions: History, Requirements, Prospects* (Santa Barbara: Praeger, 2010).

[81] Abdullah Al Faruque, "Transparency in Extractive Revenues in Developing Countries and Economies in Transition: A Review of Emerging Best Practices," *Journal of Energy and Natural Resources Law* 24 (2006), pp. 66–103.

[82] Shari Bryan and Barrie Hofmann, *Transparency and Accountability in Africa's Extractive Industries: The Role of the Legislature* (Washington, DC: National Democratic Institute for International Affairs, 2007), p. 22.

[83] *Ibid.*

future generations, and Azerbaijan's State Oil Fund for the Azerbaijan Republic intends to place most of the government's oil revenues into an account that safeguards the economic security of future generations. Although they do not always work, similar schemes are being implemented in dozens of other countries around the world.[84]

## Renewable energy

Renewable energy is just that – "renewable." It is dependent on non-depletable fuels that can be utilized through a variety of sources, approaches, systems, and technologies; in each case, renewing at a rate faster than or equal to their consumption.[85] Operators and analysts generally categorize renewable energy systems according to their fuel sources, as shown in Table 9.3: wind turbines (onshore and offshore); solar energy (including solar PV panels, solar thermal systems, and concentrated solar power); geothermal (conventional and advanced); biomass (including landfill gas, agricultural waste, refuse, and energy crops as well as biofuels such as ethanol and biodiesel); hydroelectricity (large and small); and ocean power.

The beauty is that renewable fuels are often domestically available and free; for the most part, any amount generated from sunlight or wind does not compete with the sunlight or wind available elsewhere. Countries need not expend considerable resources securing renewable supplies. Put another way, a ton of coal or barrel of oil used by

---

[84] See Heuty, *Can Natural Resource Funds Address the Fiscal Challenges of Resource-Rich Developing Countries?*; David L. Goldwyn (ed.), *Drilling Down: The Civil Society Guide to Extractive Industry Revenues and the EITI* (Washington, DC: Revenue Watch, 2008); B. Jones, *São Tomé and Príncipe – Maximizing Oil Wealth for Equitable Growth and Sustainable Socio-Economic Development* (African Development Fund, 2012); Office of the Pime Minister, *From Conflict to Prosperity – Timor-Leste's Strategic Development Plan 2011–2030* (Dili, April 2010); Timor-Leste Ministry of Finance, *2009 Annual Report* (Dili, December 2009); and Macartan Humphreys and Martin E. Sandbu, *The Political Economy of Natural Resource Funds* (New York: Columbia University, 2007).

[85] While often characterized as relying on renewal though natural processes, in fact some renewables can rely upon or be enhanced by human assistance to natural processes – an example would be multispecies reforestation to offset a wood-fired electricity generating system.

Table 9.3 *Renewable energy technologies and associated fuel cycles*

| Source | Description | Fuel |
|---|---|---|
| Onshore wind | Wind turbines capture the kinetic energy of the air and convert it into electricity via a turbine and generator | Wind |
| Offshore wind | Offshore wind turbines operate in the same manner as onshore systems but are moored or stabilize to the ocean floor | Wind |
| Solar PV | Solar PV cells convert sunlight into electrical energy through the use of semiconductor wafers | Sunlight |
| Solar thermal | Solar thermal systems use mirrors and other reflective surfaces to concentrate solar radiation, utilizing the resulting high temperatures to produce steam that directly powers a turbine; the three most common generation technologies are parabolic troughs, power towers, and dish-engine systems | Sunlight |
| Geothermal (conventional) | An electrical-grade geothermal system is one that can generate electricity by means of driving a turbine with geothermal fluids heated by the earth's crust | Hydrothermal fluids heated by the earth's crust |
| Geothermal (advanced) | Deep geothermal generators utilize engineered reservoirs that have been created to extract heat from water while it comes into contact with hot rock, and returns to the surface through production wells | Hydrothermal fluids heated by the earth's crust |

**Table 9.3 (*cont.*)**

| Source | Description | Fuel |
|---|---|---|
| Biomass (combustion) | Biomass generators combust to biological material to produce electricity, sometimes gasifying it prior to combustion to increase efficiency | Agricultural residues, wood chips, forest waste, energy crops |
| Biomass (digestion) | Biomass plants generate electricity from landfill gas and anaerobic digestion | Municipal and industrial wastes and trash |
| Biomass (biofuels) | Liquid fuels manufactured from various feedstocks | Corn, sugarcane, vegetable oil, and other cellulosic material |
| Hydroelectric | Hydroelectric dams impede the flow of water and regulate its flow to generate electricity | Water |
| Ocean power | Ocean, tidal, wave, and thermal power systems utilize the movement of ocean currents and heat of ocean waters to produce electricity | Saline water |

*Source:* Adapted from Benjamin K. Sovacool, *The Dirty Energy Dilemma: What's Blocking Clean Power in the United States* (Westport: Praeger, 2008).

one community cannot be used by another, whereas renewable resources, because they are nondepletable, do not force such enduring tradeoffs. Moreover, the fuel cost for renewables can be known for decades into the future (and in many cases is seen as zero, or free), something that cannot be said about conventional technologies where predicting spot prices in the future is about as reliable as reading crystal balls.

Furthermore, although renewable energy technologies have their own associated set of environmental and social impacts, they do not generally melt down, rely on hazardous fuels, or depend on a fuel cycle of mining or milling that must extract fuels out of the earth. When roughly quantified and put into monetary terms, the negative externalities for coal power plants are seventy-four times greater than those for wind farms, and the ones from nuclear power plants are twelve times greater than those from solar PV systems.[86] Oil, gas, coal, and uranium are susceptible to rapid escalations in price and price volatility, whereas renewable fuels are often free for the taking, widely available, and inexhaustible. For more on their benefits, readers are invited to sample the final part of Chapter 10, which discusses renewable energy as a prime way of mitigating GHG emissions.

Overall, and to an increasing degree, the world's healthiest economies are beginning to honor the concepts of renewability and sustainability by investing in renewable energy. In a very real sense, the thoughts of Dworkin, Barry, and Brown Weiss are being reflected in the office towers and the forests of the world. Abstract writings about intergenerational justice mark the physical world every time a renewable facility replaces a fossil-fired one.

[86] B.K. Sovacool and C. Watts, "Going Completely Renewable: Is It Possible (Let Alone Desirable)?," *Electricity Journal* 22(4) (May 2009), pp. 95–111.

# 10 | *Fairness, responsibility, and climate change*

Imagine for a moment that you are the governor of the state of Washington in the United States, and that you are entering the final year of your first term. You fully intend to run again. Before then, however, you need to decide your position in a fierce debate that has emerged over the 6,809 MW Grand Coulee Dam on the Columbia River, the largest hydroelectric power station in the country and a key source of energy for Washington State.[1] On the one hand, the dam itself is old – built originally between 1933 and 1942 – and most of its thirty-three hydroelectric generators are in need of expensive refurbishing and upgrades. It lacks a fish ladder, meaning that the Department of the Interior informs you that it permanently blocks fish migration, removing more than 1,700 square kilometers of critical spawning habitat for salmon.[2] Naturalists and recreationists have called the facility an "eyesore," and your officers tell you that removing it would enable the Washington State Parks Foundation to convert Franklin Delano Roosevelt Lake and Banks Lake, currently reservoirs for the dam, into a kayaking tourist attraction. You have read studies that project that closing and removing the dam will cost $100 million, but that the state will receive $310 million per *year* from increased fisheries and tourism revenues – enough to pay for the construction of new power plants in

---

[1] Most of this example is fictional and has been dramatized to tease out its justice implications, though the dam does actually exist. For *real* facts on the dam, see David P. Bilington, Donald C. Jackson, and Martin V. Melosi, *The History of Large Federal Dams: Planning, Design, and Construction* (Washington State: US Department of the Interior, 2005); Ray Bottenberg, *Images of America: Grand Coulee Dam* (Charleston, SC: Arcadia Publishing, 2008); and L. Vaugh Downs, *The Mightiest of Them All: Memories of Grand Coulee Dam* (Reston, VA: American Society of Civil Engineers, 1993).
[2] Leonard Ortolano and Kao Cushing, *Grand Coulee Dam and the Columbia Basin Project USA, Annexes* (Cape Town: World Commission on Dams, 2000).

other places, offset the cost of dam removal, and still produce extra revenue for the state.

On the other hand, closing down the dam means that you may have to approve three new coal-fired power plants to offset the reduction in electrical capacity, thus doubling the state's GHG emissions. Farmers across the Columbia River Basin warn that without the irrigable water that the dam provides, they would need to switch to more pesticide- and fertilizer-intensive crops, contributing even more to future emissions. Your advisors tell you that the remodeled Roosevelt Lake could become such an attractive tourist option that you would need to build a new highway and hotels, which would both need more energy-intensive materials (while they are being built) and sources of energy (once they are operational), again contributing to climate change.

Essentially, you're asked to take a stance on whether you, as governor, prioritize present gain over future suffering. Do you tear down the dam for recreational reasons to open its streams to salmon, facilitate white water kayaking, and expose more native rock formations, benefiting present generations? Or do you keep the dam operating to avoid massive subsequent increases in your state's GHG emissions, benefiting future generations?

Modern justice scholars such as Peter Singer, Henry Shue, and Simon Caney would suggest that you keep the dam going, and respect future generations. This chapter demonstrates how these thinkers strongly argue that our global energy system is unjust because it emits GHGs into the atmosphere which will, in the future, damage the people who contributed the least to those emissions. The buffering capacity of the planet requires that we radically reduce our GHG emissions at the same time that the energy needs of the world are crying out for vast increases in the distribution of energy. Fortuitously, the chapter shows that three tools – greenhouse development rights (GDR), mitigation of emissions through stabilization "wedges," and community-based adaptation – offer industrialized and developing countries alike a way out of this quagmire.

## What is reality?

Chapter 2 already provided an overview of climate change, and Chapter 4 explained how global greenhouse gas emissions are an externality – and therefore unjust under utilitarian grounds. But how those impacts unfold raises other, perhaps more complicated justice concerns. The impacts of emissions could last longer than Stonehenge, time capsules, and perhaps even high-level nuclear waste.[3] Once emitted, a ton of carbon dioxide takes a very long time to process through the atmosphere – according to the latest estimates, one fourth of all fossil-fuel-derived carbon dioxide emissions will remain in the atmosphere for several centuries and complete removal could take as long as 30,000 to 35,000 years.[4] Put another way, the climate system is like a bathtub with a very large tap and a very small drain.[5]

## Towards global calamity

Taken collectively, the climate change consequences of "business as usual" could be nothing short of catastrophic for the planet. A consensus of studies from the IPCC,[6] UN,[7] and other top climatologists[8] warn that continued emissions of GHGs will contribute directly to the following:

- Major changes in wind patterns, rainfall, and ocean currents, resulting in severe alterations to the distribution, availability, and precipitation of water;
- Destruction of ecosystems, species, and habitats – especially coral reefs, beaches, and intertidal zones – and widespread deaths of many types of migratory species;

---

[3] David Archer, *The Long Thaw* (Princeton University Press, 2009).

[4] See J. Hansen, M. Sato, P. Kharecha, D. Beerling *et al.*, "Target Atmospheric $CO_2$: Where Should Humanity Aim?," *Atmospheric Science Journal* 2 (2008), pp. 217–231; and D. Archer, "Fate of Fossil Fuel $CO_2$ in Geologic Time," *Journal of Geophysical Research* 110 (2005), pp. 26–31.

[5] David Victor, Granger Morgan, John Steinbruner, and Kate Ricke, "The Geoengineering Option: A Last Resort against Global Warming?," *Foreign Affairs*, 88 (2009), p. 65.

[6] IPCC, "Summary for Policymakers," in S. Solomon, D. Qin, M. Manning, Z. Chen, M. Marquis, K.B. Averyt, M. Tignor, and H.L. Miller (eds.), *Climate Change: 2007: The Physical Science Basis. Contribution of Working Group I to the Fourth Assessment Report of the Intergovernmental Panel on Climate Change* (Cambridge University Press, 2007).

[7] UN Development Program, *Energy after Rio: Prospects and Challenges* (Geneva: UN, 1997).

[8] Klaus S. Lackner and Jeffrey D. Sachs, "A Robust Strategy for Sustainable Energy," *Brookings Papers on Economic Activity* 2 (2004), pp. 215–248.

- A significant loss of agricultural and fishery productivity, along with a shift in the growing seasons for crops and increased drought in areas with marginal soils that have low buffering potential;
- Increased damage from floods and severe storms, especially among coastal areas;
- Deaths arising from changes in disease vectors, particularly diseases regulated by temperature and precipitation such as malaria and dengue fever;
- The risk of abrupt and catastrophic changes such as the sudden release of pockets of deep sea methane, collapse of the North Atlantic Ocean's thermohaline circulation, and the melting of Greenland's ice sheet.

A research team headed by the NASA/Goddard Institute for Space Studies and the Columbia Center for Climate Systems Research recently confirmed the likelihood of these impacts.[9] After analyzing 30,000 sets of data relating to biological and physical changes affecting the planet over a span of three decades, the researchers identified how many of the adverse consequences from climate change are already occurring. Plants are flowering earlier, birds are breeding prematurely, polar bear populations are declining, precipitation patterns are changing in South America and the Alps, fisheries and forests are collapsing in Europe and Africa, and migration patterns are shifting in Asia, Australia, and Antarctica. Another research team at the US Geologic Survey found that glaciers are melting much faster than anyone imagined a few years ago. Their assessment of the South Cascade glacier in Washington and the Wolverine and Gulcana glaciers in Alaska, long considered global benchmarks for glaciers worldwide because they are located in different climate zones and at various elevations, found that the rate of surface loss has greatly accelerated for each of them in the past fifteen years, even doubling for some years.[10]

---

[9] Cynthia Rosenzweig, David Karoly, Marta Vicarelli, Peter Neofotis, Qigang Wu, Gino Casassa, Annette Menzel *et al.*, "Attributing Physical and Biological Impacts to Anthropogenic Climate Change," *Nature* 453 (May 15, 2008), pp. 353–357.

[10] Edward Josberger, William Bidlake, Rod March, and Shad O'Neel, "Fifty Year Record of Glacier Change," *U.S. Geological Survey Fact Sheet 2009–3046* (July 6, 2009); E.G. Josberger, W.R. Bidlake, R.S. March, and B.W. Kennedy, "Glacier Mass-Balance Fluctuations in the Pacific Northwest and Alaska," *USA: Annals of Glaciology*, 46 (2007), pp. 291–296.

New projections suggest that the impacts from climate change could be *twice* as severe as earlier predictions from the IPCC and other groups. These new calculations, based on improved economic modeling that also accounts for volcanic activity, ocean temperature, the rapidly thawing ice sheets of the Arctic, Antarctic, and Greenland, and the interaction of soot emissions and aerosols in the atmosphere, predict a median probability that surface temperature will increase by 5.2°C (9.1°F) by 2100.[11] As one of the co-authors of the study bluntly noted: "There's no way the world can or should take these risks."[12]

A second, independent study from the authors of the IPCC offered updated projections that are just as stark.[13] As the authors stated:

There is increasing evidence of greater vulnerability of specific populations, such as the poor and elderly, to climate variability and change in not only developing but also developed countries, and that high levels of adaptive capacity may not be realized in practice in the face of stress. For example, events such as Hurricane Katrina and the 2003 European heat wave have shown that the capacity to adapt to climate-related extreme events is lower than expected and, as a result, their consequences and associated vulnerabilities are higher than previously thought.

That assessment found increased evidence of extreme weather events as well as higher sensitivity to disasters and lower adaptive capacity for communities to deal with them, especially in dry regions and mega-deltas.

A third meta-analysis and massive review of the existing scientific literature in 2011 undertaken by a team of British researchers from top universities as well as the National Oceanography Center in the United Kingdom and the Met Office Hadley Center documented even *greater*

[11] A.P. Sokolov, P.H. Stone, C.E. Forest, R. Prinn, M.C. Sarofim, M. Webster, S. Paltsev, C.A. Schlosser, D. Kicklighter, S. Dutkiewicz, J. Reilly, C. Wang, B. Felzer, J.M. Melillo, and H.D. Jacoby, "Probabilistic Forecast for Twenty-First-Century Climate Based on Uncertainties in Emissions (without Policy) and Climate Parameters," *Journal of Climate* 22(19) (October 2009), pp. 5175–5204.

[12] David Chandler, "Revised MIT Climate Model Sounds Alarm," *MIT Tech Talk* 53(26) (May 20, 2009), p. 5.

[13] Joel B. Smith *et al.*, "Assessing Dangerous Climate Change through an Update of the Intergovernmental Panel on Climate Change (IPCC) 'Reasons for Concern,'" *Proceedings of the National Academy of Sciences* 106(11) (March 17, 2009), pp. 4133–4137.

threats.[14] It cautioned that sea-level rise by 2100 may be so severe it will exceed the 95th percentile of earlier IPCC projections; that summer sea ice in the Arctic is now disappearing entirely; that tropical forests are becoming more vulnerable to extended droughts; that thawed permafrost and the release of methane gas from the seabed have started self-sustaining feedback loops; that tropical mammal species are now having to travel thousands of kilometers to find refuge; and that as much as 70 percent of the Amazon rainforest could be lost or converted to seasonal forests. The authors underscored that *none* of these events had been predicted, or incorporated, into previous models.

Basically, climate change has resulted in a massive "accidental experiment" with the entire planet, one that humans have not been biologically well evolved to handle, as it does not fit well with our "fight or flight" mentality. It is more like the method of torture known as "slow slicing," or death by a thousand cuts.[15] Under the most severe projections, the Arctic Ocean could be ice free as early as 2037,[16] and if the Greenland Ice Sheet melts, sea levels could rise a whopping 6 meters – enough to inundate almost all low-lying island states as well as coastal areas from San Francisco and New York to Amsterdam and Tokyo. Once a farfetched scenario, the destabilization of ice shelves and the sudden and unexpected collapse of the West Antarctic ice sheet now have scientists predicting "even greater likelihood of sea level rise in key regions."[17] Concentrations of carbon dioxide in the atmosphere could exceed 1,000 ppm by volume by the year 2050 if trends continue.[18]

Tragically, it is those countries and communities that have emitted the least that are likely to suffer the worst effects of climate change.

---

[14] Peter Good et al., "A Review of Recent Developments in Climate Change Science. Part I: Understanding of Future Change in the Large-Scale Climate System," *Progress in Physical Geography* 35(3) (June 2011), pp. 281–296; Simon N. Gosling et al., "A Review of Recent Developments in Climate Change Science. Part II: The Global-Scale Impacts of Climate Change," *Progress in Physical Geography* 35(4) (August 2011), pp. 443–464.

[15] William Antholis and Strobe Talbott, *Fast Forward: Ethics and Politics in the Age of Global Warming* (Washington, DC: Brookings Institution Press, 2010).

[16] "The Melting North," *Economist*, Special Report on the Arctic, June 16, 2012, pp. 3–4.

[17] Michael E. Mann, "Defining Dangerous Anthropogenic Interference," *Proceedings of the National Academy of Sciences* 106(11) (2009), pp. 4065–4066.

[18] Antholis and Talbott, *Fast Forward*.

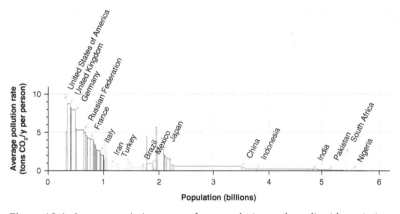

**Figure 10.1** Average emissions rates for cumulative carbon dioxide emissions by country, 1880–2004
*Source:* Adapted from David J.C. MacKay, *Sustainable Energy – Without the Hot Air* (Cambridge: UIT, 2008).

If one accepts the ideas that "the polluter should pay" and that inhabitants of nation-states share a collective responsibility, then each country's historical footprint determines its responsibility for climate change. Figure 10.1 shows cumulative emissions for a selection of countries, expressed as an average emissions rate over the period 1880 to 2004.[19] On a historical basis, the United States and Western Europe account for two-thirds of the primary buildup of carbon in the atmosphere, whereas the entire continent of Africa is responsible for a tiny sliver (just 3 percent) of global emissions.[20] However, depending on the methodology utilized, 75 to 80 percent of the costs of climate change will be borne by those in developing countries.[21]

Put succinctly, the costs of climate change will befall the weakest and least-developed countries while any benefits, if there are any, will likely

[19] David J.C. MacKay, *Sustainable Energy – Without the Hot Air* (Cambridge: UIT, 2009).

[20] Ann E. Prouty, "The Clean Development Mechanism and Its Implications for Climate Justice," *Columbia Journal of Environmental Law* 34(2) (2009), pp. 513–540.

[21] C. Hope, "How Deep Should the Deep Cuts Be? Optimal $CO_2$ Emissions over Time under Uncertainty," *Climate Policy* 9(1) (2009), pp. 3–8; K. De Brun, R. Dellink, and S. Agrawala, *Economic Aspects of Adaptation to Climate Change: Integrated Assessment Modeling of Adaptation Costs and Benefits* (Paris: OECD, 2009).

accrue to the rich and powerful.[22] One global study distinguishing between "experienced" effects of climate change and "imposed" effects – essentially separating out those causing climate change and those experiencing it – concluded that people in rich countries impose 200–300 times more health damage from climate change on others from their historical GHG emissions than they experience themselves.[23] As one of the authors of the study, Berkeley Professor Kirk Smith, mused, these aspects of climate change mean that it is "the most regressive tax in the world: the poorest pay for the actions of the rich."[24]

## What is justice?

Because climate change is such a wide-ranging and complex threat, it cuts across multiple justice concepts and dimensions. One issue is that the impacts of climate change will be distributed unevenly due to both physical processes and the different adaptive capacities of communities and countries; another is that historically only a small group of countries has been responsible for the largest chunk of these emissions; yet another is that the capacity of countries to deal with these threats is highly uneven.[25] Justice scholar Gordon Walker writes that

[22] Richard A. Matthew, "Climate Change and Human Security," in Joseph F.C. DiMento and Pamela Doughman (eds.), *Climate Change: What It Means for Us, Our Children, and Our Grandchildren* (Cambridge, MA: MIT Press, 2007), pp. 161–180.

[23] Kirk R. Smith, Manish A. Desai, Jamesine V. Rogers, and Richard A. Houghton, "Joint $CO_2$ and $CH_4$ Accountability for Global Warming," *Proceedings of the National Academy of Sciences: Early Edition*, July 11, 2013.

[24] Quoted in "Climate Change and the Poor: Adapt or Die," *Economist*, September 11, 2008, p. 51.

[25] For a survey of these arguments, see W. Neil Adger and Sophie Nicholson-Cole, "Ethical Dimensions of Adapting to Climate Change-Imposed Risks," in Denis G. Arnold (ed.), *The Ethics of Global Climate Change* (Cambridge University Press, 2011), pp. 255–271. See also Steve Vanderheiden, *Atmospheric Justice: A Political Theory of Climate Change* (New York: Oxford University Press, 2008); Eric A. Posner and Cass R. Sunstein, "Climate Change Justice," *Georgetown Law Journal* 96 (2008), pp. 1565–1612; W. Neil Adger, Jouni Paavola, and Saleemul Huq, "Toward Justice in Adaptation to Climate Change," in W. Neil Adger, Jouni Paavola, Saleemul Huq, and M.J. Mace (eds.), *Fairness in Adaptation to Climate Change* (Cambridge, MA: MIT Press, 2006), pp. 1–19; Simon Caney, "Cosmopolitan Justice, Rights and Global Climate Change," *Canadian Journal of Law and Jurisprudence* 19(2) (July 2006), pp. 255–278; Simon Caney, *Justice beyond Borders: A Global Political Theory* (Oxford University Press, 2005); A. Agarwal, S. Narain, and A. Sharma, "The Global

Climate change makes the most persuasive case for a justice framing. With climate change we are confronted with evidence of patterns of inequality and claims of environmental injustice that span the globe, that permeate daily life and which pose threats to the current and future health and wellbeing of some of the poorest and most vulnerable people in the world. Climate change demands more than ever that we think rationally about how things interconnect, about who benefits at the expense of others, and about the spatially and temporally distant impacts of patterns of consumption and production. The consequence is that, for many already economically, politically, and environmentally marginalized people, climate change presents compounding forms of injustice.[26]

In other words, the issue of climate change confronts us with fundamental questions about fairness. Climate expert W. Neil Adger and his colleagues write that "fairness is essential to reaching any meaningful solution to the problem of climate change during this century."[27] But fairness based on what, and to whom? Modern justice theorists advance three interrelated claims: an argument about future generations, an argument about human and subsistence rights, and an argument about responsibility and "corrective" justice.

## Respect for future generations

Climate change raises justice concerns for future generations in a variety of ways. Failing to mitigate emissions today inflicts actual harm on future peoples when those emissions produce dangerous changes in climate.[28] Professor and philosopher Henry Shue argues that "future generations will be more severely damaged by climate change than present generations – indeed, they will be its greatest victims, especially in the relatively near future before physical and

Commons and Environmental Justice – Climate Change," in John Byrne, Leigh Glover, and Cecilia Martinez (eds.), *Environmental Justice: Discourses in International Political Economy* (New Brunswick: Transaction Publishers, 2002), p. 173.

[26] Gordon Walker, *Environmental Justice: Concepts, Evidence, and Politics* (London: Routledge, 2012), p. 179.

[27] W. Neil Adger, Jouni Paavola, Saleemul Huq, and M.J. Mace, "Preface," in Adger, Paavola, Huq, and Mace (eds.), *Fairness in Adaptation to Climate Change*, p. xi.

[28] Tamara Steger, *Making the Case for Environmental Justice in Central and Eastern Europe* (Budapest: CEU Center for Environmental Law and Policy, March 2007).

psychological adaptations can set in for the lucky."[29] Assuming that we truly care about the sustainability of our planet beyond our current generation, Shue notes that our own self-interest depends on "achieving ecological justice for future generations."[30]

Philosopher John Nolt has framed the current situation of emissions as a "domination" of future generations. He notes that "our emissions of greenhouse gases constitute unjust domination, analogous in many morally significant respects to certain historic instances of domination that are now almost universally condemned, and, further, no benefits that we may bequeath to the future can nullify the injustice."[31] For him, "domination" implies that the four conditions of (1) power, (2) dependency, (3) rules, and (4) harms have been met. An imbalance of power exists where an agent wields a degree of superior power over the subject. This is certainly the case with future generations as the subjects, Nolt writes, because they have no power over us. Dependency means the subject is not free to exit the relationship without costs. Future generations cannot exist without having us as their predecessors, meeting that criterion. There must be an absence of rules, with no laws or conventions regulating the use of power. In the case of present generations, we yield our power almost completely and without constraining rules, given the collapse of global climate change negotiations.[32] Lastly, there must be harm – and a consensus of studies depicts immense harm for future peoples concerning climate change.

Perhaps for these reasons, explicit calls for the protection of future generations have started to seep into international climate agreements and state constitutions. Article 3(1) of the UNFCCC states that "parties should protect the climate system for the benefit of present and future generations of humankind, on the basis of equity and in accordance

[29] See Henry Shue, "Responsibility to Future Generations and the Technological Transition," in Walter Sinnott-Armstrong and Richard B. Howarth (eds.), *Perspectives on Climate Change: Science, Economics, Politics, Ethics* (Amsterdam: Elsevier, 2005), pp. 265–283; and Henry Shue, "Climate," in Dale Jamieson (ed.), *A Companion to Environmental Philosophy* (Maldon, MA: Blackwell, 2001), pp. 450–477.
[30] Shue, "Climate."
[31] John Nolt, "Greenhouse Gas Emissions and the Domination of Posterity," in Arnold (ed.), *The Ethics of Global Climate Change*, pp. 61–76.
[32] See David G. Victor, "Why the UN Can Never Stop Climate Change," *Guardian*, April 4, 2011; and David G. Victor, *Global Warming Gridlock* (Cambridge University Press, 2011).

with their common but differentiated responsibilities." Article 225 of Brazil's constitution says that "the Government and the community have a duty to defend and preserve the environment for ... future generations." The Republic of Vanuatu's constitution says that every citizen has a duty "to himself and his descendants and to others to safeguard the natural wealth, natural resources and environment in the interests of the present generation and of future generations."[33]

## Honoring subsistence rights

Climate change raises justice issues on human rights grounds. Some now argue that people have a "positive right" to a clean and safe environment and to levels of emissions that provide them a happy and healthy life, and they also have the "human right not to suffer from the disadvantages generated by global climate change."[34] UN General Assembly Resolution 45/94 states that "All individuals are entitled to live in an environment adequate for their health and well-being," and fifty-three nations (by the latest count) have included the provision of such a right in their constitutions. The Draft Declaration of Principles on Human Rights and the Environment, backed by a UN delegation, stated in 1994 that all persons should be free from any form of discrimination in regard to actions and decisions that affect the environment, and that all persons have the right to an environment adequate to meet the needs of present generations that do not impede the rights of future generations.[35]

Henry Shue has argued logically that if physical security is a basic right, then so are the conditions that create it, such as employment, food, shelter, and also unpolluted air, water, and other environmental goods, something he calls "subsistence rights."[36] The implication is that

---

[33] Lynda M. Collins, "Revisiting the Doctrine of Intergenerational Equity in Global Environmental Governance," *Dalhousie Law Journal* 30 (2007), pp. 79–140.

[34] Simon Caney, "Cosmopolitan Justice, Responsibility, and Global Climate Change," *Leiden Journal of International Law* 18 (2005), pp. 747–775.

[35] Steger, *Making the Case for Environmental Justice.*

[36] See H. Shue, *Basic Rights: Subsistence, Affluence and U.S. Foreign Policy* (Princeton University Press, 1980); H. Shue, "Subsistence Emissions and Luxury Emissions," *Law Policy* 15 (1993), pp. 39–59. See also Henry Shue, "Human Rights, Climate Change, and the Trillionth Ton," in Arnold (ed.), *The Ethics of Global Climate Change*, pp. 292–314; and Narasimha Rao and Paul Baer, "'Decent Living' Emissions: A Conceptual Framework," *Sustainability* 4 (2012), pp. 656–681.

Table 10.1 *Criteria and indicators for Shue's "standard of decent living"*

| Basic goods | Energy service(s) | Standard for decent living |
|---|---|---|
| Food | Cooking energy, methane | Adequate nutrition, 2 MJ/cap/day |
| Water/sanitation | Heat for boiled water | 50l potable water/month |
| Shelter | Floor space, lighting, space conditioning | 10 square meters of space, 100 lumens per square meter light, 20 to 27°C temp |
| Healthcare | Electricity | 70 year life expectancy |
| Education | Lighting and electricity | |
| Clothing | Mechanical energy for weaving | |
| Television | Electricity | ~100 kWh per month for all household appliances |
| Refrigerator | Electricity | |
| Mobile phone | Electricity | |
| Mobility | Personal vehicle | Motorized transport |

*Source:* Adapted from H. Shue, "Subsistence Emissions and Luxury Emissions," *Law Policy* 15 (1993), pp. 39–59.

such people are therefore entitled to a certain set of "goods" that enables them to enjoy a basic minimum of well-being, shown in Table 10.1; included in this set of goods are the right to "subsistence emissions." As Shue puts it, "Basic rights are the morality of the depths. They specify the line beneath which no one is allowed to sink."[37] And as he later wrote, "whatever justice may positively require, it does not permit the poor nations to be told to sell *their* blankets in order that rich nations may keep *their* jewelry."[38]

## Responsibility and corrective justice

Climate change raises justice issues on the grounds of responsibility and corrective justice. Essentially, the activities of one group of persons and

[37] Shue, *Basic Rights*.
[38] Henry Shue, "The Unavoidability of Justice," in *The International Politics of the Environment: Actors, Interests, and Institutions* (Oxford University Press, 1992), pp. 373–397.

countries overusing the atmosphere as their carbon "dump" have caused and continued to injure a different, much larger group. This is a matter of "corrective" justice since one group has engaged in wrongfully injuring another group, meaning they should desist from their harmful actions and also compensate them for damages.[39] Polluters and industrializing countries, the thinking goes, should be required to "clean up their own mess." Part of the argument is historical, since industrializing countries have emitted the most into the atmosphere to reach current levels; part is also an argument from ecology, since one could characterize the atmosphere as a sink with limited space. Rich countries have exhausted the capacity of this sink, have denied other countries their shares, and are required to pay compensation for this overuse.[40] Such inequalities must be "reversed" by imposing extra burdens on those countries and peoples responsible for inflicting and producing those inequalities.[41]

In sum, these complementary notions of (1) protecting future generations, (2) ensuring subsistence rights, and (3) acknowledging responsibility mean that "distance makes no moral difference in our globalized world; individual high emitters have a duty to reduce their emissions, wherever they are."[42] It means that when a party has in the past taken an unfair advantage of others by imposing costs upon them without their consent, those who have been disadvantaged can demand that the party shoulder burdens sufficient to undo the unfair advantage previously gained – put another way, historical emitters compensate for their misuse of the atmosphere; the polluter "pays." It, finally, means that when some people have less than enough for a decent human life, and other people have more than enough, an adequate

---

[39] International Council on Human Rights Policy, *Climate Change and Human Rights: A Rough Guide* (Versoix, Switzerland: International Council on Human Rights Policy, 2008).

[40] Stephen M. Gardiner, "Ethics and Global Climate Change," in Stephen M. Gardiner, Simon Caney, Dale Jamieson, and Henry Shue (eds.), *Climate Ethics: Essential Readings* (Oxford University Press, 2010), pp. 3–35.

[41] Caney, "Cosmopolitan Justice, Responsibility, and Global Climate Change"; see also E. Neumayer, "In Defence of Historical Accountability for Greenhouse Gas Emissions," *Ecological Economics* 33 (2000), pp. 185–192.

[42] Paul G. Harris, "Introduction: Cosmopolitanism and Climate Change Policy," in Paul G. Harris (ed.), *Ethics and Global Environmental Policy: Cosmopolitan Conceptions of Climate Change* (Cheltenham: Edward Elgar, 2011), pp. 1–19.

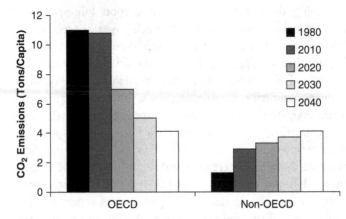

**Figure 10.2** Example of a per capita emissions "contraction and convergence" strategy, 1980–2040

minimum must be set for those that need to meet a basic standard of living.[43]

## What is to be done?

To ensure subsistence, but also adapt to the impacts of climate change and mitigate emissions, the best strategy is one known as "contraction and convergence" where rich, industrialized countries "contract" their emissions while at the same time poor, developing countries "converge" to emissions rates that guarantee a rise in living standards. Such emission levels, if based on an energy-efficient society, may be higher than current ones in developing countries, but lower than historical and current ones from developed nations. Figure 10.2 shows how such contraction and convergence would look in terms of per capita emissions for rich (OECD) and developing (non-OECD) countries. This strategy ascribes "common but differentiated responsibility" to the problem of climate change, arguing that all of us are responsible but to different degrees, based on both historical emissions rates and current capacity. We believe that three

---

[43] H. Shue, *Subsistence, Affluence and U.S. Foreign Policy*, 2nd edn. (Princeton University Press, 1996); Henry Shue, "Global Environment and International Inequality," in Gardiner, Caney, Jamieson, and Shue (eds.), *Climate Ethics*, pp. 101–111.

tools – GDR, community-based adaptation measures, and stabilization wedges – offer an optimal way of achieving this contraction and convergence.

## Greenhouse development rights

Various ethicists, including Peter Singer, Stephen M. Gardiner, and James Garvey, among others, have advocated setting equal per capita emissions allowances related to the capacity of our atmospheric sink, tied to projections of population growth, out to 2030 or 2050.[44] These proposals often discuss setting per capita entitlements, based on an acceptable overall level of greenhouse gas emissions divided equally among the world's population; or subsistence emissions, allowances tilted towards those most in need in order that they achieve an inalienable right to a happy and fulfilling life. Others have argued for global carbon taxes (such as the one discussed in Chapter 4) but for the sole purpose of funding investments in adaptation for those countries least able to cope with it themselves.[45] The UNFCCC suggests a combination of reducing emissions, expanding forests, altering individual lifestyle choices, and creating regulations and policies to restrict carbon output.[46] Similarly, in the United States, the RGGI provides states in the northeastern part of the country with action plans for designing multistate carbon cap-and-trade programs to control their carbon emissions,[47] and the EU has its regional Emissions Trading Scheme covering some 10,000 large

---

[44] See Peter Singer, *One World: The Ethics of Globalization* (New Haven: Yale University Press, 2002); Dale Jamieson, "Adaptation, Mitigation, Justice," in Sinnott-Armstrong and Howarth (eds.), *Perspectives on Climate Change*, pp. 217–248; James Garvey, *The Ethics of Climate Change: Right and Wrong in a Warming World* (London: Continuum, 2008); and Gardiner, "Ethics and Global Climate Change." We leave to another forum the discussion of whether the approach of "per capita" allowances creates a "perverse incentive" for nation-states to increase their internal population levels.

[45] Jouni Paavola, W. Neil Adger, and Saleemul Huq, "Multifaceted Justice in Adaptation to Climate Change," in Adger, Paavola, Huq, and Mace (eds.), *Fairness in Adaptation to Climate Change*, pp. 263–277.

[46] See http://unfccc.int/essential_background/feeling_the_heat/items/2907.php –. There is plenty of information under each category provided on the site.

[47] About RGGI, available at www.rggi.org/about.htm.

industrial plants representing about 40 percent of their total equivalent $CO_2$ emissions.[48]

The problems with these approaches, though they are well intentioned, are manifold. One, most attempt to divide emissions equally, which sounds fair, but avoids the historical trends that have given some, like the US and EU, the "advantage" of being able to emit with impunity for the past few centuries. Two, most do not account for variability *within* countries. The Kyoto Protocol famously divided its signatories into annexes of countries, which captures differences in economic activity between nations, but does not account for the wide variance within them. Rich elites in Buenos Aires, Argentina, are permitted to emit far more than struggling farmers in rural Minnesota or peri-urban Mexico. Similarly, the emissions profile of a Papua New Guinea is vastly different from a Malaysia or China, yet the Kyoto Protocol (and approaches similar to it) places them in the same class. This enables the wealthy to "hide behind" the poor in terms of emissions patterns. Three, and equally important, is that most of these efforts focus on *tons of carbon emitted* rather than the more scientifically informed *temperature targets* or corresponding *atmospheric concentration targets*, which matter far more than emissions in terms of climate change.

As a response, the ethicist Paul Baer and his colleagues have developed a principled framework known as greenhouse development rights (GDR).[49] This framework is based on the twin notions of capacity and responsibility. It creates an emissions budget, and then divides the allowances by income according to individuals, making it a "burden sharing" tool. The notion of *capacity* is rooted in income for an individual adjusted for power purchasing parity over a development threshold. The GDR

[48] Commission of the European Communities, Building a Global Carbon Market, November 13, 2006, available at www.euractiv.com/en/climate-change/eu-emissions-trading-scheme/article-133629; see also Christian Egenhofer, "The Making of the EU Emissions Trading Scheme: Status, Prospects and Implications for Business," *European Management Journal* 25(6) (2007), pp. 453–463.

[49] Paul Baer, Glenn Fieldman, Tom Athanasiou, and Sivan Kartha, "Greenhouse Development Rights: Towards an Equitable Framework for Global Climate Policy," *Cambridge Review of International Affairs* 21(4) (December 2008), pp. 649–669; and Paul Baer, Tom Athanasiou, and Sivan Kartha, *The Right to Development in a Carbon Constrained World: The Greenhouse Development Rights Framework* (Washington, DC: Heinrich Boll Foundation, November 2007); Paul Baer, John Harthe, Barbara Haya, Antonia V. Herzog *et al.*, "Equity and Greenhouse Gas Responsibility," *Science* 289 (5488) (2000), p. 2287.

**Table 10.2** *Characteristics of a greenhouse development rights framework based on responsibility and capacity*

| | Total income (billion $ purchasing power parity 2010) | Total capacity (billion $ purchasing power parity 2010) | Global RCI (%) | Per taxpayer bill ($ purchasing power parity 2010) |
|---|---|---|---|---|
| United States | 14,226 | 11,909 | 31.8 | 733 |
| EU-27 | 14,845 | 11,192 | 24.8 | 412 |
| Russia | 2,173 | 1,166 | 3.9 | 228 |
| Brazil | 1,891 | 926 | 1.8 | 166 |
| China | 8,567 | 2,345 | 6.6 | 124 |
| India | 3,541 | 321 | 0.8 | 65 |
| Mexico | 1,368 | 730 | 1.7 | 199 |
| South Africa | 502 | 257 | 0.9 | 320 |
| Least developed countries | 1,018 | 36 | 0.07 | 57 |
| Annex I | 39,357 | 30,112 | 74.6 | 447 |
| Non-annex I | 29,400 | 9,973 | 25.4 | 169 |
| World | 68,757 | 40,085 | 100 | 315 |

*Source:* Adapted from Paul Baer, Tom Athanasiou, and Sivan Kartha, *The Right to Development in a Carbon Constrained World: The Greenhouse Development Rights Framework* (Washington, DC: Heinrich Boll Foundation, November 2007).

framework therefore distinguishes between necessities such as food and water and luxuries such as yachts and couture dresses. Capacity in this way means the ability to reduce one's consumption, and thus emissions, without sacrificing necessities, and Bauer calculated that amount to be about $7,500 per capita. Bauer and his colleagues define *responsibility* as one's contribution to the problem of climate change, adhering to the classic "polluter pays principle." Bauer bases this on per capita emissions of carbon dioxide from fossil-fuel consumption. He then plugs all of this into a Responsibility and Capacity Indicator (RCI), shown in Table 10.2.

Essentially, Table 10.2 argues that people within the US and EU should now be responsible for 75 percent of the resources needed to address climate change, even though these regions hold less than 19 percent of the global population; and that they start paying an average of $447 per taxpayer to help other countries build their capacity. The GDR framework thus ensures that developing countries exercise their "right to development," while the higher costs and taxes for rich countries both fund that development but also create incentives to limit and lower their own energy consumption, and thus emissions. The GDR framework is concerned with enabling all countries to reach a "development threshold" at which basic rights could be achieved. It also offers numerical pointers for where different countries should cap their own greenhouse gas emissions.[50]

## Community-based adaptation

Funds from a GDR approach, or variants of it, could be put to optimal use investing in community-based climate change adaptation projects. Adaptation describes adjustments in natural or human systems in response to the impacts of climate change. The IPCC defines adaptive capacity as the ability of a system to adjust to climate change (including climate variability and extremes) to moderate potential damages, to take advantage of opportunities, or to cope with the consequences.[51] The closely related concept of resilience refers to the amount of disturbance a local system, climatic or social, can absorb and still remain within the same state, the degree that the system is capable of self-organization, and the degree that it can learn and adapt to changes.[52] "Community-based adaptation" schemes operate at the local level, rely on participatory processes of stakeholder inclusion, and build on existing cultural norms to respond to local development and resilience concerns. They attempt to address the "locally and contextually specified nature of climate change" by incorporating community-based and indigenous knowledge into "locally appropriate" adaptation

---

[50] See International Council on Human Rights Policy, *Climate Change and Human Rights*; Harris, "Introduction"; Michael W. Howard, "Sharing the Burdens of Climate Change: Environmental Justice and Qualified Cosmopolitanism," in Harris (ed.), *Ethics and Global Environmental Policy*, pp. 108–127.

[51] Henry David Venema and Moussa Cisse, *Seeing the Light: Adapting to Climate Change with Decentralized Renewable Energy in Developing Countries* (Winnipeg: IISD, 2004).

[52] Economics of Climate Adaptation Working Group, *Shaping Climate-Resilient Development: A Framework for Decision-Making* (Washington, DC: Global Environment Facility, European Commission, McKinsey & Company, The Rockefeller Foundation, Standard Chartered Bank, and Swiss Re, 2009).

projects.[53] This effort to find – or build – links between global events and local actions reflects the rising effort to turn the slogan of "think globally and act locally" from a mere generalization into operationalized activities.

Unlike mitigation efforts which are prone to public goods problems and the tragedy of the commons, adaptation efforts result in direct benefits to local communities, making them more politically acceptable.[54] As one study put it succinctly, "it is useful to adapt even if nobody else does, but mitigation is meaningless unless it is as part of collective global effort."[55] Adaptation efforts tend to be a "win-win" for they not only improve resilience to climate change but often spill over into ancillary benefits such as economic stability, improved environmental quality, foreign direct investment, and jobs. It is also cheaper to adapt now to climate change than to wait for its eventual impacts, with every \$1 invested in adaptation now yielding as much as \$40 in economic benefits by 2030 in some parts of the world.[56]

The types of adaptation technologies, systems, and practices are wide-ranging and diverse.[57] Some involve anticipatory actions, which are taken in advance of climate change events, in order to generally prepare for climate variability or to prevent irreversible damages such as species extinction and coastal land lost to rising seas. In contrast, reactive practices are deployed after climate disasters have stuck, including various types of emergency response, disaster recovery, and migration.

Anticipatory adaptation is seen as an essential part of the optimal response to climate change, as it is likely much less expensive than relying on reactive adaptation only. While the issue of timing is hotly

---

[53] Jessica Ayers and Tim Forsyth, "Community-Based Adaptation to Climate Change: Strengthening Resilience through Development," *Environment* 51(4) (July/August 2009), pp. 22–31.

[54] David Archer and Stefan Rahmstorf, *The Climate Crisis: An Introductory Guide to Climate Change* (Cambridge University Press, 2010).

[55] Asbjorn Aaheim, T. Dokken, S. Hochrainer *et al.*, "National Responsibilities for Adaptation Strategies: Lessons from Four Modeling Frameworks," in Mike Hulme and Henry Neufeldt (eds.), *Making Climate Change Work for Us: European Perspectives on Adaptation and Mitigation Strategies* (Cambridge University Press, 2010), pp. 87–112 (quote is on p. 88).

[56] Asian Development Bank, *The Economics of Climate Change in Southeast Asia: A Regional Review* (Manila: Asian Development Bank, April 2009).

[57] M.A. Brown and B.K. Sovacool, *Climate Change and Global Energy Security: Technology and Policy Options* (Cambridge, MA: MIT Press, 2011).

debated, many argue that the cost of adaptation will be lower if it is planned and implemented in coordination with other public infrastructure investments and as systems naturally evolve. Strategic planning and investment in information infrastructure and other forms of emergency preparedness can also lower the cost and improve the effectiveness of reactive adaptation. Raising bridges by adding caps to piers (as was done to Alaska's bridge at the Twenty Mile River, for example) reduces the risk of damage from storm surges, while investing in evacuation planning reduces the cost of flooding.[58]

Another way to characterize adaptation practices is according to the climate-related stresses that they address. For instance, different actions are needed to adapt to sea-level rise, drought, ocean acidification, permafrost melt, increased intensity and frequency of coastal storms, and extreme temperatures. We illustrate some of the adaptation initiatives undertaken across the globe by type of stress:

- Sea-level rise – restoring or planting mangroves in coastal embankments to reduce damage from storm surges (Bangladesh), coastal land acquisition programs (US), building storm surge barriers (Netherlands), building bridges higher to anticipate sea-level rise (Canada), and building sea walls to harden seacoast structures (the Maldives);
- Drought – expanded use of traditional rainwater harvesting (Sudan), hydroponic gardening (Philippines), development of drought-resistant strains of wheat (Australia), and adjustment of planting dates and crop variety (Mexico and Ethiopia);
- Extreme temperatures – opening of designated cooling centers (Canada) and heat wave warning systems (EU);
- Permafrost melt – erecting protection dams against avalanches and debris flows stemming from permafrost thawing (Switzerland), railway line construction with insulation and cooling systems to minimize the amount of heat absorbed by the permafrost (Tibet), and draining glacial lakes (Bhutan).

In addition to these infrastructure-oriented adaptation pathways, an array of softer adaptation pathways can reduce the cost of global climate change, encompassing activities as diverse as ecosystem adaptation and establishing and maintaining gene banks to preserve

[58] *Ibid.*

biodiversity, strengthening information infrastructures, and providing better or more comprehensive insurance.[59]

Adaptation seems to work best when it focuses not on improving technology alone, but seamlessly strengthening three types of resilience – infrastructural, institutional, and social – to bolster ecosystems, communities, and human organizations. *Infrastructural* resilience refers to the assets, technologies, or "hardware" in place that could be disrupted by climate change, such as irrigation systems, roads, or electricity networks. *Institutional* resilience refers to the endurance of an institution or set of institutions, usually government ministries or departments, in charge of planning and policy. *Social* resilience refers to the cohesion of communities and the livelihoods of the people that compose them. Resilient infrastructures can recover quickly from climate disruptions, resilient institutions can cope with new stresses and changes and still function, and resilient communities have assets such as education or income that enable them to survive or even thrive in the face of climate-related challenges.[60] Table 10.3 depicts how even least-developed countries, such as those in the Asia-Pacific, are relying on such cross-dimensional adaptation projects as they attempt to cope with climate change.

### Mitigation stabilization wedges

To address climate change we need not only invest in adaptation, but continue to mitigate emissions. Professors S. Pacala and Robert Socolow have developed a series of "stabilization wedges" that can allow us to maintain our quality of life while avoiding catastrophic climate change.[61] A stabilization "wedge" represents an activity that starts at a zero reduction of emissions today but increases linearly until it accounts for 1 gigaton of carbon per year of reduced emissions by 2055. Thus, each wedge represents a cumulative total of 25 gigatons of

[59] *Ibid.*

[60] See B.K. Sovacool, A.L. D'Agostino, H. Meenawat, and A. Rawlani, "Expert Views of Climate Change Adaptation in Least Developed Asia," *Journal of Environmental Management* 97(30) (April 2012), pp. 78–88; as well as B.K. Sovacool, A. D'Agostino, A. Rawlani, and H. Meenawat, "Improving Climate Change Adaptation in Least Developed Asia," *Environmental Science & Policy* 21(8) (August 2012), pp. 112–125.

[61] S. Pacala and R. Socolow, "Stabilization Wedges: Solving the Climate Problem for the Next 50 Years with Current Technologies," *Science* 305 (August 13, 2004), pp. 968–972.

Table 10.3 *Examples of infrastructural, organizational, and social adaptation projects in the Asia-Pacific*

| Country | Infrastructural adaptation | Organizational adaptation | Social adaptation |
| --- | --- | --- | --- |
| Bangladesh | Mangrove plantations, mound plantations, dykes, and embankments; early warning system | Capacity building through training courses for local government officials in forestry, and organizational change through setting up new functional departments | Coupling of forestry programs to income generation through forest products, fish, and food |
| Bhutan | Lowering glacial lake levels; deepening river channels; early warning system; climate shelters | Workshops for government officials at the nodal level | Community training in search and rescue, evacuations, and first aid |
| Cambodia | Climate-proofing of canals and communal ponds; experimentation with crop variation and diversity | Education sessions for provincial and local officials | Local empowerment over prioritization of climate-proofing schemes |
| Maldives | Sea walls; replenishment of sea ridges; mangrove afforestation; beach nourishment; coral reef propagation; repositioning of water tanks | Decentralization of adaptation planning and management to local political units | Community control over adaptation investments |
| Vanuatu | Roads; bridges; port infrastructure; sea walls | Consultation of adaptation options with community stakeholder | Dissemination of information kits to tribal leaders |

*Source:* Adapted from B.K. Sovacool, "Vulnerabilities to Climate Change: Adaptation in Asian Societies," in Paul Harris and Graeme Lang (eds.), *Routledge Handbook of Environment and Society in Asia* (London: Routledge, 2014, in press).

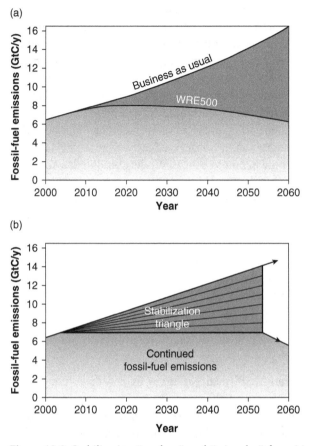

**Figure 10.3** Stabilization "wedges" and "triangles" for mitigating emissions
*Source:* Adapted from S. Pacala and R. Socolow, "Stabilization Wedges: Solving the Climate Problem for the Next 50 Years with Current Technologies," *Science* 305 (August 13 2004), pp. 968–972.

carbon reduced over fifty years, or about $2.5 trillion worth of value in a world where carbon credits trade at a cost of $100 per ton.

As Figure 10.3 shows, such efforts are called "wedges" since each one looks like a wedged triangle. The top curve of image (a) shows business as usual emissions for carbon dioxide from fossil fuels and cement growing at about 7 gigatons of carbon per year. The bottom curve is an emissions pathway consistent with an atmospheric concentration of carbon dioxide of 500 ppm by 2125. Image (b) shows how we could cut emissions out of this business as usual pathway by a combination of different stabilization wedges ranging from carbon capture to efficient vehicles to wind power. Indeed, Table 10.4 shows explicitly how sixteen of these different wedges could be deployed with today's technology to rapidly cut emissions.

Those quick at math may notice that a significant number of "wedges" come from sources of renewable energy. When the potential for these alternative energy sources is quantified, the numbers are startling. The United States has an enormous cache of renewable energy resources that it has only begun to utilize. While a bit dated, a comprehensive study undertaken by the US Department of Energy calculated that 93.2 percent of all domestically available energy within the country's borders was in the form of wind, geothermal, solar, and biomass.[62] As the nonpartisan, independent NRC concurred,

> sufficient domestic renewable resources exist to allow renewable electricity to play a significant role in future electricity generation and thus help confront issues related to climate change, energy security, and the escalation of energy costs ... Renewable energy is an attractive option because renewable resources available in the United States, taken collectively, can supply significantly greater amounts of electricity than the total current or projected domestic demand.[63]

Their conclusions were reaffirmed yet again by a four-volume 2012 National Renewable Energy Laboratory (NREL) report which concluded that "renewable electricity generation from technologies that are commercially available today, in combination with a more flexible electric system, is more than adequate to supply 80% of total US electricity generation in 2050 while meeting electricity demand on an hourly basis in every region of the country."[64]

Globally, one recent assessment which collected actual data on wind speeds at 80 meters from 7,753 surface stations identified about 72 TW

[62] US Department of Energy, *Characterization of US Energy Resources and Reserves* (Washington, DC: DOE/CE-0279, 1989).

[63] NRC, *Electricity from Renewable Resources: Status, Prospects, and Impediments* (Washington, DC: NRC, 2010), p. 4.

[64] National Renewable Energy Laboratory, *Renewable Electricity Futures Study*, ed. M.M. Hand, S. Baldwin, E. DeMeo, J.M. Reilly, T. Mai, D. Arent, G. Porro, M. Meshek, and D. Sandor, 4 vols. NREL/TP-6A20–52409 (Golden, CO: National Renewable Energy Laboratory, 2012), available at www.nrel.gov/analysis/re_futures/.

**Table 10.4** *Sixteen climate stabilization wedges*

| Sector | Option | Effort by 2055 to realize one wedge (1 gigaton of carbon dioxide) | Comments and issues |
|---|---|---|---|
| Energy efficiency | Efficient vehicles | Increase fuel economy for 2 billion cars from 30 to 60 mpg | Car size, power |
| | Reduced use of vehicles | Decrease travel for 2 billion 30 mpg cars from 10,000 to 5,000 miles per year | Urban design, mass transit, telecommuting |
| | Efficient buildings | Cut emissions by a quarter in buildings and appliances | Weak incentives |
| | Efficient baseload coal plants | Produce twice today's output at 60% efficiency (32% today) | Advanced high-temperature materials |
| Fuel switching | Gas baseload power for coal | Replace 1,400 GW 50 percent efficient coal plants with gas plants | Competing demands for natural gas |
| Carbon capture and storage | Capture carbon dioxide at baseload power plants | Introduce 800 GW coal or 1,600 GW natural gas plants with the equivalent of 3,500 Sleipner sites for storage | Technology already in use for $H_2$ production |
| | Capture $CO_2$ at $H_2$ plant | Introduce CCS at plants producing 250 million tons of hydrogen/year from coal or 500 million tons of hydrogen/year from natural gas (compared with 40 million tons of hydrogen/year today from all sources) | $H_2$ safety, infrastructure |
| | Capture $CO_2$ at coal-to-synfuels plant | Introduce CCS at synfuels plants producing 30 million barrels a day from coal (200 times Sasol), if half of feedstock carbon is available for capture | Increased $CO_2$ emissions, if synfuels are produced without CCS |

**Table 10.4** (*cont.*)

| Sector | Option | Effort by 2055 to realize one wedge (1 gigaton of carbon dioxide) | Comments and issues |
|---|---|---|---|
| | Geologic storage | Create 3,500 Sleipners | Durable storage, successful permitting |
| Nuclear fission | Nuclear power for coal power | Add 700 GW (twice current capacity) | Nuclear proliferation, terrorism, waste, accidents |
| Renewable electricity and fuels | Wind power for coal power | Add 2 million 1 MW wind turbines (50 times current capacity) | Multiple uses of land because windmills are widely spaced |
| | Solar power for coal power | Add 2,000 global warming potential solar PV systems (700 times current capacity) | PV production cost |
| | Biomass for fossil fuel | Add 100 times Brazil or US ethanol production | Biodiversity, competing land use |
| | Wind H$_2$ in fuel-cell car for gasoline in hybrid car | Add 4 million 1-MW-peak windmills (100 times the current capacity) | H$_2$ safety, infrastructure |
| Forestry and agriculture | Reduced deforestation, plus reforestation, afforestation, and new plantations | Decrease tropical deforestation to zero instead of 0.5 gigaton of hydrogen/year, and establish 300 million hectares of new tree plantations (twice the current rate) | Land demands of agriculture, benefits to biodiversity from reduced deforestation |
| | Conservation tillage | Apply to all cropland (10 times the current usage) | Reversibility, verification |

*Note:* Pacala and Socolow frame this table as having "15 options" but they do not count geologic storage, even though it is a sixteenth item in their Table 1 on p. 970.

*Source:* Adapted from S. Pacala and R. Socolow, "Stabilization Wedges: Solving the Climate Problem for the Next 50 Years with Current Technologies," *Science* 305 (August 13, 2004), pp. 968–972.

of potential.[65] One fifth of this potential could satisfy all of the world's energy demand and more than seven times its electricity needs. Excluding biomass, and looking at solar, wind, geothermal and hydroelectric energy resources, the world has roughly 3,439,685 terawatthours (TWh) of potential – about 201 times the amount of electricity humans consume each year.[66] So far, less than 0.09 percent of the potential for renewable energy to meet global energy needs has been harnessed. (However, as we will see below, that percentage is starting to increase.)

A slew of recent academic research has also confirmed both the technical feasibility and the social and economic desirability of 100 percent renewable energy systems. One peer-reviewed assessment looked at the economics of two new alternative hypothetical generation systems for 2030 for Australia: 100 percent renewable electricity versus an "efficient" fossil-fueled system, and concluded that the total annualized cost (including capital, operation, maintenance, and fuel where relevant) of the renewable energy system was only $7–10 billion per year higher than that of the "efficient" fossil scenario. For comparison, the subsidies to the production and use of all fossil fuels in Australia are at least $10 billion per year, the implication being that if governments shifted the fossil subsidies to renewable electricity, they could pay for the latter's additional costs.[67] Another study noted that renewables could meet future energy needs "everywhere in the world."[68] The IPCC's special report on renewables concluded that they could reach 43 percent of *global* energy supply in 2030 and up to 77 percent in 2050.[69] The International Energy Agency is now, in parallel, projecting

[65] Cristina L. Archer and Mark Z. Jacobson, "Evaluation of Global Wind Power," *Journal of Geophysical Research* 110 (2005), pp. 1–20.
[66] B.K. Sovacool and C. Watts, "Going Completely Renewable: Is it Possible (Let Alone Desirable)?," *Electricity Journal* 22(4) (May 2009), pp. 95–111.
[67] Ben Elliston, Iain MacGill, and Mark Diesendorf, "Least Cost 100% Renewable Electricity Scenarios in the Australian National Electricity Market," *Energy Policy* 59 (2013), pp. 270–282.
[68] Mark Z. Jacobson and Mark A. Delucchi, "Providing All Global Energy with Wind, Water, and Solar Power, Part I: Technologies, Energy Resources, Quantities and Areas of Infrastructure, and Materials," *Energy Policy* 39 (2011), pp. 1154–1169; Mark A. Delucchi and Mark Z. Jacobson, "Providing All Global Energy with Wind, Water, and Solar Power, Part II: Reliability, System and Transmission Costs, and Policies," *Energy Policy* 39 (2011), pp. 1170–1190.
[69] IPCC, *Special Report on Renewable Energy Sources and Climate Change Mitigation* (Geneva: IPCC, 2011).

that renewables will account for *at least* 35 percent of global energy supply by 2035.[70]

Consider the example of California, notable because if it was its own country it would have the twelfth largest economy in the world. It is currently on track to have 33 percent of its electricity provided by renewable sources by 2020. Moreover, a team of researchers from the University of California Berkeley projected that if expected cost improvements in renewable energy systems like solar PV continue to occur, renewables will grow to provide more than a third of electric power in the entire Pacific Northwest region, displacing natural gas in the medium term and reducing the need for nuclear and carbon capture and sequestration technologies, lowering electricity costs by up to 14 percent, and saving some $20 billion ($2010) annually by 2050 relative to business as usual.[71] Figure 10.4 shows the likely energy mix under a scenario where the Department of Energy continues to make advancements to solar panels under its SunShot program.

In line with these forecasts, recent growth in global renewable energy markets has been impressive, to say the least. From 2004 to 2010, annual renewable energy investment quadrupled to reach more than $271 billion – when large hydroelectric facilities and solar hot water collectors are included.[72] Over the same period, investments in solar PV increased by a factor of sixteen; investments in wind energy increased 250 percent; and investments in solar heating doubled.[73] From 1999 to 2004, geothermal electricity systems grew 16 percent and direct use for heating grew by 43 percent.[74] Figure 10.5 shows growth rates for 2010 to 2012; Figure 10.6 shows investment trends, which in aggregate jumped from $112 billion in 2007 to more than $300 billion in 2011.

---

[70] IEA, *World Energy Outlook 2012* (Paris: OECD, 2012).

[71] Ana Mileva, James H. Nelson, Josiah Johnston, and Daniel M. Kammen, "SunShot Solar Power Reduces Costs and Uncertainty in Future Low-Carbon Electricity Systems," *Environmental Science & Technology* 47(16) (2013), pp. 9053–9060.

[72] Renewable Energy Policy Network for the 21st Century (REN21), *Renewables 2011: Global Status Report* (Paris: REN21 Secretariat, 2011).

[73] REN21, *Renewables Global Status Report: 2009 Update* (Paris: REN21 Secretariat, 2009) (www.ren21.net/pdf/RE_GSR_2009_Update.pdf).

[74] Ingvar B. Fridleifsson *et al.*, "The Possible Role and Contribution of Geothermal Energy to the Mitigation of Climate Change," in O. Hohmeyer and T. Trittin (eds.), *IPCC Scoping Meeting 3 on Renewable Energy Sources* (Lübeck, Germany: IPCC Geothermal, January 2008).

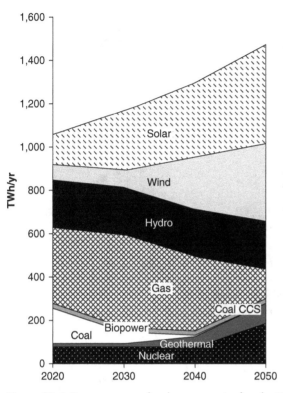

**Figure 10.4** Base energy technology scenario for the Western United States, 2020–2050

*Source:* Adapted from Ana Mileva, James H. Nelson, Josiah Johnston, and Daniel M. Kammen, "SunShot Solar Power Reduces Costs and Uncertainty in Future Low-Carbon Electricity Systems," *Environmental Science & Technology* 47(16) (2013), pp. 9053–9060.

Due to the availability of renewable resources in every country, Table 10.5 shows that such investment has occurred in almost every part of the world. To select just a few examples, China doubled its wind capacity for the fifth year in a row in 2010, and the US and EU each added more capacity from renewable electricity systems than from natural gas, coal, oil, and nuclear power plants.[75] By August 2008, no less than 160 publicly traded renewable energy companies had market

[75] REN21, *Renewables 2011*.

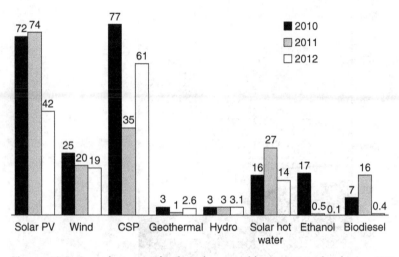

**Figure 10.5** Growth rates of selected renewable energy technologies (%), 2010–2012
*Note:* CSP: concentrated solar power.
*Source:* Adapted from various REN21 global status reports over the years 2007 to 2012.

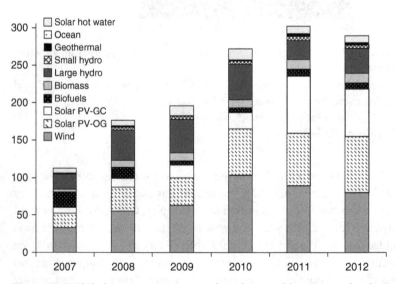

**Figure 10.6** Global investment rates in selected renewable energy technologies (billions of US$), 2007–2012
*Note:* -GC: grid connected; -OG: off-grid.
*Source:* Adapted from various REN21 global status reports over the years 2007 to 2012.

Table 10.5 *Top five countries for renewable energy growth and cumulative investment, 2010*

| | #1 | #2 | #3 | #4 | #5 |
|---|---|---|---|---|---|
| **Annual growth** | | | | | |
| New capacity investment (all renewables) | China | Germany | United States | Italy | Brazil |
| Wind | China | United States | Spain | Germany | India |
| Solar PV | Germany | Italy | Czech Republic | Japan | United States |
| Solar hot water/heat | China | Germany | Turkey | India | Australia |
| Ethanol production | United States | Brazil | China | India | France |
| Biodiesel production | Germany | Brazil | Argentina | France | United States |
| **Total capacity** | | | | | |
| All renewables | China | United States | Canada | Brazil | Germany and India |
| Wind | China | United States | Germany | Spain | India |
| Biomass power | United States | Brazil | Germany | China | Sweden |
| Geothermal power | United States | Philippines | Indonesia | Mexico | Italy |
| Solar PV | Germany | Spain | Japan | Italy | United States |
| Solar hot water/heat | China | Turkey | Germany | Japan | Greece |

*Source:* Adapted from REN21, *Renewables 2011: Global Status Report* (Paris: REN21 Secretariat, 2011).

capitalization greater than $100 million, more than doubling from only 60 in 2005.[76] From 2007 to 2009, China, Spain, and the United States all each added more wind capacity to their domestic portfolios than the world added nuclear capacity.[77] Put another way, the installation of small-scale and distributed power systems such as wind turbines and solar panels grew eighteen times faster than installations for conventional units; it is also telling that a large amount of this investment was financed not by governments but by the private sector.[78] Even in the United States, relatively slow to adopt renewable electricity compared to European countries, wind energy provided 4.4 percent of nameplate capacity in 2011 and roughly 3 percent of electricity demand, and 35 percent of all new capacity added from 2007 to 2012 was in the form of wind energy – an amount greater than *twice* the combined amount from new nuclear and coal units.[79]

Planners, policymakers, and parliamentarians have a variety of tools at their disposal to support renewable energy, with 89 countries having some type of policy target for renewable energy in 2012, a jump from only 45 in 2005.[80] Europe's target of 20 percent of final energy by 2020 is predominant among countries belonging to the OECD; Brazil is targeting 75 percent renewable electricity by 2030, China 15 percent by 2020, India 20,000 MW of solar by 2022, and Kenya 4,000 MW of geothermal by 2030.[81] Two countries, Denmark (2050) and Scotland (2020), have official targets for 100 percent renewable electricity, and to meet its formal greenhouse gas target of at least 80 percent reduction in emissions by 2050, Germany hopes to achieve close to 100 percent renewable electricity, too. Germany already receives about 25 percent of its electricity from renewable sources (up from less than 7 percent in 2000), no small feat considering that Germany has the world's fifth largest economy and is the world's third largest exporter.

---

[76] REN21, *Renewables Global Status Report*.

[77] Amory Lovins, "Does a Big Economy Need Big Power Plants?," *New York Times Freakonomics Guest Post*, February 9, 2009.

[78] Amory Lovins, "Preface to the Chinese Edition of *Winning the Oil Endgame*," February 29, 2008.

[79] R.F. Hirsh and B.K. Sovacool, "Wind Turbines and Invisible Technology: Unarticulated Reasons for Local Opposition to Wind Energy," *Technology & Culture* 54(4) (October 2013), pp. 705–734.

[80] REN21, *Renewables 2010 Global Status Report* (Paris: REN21 Secretariat, 2010); 2011 and 2012 editions.

[81] *Ibid.*

In early 2010, no less than 50 countries and 25 states and provinces had some type of feed-in tariff, and 46 countries were home to renewable portfolio standards for electricity. A number of towns and municipalities around the world – 41 at last count, including Güssing (Austria), Dardesheim (Germany), Moura (Portugal), Varese Ligure (Italy), Samsø (Denmark), Thisted (Denmark), Frederikshavn (Denmark), and Rock Port (United States) – have already implemented 100 percent renewable energy sectors or will implement them by 2015.[82] Policymakers have therefore adopted a cornucopia of other policies to promote renewable energy, many in combination. Direct capital investment subsidies, grants, and rebates are offered in 45 countries; tax credits, import duty reductions, and other tax incentives are offered in more than 30 countries; net metering laws now exist in 10 countries and in 43 US states. Biofuel blending mandates exist in 43 states and provinces and 29 countries as of 2012, with most requiring a blending of 10–15 percent ethanol with gasoline, or 2–5 percent biodiesel with diesel.[83]

Aggressively expanding renewable energy is only one way of configuring an approach to climate stabilization; many other combinations and permutations exist. Some have focused on "alternative" or "behavioral" wedges that involve altering consumption patterns and human values on the "demand side" rather than the "supply side."[84] The physicist Arjun Makhijani has calculated that twelve options deployed today – involving both technological and behavioral wedges – could achieve a "zero carbon dioxide" future within the next thirty years for countries such as the United States. These include:

- Enacting a physical limit on carbon dioxide emissions, which steadily declines to zero prior to 2060, with no free allowances, no offsets, no international purchases of carbon credits, and estimated revenues of

---

[82] Herbert Girardet and Miguel Mendonca, *A Renewable World: Energy, Ecology, Equality* (London: Green Books, 2009), pp. 162–169.

[83] REN21, *Renewables 2010*.

[84] Philip Cafaro, "Beyond Business as Usual: Alternative Wedges to Avoid Catastrophic Climate Change and Create Sustainable Societies," in Arnold (ed.), *The Ethics of Global Climate Change* (Cambridge University Press, 2011), pp. 192–215; Michael P. Vandenbergh, Paul C. Stern, Gerald T. Gardner, Thomas Dietz, and Jonathan M. Gilligan, "Implementing the Behavioral Wedge: Designing and Adopting Effective Carbon Emissions Reduction Programs," *Environmental Law Reporter* 40 (2010), pp. 10547–10554.

$30 to $50 billion funneled back into energy research, demonstration, and worker and community transition;
- Eliminating all subsidies and tax breaks for fossil fuels and nuclear power (including guarantees for nuclear waste disposal, loan guarantees, and subsidized insurance);
- Removing all subsidies for biofuels from food crops;
- Building demonstration plants for solar PVs, concentrated solar, and carbon capture and storage;
- Leveraging purchasing power to create markets for hybrid electric vehicles;
- Banning all new coal-fired power plants without carbon capture;
- Creating stricter efficiency standards for domestic appliances;
- Stipulating more stringent building efficiency standards for industry and commercial enterprises;
- Passing more stringent corporate average fuel economy standards;
- Rewarding early adopters of carbon dioxide reductions;
- Accelerating research and development of low-carbon and zero-carbon energy technologies.[85]

In short, Pacala, Socolow, Makhijani, and others are telling us that a world with far less emissions is technically possible. All that's left is the personal and political motivation to do it.

[85] Arjun Makhijani, *Carbon-Free and Nuclear-Free: A Roadmap for U.S. Energy Policy* (Takoma Park, MD: Institute for Energy and Environmental Research, July 2007).

# 11 | *The imperative of making just energy decisions*

Now we come to our closing chapter, in which we hope to summarize what we have learned about how justice theory can help us make energy decisions. As we do so, let us consider one more factual example, a clear and horrible test of life and death. With that example in mind, we will try to both recognize the diversity of advice that justice theorists might give and, moreover, find some core principles that they do seem to share.

On the evening of April 25, 1986, engineers at Chernobyl's number four reactor in the Ukraine experimented with the cooling pump system to see if it could still function without auxiliary electricity supplies. In order to proceed with the test, the operators turned off the automatic shutdown system. At the same time, they mistakenly lowered too many control rods into the reactor core, dropping plant output too quickly. This stressed the fuel pellets, causing ruptures and explosions, bursting the reactor roof and sweeping the eruption outwards into the surrounding atmosphere. As air raced into the shattered reactor, it ignited flammable carbon monoxide gas and created a radioactive fire that firefighters could not extinguish.[1]

Imagine that you are a Russian military commander taking charge of the emergency teams six days later on May 1, 1986. The radioactive fire continues to burn and is spreading dangerous levels of iodine-131, ruthenium-106, cerium-141 and -144, cesium-137, strontium-89 and -90, and plutonium-238 throughout the facility. The reactor area is a death zone, and the situation is so unsafe that more than 116,000 people have just been evacuated from a thirty square kilometer exclusion zone constituting parts of Belarus, Ukraine, and Russia. Pripyat, a

[1] David R. Marples, "Nuclear Politics in Soviet and Post-Soviet Europe," in John Byrne and Steven M. Hoffman (eds.), *Governing the Atom: The Politics of Risk* (London: Transaction Publishers, 1996), pp. 247–270.

large city in Ukraine, is in the process of being entirely abandoned. You have two options: do you leave with the evacuation, meaning you save your life and the lives of those on your team, but place those downwind at risk of more damage from the fire, since it has yet to be exterminated? Or do you stay and redeploy the army to combat the fire, sacrificing your life and those of your team on the chance that you can eliminate it and save hundreds of thousands of other people?

The justice theorists presented in this book give varying answers to this question, and may even contradict each other in their guidance.[2] Aristotle might argue that a virtuous energy system is definitely not one that spews hazardous contaminants into the air, and should therefore be abandoned – that is, the fire should be put out, and the Chernobyl facility (and indeed all other nuclear reactors) immediately and permanently closed down. Immanuel Kant could say that the sanctity of human life – the infinite value of the lives of the emergency team – means you focus on the individual good, and do not ask them to sacrifice themselves. Jeremy Bentham would say that if one life matters, two lives matter more, and that one should focus on the collective good, sacrificing the emergency team to save an even greater number of people. John Rawls would say that we should imagine a social contract and act as if we lived in a society that seems morally legitimate, regardless of whether we would be either on the emergency army team (those expected to die) or in the homes downwind of Chernobyl's radioactive plume (those who might be saved). Robert Nozick might decry the subsidized nature of both the nuclear power plant and the emergency cleanup operation, since these were guided not by the invisible hand of the market but by the iron fist of the Soviet government.

What, then, would you do? In reality, the Soviets did decide on that May Day to sacrifice the lives of the emergency team and sent them in to deal with the fire from the ground and in the air. They bore the expected radiation exposures and many of them died. In addition, one helicopter crew redeployed from Afghanistan was in the process of dropping boric acid on the exposed fissile material above Chernobyl's shattered reactor but were blinded by its smoke and crashed into it, killing everybody on board and causing yet another radioactive explosion.[3] As a result of the

---

[2] Even though extraordinary accidents such as this happen all too frequently, as residents near Three Mile Island, Pennsylvania, and in Fukushima prefecture, Japan, painfully realize.

[3] *Ibid.*

initial fire and this second explosion, the Chernobyl meltdown ended up releasing more than 200 times the radiation created by the atom bombs dropped on Nagasaki and Hiroshima. More than 5 million people, including 1.6 million children, were exposed to unhealthy levels of radiation, and about 350,000 more people had to be forcibly resettled from the area. Cesium and strontium severely contaminated agricultural products, livestock, and soil as far away as Japan and Norway; some milk in Eastern Europe is still undrinkable.[4]

What does this example tell us, apart from the fact that it is difficult to predict the consequences of one's actions? (Nobody, for instance, thought redeploying the helicopter teams could in any way make the accident *worse*). It suggests that energy justice principles are complex, and that they do not always agree with each other. Utilitarian theorists such as Jeremy Bentham hold that the rightness of an act depends upon its consequences; rights-based theorists such as Immanuel Kant maintain that individuals have fundamental rights that cannot be overridden even if measurable consequences produce net gains in happiness to society as a whole.[5] John Rawls and Robert Nozick explicitly respect pluralism, whereas other justice advocates such as Aristotle and Kant believe in universally applicable standards.[6] Rawls and others subscribing to contractionist theories of justice have a difficult time condemning externalities since two people or a society can agree unilaterally to damage the environment or emit GHGs.[7] Most libertarians are skeptical about intergenerational justice since future persons cannot have present property rights, yet those subscribing to resource egalitarianism such as Brian Barry and Edith Brown Weiss make a strong case for ethical codes protecting future generations.[8]

---

[4] B. K. Sovacool and C. Cooper, "Nuclear Nonsense: Why Nuclear Power is No Answer to Climate Change and the World's Post-Kyoto Energy Challenges," *William & Mary Environmental Law & Policy Review* 33(1) (Fall 2008), pp. 1–119.

[5] Dan M. Berkovitz, "Pariahs and Prophets: Nuclear Energy, Global Warming, and Intergenerational Justice," *Columbia Journal of Environmental Law* 17(2) (1992), pp. 245–326.

[6] Onora O'Neill, "Bounded and Cosmopolitan Justice," *Review of International Studies* 26 (2000), pp. 45–60.

[7] Dale Jamieson, "When Utilitarians Should Be Virtue Theorists," in Stephen M. Gardiner, Simon Caney, Dale Jamieson, and Henry Shue (eds.), *Climate Ethics: Essential Readings* (Oxford University Press, 2010), pp. 315–331.

[8] Clark Wolf, "Intergenerational Justice," in R. G. Frey and Christopher Heath Wellman (eds.), *A Companion to Applied Ethics* (London: Blackwell Publishing, 2003), pp. 279–294.

Still, despite these complexities, we suggest that a set of common conclusions do exist, upon which most of these theorists would agree. In this chapter, we present them as follows: (1) energy injustices continue to be both pervasive and perverse; (2) solutions to energy injustice do exist, but they require comprehensive action; (3) values can play as meaningful a role as technology in causing (and resolving) injustices; (4) adopting a synthetic framework offers us a chance to realign our values in ways that enhance justice; and (5) ethics must be more than simply abstract theories, for, in a functional sense, it has value only when put to use in actual decisions. Or, as the ethicist Peter Singer wryly notes, with ethics "the proof of the pudding lies in the eating."[9]

## The perversity of energy injustice

To help readers comprehend the importance of energy justice as a concept and a tool, the book has compiled numerous examples indicating the *opposite*, describing the myriad ways existing patterns of energy production and use are unjust and unfair. Chapter 3 revealed a number of cruel inefficiencies in the way we supply, convert, distribute, and use energy. Chapter 4 listed a series of negative externalities associated with the global energy system including automobile accidents, nuclear waste, air pollution, and greenhouse gas emissions. Chapter 5 summarized how the energy system can contribute to human rights abuses, social instability, and even military conflict. Chapter 6 noted how some forms of energy decision-making are hostile and exclusionary for minorities and the disenfranchised. Chapter 7 illustrated how many people lack equitable or affordable access to electricity and heating fuels. Chapter 8 detailed a long list of subsidies that involuntarily transfer wealth and distort market signals for energy systems. Chapter 9 demonstrated how the international economy continues to deplete energy resources which took billions of years to form. Chapter 10 warned of how our energy production and use continues to poison our climate with grave implications for global civilization.

Indeed, if the global energy system were to remain configured as it is exactly today until the end of the century, by the year 2100 – a date closer than the birth of our grandparents, a year we hope our grandchildren will enjoy:

[9] Peter Singer, *Practical Ethics*, 2nd edn. (Cambridge University Press, 1993), p. 8.

- The consumption of energy in our homes and automobiles would continue to waste in some instances more than 90 percent of the original energy content embodied in fuels such as coal and oil;[10]
- The economic losses associated with blackouts and power outages would exceed more than $1 trillion each year;[11]
- The number of traffic-related deaths would exceed 3.6 million per year, the planet would be home to roughly 6 billion automobiles, and the global economy would consume 252 million barrels of oil per day;[12]
- More than 3 billion people would lack access to electricity networks and more than 6 billion would depend on solid fuels whose use directly threatens their health and prosperity, with more dying from IAP than malaria, tuberculosis, and HIV/AIDS;[13]
- Egregious human rights abuses associated with energy production – including the denial of free speech, torture, slavery, forced labor, executions, and rape – would continue to afflict thousands of people around the world;[14]
- Massive energy subsidies would cost taxpayers $5.7 trillion, in some cases making oil and gasoline cheaper than bottled water, and three-quarters of these subsidies would continue to support the dirtiest and least efficient energy systems;[15]
- Natural and humanitarian disasters associated with climate change, driven largely by greenhouse emissions from the energy sector, would affect billions of people.[16]

Our book, therefore, seriously questions whether many energy companies – and the governments that partner with them – will strive for energy justice on their own. On the contrary, many of the examples of corruption, social exclusion, human rights abuses, and conflict occurred

---

[10] See Chapter 3 on inefficiencies for a fuller explanation.
[11] Oracle Utilities, *The Future of Energy*, October 14, 2011, reports that in the EU power outages cost €150 billion per year. Also, in the United States the cost of annual blackouts was estimated at about $206 billion. We triple these numbers to get to 2100 levels.
[12] We have merely tripled the existing externalities from today's levels to correspond with a trebling in energy demand.
[13] See Chapter 7 on energy poverty, with numbers tripled from today's levels.
[14] See Chapter 5 for more on human rights abuses.
[15] See Chapter 8 for more on subsidies.
[16] See Chapter 10 for more on climate change and the necessity of community-based adaptation.

on the part of governments and companies. Their actions are antithet-
ical to initiatives promoting better transparency, accountability, and
stakeholder involvement throughout parts of the energy sector. Which
brings us to a troubling thought: neither individuals, nor companies and
governments, seem able to provide energy justice on their own. Energy
projects operating in the "free market" without proper public oversight
can turn a profit and please their shareholders while violating many of
the principles of energy justice introduced in this book.

Yet, with all that said, the global energy system also has enabled
people to live longer and healthier than in any earlier civilization, and
the supply of modern energy services remains central to our economies
and our lifestyles. So how can the energy sector be reconstructed to
minimize its perils and maximize its potential?

## The necessity of comprehensive intervention

Both policy and individual solutions to energy injustices do exist,
thankfully. Regulators, policymakers, and parliamentarians can implement some of these from the "top down," whereas individuals, families,
and companies can implement others from the "bottom up." For
instance, some of the major "top-down" policy initiatives that can
address injustices include national fuel economy standards for automobiles and energy-efficiency labeling programs to improve the virtuous-
ness of the energy system. Regulators can change the price of energy so it
reflects externalities, pass a carbon tax to provide more accurate price
signals, and incentivize extractive industries transparency initiatives
and inspection panels to protect human rights. National governments
can form 5Ps to promote energy systems in the developing world suffering from acute energy poverty, and they can eliminate inappropriate
subsidies. They can create national resource funds, endorse renewable
electricity and biofuels, and mitigate greenhouse gas emissions through
the adoption of stabilization wedges.

These efforts can be complemented with "bottom-up" actions such as
companies sponsoring energy-efficiency retrofits and environmental
bonds, and electric utilities adopting or expanding their demand-side
management and energy-efficiency programs. Homeowners can invest
in smart-grid systems and advanced metering which enable them to
better track their energy use, and to integrate solar panels and other
forms of distributed generation into the electricity grid. Local civil

society groups can provide legal aid to vulnerable groups damaged by energy production, and help ensure that minorities are represented in energy decisions. Communities can also invest in climate change adaptation to bolster their resilience. Individuals can even accept their own responsibility for emissions under a GDR scheme which tracks and makes them accountable for per capita carbon dioxide figures.

However, this suite of packages and actions faces a pernicious set of social, political, and behavioral barriers. Too often, regulators and advocates of particular policies tend to view different options as substitutes for each other, rather than components or pieces of an effective whole.[17] In the case of promoting renewable energy and energy efficiency, pursuing the solutions identified here will not work in isolation. Making renewable power mandatory through a national FIT, for example, but not removing conventional subsidies and continuing to price electricity inaccurately decreases the economic viability of renewable power projects and interferes with the ability of users to sell power back to the grid (or conserve it).

Simply changing the price of energy is insufficient as well. For most people, the only visible sign of electricity use is at payment time, when utility bills periodically reach the household.[18] Extensive interviews with residential electricity consumers have found more than half of electricity customers (55 percent) pay all of their bills the same time each month. This "processing and batch" treatment implies that for the majority of consumers, electricity prices will be ignored because they are injected into an activity primarily concerned with verifying dollar amounts and writing checks. Only 40 percent of those surveyed, for instance, looked at their actual usage of electricity when paying the bill.[19] The explanation may lie in the fact that a typical middle-class European family may pay more than $15,000 per year for housing/land and rent, more than $10,000 per year for medical matters, more than $10,000 per year for clothing and food, but less than $2,000 per year for electricity. The effect is that, at monthly bill paying time, utility costs

[17] Michael P. Vandenbergh, "From Smokestack to SUV: The Individual as Regulated Entity in the New Era of Environmental Law," *Vanderbilt Law Review* 57 (2004), pp. 515–610.

[18] Eugene A. Rosa, Gary E. Machlis, and Kenneth M. Keating, "Energy and Society," *Annual Review of Sociology* 14 (1988), pp. 149–172.

[19] Willett Kempton and Linda Layne, "The Consumer's Energy Analysis Environment," *Energy Policy* 22(10) (1994), pp. 857–866.

are often treated to electronic or mental "autopay" without serious analysis of alternatives. In a perverse way, electricity has become "too cheap to analyze" even as it has become easier to meter.

Further complicating matters, honest accounting by those rare customers that do attempt to track their energy use is compounded by the invisibility and difficulty of quantifying energy savings, which are for all intents and purposes invisible. Many people, including experts, generally understand the services provided by energy and electricity in nonmonetary terms, and instead make decisions based on the amount of time saved and the avoidance of inconvenience.[20] Furthermore, decisions about energy efficiency are often made by people who are not paying the energy bills, such as landlords or developers of commercial office space. Many buildings, moreover, are occupied for their entire lives by temporary owners and renters, each unwilling to make long-term investments in efficiency.[21]

Without compensatory modification, rising (and more accurate or "just") prices are inherently inequitable to low-income families, and relying on financial mechanisms alone can entrench classism. One study evaluated the effectiveness of energy-efficiency tax credits in the United States, intended to motivate homeowners to install more efficient windows, caulking and weather stripping, and found not a single respondent considered the tax credit important enough that their energy-efficiency purchases would not have been made without it (40 percent actually learned about the credit only after they had completed the installation).[22] Furthermore, the authors noted that almost no low-income families took advantage of the tax credit, since they had less capital available to retrofit their homes, and could not wait until the end of the year for reimbursement. Furthermore, most had little or no tax obligations against which to apply the credit.

Relying solely on changes in pricing, or subsidy removal, also becomes risky when prices or end-use patterns unexpectedly change. Pricing energy more accurately but not coupling it with information programs

---

[20] Loren Lutzenhiser, "Social and Behavioral Aspects of Energy Use," *Annual Review of Energy & Environment* 18 (1993), pp. 247–289.

[21] Ralph Cavanagh, "Energy-Efficiency Solutions: What Commodity Prices Can't Deliver," *Annual Review of Energy and Environment* 20 (1995), pp. 519–525.

[22] Robert E. Pitts and James L. Wittenbach, "Tax Credits as a Means of Influencing Consumer Behavior," *Journal of Consumer Research* 8 (December 1981), pp. 335–338.

does nothing to eliminate unrealistic payback rates among property owners and investors. Removing subsidies without reforming electricity prices or informing consumers still clouds the price signals that are sent to them. Moreover, Bigdeli determined that the effect of removing energy subsidies in five European countries, by themselves, would have a minimal effect on reducing the use of coal, and could even increase greenhouse gas emissions, since those countries would merely switch to cheaper (lower-quality) international imports if domestic prices rose.[23] The evidence suggests that changes in behavior and significant greenhouse gas reductions will happen only if policy reforms encompass more than the removal of subsidies and alterations in pricing in isolation.

Energy efficiency by itself is vital, but insufficient, partially because new sources of energy supply are needed to expand access to modern energy services for the billions of people that do not have it, and also because increases in personal consumption – driven by larger houses, and more electronic devices such as laptops and mobile phones – continue to partially offset improvements in efficiency. Moreover, one interdisciplinary study, good enough to meet the rigorous standards of *Science*, recently analyzed the technology pathways required to meet California's goal of an 80 percent reduction in greenhouse gas emissions below 1990 levels, using detailed modeling of infrastructure stocks, resource constraints, and electricity system operability. The team found that "feasible levels of energy efficiency and decarbonized energy supply alone are not sufficient; widespread electrification of transportation and other sectors is required."[24] Efficiency cannot do it alone.

Improved information and education, by themselves, are also inadequate. An assessment of energy-efficiency programs involving refrigerators, natural gas ranges, washers and dryers, dishwashers, and room air conditioners found that energy labels were incapable of causing substantial changes in consumer preferences.[25] One researcher interviewed

[23] Sadeq Z. Bigdeli, "Will the Friends of Climate Emerge in the WTO? The Prospects of Applying the Fisheries Subsidy Model to Energy Subsidies," *Carbon & Climate Law Review* 2(1) (2008), pp. 78–88.

[24] James H. Williams, Andrew DeBenedictis, Rebecca Ghanadan, Amber Mahone, Jack Moore, William R. Morrow, Snuller Price, and Margaret S. Torn, "The Technology Path to Deep Greenhouse Gas Emissions Cuts by 2050: The Pivotal Role of Electricity," *Science* 335 (January 6, 2012), pp. 53–59.

[25] Everett Shorey and Tom Eckman, *Appliances & Global Climate Change: Increasing Consumer Participation in Reducing Greenhouse Gases* (Washington, DC: Pew Center on Global Climate Change, October 2000).

500 people about their personal responsibility to stop littering, and found that while more than 90 percent acknowledged such responsibility, only 2 percent picked up litter that had been "planted" by the researcher after the interview.[26]

These studies all suggest that only comprehensive solutions implemented holistically and simultaneously can successfully eradicate energy injustice. They also reveal that just actions are impeded by a sobering array of barriers, obstacles, and impediments.

## The import of values behind technologies

Due to the presence of these barriers, and our own moral involvement in energy injustices, technology cannot entirely resolve society's energy problems. This is partly because people actually do not want a particular energy technology or system at all; what they really desire is the luxury, comfort, happiness, and convenience such fuels and technologies provide. It is also partly because energy technologies can be interpreted not as neutral devices that produce, transport, or convert energy, but as forms of congealed culture where the social interests of those designing the technology get built into the system, rather than becoming a latent or unintended result.

In other words, the manner in which energy technologies redistribute social, political, and economic power is as important as how such technologies generate electricity or transport liquid fuel. A key implication here is that the global energy system not only satisfies our wants, desires, and needs; it can also influence our behavior. Economist E.J. Mishan captured this double-faced nature of technology well when he remarked "while new technology is unrolling the carpet of increased choice before us by the foot, it is often simultaneously rolling it up behind us by the yard."[27] This means that, as Lynton K. Caldwell wrote during the peak of the energy crisis of the 1970s, "if there is a comprehensive energy problem, it is a problem of choice and value in a world of finite capabilities. It is therefore also a moral and political problem, and for this reason will not yield to a purely technical solution."[28]

[26] L. Bickman, "Environmental Attitudes and Actions," *Journal of Social Psychology* 87 (1972), pp. 323–324.

[27] E.J. Mishan, *The Costs of Economic Growth* (New York: Praeger, 1967).

[28] Lynton K. Caldwell, "Energy and the Structure of Social Institutions," *Human Ecology* 4(1) (1976), pp. 31–45.

The implication that energy systems are simultaneously technological as well as *political* and *ethical* reminds us that more efficient energy devices and improved economic signals are necessary but incomplete conditions to achieve energy justice. Utility managers, systems operators, business leaders, and ordinary consumers do not function merely like automatons that rationally calculate price signals and change their behavior to optimize benefits and minimize costs. Instead, they are embroiled in a complicated social and cultural environment that is shaped by and helps to shape technological change, rituals, behaviors, values, attitudes, emotions, and interests.

Consequently, the contest between energy technologies is about more than merely hardware. As we exhaust energy resources and have to find substitutes to them, change our way of life, or transition to renewable energy, the biggest challenge will be determining how we make this transition, and more specifically *who* gets to make it, and *who* has to pay for it. This is not a question that can ever be answered by economics or engineering. Such disciplines can tell us how large energy reserves may be or how much energy fuels may cost today, but they treat supply as a function of geologic availability or of price and demand, not of morality.[29] Economics offers an excellent set of tools for estimating costs and benefits, but tells us little about who benefits and who suffers.[30] Imagine trying to explain to a farmer in Bangladesh who had lost three children in a "post-climate-change cyclone" in cost-benefit language that your extra pleasure in driving a bigger car outweighs his loss. Economics is concerned with accounting, justice with accountability.

As such, we need a shift in values as much as – perhaps even more than – we need to alter our energy technologies and systems. Philosopher Dale Jamieson explains that "a system of values provides a standard for assessing our behavior and that of others," and it also "provides a measure of the acceptability of government action and regulation."[31] Three recent anecdotes help put this claim in perspective.

---

[29] Douglas MacLean, "Introduction," in Douglas MacLean and Peter G. Brown (eds.), *Energy and the Future* (Totowa, NJ: Rowman and Littlefield, 1983), pp. 1–14.

[30] David Archer and Stefan Rahmstorf, *The Climate Crisis: An Introductory Guide to Climate Change* (Cambridge University Press, 2010).

[31] Dale Jamieson, "Ethics, Public Policy, and Global Warming," in Gardiner, Caney, Jamieson, and Shue (eds.), *Climate Ethics*, pp. 77–86.

In 2009, at the Fifteenth Session of the Conference of Parties to the UNFCCC (COP15), where global lawmakers met to hammer out an international climate change treaty, they rented 1,200 limousines. One delegation wanted 42 vehicles to themselves, and almost none of the vehicles ferrying around delegates were electric cars or hybrid vehicles. Copenhagen's Kastrup airport saw 140 extra private jets and was quickly overcapacity, meaning most planes flying into Copenhagen simply dropped people off and then flew to Sweden to park. Menus at the conference featured fish, scallops, caviar, and *foie gras*. It has been estimated that by the end of the eleven-day conference, more than 41,000 tons of carbon dioxide equivalent had been emitted,[32] an amount greater than the national emissions of some small countries for an entire year. Thus, the very conference intended to stop climate change was not only what one newspaper called "a useless gabfest,"[33] it also contributed to the very problem it was trying to address.

A second anecdote concerns the United States in 2012. That year, when the US EPA withheld permits for coalmines, tightened pollution controls for coal-fired power plants, and backed legislation that would place a price on greenhouse gas emissions, one of West Virginia's two federal senators responded by showing an advertisement where he took a rifle and shot hundreds of bullets through a copy of a proposed climate change bill. Ten counties also voiced their disapproval for President Obama, who they blamed for the decision, by voting for Keith Judd, a convict serving a seventeen-year sentence for extortion at the Correctional Institution in Texarkana. This, in essence, meant that to many West Virginians President Obama had become so unpopular due to his actions phasing out coal that a convicted felon seemed a better choice to them for president.[34]

A third anecdote concerns the Yasuní-ITT initiative in Ecuador. That initiative, promoted by President Rafael Vicente Correa in 2007, would have left almost 1 billion barrels of crude oil in the ground beneath the Ishpingo Tambococha Tiputini (ITT) oilfield within the country's Parque Nacional Yasuní, or Yasuní National Forest, one of the most

[32] Andrew Gilligan, "Copenhagen Climate Change Conference: Not the Science but the Vision," *Daily Telegraph* (London), December 7, 2009.
[33] Nitin Sethi, "After Five Days, Nothing to Show at Climate Meet," *Times of India*, December 12, 2009, p. 1.
[34] "What's Eating Appalachia? Many Democrats in the Region Seem to Hate their President," *Economist*, July 7, 2012, p. 35.

treasured biological hotspots on the planet. The proposal would have brought $32.8 billion in benefits, including displaced greenhouse gas emissions, prevented deforestation, the protection of indigenous communities residing in the forest, and investments in a clean energy and social development fund.[35] In exchange for not developing the ITT oilfield, President Correa asked the international community only for "fair compensation" of $3.6 billion. After raising a mere $336 million over five years – less than 10 percent of the needed funds – the President was forced to cancel the project in August 2013 and proceeded to develop the ITT oilfield "within weeks."[36] As the President tearfully stated when he made his announcement in Quito, "we have waited long enough ... the world has failed us."[37]

These three sobering examples indicate that we do not always make energy decisions based on facts; instead, we base them on values. In the first instance, the values of luxury and expediency were given greater priority at COP15 than sustainability and frugality. In the second instance, local employment was valued more than protection of the environment and the earth's climate. In the third example, the lure of economic development and revenue were deemed more important than the protection of indigenous people and maintenance of a national wilderness area. Indeed, Marybeth Long Martello and Sheila Jasanoff have even argued that the COP process under the UNFCCC is values-based since it treats all emissions alike – regardless of their source – so that it in essence penalizes subsistence activities just as severely as luxury ones. Farmers producing GHGs from rice paddies are to be held just as accountable as yacht owners on a luxury fishing trip, a decision that conceals an intention, based on *values*, not to distinguish emissions sources.[38]

[35] B. K. Sovacool, "Responsibility and Ecuador's Yasuni-ITT Initiative," in *Energy & Ethics: Justice and the Global Energy Challenge* (New York: Palgrave MacMillan, 2013), pp. 194–217.

[36] "Ecuador President Pulls Plug on Innovative Yasuni-ITT Initiative, Authorizes Drilling in National Park," *Amazon Watch*, August 16, 2013.

[37] Joan Martinez-Alier, Nnimmo Bassey and Patrick Bond, "Yasuni ITT Is Dead. Blame President Correa," Ejolt, August 2013, available at www.ejolt.org/2013/08/yasuni-itt-is-dead-blame-president-correa/.

[38] Marybeth Long Martello and Sheila Jasanoff, "Globalization and Environmental Governance," in S. Jasanoff and M. Long Martello (eds.), *Earthly Politics: Local and Global in Environmental Governance* (Cambridge, MA: MIT Press, 2004), pp. 1–29.

In each case, one set of values was given precedence over another set of values. Back in the 1970s, the physicist Amory Lovins somewhat famously argued that the true contest between promoting centralized fossil-fuel and nuclear generators and decentralized energy-efficiency and renewable systems had little to do with the technologies themselves, and much more about the values behind different energy pathways. One could conceivably integrate a collection of 1 kW solar panels on the cooling tower of a large nuclear facility. Yet these two approaches were deemed "culturally incompatible" since "each path entails a certain evolution of social values and perceptions that make the other kind of world harder to imagine."[39] Similarly, Lutzenhiser surveyed dozens of studies relating to energy and electricity consumption where energy conservation or improved efficiency took place, and he found numerous examples of where it was values such as "reducing waste" and "being independent" motivating behavioral change, not particular policies or cost-benefit calculations.[40]

Unfortunately, traditional energy policymaking gives us no easy answer to energy injustices, no way out. As we shall see in the next subsection, we must look beyond the status quo, beyond its energy markets and institutions; hence the need for justice theory and concrete thoughts about just energy futures.

### Presenting an energy justice framework

In that vein, we present an energy justice framework in this penultimate section of the chapter. Drawing from each of our previous chapters, our framework – presented in Table 11.1 – argues that that we need to embrace a different set of energy values. We need to start making energy decisions that promote:

1) Availability;
2) Affordability;
3) Due process;
4) Information;
5) Sustainability;

---

[39] A. B. Lovins, "A Target Critics Can't Seem to Get in Their Sights," in H. Nash (ed.), *The Energy Controversy: Soft Path Questions and Answers* (San Francisco, CA: Friends of the Earth, 1979), pp. 15–34.
[40] Lutzenhiser, "Social and Behavioral Aspects of Energy Use."

Table 11.1 *Energy justice conceptual framework*

| Principle | Explanation |
| --- | --- |
| Availability | People deserve sufficient energy resources of high quality |
| Affordability | All people, including the poor, should pay no more than 10 percent of their income for energy services |
| Due process | Countries should respect due process and human rights in their production and use of energy |
| Information | All people should have access to high-quality information about energy and the environment and fair, transparent, and accountable forms of energy decision-making |
| Sustainability | Energy resources should not be depleted too quickly |
| Intragenerational equity | All people have a right to fairly access energy services |
| Intergenerational equity | Future generations have a right to enjoy a good life undisturbed by the damage our energy systems inflict on the world today |
| Responsibility | All nations have a responsibility to protect the natural environment and minimize energy-related environmental threats |

6) Intergenerational equity;
7) Intragenerational equity; and
8) Responsibility.

While all eight principles are important, the idea is to start with the simplest and most accepted ones, such as availability and affordability, before moving towards the more controversial or complex ones such as intragenerational equity and responsibility.

## *Availability*

Availability is the most basic element of our energy justice framework, for it involves the ability of an economy, market, or system to guarantee sufficient energy resources when needed. It therefore transcends concerns related to security of supply, sufficiency, and reliability, and it encompasses a range of different dimensions. It includes the physical resource endowment of a particular country or region, as well as the technological solutions that region utilizes to produce, transport, conserve, store, or distribute energy. It includes the amount of invest-ment needed to keep the system functioning, essentially having a robust and diversified energy value chain, as well as promoting infrastructure that can withstand accidental and intentional disruption.[41]

## Affordability

A second core element of energy justice is the basic affordability of energy services, a term that means not just lower prices so that people can afford warm homes and well-lit dwelling spaces, but also energy bills that do not overly burden consumers. Affordability thus encom-passes stable prices (minimal volatility) as well as equitable prices that do not require lower-income households to expend disproportionately larger shares of their income on essential services. Implicit with this criterion is that the idea of highly available energy fuels and services is meaningless unless households and other consumers can afford to access and utilize them.

## Due process

The notion of due process – respect for human rights and basic ele-ments of national and international law – dates back thousands of years, yet abuses of those rights and impact assessments that do not adequately protect people occur frequently within the energy sector. Due process revolves around deciding what process is "due." Thus, discussions tend to move from the generalized idea of "respect" and focus more on questions about "how important is the matter?" and "how irrevocable is a decision?" From an energy justice perspective, due process seeks to ensure that the potential for stakeholder partic-ipation in the energy policymaking process at least roughly matches the importance (in aggregate and to each person affected) of the matter at stake and the irrevocability of any decisions that may be reached. It also necessitates effective recourse through judicial and administrative remedies and forms of redress. More specifically, the principle suggests that communities must be involved in deciding about projects that will

[41]  J. Elkind, "Energy Security: Call for a Broader Agenda," in C. Pascual and J. Elkind (eds.), *Energy Security: Economics, Politics, Strategies, and Implications* (Washington, DC: Brookings Institution Press, 2010), pp. 119–148.

affect them; they must be given fair and informed consent; environmental and social impact assessments must involve genuine community consultation; and neutral arbitration should be available to handle grievances.

## Information

This principle suggests that, to minimize corruption and improve accountability, all people should have access to high-quality information about energy and the environment. Information has become a central element of promoting "good governance" throughout a variety of sectors, a term that centers on democratic and transparent decision-making processes and financial accounting, as well as effective measures to reduce corruption and publish information about energy revenues and policies.[42] Access to information and transparent frameworks for preserving that access have been known under certain conditions also to encourage democracy, increase business confidence, and enhance social stability.

## Sustainability

Sustainability refers to what the Brundtland Commission termed "development that meets the needs of the present without compromising the ability of future generations to meet their own needs."[43] In an energy context, it refers to the duty of states to ensure the sustainable use of natural resources. It means that countries have sovereign rights over their natural resources, that they have a duty not to deplete them too rapidly, and that they do not cause undue damage to their environment or that of other states beyond their jurisdiction. Ecologist Paul Hawken eloquently summed up sustainability when he wrote that it involves achieving a state where "the demands placed upon the environment by people and commerce can be met without reducing the capacity of the environment to provide for future generations. It can also be expressed in the simple terms of an economic golden rule for the restorative

---

[42] P. Wolfowitz, "Good Governance and Development – A Time for Action," *World Bank Press Release*, April 11, 2006.
[43] World Commission on Environment and Development (WCED), *Our Common Future* (Oxford University Press, 1987), p. 43.

economy: Leave the world better than you found it, take no more than you need, try not to harm life or the environment, make amends if you do."[44]

## Intragenerational equity

Intragenerational equity – that present people have a right to access energy services fairly – finds its roots in modern theories of distributive justice. Philosophers call it "distributive" justice because it deals intently with three aspects of distribution:

1. What goods, such as wealth, power, respect, food, or clothing, are to be distributed?
2. Between what entities are they to be distributed?
3. What is the proper mode of distribution – based on need, based on merit, based on property rights, or something else?

Distributive justice argues that, if physical security is a basic right, then so are the conditions that create it, such as employment, food, shelter, and also unpolluted air, water, and other environmental goods. People are, therefore, entitled to a certain set of minimal energy services which enable them to enjoy a basic minimum of well-being.

## Intergenerational equity

Instead of emphasizing distributive justice between different communities in the present, intergenerational equity is about distributive justice between present and future generations. It holds that future people have a right to enjoy a good life just like us contemporaries, yet one undisturbed by the damage our energy systems will inflict over time. Consequently, each of us has a moral responsibility to ensure that today's children and future generations inherit a global environment at least no worse than the one we received from our predecessors – and that responsibility extends to preventing climate change and making strategic investments in something known as "adaptation" to increase the needed resilience of communities.

---

[44] P. Hawken, *The Ecology of Commerce: A Declaration of Sustainability* (New York: Harper Collins, 1994), p. 112.

## Responsibility

The final principle – responsibility – holds that nations have a responsibility to protect the natural environment and minimize the production of negative externalities, or energy-related social and environmental costs. This element of energy justice is perhaps the most controversial and complex, as it blends together four somewhat different notions of "responsibility": a responsibility of governments to minimize environmental degradation, a responsibility of industrialized countries responsible for climate change to pay to fix the problem (the so-called "polluter pays principle"), a responsibility of current generations to protect future ones, and a responsibility of humans to recognize the intrinsic value of nonhuman species, adhering to a sort of "environmental ethic."

## Synthesis

In laying out our energy justice framework, some priorities – such as availability and affordability – come before others, and some concepts (such as distributive justice) are mixed with others (such as procedural justice). This makes our framework hierarchical, cosmopolitan, and synthetic.

By being hierarchical, our framework intends to help those most in need first. It is based on a "lexical" or "lexicographical" ordering of energy needs so that the most vulnerable – those lacking energy access entirely or those threatened by human rights abuses – must be totally satisfied before one addresses other injustices.[45] Some philosophers have called this a "vulnerability based leximin rule" because it means that when the neediest are best taken care of, one must then help the second neediest, and so on, to assist the most vulnerable groups first.[46]

---

[45] Scott Gordon, *Welfare, Justice, and Freedom* (New York: Columbia University Press, 1980), pp. 146–148.

[46] Such a rule has shown how to construct a continuum of intermediate social welfare functions between sum-utilitarianism and the maximin criterion (or its lexicographic refinement, the leximin criterion), which ranks distributions of well-being by examining first the worst-off position, then the position which is just above the worst-off, and so on. For instance, the maximin is indifferent between the three distributions (1,2,5), (1,3,5) and (1,3,6), whereas the leximin ranks them in increasing order. See Marc Fleurbaey, "Economics and Economic Justice," in Edward N. Zalta (ed.), *The Stanford Encyclopedia of Philosophy* (Summer 2012 edn.), as well as Serge-Christophe Kolm, *Modern Theories of Justice* (Cambridge, MA: MIT Press, 1996).

Such a hierarchy of principles does exist in other areas; the US Constitution is one example (indicating, in its Supremacy Clause, that it comes "first" before all other laws within the nation). Another example is Isaac Asimov's three laws of robotics (yes, both of us are science fiction fanatics), which are also hierarchically ordered in importance,[47] as is Abraham Maslow's psychological "hierarchy of needs," which argues that basic needs such as food and shelter come before those such as friendship and self-actualization.[48]

Secondly, our framework is cosmopolitan, for we argue that it should apply to everyone, equally, across the globe. Cosmopolitan justice theorists argue that justice principles must apply universally to all human beings in all nations. Cosmopolitan theories of justice acknowledge that all ethnic groups belong to a single community based on a collective morality. Cosmopolitanism implies that "duties of justice are global in scope, and these duties require adherence to general principles including respect for civil and democratic rights and substantial socio-economic egalitarianism."[49] Put another way, cosmopolitan justice accepts that all human beings have equal moral worth and that our responsibilities to others do not stop at borders. Cosmopolitans believe that to be worthwhile and meaningful, some moral judgments and frameworks must be absolute. Otherwise, morality threatens to become what Oscar Wilde called "simply the attitude we adopt towards people whom we personally dislike." As Brian Barry put it succinctly, "I believe that the core idea of universalism – that place and time do not provide a morally relevant basis on which to differentiate the weight to be given to the interests of different people – has immense rational appeal."[50] Or, as the late ethicist Louis Pojman put it, "a core set of moral principles [is] necessary to the good society and the good life ... We may well agree

---

[47] These laws state that "A robot may not injure a human being or, through inaction, allow a human being to come to harm; A robot must obey the orders given to it by human beings, except where such orders would conflict with the First Law; A robot must protect its own existence as long as such protection does not conflict with the First or Second Law."

[48] A. Maslow, *Motivation and Personality*, 3rd revised edn. (New York: Harper & Row, 1954/1987).

[49] Darrel Moellendorf, *Cosmopolitan Justice* (Boulder: Westview Press, 2002), p. 171.

[50] Brian Barry, "Sustainability and Intergenerational Justice," in Andrew Dobson (ed.), *Fairness and Futurity: Essays on Environmental Sustainability and Social Justice* (Oxford University Press, 1999), pp. 93–117.

that cultures differ and that we ought to be cautious in condemning what we do not understand. But this agreement in no way needs to imply that there are not better and worse ways of living."[51]

Thirdly, by synthetic, we mean that our framework intertwines (or "synthesizes") many aspects of justice sprinkled throughout this book. It includes distributive justice, which is about how energy harms and energy services are distributed, whether the energy system is equitable or not, and whether it is fair to future generations or not. It includes procedural justice, which is about FPIC for energy projects, representation in energy decision-making, and access to high-quality information about energy. Cosmopolitan justice applies these two concepts (distributive and procedural) globally, arguing that each individual person has inviolate worth that must be respected and protected. Enfolded in our framework are other elements of justice. We include the idea that guilty people should be held accountable for wrongful acts, or "justice as an outcome"; that individuals will be protected to prevent innocent people from being wronged, or "justice as due process"; and that all people should be treated equally under the law, or "justice as fairness."[52]

Such a synthetic or multifaceted notion of justice is necessary because "redistribution without empowerment can be short-lived, and empowerment without redistribution can be an insult."[53] That is, proper distribution of outcomes – distributive justice – and impartiality in decision-making – procedural justice – are interconnected. One philosopher admits that "my utility may not only depend on what I get but on the manner in which I get it. That is my utility may not only depend on the consequences of policy but on the policy itself."[54]

---

[51] Louis Pojman, "Ethical Relativism versus Ethical Objectivism," in Louis P. Pojman (ed.), *Introduction to Philosophy: Classical and Contemporary Readings* (Belmont: Wadsworth Publishing, 1991), pp. 506–516.

[52] See Matthew B. Robinson, "Justice as Freedom, Fairness, Compassion, and Utilitarianism," *Contemporary Justice Review* 6(4) (2003), pp. 329–340; B. Arrigo (ed.), *Social Justice, Criminal Justice: The Maturation of Critical Theory in Law, Crime, and Deviance* (Belmont, CA: Wadsworth, 1999).

[53] Jouni Paavola, W. Neil Adger, and Saleemul Huq, "Multifaceted Justice in Adaptation to Climate Change," in W. Neil Adger, Jouni Paavola, Saleemul Huq, and M. J. Mace (eds.), *Fairness in Adaptation to Climate Change* (Cambridge, MA: MIT Press, 2006), pp. 263–277.

[54] F. Hahn, "On Some Difficulties of the Utilitarian Economist," in A. Sen and B. Williams (eds.), *Utilitarianism and Beyond* (Cambridge University Press, 1982), pp. 187–198.

A synthetic notion of justice is also needed because energy injustices are interrelated: the degradation of the environment can be wrong for reasons of posterity (hurting future generations), human rights (violating a "right" to a clean environment), and utility (externalities which produce human suffering and misery). Similarly, the exclusion of vast populations of people from accessing modern forms of energy can be wrong for reasons of virtue (failing to meet the essential purpose of what energy systems are for), welfare (denying them the ability to realize their functionings and capabilities), and equity (failing to promote resource egalitarianism).

Lastly, a synthetic framework is needed to incorporate the sheer diversity of concepts and justice principles. In a commonality that spans millennia and continents, there is a common belief that "right" and "wrong" do exist objectively, even if they are hard to distinguish.[55] For example, as already mentioned, utilitarian theorists such as Bentham hold that the rightness of an act depends upon its cumulative beneficial impact; rights-based theorists such as Kant hold that individual rights cannot be overridden even if the consequences would be cumulatively beneficial. The two ideas seem insurmountably inconsistent – yet both in the end consider freedom from bodily harm a fundamental right.[56] They arrive at the same destination despite taking different routes. Thus, we hold that the view that ethics and moral principles are always relative to a specific society is dangerous and implausible; such relativism permits no basis for denouncing cultures that condone slavery or genocide, for instance.

In sum, our framework has elements of Kantian ethics, which takes each person as an end, looking at the opportunities available to them. It has libertarian elements of freedom and choice, suggesting that good societies present people with a set of opportunities or substantial freedoms; people can choose to exercise these or not. It is pluralist about value, holding that capabilities for people are different and also that their own interests vary. It is concerned with justice as recognition and respect, noting that failures of procedural justice can result in discrimination and marginalization. It, also, has elements focused on

---

[55] See, among others, John Alder and David Wilkinson, *Environmental Law and Ethics* (Basingstoke: Macmillan, 1999); John Ash, "New Nuclear Energy, Risk, and Justice: Regulatory Strategies for an Era of Limited Trust," *Politics & Policy* 38(2) (2010), pp. 255–284.

[56] Berkovitz, "Pariahs and Prophets."

utilitarianism and welfare, attempting to improve the quality of life for all people, as defined by their capabilities.[57]

## The criticality of choice

Our final conclusion calls on all of us to recognize our involvement in energy injustices and to *act* accordingly. All of us participate in the global energy system, and thus each of us contributes to some – perhaps even many – of the injustices highlighted above. We each consume varying levels of energy to warm our homes, to cook our meals, and to travel to and from work. The decisions we make about which home appliance to purchase, which electricity company to patronize, and which car to buy have very real moral and ethical implications. The heating oil we purchase to thaw our homes in the winter contributes to PM being inhaled by children living near refineries. The firewood we collect and burn exposes our mothers and children to IAP and contributes to the deforestation of tropical rainforests. The electricity we consume is partially responsible for the impacts of climate change – the tidal inundations and storm surges flooding our low-lying cities – as well as the forcible relocation of indigenous communities near a coalmine or hydroelectric dam. The automobile we covet contributes to the acid rain bleaching streams, forests, and coral reefs, or to human rights abuses in oil-producing countries which extracted the fuel. The Nobel laureate Elinor Ostrom once wrote that the decisions made within a family about the type of investments to make in their home, their choice of electricity provider, and deciding what car to purchase have a *significant* effect on global atmosphere, accounting for 40 to 70 percent of emissions in most countries.[58]

Because of our own involvement in the energy system, and our collective responsibility, energy problems inescapably have a technical element – involving technologies and infrastructure, and a moral element – involving how we value other human beings (now, and in the future) and the natural environment. This may be part of the reason why

[57] Gordon Walker, *Environmental Justice: Concepts, Evidence, and Politics* (London: Routledge, 2012).
[58] Elinor Ostrom, *A Polycentric Approach for Coping with Climate Change* (Report Prepared for the WDR2010 Core Team at the World Bank, February 2009, W09–4).

the ethicist Peter Singer has called climate change "the greatest *moral* challenge our species have ever faced," or why philosopher Stephen M. Gardiner has called climate change a perfect "*moral* storm."[59]

Philosopher Dale Jamieson has also noted that improving energy security and responding to climate change present unique moral dilemmas. Classic morality is about people harming others directly, and where they act intentionally. It is where both the individuals and the harm can be identified, and the two are closely related in time and space. It is where cause and effect are clear. One example would be Arnold stealing bread from his coworker Amanda, or Benjamin stealing a bicycle from Bob. The case of energy and climate, Jamieson notes, is much different. It is more akin to Benjamin and Arnold and a large number of other unacquainted people setting in motion a chain of events that prevents a large number of future people who will live far away from ever having bicycles or loaves of bread. It thus does not fit classic notions of (im)morality.[60]

What does all this mean for energy justice in the end, readers may rightly ask at this point? It means that energy systems ought to maximize welfare – not necessarily in a narrow utilitarian way, but their ability to realize happiness and well-being.[61] It means that energy planners ought to direct most of their effort to benefiting the *least-well-off*, adhering to a global application of a leximin rule.[62] As one group of scholars put it, "a society is just only if it is arranged in such a way that the position of the least advantaged is optimized."[63] It implies that every person has the right to a "social minimum" of energy or electricity so that they can enjoy a modern, healthy lifestyle.

It also means that energy justice boils down to *choice*. As the saying (from Benjamin Franklin) goes, "the great advantage of being a

---

[59] Quoted on the back cover of Stephen M. Gardiner, *A Perfect Moral Storm: The Ethical Tragedy of Climate Change* (Oxford University Press, 2011).

[60] Dale Jamieson, "Energy, Ethics, and the Transformation of Nature," in Denis G. Arnold (ed.), *The Ethics of Global Climate Change* (Cambridge University Press, 2011), pp. 16–37.

[61] Sven Ove Hansson, "Welfare, Justice, and Pareto Efficiency," *Ethical Theory and Moral Practice* 7(4) (August 2004), pp. 361–380.

[62] Thomas C. Grey, "Property and Need: The Welfare State and Theories of Distributive Justice," *Stanford Law Review* 28(5) (May 1976), pp. 877–902.

[63] Kirstin Dow, Roger E. Kasperson, and Maria Bohn, "Exploring the Social Justice Implications of Adaptation and Vulnerability," in Adger, Paavola, Huq, and Mace (eds.), *Fairness in Adaptation to Climate Change*, p. 81.

reasonable creature is that you can find a reason for whatever you do," implying that we all tend to justify the choices we make, after the fact, as if they were the inevitable outcome of reason. In reality, the process of making choices is more tenable, iterative and uncertain; it is, in short, a quandary. As the late biologist Edward O. Wilson eloquently put it:

Each of us finds a comfortable position somewhere along the continuum that ranges from complete withdrawal and self-absorption at one end to full civic engagement and reciprocity at the other. The position is never fixed. We fret, vacillate, and steer our lives through the riptide of countervailing instincts that press from both ends of the continuum … [Our lives] are neither a celebration nor a spectacle but rather, as a later philosopher put it, a predicament. Humanity is the species forced by its basic nature to make moral choices and seek fulfillment in a changing world by any means it can devise.[64]

Applied to energy, we can *choose* to adopt the view that markets adequately distribute energy fuels and services, and continue to value lumps of coal, barrels of oil, and cubic meters of natural gas for the motive power or electricity they give us through dollars and cents. Or we can *choose* to acknowledge that markets are inherently amoral, and recognize that the global energy system is replete with extreme injustices and asymmetries that we are all complicit in.

Given that we started the book with a quotation from Edmund Burke, we thought it fitting to also end with one. As Burke wrote almost three centuries ago:

Men are qualified for civil liberty in exact proportion to their disposition to put moral chains upon their own appetites. Society cannot exist unless a controlling power on will and appetite be placed somewhere, and the less of it there is within, the more there must be without. It is ordained in the eternal constitution of things, that men of intemperate minds cannot be free. Their passions forge their fetters.[65]

Burke's remark suggests that justice may very well be central to the orderly and fair working of our entire society, but to achieve it, we must all choose to constrain our own – and, collectively, each other's – appetites.

---

[64] E. O. Wilson, *The Future of Life* (New York: Random House, 2002), pp. xxi–xxii.

[65] Quoted in Herman E. Daly, *Steady-State Economics* (Washington, DC: Island Press, 1991), p. 171.

# Index

Locators with the suffix 'f' indicate a figure and 't' a table.

5P (pro-poor public private partnership)
249–253

Aarhus Convention 211
acid rain 75, 148
  *see also* sulfur dioxide (SO$_2$)
    emissions
Adger, W. Neil 327
Afghanistan, Talisman Oil Company 167
Africa
  energy poverty 226t, 227–228
  indoor air pollution 139
  oil and natural gas reserves 50t, 51t
  petroleum production 63t
agriculture, energy needs 65–68
air conditioning 105–106, 119
air pollution
  effects of 75–77, 130–131
  and energy use 68t
  sources of 74–76
  sources of human disruption 84t
  *see also* indoor air pollution (IAP)
aircraft industry, jet turbines 40–41
Algeria, natural gas production 51t
aluminium 58t
Ambrozic, Jose 246
Anderson, Kevin 74
Angola
  civil war 173
  corruption 169
*Anthropocene* era 86–87
Aristotle 14t, 354
  and first principles 38
  and happiness 110–111
  and justice 108–109
  and virtue 3, 18, 88–90, 111–113
Armenia, subsidy reform 283t
arms race 174

Asia
  air pollution 77, 78f
  energy poverty 226t
  indoor air pollution 139
  oil and natural gas reserves 50t, 51t
Australia
  coal subsidies 271
  energy trade 27
  petroleum liquids production 63t
  renewable energy 345, 349t
  uranium mining 135–136, 162, 168
automobile industry 40, 236–237
automobiles
  and consumer behavior 102–103
  dominance 61, 62–65
  energy efficiency measures 116–117
  energy inefficiencies 92, 93f
  fuel economy 119
  growth in ownership 65
  negative externalities 130–131
  opportunity costs 108
  safety 278
  *see also* electric vehicles
Azerbaijan
  BTC pipeline 167, 172–173,
    201–202
  oil and gas production 132–133,
    133f
  State Oil Fund 315

Baer, Paul 14t, 334–336
Bakun Hydroelectric Project 196
Bangladesh
  climate change adaptation projects
    340t
  energy poverty 226t
  Phulbari Coal Project 168
  small-scale renewable energy 247

Barbour, Ian G. 210
Barry, Brian 14t, 20, 291, 303–305,
    311, 355, 372
Bentham, Jeremy 2–3, 14t, 126,
    141–143, 354, 355
Berkovitz, Dan 174, 176
Bhutan 340t
Bigdeli, Sadeq Z. 361
biodiesel 348f, 349t
biofuel 351
biomass energy
    critical materials needs 58t
    energy payback ratio (EPR) 100, 101f
    and environmental costs 150–151
    growth and investment 348f, 349t
    negative externalities 149t
    technologies 316t
    *see also* fuel collection
Boulding, Elise M. 308
Brazil
    constitution 329
    deforestation and GHGs 82–83, 83t
    greenhouse gas emissions 69, 70f
    petroleum production 63t
    renewable energy 349t, 350
    subsidy reform 283t
Brighouse, Harry 239
British Petroleum, *Deepwater Horizon*
    51–53
British Thermal Unit (BTU) 34
Brock, Gillian 209
Brookings Institute 146
Brown Weiss, Edith 14t, 291, 305–306,
    310–311, 355
Burke, Edmund 30, 377
Burma *see* Myanmar (Burma)

cadmium 58t, 84t
Caldwell, Lynton K. 362
California
    GHG emissions reduction 361
    renewable energy 346
    San Diego electricity supply 191–193
calorie, unit of measurement 34
Cambodia 340t
Canada
    carbon taxation 146–147
    greenhouse gas emissions 70f
    Impact-Benefit Agreements (IBAs)
        184, 185t

oil and gas production 50t, 51t, 63t
renewable energy 349t
Saskatchewan Rate Review Panel
    (SRRP) 218
Caney, Simon 14t, 320
carbon capture and storage (CCS) 107t,
    108t, 343t, 352
carbon credits 198–199
carbon dioxide emissions
    by sector 70f
    cap-and-trade systems 147
    carbon-cost ratios 108t
    causes 84t
    contraction and convergence
        332–333, 332f
    cumulative rates 325, 325f
    and deforestation 82–83, 83t
    effect of subsidy removal on 280
    entitlement allowances 333–334
    from international trade 27–28
    increased by subsidies 271
    lifecycle equivalent for clean energies
        107t
    rising levels 71–73, 72f
    safe limit 69
    sources 68t
    stabilization wedges 339–342, 343t,
        341f
    timescale for removal 321
    zero carbon dioxide measures 352
carbon taxation 145–147
carbon-offset plantations 198–199
Chad
    future generation fund 314
    transparency initiative 187
chemical pollution 214
Chernobyl 138, 200–201, 353–355
childbirth 230
Chile
    petroleum liquids production 63t
    Ralco Dam 197
    subsidy reform 283t
China
    air conditioning 106
    air pollution 77
    Beijing's energy efficiency measures
        115–116
    carbon dioxide emissions 28f
    coal production 54–55
    coalmine hazards 159

China (cont.)
  coalmine numbers 54t
  cookstoves 247
  energy subsidies 266
  greenhouse gas emissions 69, 70f
  indoor air pollution 229
  land rights and nuclear plants 201
  military conflict 173
  motor vehicle ownership 65
  negative effects of climate change
    129
  oil and gas production 50t, 51t, 63t
  renewable energy 349t, 350
  Three Gorges Dam 196–197, 197f
chromium 58t
civil wars 173
climate change
  adverse consequences 321–326
  community-based adaptation projects
    336–339, 340t
  and energy justice 326–329
  and energy use 68t
  and fairness and responsibility 14t
  and human moral systems 4–5
  negative externalities 127–129
  and social inequity 29
  UN Framework Convention on
    Climate Change (UNFCCC) 194,
    328–329, 333–334, 364, 365
  *see also* carbon dioxide emissions;
    greenhouse gases (GHG)
coal-fired power plants
  aging stock 95, 96f
  emissions reduction 343t
  environmental costs 150–151
  healthcare costs 129
  opportunity costs 107t
  subsidies 269, 271
coalmining
  coalmine numbers and types 54t
  companies 53, 54t
  and involuntary resettlement 179
  negative externalities 149t
  occupational hazards 159–162, 165f
  Phulbari Coal Project 168
  reserves 294–295, 295f, 296t
  techniques 53–54, 86
  US accidents 159, 160t
  water use 81
  *see also* mountaintop removal

cobalt 59
Coke, Edward 14t, 206–207
Colgan, Jeff D. 173
Colombia, military conflict 174
communication 207–208
community-based adaptation projects
    336–339, 340t
concrete, energy industry needs 57, 58t
Congo, Republic of
  corruption 171
  energy poverty 225, 226t
  military conflict 174
consumers
  behavior and morality 375–377
  and electricity prices 359–360
  and energy efficiency 101–103
  information and awareness 101–103,
    105, 123–124, 212–213, 254,
    361–362
  *see also* public involvement
contractarian theory 237–238,
    304–305, 355
cookstoves 246–248, 313
copper 57, 58t, 173
Cornwell, Laura 153–154
corrective justice 330–332
corruption 169–172, 170t
cosmopolitanism 372–373
Costanza, Robert 153–154
critical materials 57–59, 58t
crops, and acid rain 148
Czech Republic
  renewable energy 349t
  subsidies 266

Daly, Herman E. 294
de Moor, André 272
deaths
  and fuel poverty 231–233
  heat-wave 205
  and indoor air pollution 228f
  PM emissions 130, 131t
  winter mortality rates 232t
decision-making 25–26
deforestation 68t, 82–83, 83t, 198–199,
    343t
Denmark
  consensus conferences 216
  energy tax shifting 152t
  energy taxes 123

renewable energy 350
wind energy 220, 247
de-Shalit, Avner 308
developing countries
 and climate change 128–129
 costs of oil dependence 298–299
 disadvantaged in international
  negotiations 193–195
 energy inefficiencies 99
 lack of technology 233
diesel, subsidies 263, 264f
diesel engines 40
difference principle (Rawls) 240–241
disasters
 Environmental Impact Assessments
  (EIAs) 183
 *see also* natural disasters; nuclear
  safety
distributive justice 11, 275, 370, 373
Driver, Julia 142
drought 338
due process 14t, 206–208, 210–211,
 368–369
Dworkin, Ronald 14t, 174–175, 291,
 301–303

ecological footprint 66–67
ecological justice 12–13
Ecuador, Yasuní-ITT initiative
 364–365
Egypt
 corruption 170t
 energy subsidies 266
Eisenhower, Dwight D. 256–257
electric appliances 41, 43–44, 118–119
 *see also* refrigerators; televisions
electric vehicles 59, 60, 123, 352
electricity
 lack of access 225, 226t
 lack of consumer knowledge 102
electricity grids 119, 120t, 220
electricity industry
 aging stock 95–99
 billing system improvements 121
 blackouts 98–99, 130, 192–193
 customer demand (load) 46–47, 95,
  96f, 105
 decoupling sales from profits
  121–123
 disconnection 223–224

energy efficiency measures 113–116,
 117–118
human dependence upon 60–61
inefficiencies 90–92
negative effects of climate change
 129–130, 149
power frequency 47
pricing 119–121, 151–153, 213–214,
 359–360
sources of power 129–130
subsidies 269
supply 60–61, 86
transmission lines 47, 150, 191–193
units of measurement 34–35
voltage 47
water use 79–81
end-use energy, definition 6–7
energy
 concept of 32–34
 definition 6–8
 delivery mechanisms 44–47
 laws of thermodynamics 33–34, 90
 measurement 34
 prime movers 38–44
energy density 37, 39f
energy efficiency
 consumer awareness and education
  101–103, 105, 123–124, 254,
  361–362
 effective policies 281
 electricity industry 113–116
 and emissions reduction 343t
 energy conversion and use 90–95,
  93f, 94f
 energy intensity reduction 117–118
 labeling 118–119
 McKinsey recommendations 114,
  115f
 and new technologies 311–314
 principal-agent problem 103–104
 savings 117–118, 118f
 summary 14t
 and tax credits 360
energy intensity 117–118
energy justice
 and accessibility 14t, 225, 226t
 affordability 368
 availability 367–368
 barriers to effective intervention
  359–360

energy justice (cont.)
  and climate change 326–329
  definition 13
  due process 14t, 206–208, 210–211,
    368–369
  framework 366–367, 367t,
    371–375
  hierarchy of needs 371–372
  intergenerational equity 370
  intragenerational equity 370
  multifaceted notion 373–374
  perversity of 356–358
  responsibility 14t, 371
  summary of concepts and
    contexts 14t
  sustainability 369–370
  top down and bottom up solutions
    358–359
  and transparency 184–187, 211,
    213–214, 282–285, 369
  *see also* equality; posterity
energy payback ratios (EPRs) 100–101,
  101f
energy poverty
  extent 225–228, 226t
  and fuel poverty 231–233
  health consequences 229
  and income inequality 230–231
  summary 14t
environmental audits 214
environmental bonds 153–156
environmental externalities *see*
  externalities
Environmental Impact Assessments
  (EIAs) 181–184, 196
environmental justice 12
equality
  and climate change 29
  income inequality 230–231
  of opportunity (liberty) 240
  of resources 302–303, 307
Equatorial Guinea 174
ethanol 348f, 349t
Ethiopia
  corruption 169
  energy poverty 226t, 229
European Union
  Emissions Trading Scheme 333–334
  participatory technology assessments
    217t

externalities
  automobiles and transport 130–131
  climate change 127–129
  costs 147–151
  definition 126–127
  effects of 139–141
  electricity industry 129–130
  and environmental bonds
    153–156
  health effects of 204–205
  included in energy pricing
    151–153
  mountaintop removal 81, 133–135
  nuclear power 136–139
  oil and gas production 132–133
  and pricing 147–153
  summary 14t
  uranium mining 135–136
extractive industries 49–60
  transparency initiatives (EITIs)
    184–187
  *see also* coalmining; fossil fuels; oil
    and gas; uranium

Farrington, John and Conor 208
fertilizers 67
fiberglass 58t
finance
  consumer protection 253–254
  models of 249–253
  pro-poor public private partnership
    (5P) 249–253
  social pricing 253
  World Bank funding 233–234
  *see also* investment; subsidies
Finland
  energy tax shifting 152t
  nuclear waste 292–293
food miles 66
food production 65–68
fossil fuels
  depletion 295–297, 297f
  energy payback ratio (EPR) 101f
  energy payback ratios (EPRs) 100
  life expectancy 296t
  *see also* coalmining; oil and gas;
    uranium
Fouqout, Roger 312
France
  carbon dioxide emissions 28f

energy tax shifting 152t
health effects of automobile emissions
130–131
heat-wave deaths 205
lack of consultation in nuclear sector
200
nuclear waste 292
uranium decommissioning costs
138–139
free prior informed consent (FPIC)
220
freedom 14t, 144, 176–178, 238–239
*see also* libertarianism
Friedman, Milton 14t, 275–276
fuel collection 225, 229–230
fuel poverty 231–233

Gagnon, Luc 100
gallium 58t
Gambia, indoor air pollution 229
Gardiner, Stephen M. 14t, 333
Garvey, James 333
gasoline, subsidies 263, 264f
Gazprom 171
geothermal energy
carbon-cost ratios 108t
critical materials needs 58t
growth and investment 346–351,
348f, 349t
opportunity costs 107t
technologies 316t
germanium 58t
Germany
carbon dioxide emissions 28f
coal subsidy removal 287
greenhouse gas emissions 70f
renewable energy 349t, 350
solar power 219–220
tax shifting 151, 152t
Ghana
development fund 315
subsidy reform 283t
gigawatts (GW) 34–35
glass materials
refundable deposits for bottles 154
in solar energy 58t
gold 173
Goldman, Michael 234
Goodin, Robert E. 307
Gordon, Ruth 194

Greece, renewable energy 349t
green bonds 155–156
greenhouse gases (GHG)
greenhouse development rights
(GDR) 334–336, 335t
projected increase 71, 72f, 127
share of emissions by sector, gas and
country 69, 70f
and subsidies 271
unjust domination 328
*see also* carbon dioxide emissions

Habermas, Jürgen 14t, 207–208
Haggett, Claire 209
Haiti, corruption 170t
happiness 141, 143, 177, 179
Hawden, Paul 369–370
health
and air pollution 75–77
and automobile emissions 130–131
coal dust effects 129, 159, 162
and fuel poverty 230
healthcare expenditure 265
and indoor air pollution 74, 77–79,
139, 140f, 228f
minorities and pollution 204–205
and uranium mining 162–163
*see also* deaths; occupational hazards
heat waves 205, 338
heating, improvements 312t
Hornberger, Jacob G. 206
household devices *see* electric
appliances; refrigerators;
televisions
housing, weatherization programs
254–255
Hubbert, M. King 296–297
human rights
and climate change 329–330
and energy sector 14t
indigenous people 184, 221–222
and justice 174–179
Mining Minerals and Sustainable
Development (MMSD) 189–190
oil and gas company abuses 165–168
and pollution control 157–158
protect, respect, and remedy
187–189
Shue's decent standard of living
329–330, 330t

hydroelectric energy
  accident risks 164, 165f
  aging stock 95, 97
  carbon-cost ratios 108t
  critical materials needs 57, 58t
  energy payback ratio (EPR) 100, 101f
  Grand Coulee Dam dilemma
    319–320
  growth and investment 348f
  and involuntary resettlement
    125–126, 195–199
  negative externalities 149t
  opportunity costs 107t
  technologies 316t
  water use 79

Ikeda, Daisaku 308
Impact-Benefit Agreements (IBAs)
  183–184, 185t
income inequality 230–231
India
  air conditioning 106
  carbon dioxide emissions 28f
  coalmines 54t
  energy poverty 226t
  energy subsidies 266, 267
  fuel collection 229–230
  greenhouse gas emissions 70f
  Hyrakud Dam, Orissa 125–126
  involuntary resettlement 198
  lack of consultation in nuclear sector
    200
  LPG cylinders 269
  negative effects of climate change 129
  petroleum production 63t
  power outages 99
  renewable energy 349t, 350
indigenous people 184, 191–192,
    221–222
  *see also* human rights
indium 58t, 59
Indonesia
  Cinta Mekar Project 250–251, 252t
  civil war 173
  corruption 170t
  deforestation and GHGs 82–83, 83t
  energy poverty 226t
  greenhouse gas emissions 69, 70f
  involuntary resettlement and coal
    mining 197–198

natural gas production 51t
negative effects of climate change
    128–129
renewable energy 349t
subsidy reform 283t
indoor air pollution (IAP)
  causes 77–79
  health consequences 139, 140f, 228f
  *see also* cookstoves
industry, energy inefficiencies 92–94,
    93f, 104–105
inspection panels 180–181
insurance, and natural disasters 128
intellectual property 235–237
internal combustion engines 38–40
International Labor Organization 211,
    221–222
international law 210–211, 221–222,
    309
investment 48, 346–351, 348f, 349t
Iran
  corruption 169
  energy subsidies 266
  oil and natural gas production 50t,
    51t
  subsidy reform 283t
Iraq
  military conflict 173, 174
  Oil-for-Food Program 172
Israel, energy deprivation 225, 227f
Italy
  energy tax shifting 152t
  renewable energy 349t

Jacobson, Mark 107
Jamieson, Dale 14t, 363, 376
Japan
  carbon dioxide emissions 28f
  Fukushima accident 27, 138
  greenhouse gas emissions 70f
  petroleum liquids production 63t
  renewable energy 349t
Jasanoff, Sheila 365
Jefferson, Thomas 14t, 207
jet turbines 40–41
justice
  concept 9–13
  and conflicting values 362–366
  contractarian theory 237–238,
    304–305, 355

corrective justice 330–332
cosmopolitanism 372–373
definition 11
difference principle (Rawls) 240–241
distributive justice 11, 275, 370, 373
equality of opportunity principle (Rawls) 240
and human capabilities 243–244
and human rights 174–179
and ideal states 109
literature of 22–24
and posterity 144–145, 300–311, 356–358, 370
procedural justice 11–12, 14t, 208–211, 373
unfair negotiations 193–195
veil of ignorance 239–240
*see also* energy justice; morality; virtue

Kant, Immanuel 3, 14t, 18, 158, 175–179, 301, 354, 355
Kent, Jennifer 280
Kenya
corruption 169
energy poverty 226t
renewable energy 350
subsidy reform 283t
kilowatts (kW) 34–35
Koplow, Douglas 257–258
Kyoto Protocol 334

Ladd, John 178–179
land, pollution 135–136
land rights 168, 191–192, 201
land use
for agriculture 65–66, 68t
and energy costs 148
and energy use 68t
and forest carbon revenues 198–199
*see also* deforestation
Lane, Janica 194
law
due process 14t, 206–208, 210–211, 368–369
free prior informed consent (FPIC) 220
procedural justice 208–211
*see also* international law
lead 58t, 84t, 205

Lewis, Sanford 210
libertarianism 14t, 273–279, 355
Libya, corruption 170t
lighting technology
consumer behavior 105
improvements 41–43, 42f, 312
inefficiencies 91–92, 93f
and rare earth minerals 59, 60
lithium 59
Locke, John 300
Long Martello, Marybeth 365
Lovins, Amory 106–107, 366
LPG 248, 269
Lutzenhiser, Loren 366

MacIntyre, Alasdair 142
McKibben, Bill 69–71
McKinsey & Company 114, 115f
MacLean, Douglas 305
*Magna Carta* 206
Makhijani, Arjun 352
Malaysia
electricity pricing 121, 122f
hydroelectric power 196
Maldives 340t
manganese 58t
marine pollution 46, 84t
Mauritania, subsidy reform 283t
mechanical power 248
megawatts (MW) 34–35
Menezes, Fradique 288–290
mercury 84t, 204, 205
methane 69, 84t, 159
Mexico
energy consultation 219
oil and gas production 50t, 51t, 63t
renewable energy 349t
Middle East
carbon dioxide emissions 28f
energy subsidies 266–267
oil and natural gas reserves 50t, 51t
petroleum production 63t
military, energy use 94–95
military conflict, and energy resources 172–174
Mill, John Stuart 14t, 126, 143–144
*On Liberty* 144
Mishan, E.J. 362
molybdenum 58t

morality 22–24, 276, 362–366,
    375–377
Morocco 173
mortality rates *see* deaths
motor vehicles *see* automobile industry;
    automobiles
mountaintop removal 53, 81, 133–135,
    134f
Myanmar (Burma)
    energy poverty 226t
    energy shortages 269–270
    military conflict 172
    reaction to subsidy removal 287
    Unocal and human rights abuses 166
Myers, Norman 280

Namibia, subsidy reform 283t
natural disasters 128
natural gas
    definition 49
    production 50t, 51t, 52t
    reserves 50t, 51t, 52t, 294, 295f, 296t
    safety 164, 165f
    subsidies 269
Nepal
    community-owned grids 220
    energy consultation 218–219
    power outages 99
Netherlands, energy tax shifting 152t
New Caledonia, France 173
New Zealand, petroleum liquids
    production 63t
nickel 58t, 173
Niger, subsidy reform 283t
Nigeria
    Akassa Project 219
    corruption 169, 170t
    energy poverty 226t, 228
    military conflict 174
    oil and gas production 50t
    power outages 98–99
    Shell and human rights abuses 166
    subsidy reform 283t
    transparency initiative 187
nitrogen 67
nitrogen fixation 84t
nitrogen oxide (NO$_x$) emissions 68t,
    75
nitrous oxide 69, 84t
Nolt, John 328

nonrenewable energy 36–37, 36t
    *see also* electricity industry; fossil
        fuels; nuclear power
Nordhaus, William D. 41–42
Norton, Bryan 279, 306–307
Norway, natural gas production 51t
Nozick, Robert 14t, 258–259, 274–275,
    279, 354, 355
nuclear power
    aging stock 95–99
    carbon-cost ratios 108t
    critical materials needs 57, 58t
    decommissioning costs 137–138
    for electricity 61
    emissions reduction potential 343t
    energy payback ratio (EPR) 100–101,
        101f
    improper licensing 199–201
    negative externalities 136–139, 147,
        149t
    opportunity costs 106–107, 107t
    and peripheral communities 203
    and the public 218
    rare earth minerals needs 59
    subsidies 257–258
Nuclear Regulatory Commission 155
nuclear safety
    accidents 164, 165f
    Chernobyl 138, 200–201, 353–355
    Fukushima accident 27, 138
    Soviet Union coverups 200–201
nuclear waste 81, 136–137, 291–294,
    293f
Nussbaum, Martha 15t, 224, 243–245

Obama, Barack 364
O'Brien, Mary 231
occupational hazards 159–165f, 165f
ocean power 316t, 348f
OECD, Guidelines for Multinational
    Corporations 188
oil
    prices and subsidies 272–273
    reserves 294–295, 295f, 296t
    supply disruptions 299–300
    Yasuní-ITT initiative 364–365
oil companies 294
oil and gas
    BTC pipeline 167, 172–173, 201–202
    companies 50–53, 52t

environmental bonds 155
global trade 26–29
negative externalities 132–133, 133f,
  149t, 150
occupational hazards 163–164,
  165f
pipelines 44–45, 164
production 49–50, 50t, 52t
production projections 63t
reserves 50t, 51t, 52t
revenues and military conflict
  172–174
safety 164, 300
subsidies 269
tankers 45–46
uses 49
water use 79, 80–81
*see also* natural gas; oil
O'Leary, Shannon 173

Pacala, S. 339, 341f
Page, Edward 303
Pakistan, energy poverty 226t
Palast, Greg 231
Papua New Guinea
  childbirth 230
  natural resources conflict 173
  petroleum project funds 315
participatory technology assessment
  (PTA) 215–216, 217t
patents 235–237
paternalism 276, 278
Paton, H.J. 178
permafrost melt 338
Peru, subsidy reform 283t
petro-states 173
petrol, subsidies 263, 264f
Philippines
  corruption 170t
  negative effects of climate change
    128–129
  power outages 99
  renewable energy 349t
  subsidy reform 283t
phosphates 173
pipelines
  BTC pipeline 167, 172–173,
    201–202
  environmental effects 150
  global extent 44–45

and human rights abuses 166–167
military conflict 172–173
safety 164, 300
plastic 58t
Plato 14t, 108–109
plutonium 138
PM (particulate matter) emissions 68t,
  75–77, 78f, 84t, 130, 131t
Pojman, Louis 372–373
Poland, subsidy reform 283t
pollution
  chemical 214
  and human rights 157–158
  major sources 84t
  and peripheral communities
    203–205
  *see also* air pollution; marine
    pollution; water pollution
population growth, and energy use 48f
posterity
  hopes for 356–357
  ignorance problem 306
  and immorality of energy activities
    305–306
  international agreements 329
  international law 309
  and justice 144–145, 300–311,
    370
  and natural resources funds 290–291,
    314–315
  property leases 308–309
  resource egalitarianism 302–303, 307
  restoration measures 311
  São Tomé's Permanent Oil Fund
    290–291
  summary 14t
  theory of intergenerational justice
    303–305, 306–307
  'two-hundred-year-present' concept
    308
  *see also* nuclear waste
pricing
  and cost of externalities 147–153
  electricity 119–121, 213–214,
    359–360
primary energy 6–7, 36–37, 36t, 48f
prime movers 38–44
privatized enterprises 235
procedural justice 11–12, 14t, 208–211,
  373

public involvement
  advantages of 209–211
  community marginalization 202–205
  community-based research 215
  consensus conferences 216
  consultation examples 218–220
  and free prior informed consent
    (FPIC) 220–222
  information campaigns 123–124,
    212–213
  information disclosure 213–214
  just society 208
  and local communities 191–192,
    199–201
  and nuclear power 218
  ownership of energy infrastructure
    219–220
  participatory technology assessment
    (PTA) 215–216, 217t
  stakeholders 211–212
public transport 65, 116

Qatar, natural gas production 51t

rail transport 65
railway industry, diesel engines 40
rare earth minerals 59–60
Rawls, John 14t, 18
  *A Theory of Justice* 238–239
  criticisms 241–242, 245
  difference principle 240–241
  distribution of primary goods 11
  and energy justice 224, 355
  equality of opportunity (liberty)
    principle 240
  and nuclear safety 354
  savings principle 301
  veil of ignorance 239–240
refrigerators 43, 119, 312–313, 313f
religion 112, 175, 301
renewable energy
  benefits 315–318
  growth and investment 346–351
  lack of consumer knowledge 102
  negative externalities and costs 147
  potential sources 342–346
  Renewable Energy and Energy-
    efficiency Partnership (REEEP)
    251–253
  research subsidies 269, 270f

resources 36–37, 36t
  small-scale renewables 246–248
  *see also* solar energy; wind energy
research 215f, 269, 270f
reservoirs, evaporation from 68t,
    79–80, 80f
resource egalitarianism 355
responsibility 14t, 371
rights 274–275
  *see also* human rights
Rio Declaration 210–211
roads 62, 261, 263
Roma communities 202–203
Ross, Michael L. 174
Ruggie, John 188–189
Russia
  carbon dioxide emissions 28f
  Chernobyl accident 138, 200–201,
    353–355
  energy subsidies 265–266
  energy trade 27
  Gazprom 171
  greenhouse gas emissions 70f
  nuclear secrecy 200–201
  oil and gas production 50t, 51t, 63t
  uranium mining 163

Sachs, Jeffrey 289–290
Sandel, Michael J. 11, 18, 110, 177,
    276, 277
São Tomé and Príncipe
  lack of resources 288–290
  Oil Revenue Management Law
    (ORML) 290–291
  transparency initiative 187
Sarawak Corridor of Renewable Energy
    196
Saudi Arabia
  aid to Afghanistan and Pakistan 173
  energy subsidies 266
  oil and gas production 50t, 51t
  oil and gas trade 27
Schneider, Stephen H. 194
Schumacher, E.F. 8
Scotland, renewable energy 350
sea-level rise 324, 338
secondary energy, resources 36–37, 36t
Sen, Amartya 14t, 143, 224, 242–243
shale gas 295f
Shell 166

shipping industry, diesel engines 40
Shue, Henry 14t, 194–195,
   320, 327–328, 329–330,
   330t
Sidgwick, Henry 14t, 126, 300–301
   *Methods of Ethics* 144–145
silicon 58t
silver 58t
Singapore, urban transport policy 116
Singer, Peter 14t, 320, 333
Sioshansi, Fereidoon P. 28
Slovak Republic, subsidies 266
smuggling 267
Socolow, Robert 339, 341f
Soddy, Frederick 34
Soderholm, Patrik 149–150
solar energy
   carbon-cost ratios 108t
   critical materials needs 58t, 59
   emissions reduction potential 343t
   green bonds 155
   growth and investment 346–351,
      348f, 349t
   installations 247
   and local ownership 219–220
   negative externalities 149t
   opportunity costs 107t
   subsidies 257
   technologies 316t
Somalia, fuel collection 229
South Africa, subsidy reform 283t
South Korea
   nuclear waste 292
   petroleum liquids production 63t
South Sudan, corruption 169
Spain
   energy tax shifting 152t
   renewable energy 349t
stabilization wedges 339–342, 343t
steel industry 57, 58t
Stern Report 128
Stiglitz, Joseph 277–278
Stockholm Declaration 309
subsidies
   adjustment packages for subsidy
      removal 286–287
   for conventional vs new technologies
      267–269
   definition 258

elimination 280–287, 352,
   360–361
encourage increased consumption
   265–266
and energy shortages 269–271
for gasoline and diesel 264f
and GHG emissions 271
and government debt 265
impact studies 282–285
lock in and dependency 272–273
negative impact 261–265, 270–271
nuclear power 257–258
perverse subsidies 280
research subsidies 269, 270f
solar power 257
successful reforms 281–282, 282t,
   283t
summary 14t
sunset clauses 285–286
and transport of fuels 261
types 259t
US trends 262
wind energy 257
Sudan
   military conflict 172, 173, 174
   oil and gas human rights abuses 166
sulfur dioxide ($SO_2$) emissions 68t,
   74–75
   *see also* acid rain
sulfur emissions 84t
Sundqvist, Thomas 149–150
Sweden
   nuclear power 218, 292–293
   renewable energy 349t
   tax shifting 151, 152t

tankers 45–46
Tanzania, energy poverty 226t
taxation
   carbon taxation 145–147
   and energy subsidies 259t, 261
   and redistribution of wealth 277
   tax credits 360
   tax shifting 151–153, 152t
   to encourage energy saving 123,
      360
   VAT subsidy removal 281–282,
      282t
televisions 43, 105

tellurium 58t
temperature change 73–74, 73f, 205,
    323, 338
terawatts (TW) 34–35
Thailand
    air conditioning 106
    negative effects of climate change
        128–129
thermodynamics laws 33–34, 90
Three Gorges Dam 196–197, 197f
tidal power 316t
Total 171
trade
    and global emissions 27–28
    and subsidies 259t
transmission lines, electricity 47, 150,
    191–193
transparency 184–187, 211, 213–214,
    282–285, 369
transport 61–65, 116–117, 261,
    312t
    *see also* automobiles; rail transport
tritium-contaminated wastewater 81
truth commissions 180
Tunisia, corruption 170t
Turkey
    hydroelectric energy 197
    renewable energy 349t
    subsidy reform 283t
Tuvalu 246–247
'two-hundred-year-present' concept
    308

Uganda
    carbon-offset plantations 199
    subsidy reform 283t
United Arab Emirates, oil and natural
    gas production 50t
United Kingdom
    carbon dioxide emissions 28f
    coal subsidies 266, 286
    energy tax shifting 152t
    nuclear energy 137, 139
    private security company guidelines
        189
    Scotland's renewable energy target 350
    Warm Front program 255
    wind power 216
    Woking's energy efficiency measures
        114–115

United Nations
    environmental conventions 309, 329
    Framework Convention on Climate
        Change (UNFCCC) 194, 328–329,
        333–334, 364, 365
    and free prior informed consent 222
    Global Compact 189
    Oil-for-Food Program 172
United States
    air conditioning 106
    air pollution 76–77
    automobile driver behavior 102–103
    automobiles 130–131, 131t
    carbon dioxide emissions 28f
    carbon taxation 146
    coal pollution control 364
    coalmine numbers and types 54t
    coalmining accidents 159, 160t
    community-based research projects
        215
    Constitution 207
    corruption 171
    dependence on foreign oil 298–299,
        298f
    electricity industry 61, 213–214
    energy inefficiencies 92
    energy intensity 117–118
    energy pricing 151–152
    Energy Star Program 118–119
    energy subsidies 267
    environmental bonds 154–155
    fuel assistance program (LIHEAP)
        253, 261
    Grand Coulee Dam dilemma
        319–320
    greenhouse gas emissions 69, 70f, 333
    Miller Act (1935) 154
    National Environmental Policy Act
        (1969) 154–155
    nuclear reactors, improper licensing
        199
    nuclear waste 292
    OHIO state pollution 205
    oil and gas production 50t, 51t, 63t
    pollution and peripheral communities
        204–205
    private security company guidelines
        189
    renewable energy 342, 346, 347f,
        349t, 350

San Diego electricity supply 191–193
subsidy sunset clauses 286
Surface Mining Control and
    Reclamation Act (1977) 155
Three Mile Island 137–138
Toxics Release Inventory (TRI) 214
transport policy 116–117
uranium mining 163
weatherization programs 254
uranium
    declining quality 100–101
    effects of Fukushima accident 27
    production 56t
    reserves 295, 295f, 296t
uranium mining 55–57, 57t, 135–136,
    162–163, 168
uranium processing, decommissioning
    costs 138
utilitarianism 2–3, 126, 141–145,
    178–179, 304–305, 355
utility 14t, 18

values 362–366
van Beers, Cees 272
vanadium 58t
Vanuatu 329, 340t
Varian, Hal R. 277
veil of ignorance 239–240
Venezuela
    energy subsidies 266
    oil and natural gas production 50t
Vietnam, negative effects of climate
    change 128–129
virtue 14t, 18, 88–90, 111–113, 112
voltage 47

Walker, Gordon 12, 20–21,
    326–327
Walras, Leon 300
war, and natural resources 148
waste
    from transport system 62
    *see also* nuclear waste

water pollution
    and energy costs 148
    from energy use 68t, 79–81
    from oil and gas production 132
    mountaintop removal 133–135
    and nuclear plants 81
    uranium mining 135–136, 163
    *see also* marine pollution
Watts, Michael J. 174
weatherization programs 254–255
Weinberg, Alvin M. 293
welfare 14t
Western Sahara 173
Weston, Burns H. 310
Wheelan, Charles 131
Whitehead, Alfred North 112
Wilson, Edward O. 377
wind energy
    carbon-cost ratios 108t
    critical materials needs 58t, 60, 59
    emissions reduction potential 343t
    energy payback ratio (EPR) 100, 101f
    and environmental costs 150–151
    growth and investment 346–351,
        348f, 349t
    improvements 313
    and local ownership 220
    negative externalities 149t
    opportunity costs 107t
    and public consensus 216
    rare earth minerals needs 57–59
    subsidies 257
    technologies 316t
Wolf, Clark 237
women, and indoor air pollution 77–79,
    139, 140f
Wood, Allen 178, 179
World Bank 73, 155, 180–181, 189,
    233–234

Yemen, subsidy reform 283t

Zaire, corruption 170t

CPSIA information can be obtained
at www.ICGtesting.com
Printed in the USA
LVHW011101090822
725507LV00008B/111

9 781107 665088